SAMS
Teach Yourself

Red Hat® Linux® 8

Aron Hsiao

in 24 Hours

SAMS   201 West 103rd Street, Indianapolis, Indiana 46290 USA

Sams Teach Yourself
Red Hat® Linux® 8 in 24 Hours
Copyright © 2003 by Sams Publishing

International Standard Book Number: 0-672-32475-X

Library of Congress Catalog Card Number: 2002110481

Printed in the United States of America

First Printing: January 2003

04   03   4   3   2   1

Trademarks

Warning and Disclaimer

ACQUISITIONS EDITOR
Katie Purdum

DEVELOPMENT EDITORS
Lorna Gentry
Scott Meyers

MANAGING EDITOR
Charlotte Clapp

PROJECT EDITOR
Tricia Liebig

COPY EDITOR
Nancy Albright

INDEXER
Kelly Castell

PROOFREADERS
Leslie Joseph
Katie Robinson

TECHNICAL EDITOR
Dave Taylor

TEAM COORDINATOR
Pamalee Nelson

MEDIA DEVELOPER
Dan Scherf

INTERIOR DESIGNER
Gary Adair

COVER DESIGNER
Gary Adair

PAGE LAYOUT
Ayanna Lacey

Contents at a Glance

Introduction   1

Part I Installing Red Hat Linux

Hour 1   Preparing to Install Red Hat Linux   5

Hour 2   Installing Red Hat Linux   25

Hour 3   Booting, Logging In, and Configuring   59

Part II Using Linux at the Console

Hour 4   Navigating Linux at the Console   75

Hour 5   Making the Console Work for You   103

Hour 6   Getting Help at the Console   131

Hour 7   Working Without the Mouse   145

Hour 8   Networking Without Graphics   171

Hour 9   Harnessing the Power of the Shell   197

Part III Using Linux on the Desktop

Hour 10   Introducing the Red Hat Desktop   221

Hour 11   Working with Files on the Desktop   239

Hour 12   Introducing OpenOffice   265

Hour 13   Networking on the Desktop   293

Hour 14   Getting Help on the Desktop   321

Hour 15   Customizing the Desktop   339

Hour 16   Advanced Linux Desktop Use   365

Hour 17   Using Desktop Applications Remotely   385

Part IV Advanced Topics

Hour 18   Command-Line System Administration   403

Hour 19   Desktop System Administration   431

Hour 20   Security Basics   449

Hour 21   Installing Software   465

Hour 22   Offering Network File Services   485

Hour 23   Offering Web and FTP Service   507

Hour 24   Backups, Troubleshooting, and Rescue   525

Appendix A   Installer Troubleshooting   545

Index   551

Contents

Introduction   **1**

Part I   Installing Red Hat Linux

Hour 1   Preparing to Install Red Hat Linux   **5**

Taking a Hardware Inventory 6
    Memory Capacity 6
    CPU (Processor) Speed 8
    Hard Drive Capacity 9
    Communications Hardware 9
Evaluating Your Hardware 10
Making Space for Linux 11
    Understanding Partitions 11
    Nondestructive Repartitioning 12
    Defragmenting Prior to Using FIPS 13
    Creating a FIPS Floppy and Starting FIPS 14
    Using FIPS 16
    Destructive Repartitioning 18
    Avoiding Repartitioning by Adding a Hard Drive 21
Launching the Red Hat Linux Installer 22
Summary 23
Q&A 23
Workshop 24
    Quiz 24
    Answers 24
    Activities 24

Hour 2   Installing Red Hat Linux   **25**

Starting the Red Hat Linux Installer 25
Beginning the Installation 26
    Language Selection 27
    Keyboard Configuration 27
    Mouse Configuration 27
    Installation Type 29
    Disk Partitioning Setup 30
    Disk Setup 32
    Boot Loader Configuration 39
    Network Configuration 41
    Firewall Configuration 43
    Additional Language Support 44
    Time Zone Selection 45

Account Configuration 46

Authentication Configuration 48

Package Group Selection..48

About to Install 51

Installing Packages 51

Boot Diskette Creation 53

Graphical Interface (X) Configuration 53

Monitor Configuration..54

Customize Graphics Configuration 55

Congratulations! 57

Summary 57

Q&A 57

Workshop 58

Quiz 58

Answers 58

HOUR 3 Booting, Logging In, and Configuring   59

Booting Red Hat Linux..60

Welcome to Red Hat Linux!..61

Finishing First-Run Configuration 61

Logging In for Configuration 64

Identifying the Parts of the Login Screen 64

Configuring Your Printer and Internet Service 66

Configuring Your Printer 67

Configuring Your Dial-Up Internet Service 69

Starting the Network Configuration Tool 72

Logging Out..72

Summary 72

Q&A 73

Workshop 73

Quiz 74

Answers 74

Activities 74

Part II Using Linux at the Console

HOUR 4 Navigating Linux at the Console   75

Why Learn to Use Linux at the Console? 76

Understanding Virtual Consoles 76

Switching Between Consoles 77

Logging In at a Virtual Console 77

Introducing the Shell..78

The Shell's Role: Command Interpreter 78

Fundamentals of Using the Shell 78

Working with the Filesystem 79

   Many Trees, Many Roots: The Windows File System 79

   One Tree, One Root: The Linux File System 80

   Files and Directories 80

   The Home Directory 83

   The Current Working Directory 83

   Manipulating Files and Directories 85

   Using Relative Paths 86

   Deleting Files and Directories..90

   Executable Files..91

   Symbolic Links 91

Understanding Permissions..93

   Long File Listings 93

   Identity and File Ownership 94

   Ownership and File Permissions...95

   More Permissions Examples 97

   Changing Permissions 98

Summary 100

   Q&A 101

Workshop 101

   Quiz 101

   Answers 101

   Activities 102

HOUR 5 Making the Console Work for You   103

Creating, Editing, and Saving Text Files 104

   Using vi to Create or Edit Text Files 104

   Inserting Text in vi 105

   Editing Text in vi 106

   Saving and Quitting, and Further Reading 107

   Using emacs to Create Text Files..108

   The emacs Menu System 110

   Essential emacs Keystrokes 111

Grouping Files for Efficient File Management 113

   Grouping Files on the Command Line 113

   Preventing Filename Expansion 116

Searching Files and Directories Quickly 116

   Searching for Files with find 117

   Searching the Entire Filesystem with locate 117

   Saving a List of Found Files 119

   Searching Text Files for Word Patterns...119

   Searching for Text Files That Contain Specific Words....................120

Using Command Output for Complex Tasks 121

    Using Pipes to Link Commands 121

    Using One Command's Answers As Another's Arguments 122

Keeping Your Shell Programs Under Control 124

    Moving Between Multiple Open Applications 124

    Resuming a Job with `fg` 125

    Running a Job in the Background with `bg` 126

    Final Job Control Notes..127

Summary 127

Q&A 128

Workshop 128

    Quiz 129

    Answers 129

    Activities 129

HOUR 6 Getting Help at the Console   **131**

Introducing Manual Pages 132

    Using Manual Pages: The Basics 132

    Understanding Manual Page Sections..133

    Locating Manual Pages Through Topic-Based Searches 135

Using the GNU `info` System 136

    Navigating the `info` System 136

    Using `info` Efficiently 138

Using the `/usr/share/doc` Tree 138

    Reading Extra Application Documentation..138

    Searching the `/usr/share/doc` Tree 140

Getting Help from the Commands 141

Summary 142

Q&A 143

Workshop 143

    Quiz 143

    Answers 143

    Activities 144

HOUR 7 Working Without the Mouse   **145**

Printing at the Command Line 146

    Creating Print Jobs 146

    Listing Print Jobs...147

    Dequeueing Print Jobs..147

Creating High-Quality Documents at the Command Line...................................148

    Introducing the LaTeX-2e Formatter 149

    Understanding LaTeX Basics 149

    Creating an Empty Latex Document..150

Formatting and Printing Your First Document 152
Selecting a Page Style 153
Creating Title and Author Information 154
Controlling LaTeX Paragraphs, Line Breaks, and Pages 154
Organizing Larger Texts 156
Formatting the Body of Your Text..158
Inserting Special Characters 159
Putting It All Together..160
More Information About LaTeX 162
Performing Math Tasks Using the Binary Calculator 162
Starting bc and Performing Basic Calculations 162
Using Variables 163
Automating Calculations with bc 164
Advanced Scripting in bc 165
Creating and Sorting Lists of Data..165
Creating Searchable or Sortable Lists..165
Displaying Specific Entries 166
Sorting List Data 166
Summary 168
Q&A 168
Workshop 169
Quiz 169
Answers 169
Activities 169

HOUR 8 Networking Without Graphics **171**

Browsing the Web at the Console..172
Starting the Lynx Web Browser 173
Using the Lynx Web Browser 173
Handling Cookies with Lynx..175
Managing Bookmarks with Lynx 176
Managing Email at the Console 176
Fetching Post Office Protocol 3 (POP3) or Internet Message Access
Protocol (IMAP) Mail...177
Creating the .fetchmailrc File 177
Using Pine to Manage Email from the Console 179
Starting Pine 179
Setting Pine Preferences 180
Specifying a From Address in Pine..181
Composing Mail Using Pine 182
Reading Mail Using Pine 183
Getting Help and Quitting Pine..184

Logging In to a Remote Linux or Unix System 185
    Logging In Remotely Using `telnet` 186
    Logging In Remotely Using `ssh` 187
Exchanging Files with Linux/Unix Hosts Using `ftp` 188
    Starting `ftp` and Logging In 189
    Navigating an `ftp` Login 189
    Sample `ftp` Session 191
Exchanging Files with Windows Hosts Using `smbclient` 193
    Listing the Shares on a Windows Host 193
    Connecting to a Windows Share 194
    Navigating and Copying Files with `smbclient` 194
Summary 194
Q&A 195
Workshop 195
    Quiz 195
    Answers 196
    Activities 196

HOUR 9 Harnessing the Power of the Shell   **197**

Adding to Your Command Repertoire 198
    Sending Text to Standard Output with `echo` 198
    Performing Simple Calculations with `expr` 198
    Displaying Text File Beginnings or Endings with `head` and `tail` 199
    Editing Streams of Data with `sed` 200
Using Shell Variables and Quoting 201
    Creating and Substituting Variables 202
    Quoting Carefully 204
    Environment Variables 205
Creating Your Own Commands Using Shell Scripting 206
    Beginning a Shell Script 206
    Processing Command-Line Arguments 207
    Making `myscript` Easily Executable 208
    Using Conditional Statements 209
    Testing Over and Over Again 211
    Repeatedly Executing for a Predefined Set 214
    Beyond Shell Scripting 216
Summary 217
Q&A 217
Workshop 218
    Quiz 218
    Answers 218
    Activities 219

Part III Using Linux on the Desktop

HOUR 10 Introducing the Red Hat Desktop   **221**

Notes on GNOME and KDE in Red Hat Linux 8 222
Logging In to the Desktop 223
Navigating the Desktop 225
    Launching Applications...226
    Using Window Controls 228
    Moving, Resizing, Minimizing, and Maximizing Windows........................228
    Application Menus 229
Working with Multiple Windows 229
    Changing the Active Application 230
    Minimizing and Restoring with the Taskbar...231
    Shading a Window..231
Understanding Virtual Desktops..232
    Knowing Which Desktop Is Active...233
    Selecting a New Desktop 233
    Moving a Running Application to a New Desktop......................................234
    Using the KDE Window Management Menu 234
Logging Out of the GNOME Desktop 235
Summary..236
Q&A 236
Workshop 237
    Quiz 237
    Answers 237
    Activities 237

HOUR 11 Working with Files on the Desktop   **239**

Creating a New Text File Using the Text Editor 240
Using the File Manager 243
    Opening a File Manager Window 244
    Navigating the Directory Tree...245
Working with Files and Directories 247
    Opening, Editing, and Closing an Existing File 248
    Cutting, Copying, and Pasting Files 249
    Duplicating a File in the Current Directory 250
    Selecting Multiple Files...251
    Creating a Symbolic Link 252
    Renaming an Item 252
    Deleting Items 253
    Changing File Permissions 253
    Creating a New Directory 255
    Rearranging or Sorting Icons 256

Manipulating Files Using Drag and Drop 257

Moving a File into a Directory or to the Desktop............................257

Moving a File Between Two Directory Windows............................258

Context Drag and Drop 259

Working with Trash Contents..260

Restoring Files That Have Been Thrown Away 260

Emptying the Trash 260

Summary..261

Q&A 262

Workshop 262

Quiz 262

Answers 262

Activities 262

Hour 12 Introducing OpenOffice   265

The OpenOffice Applications 266

Launching an OpenOffice Application 267

Creating and Formatting an OpenOffice Writer Document 267

Launching OpenOffice Writer..268

Entering Text 269

Editing Text 270

Changing the Appearance of Text 271

Changing Paragraph Formatting 273

Changing Margin Size and Page Layout............................274

Saving a File 275

Opening a File 277

Printing a File 278

Working with OpenOffice Calc 279

Familiarizing Yourself with Calc..279

Entering Text Labels 281

Entering and Formatting Numeric Data in Cells 282

Entering Formulas 285

Using Functions in Formulas 286

Copying Formulas 288

Printing, Saving, and Opening Spreadsheets 289

Summary..290

Q&A 291

Workshop 292

Quiz 292

Answers 292

Activities 292

Hour 13 Networking on the Desktop   293

   Introducing Mozilla 294
      Launching the Mozilla Browser 294
   Browsing the Web with Mozilla 294
      Visiting a Web Site 295
      Navigating Web Sites 296
      Remembering URLs You Like 298
      Browsing with Tabs..298
      Disabling Pop-up Windows...299
      Exiting Mozilla 300
   Reading and Writing Email 300
      Launching Evolution 301
      Configuring Evolution...301
      Composing a New Email..306
      Using HTML Formatting in Your Message..308
      Attaching a File to Your Message 309
      Sending Your Message 310
      Downloading New Mail 310
      Replying To or Forwarding a Message 311
      Accessing an Attachment 312
      Printing and Deleting..312
      Exiting Evolution..314
   Accessing Windows Networks 314
      Accessing Files on Windows Machines in GNOME 314
   Using File Transfer Protocol (FTP) on the Desktop 315
      Connecting to a Remote System 315
      Copying Files to a Remote System 316
      Copying Files from a Remote System 317
      Closing an FTP Connection 318
   Summary..318
   Q&A 319
   Workshop 319
      Quiz 319
      Answers 319
      Activities 319

Hour 14 Getting Help on the Desktop   321

   Using Application Help 322
      Finding and Launching Application Help..322
      Using the About Option in Help Menus 323
      Using What's This? in KDE Applications..324
      Viewing Help Contents in GNOME Applications 325
      Viewing KDE Application Handbooks 326

Using Systemwide Help in GNOME and KDE 327
    Launching and Using GNOME's Help Browser.....................................328
    Launching and Using KDE's HelpCenter...330
Reading Other Documentation on the Desktop 332
    Reading man and info Pages Using the GNOME Help Browser 332
    Reading man and info Pages Using KDE's Konqueror 335
Summary...336
Q&A 337
Workshop 337
    Quiz 337
    Answers 338
    Activities 338

HOUR 15 Customizing the Desktop 339

Using the GNOME Control Center 340
    Changing Mouse Behavior 340
    Changing Window Appearance 343
    Changing Your Desktop Wallpaper 345
    Changing Your Screensaver..347
    Changing Other Desktop Preferences 348
Using the KDE Control Center..349
    Changing Mouse Behavior 349
    Changing Window Style 352
    Changing Application Colors 354
    Changing Window Borders and Title Bars 355
    Changing Desktop Wallpaper 356
    Changing Your Screensaver..359
Configuring the Desktop Taskbar...360
    Adding an Icon to the Taskbar in GNOME 360
    Adding an Icon or Menu to the Taskbar in KDE 361
    Moving an Icon on the Taskbar...362
    Removing an Icon from the Taskbar..362
    Additional Taskbar Configuration..362
Summary...363
Q&A 363
Workshop 364
    Quiz 364
    Answers 364
    Activities 364

HOUR 16 Advanced Linux Desktop Use 365

Introducing the Desktop Terminal Application 366
    Starting the Terminal Application 366
    Launching Desktop Applications with the Terminal...............................368

Job Control at the Terminal Command Line..369
Using nohup to Keep Jobs Running 370
Accessing Desktop Files from the Command Line 370
Using Basic X Window System Applications 371
Using a Desktop Terminal Without GNOME or KDE 372
Using Emacs on the Desktop 373
Using X Window System Convenience Applications 374
Interacting with the User in Shell Scripts...376
Using xmessage in Shell Scripts 376
Sample xmessage Script 376
Second Sample xmessage Script 378
Scripting the Nautilus File Manager..379
Creating and Using Shell Scripts with Nautilus 380
Sample Nautilus Shell Script...380
Summary 382
Q&A 382
Workshop 383
Quiz 383
Answers 383

HOUR 17 Using Desktop Applications Remotely   385

Understanding the X Window System Protocol....................................386
Networking X Using the Secure Shell 387
Displaying Single Remote Applications Using ssh 388
Displaying Remote Applications Locally Using ssh 389
Displaying Local Applications Remotely Using ssh 390
Configuring Firewall Security for Remote Display 390
Networking X Manually 392
Allowing Incoming X Connections with xhost 392
Displaying Local Applications Remotely 394
Displaying Remote Applications Locally 395
Allowing and Starting Remote X Sessions 396
Configuring the Login Manager for XDMCP............................396
Querying a Remote X Session 398
Summary...399
Q&A 399
Workshop 400
Quiz 400
Answers 401
Activities 401

Part IV Advanced Topics

HOUR 18 Command-Line System Administration **403**

Using the su Command 404

Managing System Processes...405

   Listing Running Processes 405

   Adjusting Process Priority...407

   Killing Running Processes 408

Managing Running Services..410

   Understanding Runlevels...410

   Selecting Automatically Started Services 412

   Stopping, Starting, and Restarting Running Services.......................414

Managing Filesystems 415

   Creating Filesystems 415

   Mounting and Unmounting Filesystems 418

   Maintaining the /etc/fstab File...420

Managing Accounts 421

   Adding and Removing User Accounts 422

   Adding and Removing Groups 423

   Administering Groups 423

   Changing Group Membership..424

Using cron to Manage Periodic Jobs 425

   Adding Systemwide cron Processes 425

   Editing Per-User cron Processes 425

Shutting Down and Restarting 427

Summary...428

Q&A 429

Workshop 429

   Quiz 429

   Answers 429

   Activities 430

HOUR 19 Desktop System Administration **431**

Managing System Processes...432

   Adjusting Process Priority...433

   Killing Running Processes 434

Managing Running Services...435

   Launching and Quitting the Service Configuration Tool 435

   Enabling or Disabling Services..436

   Stopping, Starting, and Restarting Services 436

Managing Network Interfaces 437

   Editing Static IP or DHCP Properties..439

   Manually Configuring DNS Information 440

   Enabling or Disabling Network Interfaces 440

Managing Accounts 441
    Adding and Removing Users 442
    Adding and Removing Groups 442
    Editing Group Membership..443
Reading System Logs 444
Mounting and Unmounting Filesystems..445
    Formatting a Device or Partition 445
Summary 446
Q&A 447
Workshop 447
    Quiz 447
    Answers 448

HOUR 20 Security Basics   **449**

Managing the Red Hat Linux Firewall 450
    Starting the Security Level Configuration Tool 450
    Choosing Security Level and Common Services 451
    Allowing Additional Traffic Exceptions 451
Understanding Advanced Permissions 452
    Changing File Ownership 453
    Using chmod in Numeric Mode 453
    Understanding Special Permissions 455
Protecting the Root Account..457
    Enabling the wheel Group 457
    Adding Users to wheel 458
    Changing Ownership and Permissions of su 458
Logging Out Users Automatically 459
    Setting a Login Timeout 459
    Removing Minor Shells..460
Summary 461
Q&A 461
Workshop 462
    Quiz 462
    Answers 462
    Activities 463

HOUR 21 Installing Software   **465**

Installing and Removing Red Hat Components 466
    Starting the Package Management Tool 466
    Installing and Removing Software in Groups................................468
    Using the Details Dialog 468
    Updating Your System..470

Using Third-Party Software 471
    Installing Software Packages...472
    Dealing with Failed Dependencies 473
Using the rpm Command 474
    Installing RPM Packages with rpm 474
    Upgrading RPM Packages with rpm 474
    Dealing with Failed Dependencies Using rpm 475
    Getting Information with rpm 475
    Uninstalling Software with rpm..476
    Resolving Circular Dependencies 477
Using Application Launchers 478
    Creating an Application Launcher in GNOME............................478
    Creating an Application Launcher in KDE 480
Summary 481
Q&A 482
Workshop 482
    Quiz 482
    Answers 483
    Activities 483

HOUR 22 Offering Network File Services   485

Before You Begin 486
Offering Network File System Service 486
    Starting the NFS Server Configuration Tool..............................487
    Adding and Configuring NFS Shares 488
    Starting NFS Automatically via the Desktop 490
    Configuring NFS at the Command Line 491
    Starting NFS Automatically via the Command Line 492
    Allowing NFS Through Your Firewall 492
Offering Windows File Sharing Service..494
    Installing Windows File Sharing Service 494
    Using Desktop Tools to Install SWAT..495
    Using the Command Line to Install SWAT.................................496
    Starting SWAT and Configuring Samba Basics 497
    Configuring Samba Shares 499
    Starting and Autostarting Windows File Service 501
    Creating Windows File Service Accounts...................................502
    Allowing Windows File Service Through Your Firewall 503
Summary 504
Q&A 505
Workshop 505
    Quiz 505
    Answers 506

HOUR 23 Offering Web and FTP Service   **507**

Before You Begin 508
Running a Web Server 508
    Installing Apache...509
    Configuring Apache to Start Automatically 510
    Allowing Web Requests Through Your Firewall..511
    Using the Apache Web Server..512
    Enabling Home Directory Web Sites 512
    Introducing the Apache Configuration Tool 515
    Basic Apache Security..516
    Additional Apache Configuration Information 518
Running a File Transfer Protocol (FTP) Server 519
    Enabling or Disabling FTP 519
    Configuring wu-ftpd to Answer Requests 520
    Allowing FTP Through Your Firewall..521
    Controlling FTP Access..521
    Using or Disabling Anonymous FTP 521
Summary 522
Q&A 522
Workshop 523
    Quiz 523
    Answers 523

HOUR 24 Backups, Troubleshooting, and Rescue   **525**

Backing Up and Restoring Your Data 526
    Backing Up to Disk..527
    Creating Backups with tar 528
    Backing Up with tar Examples 529
    Restoring tar Backups 530
    Restoring tar Backups Examples 531
    Testing and Listing Backups 532
    Automating tar Backups 533
Dealing with Catastrophic Failures 534
    Starting Rescue 534
    Attempting Filesystem Repairs 536
    Salvaging Files 537
Recognizing Other Critical Problems...538
    Recognizing Filesystem Trouble 538
    Recognizing Malicious Network Activity...539

Summary 541

Q&A 541

Workshop 542

   Quiz 542

   Answers 542

   Activities 543

Appendix A Installer Troubleshooting   545

        Index   551

About the Author

ARON HSIAO is a longtime Unix and Linux enthusiast with 15 years of experience using Unix-like operating systems. Over the years, he has worked in network deployment, software development, Web development, and Internet advertising. He has also worked as a volunteer in a number of computer-related capacities in his community and served as the About.com guide to Linux for several years. He holds a degree in English and Anthropology from the University of Utah, but finds his technology skills to be more marketable. He is also the author of *The Concise Guide to XFree86 for Linux* and *Sams Teach Yourself Linux Security Basics in 24 Hours*.

Dedication

To everyone I've ever loved. You know who you are. ;)

Acknowledgments

With each writing project I undertake, the challenges are different but many of the people remain the same. Thanks to my family members, who have been extra editors, and to Carlos and Lydia, whose contributions are unique and immeasurable—without all of you, this book wouldn't have happened.

The rest of the Sams team also had a lot to do with the ultimate course of this book. Many thanks are due to Katie, Lorna, Dave, Nancy, Tricia, and everyone else who worked on this title and helped to propel it forward in spite of the difficulties we've encountered. Thanks, everyone, for giving it your all!

We Want to Hear from You!

As the reader of this book, *you* are our most important critic and commentator. We value your opinion and want to know what we're doing right, what we could do better, what areas you'd like to see us publish in, and any other words of wisdom you're willing to pass our way.

You can email or write me directly to let me know what you did or didn't like about this book—as well as what we can do to make our books stronger.

Please note that I cannot help you with technical problems related to the topic of this book, and that due to the high volume of mail I receive, I might not be able to reply to every message.

When you write, please be sure to include this book's title and author as well as your name and phone or email address. I will carefully review your comments and share them with the author and editors who worked on the book.

Email: opensource@samspublishing.com

Mail: Mark Taber
          Associate Publisher
          Sams Publishing
          201 West 103rd Street
          Indianapolis, IN 46290 USA

Reader Services

For more information about this book or others from Sams Publishing, visit our Web site at www.samspublishing.com. Type the ISBN (excluding hyphens) or the title of the book in the Search box to find the book you're looking for.

Introduction

Welcome to Linux.

You're reading this introduction, so it's likely that you've heard the hype: Linux is a fast, free, stable operating system that is working better for you and me every day. Linux powers a large portion of the servers that form the backbone of the World Wide Web and the Internet. Linux can be found operating manufacturing equipment, point of sale equipment, automotive equipment, personal data management equipment, and even scientific research equipment at secretive government agencies. Vendors, too, are now heavily invested in Linux; large, traditional companies such as IBM have adopted Linux as the basis for entire large-scale computing product lines.

This book will help anyone wanting to use Red Hat Linux for any of these purposes. Its real target audience, however, is somewhat more accessible: the ever-growing body of average computer users, small business owners, and network administrators who want to use Red Hat Linux to do everyday work of all kinds. This book assumes that you have no previous experience working with Red Hat Linux; it presents all of the information you need to get acquainted and become productive with the system—right away.

This book is organized into 24 follow-along lessons, each approximately an hour in length. Each of these lessons begins with a list of topics you'll cover over the course of an hour; each lesson is designed to instruct you in one major topic related to Red Hat Linux. As you progress through the lessons presented here, you'll learn to install Red Hat Linux for yourself; to perform everyday tasks, such as Web browsing, word processing, or file management at the command line and on the desktop; and to troubleshoot and administer a Linux PC or small Linux server.

Why Red Hat Linux?

If you have studied Linux at all, you are probably aware of the number of popular "distributions" of Linux, each of which is an operating system in its own right. Red Hat is one of the most popular Linux distributions. Others that might sound familiar to you are Debian Linux, S.u.S.E. Linux, Linux Mandrake, Connectiva Linux, and Slackware Linux. Make no mistake—each of these products is *Linux*, built from the same rock-solid code and with many of the same goals in mind. These products also are largely compatible with one another, both in hardware and software terms. Still, each maintains its own unique focus and personality as well—Debian for Linux purists; Mandrake for those seeking ease of use above all else; Slackware for converts from other, more traditional Unix operating systems; and so on.

In the final analysis, however, Red Hat Linux remains by far the most visible of the Linux operating systems. Red Hat is by most accounts largely responsible for bringing Linux from the marketplace of ideas to the marketplace of commerce. Red Hat is also among the most popular of Linux operating systems, thanks to its completeness, balance and ease of installation and administration. If you're thinking of giving Linux a try, you can't go wrong with Red Hat.

What You'll Learn in 24 Hours

As a set of 24 one-hour lessons, this book is written to be studied one chapter at a time, in order, from beginning to end. Early lessons ground you in Red Hat Linux basics, and later lessons build on the foundations laid by those earlier lessons. Together, these lessons represent a general introduction to Linux use and to the nuances of Red Hat Linux in particular. Again, the information in this book is targeted toward readers with no prior experience with Linux or other Unix-like operating systems.

There are four major topics to discuss when learning to use a Unix-like operating system; they are presented in logical order in this book's four parts:

- Chapters 1–3 cover basic installation, configuration, and troubleshooting of Red Hat Linux. This is an important topic because so few PCs and only a relatively small number of low-end servers come bundled with Linux today, meaning you'll likely be installing and configuring Linux yourself.

- Chapters 4–9 cover the basics of the command line for file management and day-to-day computing and networking tasks. For all the discussion of Linux (and Unix) on the desktop, the command line still lies at the center of the Linux universe. Though efforts have been underway to change this for some time, only from the command line are *all* aspects of a Linux system accessible and configurable.

- Chapters 10–17 introduce the Linux desktops bundled with Red Hat Linux, GNOME and KDE, and the X Window System technology, which represents the foundation of all. These environments are designed to be friendly and accessible to Windows users; they include or work with a number of business-oriented and network-oriented applications similar to those found in the Windows and Mac OS worlds.

- Chapters 18–24 cover system administration and related advanced topics in Linux. The term *system administration* refers loosely to the set of skills necessary to keep a Linux system securely and robustly operating, often while providing specific services to multiple users, usually on a network. Though it isn't always necessary to understand Linux system administration in order to perform everyday tasks such as word processing or Web browsing, system administration remains an essential skill for users hoping to employ Linux for anything other than purely personal computing. Even casual Linux users are likely to need some system administration skills—for example, the ability to install software or to back up important data.

Users with some Linux experience already might find that they want to study only particular lessons, or to study lessons in a different order. Each of these lessons should be self-contained enough to make this type of study possible. For those with no previous Linux experience, however, I prefer to repeat the sage advice of Lewis Carroll:

"Begin at the beginning, and go on till you come to the end: then stop."

Enjoy teaching yourself Red Hat Linux!

Conventions Used in This Book

This book uses the following conventions:

Text that you type and text that you see onscreen appears in monospace type:

```
It will look like this.
```

Variables and placeholders (words that stand for what you will actually type) appear in *italic monospace*.

Each chapter ends with questions pertaining to that day's subject matter, with answers from the author. Most chapters also include an exercise section and a quiz designed to reinforce that day's concepts.

A **Note** presents interesting information related to the discussion.

A **Tip** offers advice or shows you an easier way of doing something.

A **Caution** alerts you to a possible problem and gives you advice on how to avoid it.

NEW TERM New terms are introduced using the New Term icon. The new term appears in *italic*.

INPUT The Input icon identifies code that you can type in yourself. It usually appears next to a listing.

OUTPUT The Output icon hightlights the output produced by running the Java application or applet.

ANALYSIS The Analysis icon designates the author's line-by-line analysis.

When a line of code is too long to fit on one line of this book, it is broken at a convenient place and continued to the next line. The continuation is preceded by a special code continutation character (➥).

HOUR 1

Preparing to Install Red Hat Linux

Few computer users in the world have ever installed an operating system from scratch. Even today, with Linux enjoying more popularity than ever before, most computers of any kind are delivered with another operating system already installed. As a Red Hat Linux user, you probably will be installing Linux yourself. Because the world of PC hardware is diverse, and because it is often helpful to have both Linux and Windows installed at once, preinstallation preparation will help your Linux experience proceed smoothly.

In this hour, you

- Create a simple inventory of the central hardware items in your computer system to aid in installing Linux.
- Compare the hardware inventory that you create against the requirements for installing Red Hat Linux and perform upgrades to your hardware if necessary.

- Learn to make space on an existing hard drive for Red Hat Linux through a process called *repartitioning*.
- Launch the Red Hat Linux installer in preparation for your next hour, "Installing Red Hat Linux."

If you are not experienced with PC hardware or installing operating systems, hang in there. The first few hours might seem challenging, but it gets easier from there.

Taking a Hardware Inventory

In the past, you typically had to create a detailed and technical inventory of your computer system's hardware before attempting to install Linux because the software used to install Linux wasn't particularly clever; most users therefore had to explicitly tell Linux about their hardware configuration before Linux would function properly. Thankfully, this is no longer the case; the Red Hat Linux 8.0 installer is likely to discover and accommodate most of your hardware without needing extra help. You still need to know a few basic details about your computer system, however, so that you can make good decisions about swap space, package selection, and other details that you'll encounter while installing Linux.

Prospective Linux users are often experienced PC users who are knowledgeable about their computer hardware; similarly, users who purchased their computer system through retail channels are likely to have such hardware details already close at hand. If you fall into either of these categories, feel free to proceed to the next section; the remainder of this section is designed to help users who aren't extremely familiar with the hardware on which they plan to install Linux.

> Most of the step-by-step directions in this section are targeted at users who already have Windows installed on their computer system. Because there are several different versions of Windows, each of which behaves differently, you might find that you have to make minor adjustments to some of the steps. For example, users of Windows XP might need to click on the Switch to Classic View link in the Windows control panel in order to follow along completely.

Memory Capacity

The memory capacity of a computer system is commonly expressed in megabytes (MB) or kilobytes (KB); one megabyte equals 1,024 kilobytes. Common memory capacities in today's PCs range from 32MB (32,768KB) to 256MB (262,144KB), though it is no longer uncommon to see systems with memory capacities as high as 768MB (786,432KB) or more.

If you don't know your system's memory capacity, you probably can determine it by watching your computer system's BIOS (basic input/ouput system) display; this is generally the first thing you see on your monitor as you power on the computer system. Most PCs today perform a quick memory check before attempting to load an operating system. Look for the appearance of small numbers in multiples of 16 (32, 64, 96, 128), which indicate your memory size in MB, or large numbers in multiples of 1,024 (32,768, 65,536, 98,304, 131,072), which indicate your memory size in KB.

A BIOS display containing memory capacity information is shown in Figure 1.1.

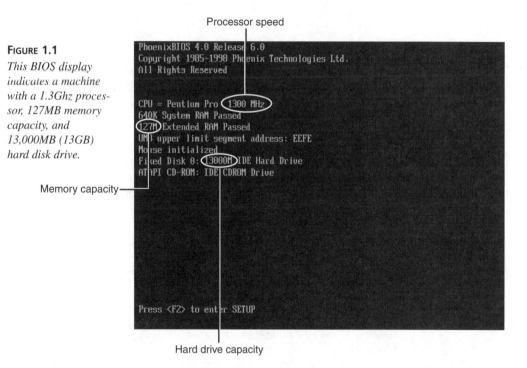

FIGURE 1.1

This BIOS display indicates a machine with a 1.3Ghz processor, 127MB memory capacity, and 13,000MB (13GB) hard disk drive.

Processor speed

Memory capacity

Hard drive capacity

If your PC has an existing installation of Windows, you can find the memory capacity listed in the System and device manager tool by following these steps:

1. Double-click the My Computer icon on your Windows desktop. The Windows Explorer appears, displaying icons for each storage device in your system plus an icon labeled Control Panel that can be used to launch the Windows control panel.

2. Double-click the Control Panel icon in the Windows Explorer. The Windows control panel appears, displaying icons for a number of different configuration dialogs.

3. Double-click the System icon in the Windows control panel to open the System and device manager tool. The System Properties dialog box appears, displaying the amount of memory detected by Windows, as shown in Figure 1.2.

FIGURE 1.2

The System Properties dialog box will show the amount of memory present and in some versions of Windows, the CPU type and speed.

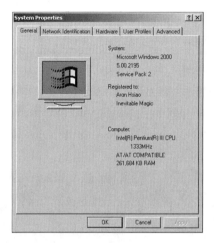

CPU (Processor) Speed

Most PCs today contain a processor made by one of two companies, Intel or Advanced Micro Devices (AMD). The Intel line of processors includes the Celeron, Pentium, and Pentium Xeon families, and the AMD line of processors includes the K6, Duron, and Athlon families. In the end, however, it is the speed of the CPU in megahertz (Mhz) or gigahertz (Ghz) that matters most to your ability to run Red Hat Linux.

One gigahertz is equivalent to 1,000MHz; a 2Ghz processor is thus equivalent to a 2,000Mhz processor. If you are unsure about the speed and model of your processor, you should look again at your BIOS display for this information.

Some users might find that their BIOS does not display hardware information as they power on. In such cases, it might be necessary to enter your BIOS setup area to learn about your installed memory capacity and CPU model and speed.

This can generally be accomplished by pressing a designated key as the computer system starts. Often, there is a message such as the following explaining how to do this on the screen:

```
Press F1 to enter setup.
```

Common BIOS setup keys include F1, F2, Delete, Insert, End, and Esc. The required keystroke will usually be discussed in system or mainboard documentation.

Hard Drive Capacity

If you have an existing Windows installation, finding your hard drive capacity and available free space are simple tasks:

1. Double-click the My Computer icon on your Windows desktop. The Windows Explorer appears, displaying icons for each storage device in your system. Your first hard drive is normally drive C, and additional hard drives, if any, may have icons as well.

2. Right-click the icon for the hard drive where you plan to install Red Hat Linux. In the context menu that appears, choose the Properties option.

3. A pie chart appears, showing the capacity of the hard drive in question, along with the relative amounts of used and available storage space.

If you do not have an existing installation of Windows, you might also be able to obtain information about your hard drive capacity by watching your BIOS display. Many newer systems display either hard drive capacity or hard drive make and model information as the computer starts. Armed with make and model details, you can visit a hard drive manufacturer on the World Wide Web or contact it by telephone in order to find capacity information.

If you are unable to find any hard drive capacity information using these methods, you might be able to find it later in this hour when we discuss using FIPS, a tool for resizing Windows partitions to make room for Linux.

Communications Hardware

Nearly every modern PC contains either ethernet hardware, modem hardware, or both. As a Linux user, you'll use the Internet early and often for software and for support, so it's important that your communications hardware be compatible with Linux. Nearly any PCI ethernet card or on-motherboard ethernet controller will work with Linux.

Modems, however, are a more complex issue:

- External serial port (RS-232) modems are ideal; these are well supported by Linux and require no special drivers or configuration work. Unfortunately, they require traditional serial ports, which are being phased out on newer PCs.

- Very old internal ISA (16-bit) slot modems will also generally work with Linux, though some Plug and Play modems might require additional configuration to work properly. Unfortunately, most PCs new enough to run Red Hat Linux 8.0 will not have ISA slots.

- External USB modems might also work, but only if they conform to the USB Abstract Control Model (ACM) standard.

- Internal PCI modems—the most common type shipping with PCs today—are also the most problematic. Many of these require special software to function; more often than not, this software is made available only for Windows. If you have an internal PCI modem and find yourself unable to use it after you finish installing Red Hat Linux, you might have to purchase another type of modem if you plan to use the Internet with Linux (see the Note for additional information).

The process of identifying the hardware used in an internal modem can be involved and is therefore beyond the scope of this book. Adventurous and determined users with internal modems can visit `http://linmodems.org` for details on using modern internal modems with Linux.

For most other users, the answer is to use an external modem with Linux, preferably of the traditional serial port (RS-232) variety. USB modems can also work so long as they conform to the USB Abstract Control Model (ACM) standard. Most USB modems for Mac OS computers fall into this category; these modems will also work with Red Hat Linux, even on computers that originally shipped with Windows.

The most complete reference for using modems of various types with Linux is the Linux Modem-HOWTO, which can be found online at the Linux Documentation Project: `http://www.tldp.org/HOWTO/Modem-HOWTO.html`.

Evaluating Your Hardware

Red Hat Linux 8.0 is a modern network operating system with a powerful Graphical User Interface (GUI). Though Linux operating systems are generally quite modular and have been known to run on very small or very old computing hardware, such minimalist feats are generally better left to the experts. You can compare your computer's hardware inventory against the list in Table 1.1 of suggested requirements for running Red Hat Linux 8.0.

TABLE 1.1   Suggested Requirements for Running Red Hat Linux 8.0

Hardware Item	Suggested Minimum
CPU (processor)	Celeron, Pentium, K6, Duron, or Athlon processor running at 300Mhz (0.3Ghz) or faster. Processors slower than 300Mhz might feel very sluggish; ancient 386 or 486 processors will be unbearably slow.
Memory capacity	128MB (131,072KB) or more. Frugal users might be able to get by with 64MB, (65,536KB) but less memory availability will certainly incur severe performance penalties.

TABLE 1.1   continued

1

Hardware Item	Suggested Minimum
Hard drive space	2GB (2,000MB) or more of free disk space is the comfortable minimum. Ideally, 5–10GB (5,000–10,000MB) of disk space should be available for serious work.
Ethernet or modem	Internet access is really a necessity for the serious Linux user. Most common ethernet hardware is supported by Linux, but modems are much more problematic. If you find that yours will not function after you installed Linux, check with the manufacturer for Linux compatibility. If your hardware isn't compatible with Red Hat Linux, you need to replace it.

As a beginner, if your hardware inventory falls short in one or several areas when compared against this list of suggested requirements, you should give serious consideration to upgrading or replacing the computer system in question before installing Red Hat Linux 8.0.

Making Space for Linux

After you've made sure your hardware is suitable for use with Red Hat Linux 8.0, you must ensure that there is space available on your hard drive for a Linux installation. Unfortunately, this is not as simple as it might seem. Merely having unused space on your hard drive is not enough; a proper Linux installation requires *unpartitioned* space.

Understanding Partitions

Every PC operating system, from Windows to OS/2 to Linux, must be installed on a hard drive partition. A *partition* is an area of the hard drive that has been set aside specifically for one operating system; in a sense, it is space that is "owned" by the operating system in question.

Most PCs today ship with Windows preinstalled. The entire hard drive has therefore been given to Windows; such drives contain only one partition, which occupies the entire drive.

Because of this, when you install Linux on a system that already contains Windows, you have only two courses of action:

- Delete the Windows partition that occupies the entire hard drive and replace it with Linux partition(s) that occupy the entire hard drive. This has the effect of *removing* Windows from the computer system. The entire computer system and its hard drive are owned exclusively by Linux. When the computer is powered on, it starts Linux immediately.

- Resize or rebuild the Windows partition so that it no longer occupies the entire hard drive, and then create additional partition(s) in the resulting free space that can be owned by Linux. The effect is like placing a large wooden screen across the middle of a room and declaring one section of the room yours and the other section mine. One section of a repartitioned hard drive belongs to Windows and the other section to Linux. The user can choose to start either Linux or Windows each time the computer is switched on. This is commonly referred to as *dual-booting*.

Most users interested in building a Linux network server replace the Windows partition completely so that Linux has exclusive control of the computer. If this is what you plan to do, feel free to skip the rest of this section—you do not need to worry about repartitioning because the Red Hat Linux installer can delete existing Windows partitions for you.

If you plan to dual-boot Linux and Windows—that is, share one hard drive between them—you need to repartition. Most desktop and laptop computer users who are installing Linux for the first time choose this option.

> Dual booting is a good choice for the beginner because it enables Windows to act as a failsafe. If you have trouble installing or configuring Linux, for example, you can visit Red Hat's Web page for technical support. On the other hand, dual booting means that less space will be available to Linux because some of your existing hard drive space has been reserved for Windows.
>
> Some users prefer not to dual boot but still want to run Windows applications. Two solutions stand head and shoulders above the rest for such needs: Win4Lin, which can be found at `http://www.netraverse.com`, and VMWare, which can be found at `http://www.vmware.org`.

Nondestructive Repartitioning

Users of Windows 95, 98, and ME can easily make room for Linux by using a utility called FIPS, which is included with the Red Hat Linux 8.0 media. FIPS shrinks an existing Windows partition while preserving the data stored there. Linux partition(s) can then be created in the resulting unassigned space.

Unfortunately, FIPS does not work with most Windows 2000 or XP systems because FIPS does not support resizing NTFS partitions, which are used by default in newer Windows versions. If you are not using Windows 95, 98, or ME, you can determine whether FIPS will work for you by following these steps:

1. Double-click the My Computer icon on your Windows desktop to open Windows Explorer and display icons for each storage device in your system.

2. Right-click the icon representing the hard drive you want to repartition and select Properties from the popup context menu.

3. Look for the phrase `File system` in the Properties dialog box. If the file system listed is FAT or FAT32, FIPS *can* be used to resize your Windows partition while preserving all your data. If the file system listed is NTFS, FIPS *cannot* be used on your existing partition. Figure 1.3 shows a Properties dialog box for an unresizable NTFS file system.

FIGURE 1.3

If you see the word NTFS in your Properties dialog box, your hard drive partition cannot be resized using FIPS.

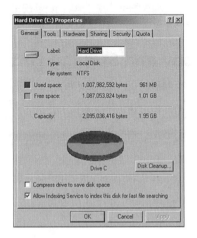

Defragmenting Prior to Using FIPS

Before you actually use FIPS, you must defragment the drive partition. Defragmentation is necessary prior to running FIPS because FIPS can shrink a Windows partition only if there is a contiguous area of unused space available. Defragmenting packs existing data toward the beginning of the partition, leaving all the unused space toward the end, where FIPS can trim it away.

You launch the Windows defragmentation tool by following these steps:

1. Double-click the My Computer icon on your Windows desktop to open Windows Explorer and display icons for each storage device in your system.

2. Right-click the icon representing the hard drive you want to defragment; select Properties from the popup context menu.

3. Select the Tools tab from the dialog box that appears.

4. Click the Defragment Now button. A progress indicator shows that your hard drive is being defragmented. When Windows indicates that defragmentation has finished, exit the defragmentation tool.

FIPS is a well-tested program that does a remarkably good job of resizing existing partitions while preserving data. But don't forget that *you* are responsible for protecting your data. Be absolutely sure that you have backed up any important files before attempting to resize your Windows partition.

Most users choose at least to copy the contents of their My Documents folder to removable storage media, such as Zip or CD-ROM. That way, if a hard drive is accidentally erased, the most important files are preserved.

Creating a FIPS Floppy and Starting FIPS

The FIPS program is on your Red Hat Linux 8.0 install CD. While you're running Windows, insert the disk into your PC, open the dosutils folder, and then open the fips20 folder. Double-click the fips.doc file in that folder and print it; you need to be familiar with this documentation before you use FIPS to resize your partition.

FIPS must be run from a DOS boot floppy. Such a floppy can be created only on an MS-DOS, Windows 95, 98, or ME system; Windows 2000 and Windows XP do not provide utilities for creating DOS boot floppies. Windows 2000 and XP users not intending to use FIPS can move to the section "Destructive Repartitioning," later in this hour.

Windows 2000 and Windows XP users will need to gain temporary access to an MS-DOS, Windows 95, 98, or ME computer system in order to create a boot floppy following the directions given below. If you use Windows 2000 or Windows XP and don't have access to a computer system suitable for creating a boot floppy, destructive repartitioning is the only way to provide space for Linux on an existing Windows hard drive.

To create a DOS boot floppy containing FIPS from within Windows 95, 98, or ME, follow these steps:

1. Insert a blank floppy disk into your PC.
2. Double-click the My Computer icon on your Windows desktop; then right-click the icon representing the floppy drive. A context menu will appear.
3. Choose the Format option from the pop-up context menu. A dialog box appears presenting floppy formatting options, as shown in Figure 1.4.
4. Select Full as the format type and check the Copy system files box. Click Start to format the floppy.

5. When the format has finished, return to the fips20 folder on the Red Hat Linux install CD, select all of the files in that folder, and drag the files from the fips20 folder to the newly formatted floppy, as shown in Figure 1.5.

FIGURE 1.4

The Format Floppy dialog box allows you to format a DOS boot floppy.

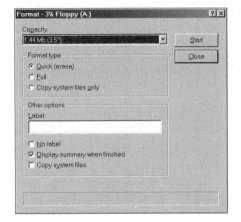

When you have created your FIPS floppy and printed the `fips.doc` file, switch off your computer. Insert the FIPS floppy disk into the PC, and power on again. When you reach the DOS prompt, type **fips** and press Enter. Carefully follow the directions in fips.doc to resize partition(s) according to your needs.

FIGURE 1.5

Select all the files in the fips20 directory with the mouse, and then drag them to the empty floppy disk.

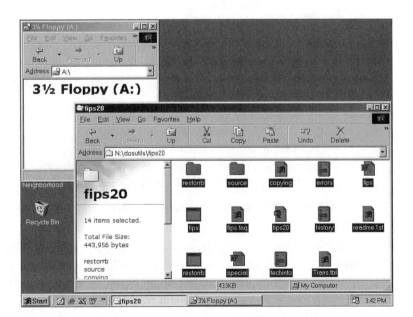

The following FIPS walk-through assumes that you have only one hard drive in your system. If you will be resizing partitions on a hard drive other than your primary hard drive, consult the FIPS documentation for instructions.

Using FIPS

When you first start FIPS, you're asked to page (by pressing Enter) through a small amount of information, and then you're shown a range of information about your hard drive as FIPS performs a couple of basic sanity checks:

```
Boot sector:

Bytes per sector: 512
Sectors per cluster: 8
Reserved sectors: 32
Number of FATs: 2
Number of rootdirectory entries: 0
Number of sectors (short): 0
Media descriptor byte: F8h
Sectors per FAT: 3993
Sectors per track: 63
Drive heads: 64
Hidden sectors: 63
Number of sectors (long): 4092417
Physical drive number: 80h
Signature: 29h
Checking boot sector ... OK
Checking FAT ... OK
Searching for free space ... OK
```

FIPS then asks whether you want to back up the root and boot sectors of your hard drive:

```
Do you want to make a backup copy of your root and boot sector before
proceeding (y/n)?
```

Should FIPS fail to correctly repartition your hard drive, you will need these backups to restore your original partition information and avoid data loss. To protect yourself against such loss, choose y. FIPS then prompts you to insert a bootable floppy disk:

```
Do you have a bootable floppy disk in drive A: as described in the
documentation (y/n)?
```

You can answer y to this question as well, because you started FIPS from the bootable floppy. FIPS creates a root and boot sector backup file on your floppy called root-boot.000. You can use the rootboot floppy to restore some of your hard drive's structure if anything goes wrong and you find that your system no longer boots as expected (see the FIPS documentation for details on restoring from backups).

After the rootboot.000 backup file is created, FIPS presents you with a simple table listing old partition size, cylinder boundary, and new partition size.

```
Old partition       Cylinder        New partition
  397.7 MB            202             1600.6 MB
```

The old partition size is the amount of disk space that is allocated to Windows. Remember, this number does not represent the *free* space available to Windows, but rather *all* space allocated to Windows (including space used by existing files and folders). The new partition size is the amount of space that is unallocated and available to the Red Hat Linux installer for Linux use. Use your left- or right-arrow key to adjust these values to allocate space as desired to the old and new partitions. Remember that you should ideally have at least 2,000MB of disk space for Linux—or more if you plan to use Linux seriously.

When you are satisfied with the numbers FIPS shows, press Enter to confirm the changes. FIPS is not the most user-friendly application, but it is an essential tool. FIPS performs several more sanity checks and displays a table showing your proposed new partitions, as shown in Figure 1.6.

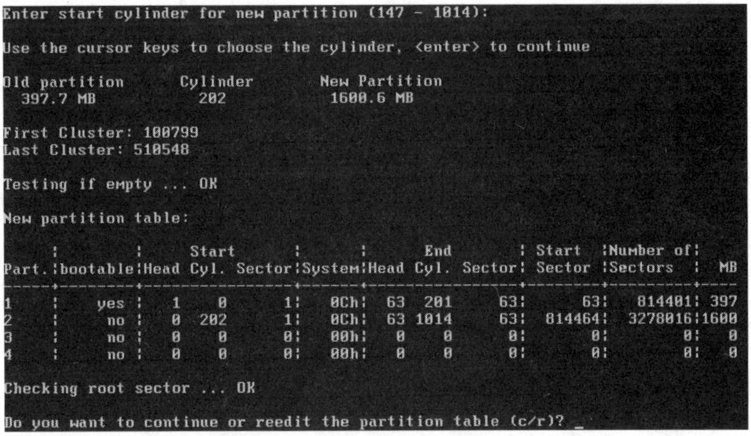

FIGURE 1.6

FIPS displays the proposed new partition table for user review. Check the sizes shown in the rightmost column to make sure they match the numbers you've selected.

After displaying the new partition details, FIPS asks whether you want to continue (you have one more chance to abort before changes are saved) or reedit the partition table:

```
Do you want to continue or reedit the partition table (c/r)?
```

Select r to re-edit if you have changed your mind about the sizes of the partitions you want to create. If you select c to continue, you are shown an updated range of information about your hard drive as it will appear after the changes are made. FIPS then asks you one final time to confirm your changes:

```
Ready to write new partition scheme to disk
Do you want to proceed (y/n)?
```

This is your last chance to change your mind, by selecting n at the prompt. If you have not yet backed up your data, you should seriously consider selecting n now, exiting and backing up your data before running FIPS again. If you are ready to save your changes and resize your Windows partition, select y to proceed. You quickly see a success message:

```
Repartitioning complete
With FAT32 partitions, you should now run scandisk on the shortened partition
```

Remove the floppy disk, reboot into Windows, and perform a file system integrity check by following these steps:

1. Double-click the My Computer icon on your Windows desktop.
2. Right-click the icon representing the hard drive you want to defragment; then select Properties from the popup context menu.
3. Select the Tools tab from the dialog box that appears.
4. Click the Check Now button in the Error-checking status section of the dialog box, as shown in Figure 1.7. A dialog box appears; click Start to begin. The check takes several minutes, and a summary is displayed when it is complete.

FIGURE 1.7
Click the Check Now button to begin a filesystem check.

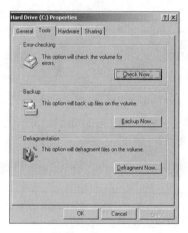

After you run FIPS to make space for Linux and check your newly resized Windows partition for errors, you are ready to launch the Red Hat Linux installer.

Destructive Repartitioning

Destructive repartitioning works just as horribly as it sounds: you must use your Windows 2000 or XP install CD to *erase your hard drive completely and install Windows from scratch*, taking care to specify that you want Windows to use only a portion of your hard drive rather than the entire thing.

Destructive repartitioning lives up to its name—it *erases* all your existing Windows data. You must therefore back up any data that you want to preserve, or you will lose it forever!

Most users choose at least to copy the contents of their My Documents folder to removable storage media such as Zip or CD-ROM. That way, if a hard drive is accidentally erased, the most important files are preserved.

The process of installing and partitioning Windows varies among the different releases of the operating system. Full instructions for installing and partitioning your version of Windows can be found in the installation guide that accompanied your Windows CD-ROM. To repartition using a Windows 2000 install CD, follow these steps:

1. Insert and boot from the Windows install CD-ROM. A number of drivers will be loaded; this may take some time. After the drivers are loaded, the Welcome to Setup screen is displayed.

2. At the Welcome to Setup screen, press Enter to indicate that you want to install Windows 2000. A list of existing partitions is displayed.

3. Use the up and down arrows to select the partition marked C:, and press the d key to delete the partition. A warning screen is displayed.

4. Press Enter to confirm that you want to delete the partition. A second warning screen is displayed. Press l to delete the partition.

5. The partition list is displayed once again. Use the arrow keys to select the Unpartitioned Space entry, as shown in Figure 1.8. Then press c to create a partition of your own choosing.

6. The partition sizing screen appears (see Figure 1.9). This screen enables the user to select a partition size for Windows.

7. After you have entered the partition size you want, press Enter to redisplay the partition list. Be sure to create a partition large enough to hold Windows plus any applications that you want to install—usually no smaller than 2,000MB.

8. Select the C: entry in the partition list and press Enter once more to proceed with Windows installation, using your Windows installation guide.

FIGURE 1.8

Select the unpartitioned space, and then press C to create a new partition for Windows in that space.

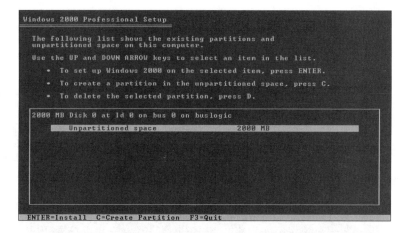

FIGURE 1.9

The Windows 2000 installer enables the user to allocate only a portion of the drive to Windows. Here, 4.0GB of storage space is being allocated for the Windows 2000 partition. The remaining 6GB is available for Linux.

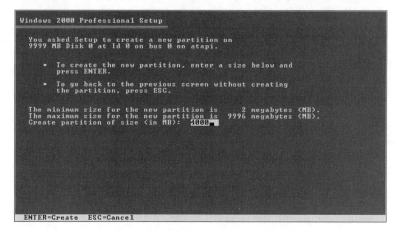

If you are reinstalling Windows 2000 or Windows XP as part of a destructive repartitioning of your hard drive, be sure to specify that you want Windows installed on a FAT32 partition, rather than on an NTFS partition. This allows you to use FIPS in the future to resize your Windows partition, should you need to do so; it also allows Linux to access your Windows data—something that can't currently be accomplished with an NTFS partition.

There are several commercial software packages that can nondestructively resize Windows 2000 or XP NTFS partitions with varying degrees of success. Partition Magic is one of these; more information can be found at http://www.partitionmagic.com. Another such utility is called BootIt Next Generation; a demo version, available from http://www.bootitng.com will help you decide whether BootIt is the right product for you.

After selecting the Windows partition size, simply install Windows using the installation instructions that accompany your Windows CD-ROM. After you finish reinstalling Windows to make space for Linux, the destructive repartitioning process is complete and you are ready to launch the Red Hat Linux installer.

Avoiding Repartitioning by Adding a Hard Drive

If all this talk of repartitioning has you running scared, you are not alone. Even pros who have installed Linux many times dread repartitioning for a dual-boot system. There are so many variables that sooner or later you are bound to erase a hard drive completely and find yourself restoring data from a pile of Zip and CD-ROM discs. Even when your data has been recently backed up, this process can be time-consuming and frustrating.

But there is an easier way, if you're willing to allow a modest hardware budget. Most PCs today can accommodate four Enhanced Integrated Device Electronics (EIDE) devices, such as hard drives, CD-ROM/RW drives, or DVD drives. Yet most PCs ship with only two drives connected—one hard drive and one removable drive (CD or DVD). This leaves room for up to two more EIDE devices in the typical PC.

Though the actual nuts and bolts of installing an additional hard drive are beyond the scope of this chapter, many experienced PC and Windows users are capable of adding a second hard drive to a PC system. Most computer retail shops can also install any hard drive you purchase for a modest labor fee. By adding a second hard drive, you gain several advantages:

- You can proceed directly to Red Hat Linux installation without needing to modify your Windows partitions at all.
- Your Linux data is kept separate from your Windows data, so that bugs in either operating system are less likely to affect data stored by the other.
- You lose no space in Windows to gain space for Linux.

If you can afford to have an additional hard drive installed, or if you can install one yourself, you should consider doing so instead of repartitioning.

Launching the Red Hat Linux Installer

As the finale to your first hour, it's time to install. For users of modern systems, this is a simple task.

Insert the Red Hat Linux 8.0 CD and restart your computer. If your computer is capable of booting from CD-ROM, you will quickly find yourself face-to-face with the Red Hat Linux logo. If this is the case, congratulations—your installation is complete!

If you're not lucky enough to have a PC capable of booting from CD, don't worry; bootable floppy disk images are stored in the images\ directory of the install CD. With these images and the rawrite tool found in the dosutils\ directory of the install CD, you can create a set of boot floppies to start the Red Hat Linux installer. From any Windows computer, follow these steps:

1. Insert the Red Hat install CD into your CD-ROM drive.

2. Double-click the My Computer icon on your Windows desktop; then double-click the icon for your CD-ROM drive to open the Red Hat Linux install CD.

3. Double-click the dosutils folder; then double-click the rawrite utility. A DOS window containing the rawrite utility opens, as shown in Figure 1.10.

4. At the Disk Image Source File Name prompt, type **\images\boot.img** and press Enter. The Enter Target Diskette Drive prompt is displayed.

5. At the Enter Target Diskette Drive prompt, type the letter of your floppy drive (usually **a**) and press Enter.

6. Insert a blank or newly formatted floppy disk and press Enter once more. The rawrite program reads the boot.img file and uses it to create a boot floppy; a numeric progress indicator is displayed as the disk is written.

7. Repeat the last three steps using the source file name **\images\drvblock.img** to create a separate drivers disk.

8. If you will be installing Red Hat Linux on a laptop or notebook computer, repeat steps 4 through 6 twice more, typing **\images\pcmcia.img** first, and then **\images\pcmciadd.img** to create two additional floppies that will contain drivers for common laptop and notebook hardware.

9. After you have created the Red Hat install floppies, close the window you've been working in.

When you finish creating the boot floppy, insert it in your PC and restart your computer. You should shortly find yourself staring at the Red Hat Linux logo. Congratulations—next hour, it's time to install Linux!

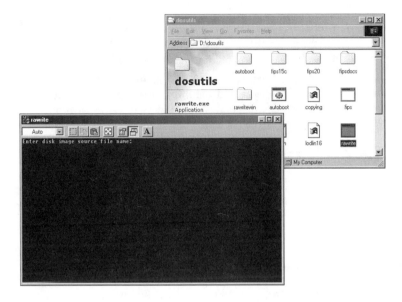

FIGURE 1.10
Creating the Red Hat Linux installation boot floppy.

Summary

This hour, you took a rough inventory of your computer's hardware and compared it to the minimal configuration required to install and run Red Hat Linux comfortably.

You learned how to make space for a Linux installation on a dual-boot system in one of several ways: by repartitioning with FIPS, by destructively repartitioning using a Windows install CD, or by adding an additional hard drive to your computer system.

Finally, you launched the Red Hat Linux installer, first creating boot floppies if your system was unable to boot the install CD.

Q&A

Q My computer system has a slower processor and/or less memory than is suggested. I am a patient person. Can't I install Red Hat Linux anyway, even if it's slow?

A Maybe, but probably not. A 386 or 486 processor will certainly get there in the end if simple arithmetic is the only task at hand. *However*, an older processor or limited amount of memory is usually indicative of an entire system full of older, slower components. You will find that some intensive tasks that take minutes on a 300Mhz Pentium system require *days* or even *weeks* on a 66Mhz 486 system.

Q **I've heard that Linux can be installed "on top of" a Windows file system, thereby eliminating the need to repartition. Is this true?**

A Several Linux operating systems are designed to be installed within a Windows file system. However, there are problems with such installations, not the least of which are performance and stability issues. If you're serious about Linux, you want partitions.

Workshop

The Workshop is designed to help you anticipate possible questions, review what you've learned, and begin learning how to put your knowledge into practice.

Quiz

1. What is the difference between nondestructive and destructive repartitioning?
2. What is the FIPS tool used for?
3. Which operating systems may not easily support nondestructive repartitioning?
4. In what circumstances are the Red Hat boot floppy disks needed?

Answers

1. Nondestructive repartitioning makes room for Linux without placing Windows data at risk; destructive repartitioning requires a complete erasure of the hard drive and a reinstallation of Windows.
2. The FIPS tool is the most popular tool among Linux users for nondestructive repartitioning.
3. Windows 2000 and Windows XP
4. They are needed for computers not able to boot from CD-ROM media.

Activities

1. Find out your computer's CPU type and speed, and memory and hard drive capacities.
2. Find out what type of modem is installed in your computer. If it is a PCI modem, visit http://www.linmodems.org and find out whether it's supported by Linux.

Hour 2

Installing Red Hat Linux

Last hour you prepared to install Red Hat Linux on your computer system.
This hour, it's time for the main event. By the end of this hour, you will have

- Created new partitions on your hard drive to hold the Linux operating
  system
- Selected a list of packages that are to be installed as your Red Hat
  Linux operating system
- Copied the Red Hat Linux operating system to your hard drive,
  including the list of packages you selected
- Configured Red Hat Linux for your graphics display hardware

It is during this hour that your Linux adventure truly begins; when this hour
is complete you should have a bootable installation of the Red Hat Linux
operating system on your computer.

Starting the Red Hat Linux Installer

At the end of Hour 1, "Preparing to Install Red Hat Linux," you found
yourself looking at the Red Hat Linux logo and facing a boot prompt after

having booted from your Red Hat install CD or install floppy. In order to install Linux, you must now boot Linux and start the installer.

Press Enter at the boot prompt to start the installer using the default options, which should work for most users. If Linux is able to locate your hard drive and your CD-ROM drive, the installer will find your Red Hat Linux install CD-ROM and ask whether you want to test your install media.

Unless your CD-ROM media is very scratched, feel free to skip the media test. This can be accomplished by pressing the Tab key until the word Skip is highlighted and then pressing Enter. If all goes as expected, you will see the screen clear and a Red Hat logo will be displayed as the graphical installer anaconda starts.

Beginning the Installation

After the graphical installer starts, you are shown a full-screen copyright notice with the Red Hat Linux logo for a few moments before the first screen of the installation process is displayed, as shown in Figure 2.1.

FIGURE 2.1

Welcome to the Red Hat Linux installer.

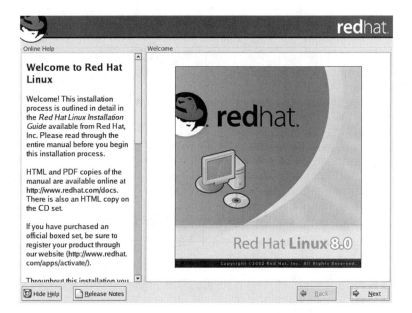

Screens in the default installer contain the following components or areas:

- The Release Notes button can be used at any time to display a dialog containing specific additional information about this release of Red Hat Linux.
- The Activity Panel is the area of the screen that you, the user, interact with as the installation process progresses.
- The Help Panel displays help information about the decisions you are making in the Activity Panel at any given time. You should always read the information in the Help Panel before making any changes in the Activity Panel.
- The Next button becomes active when you have completed all the necessary configuration in the Activity panel in this step of the installation; you can then click it to proceed to the next step of the installation.
- The Back button is used if you realize that you have made a mistake in a previous step of the installation and want to go back to remedy the mistake.

When you have read the information in the first screen's Help Panel and are ready to proceed with installation of Red Hat Linux, click the Next button to continue to the first step.

Language Selection

The first step of the installation process is to select the language that will be used by the installer itself as you proceed.

This is not the language that is used by Red Hat Linux itself after the operating system has been installed on your computer; your choice here applies only to the rest of the installation process. Click the Next button when you have selected the language you want to use.

Keyboard Configuration

Next, you are asked to select a national keyboard layout, as shown in Figure 2.2.

If you will be using a keyboard layout other than the standard U.S. English keyboard, you should select the layout that you want to use now. When you have made your selection, click the Next button to continue.

Mouse Configuration

Next, you are asked to configure your mouse or pointing device for use with Red Hat Linux—such things as the type of mouse you are using and the number of buttons it has. The Mouse Configuration screen is shown in Figure 2.3.

FIGURE 2.2

Installing a keyboard layout.

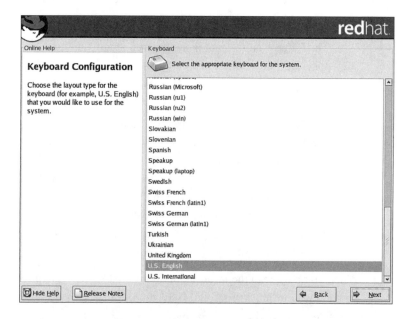

FIGURE 2.3

The Mouse Configuration dialog enables you to config- ure your pointing device. The default selection is often the safest.

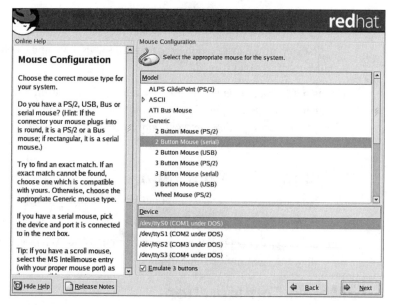

The default selection represents the method that the Red Hat Linux installer is using to communicate with your mouse right now; this selection is the result of the installer's best guess with respect to the type of mouse you are using.

If you know that the default selection is wrong or inadequate—for example, if the option for a two-button serial mouse has been selected but your serial mouse has three buttons, change the selection as needed. Users of mice with scroll wheels especially should choose one of the Microsoft Intellimouse options if their own make and model isn't listed.

If you are unsure about the type of mouse or pointing device you are using or can't find an entry in the list that seems to match it closely, you should leave the default option selected.

Users with only two mouse buttons should ensure that the Emulate 3 Buttons option near the bottom of the Activity Panel is checked. The third mouse button is actually used in a number of ways by the Linux desktop; checking this option enables you to simulate a third button by pressing the other two mouse buttons simultaneously.

> If your mouse or pointing device is working in the installer—if you can move the pointer and click buttons—you should consider leaving the default setting selected, especially if you can't find your particular model in the list of choices.

When you finish configuring your mouse or pointing device, click Next to continue with the installation.

Installation Type

After you select an installer language, a keyboard layout, and a mouse type, you are asked to indicate the type of Red Hat Linux installation you want to perform. The Installation Type screen is shown in Figure 2.4.

Each of these installation types differs significantly with regard to the software that will be installed and the way in which Red Hat Linux will behave when running.

- A Personal Desktop installation is well-suited to everyday productivity and office-related tasks—word processing, spreadsheets, Web browsing, emailing, and similar tasks commonly associated with personal computing.

- A Workstation installation tries to emulate the functionality found in traditional Unix workstations—in addition to everyday productivity tools, a more advanced set of system-oriented tools and utilities is installed, including a full development environment for writing software using the ANSI C and C++ programming languages that are popular in the Unix world.

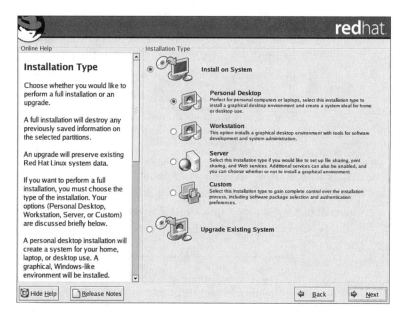

- A Server installation includes tools for offering and managing network services, allowing your computer to act as a Web server, file server, domain name server, or other type of server. By default, however, it installs little else. You are given a chance to select additional packages to install, such as the X Window System and GNOME or KDEs, later in the install process.

- A Custom installation enables those already somewhat familiar with Linux to control more closely the list of components that will be installed. Rather than provide a role-oriented default set of packages for installation, this option enables the user to choose which packages are to be installed later in the install process.

- The Upgrade Existing System option enables you to upgrade an earlier installation of Red Hat Linux. This book doesn't cover the upgrade process.

For most beginning Linux users, the correct choice is the Personal Desktop installation. Ambitious users who plan to do software development or want to gain experience with more Unix-like environments should choose the Workstation option. Users wanting to create a Linux server or who feel comfortable installing and customizing Linux can choose the Server or Custom options.

After you select the type of installation you want to perform, click Next to proceed.

Disk Partitioning Setup

Next you are asked which method you want to use to allocate disk space to Linux, as shown in Figure 2.5.

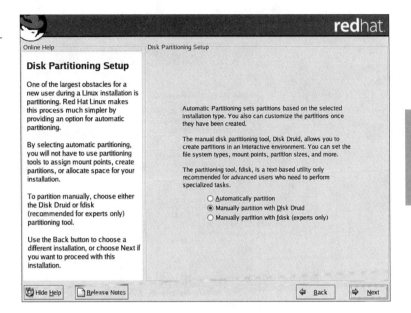

FIGURE 2.5

Selecting the partitioning method you want the installer to use.

Users who are installing Red Hat Linux alongside Windows or another operating system on a single hard drive should select Manually Partition with Disk Druid and click Next to proceed; the use of the `fips` utility to repartition a hard drive (as discussed in Hour 1) leaves the hard drive organized in a way that is not well-suited to the installer's automatic partitioning scheme. Proceed to the next section, "Disk Setup," if this is the option you have selected.

Users who have used destructive repartitioning or are installing Linux on a newly added hard drive can choose Automatically Partition and click the Next button to proceed to the Automatic Partitioning screen, shown in Figure 2.6.

If the size of your hard drive or the amount of free space available to Red Hat Linux is less than 4GB (4,000MB), automatic partitioning is not recommended because the automatic partitioning tool can make mistakes when space is limited. Instead, it is recommended that you partition manually using the Disk Druid tool, as outlined in the next section.

If you have more than one hard drive in your system, select the drive that should eventually hold Red Hat Linux. Additional hard drives are shown alongside the primary hard drive in the box in Figure 2.6. Then, choose among the following options:

Select partitioning behavior

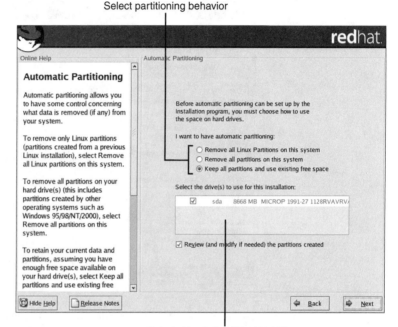

FIGURE 2.6

After selecting auto-
matic partitioning, the
installer asks you
questions about how it
should proceed.

Select drive to hold Red Hat Linux

- Select Remove All Linux Partitions on This System if you have an existing Linux installation on the drive in question and want to overwrite it with Red Hat Linux.
- Select Remove All Partitions on This System if you want to completely erase the selected hard drive, replacing its existing contents with Red Hat Linux.
- Select Keep All Partitions and Use Existing Free Space if you performed destructive repartitioning in Hour 1 or have unused, unpartitioned space on the selected hard drive.

Be sure to leave the Review (and modify, if needed) the Partitions Created check box checked so that you can preview the partitioning scheme the installer creates for you. When you are ready to continue, click Next to proceed to the Disk Setup screen.

Disk Setup

Next, you are shown the Disk Setup screen, which provides an interface to the Disk Druid tool. If you selected Manually Partition with Disk Druid at the Disk Partitioning Setup screen, you see a list of your existing partitions, as shown in Figure 2.7.

Disk partitions diagram

FIGURE 2.7
*The Disk Druid tool
enables you to review,
delete, create, or edit
partitions on a hard
drive.*

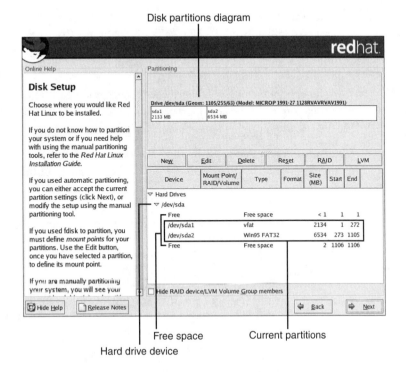

Hard drive device

Free space

Current partitions

If you select Automatically Partition at the Disk Partitioning Setup screen, you see a list of the partitions that Disk Druid has automatically created for you. These don't normally need to be changed; this section is intended to direct those who opted to use manual partitioning. You can therefore click Next and proceed to the next section.

However, you might want to read along with this section anyway to better understand the list of partitions that are automatically created and to get a feel for the way that Disk Druid works, in case you want to edit this list.

Understanding the Partition List

The partition list in the Disk Druid tool is broken into a number of separate columns:

- The Device column lists the hard drive or partition in question by Linux device name (see the following Note). If you have more than one hard drive, be sure to check the device column as you add, remove, or edit partitions in Disk Druid. This ensures that you are making changes to the correct hard drive!

- The Mount Point/RAID/Volume column lists the place in the Linux filesystem where the data stored on the partition in question appears. For an introduction to the structure of the Linux filesystem, see the section titled "Working with the Filesystem" in Hour 4, "Navigating Linux at the Console."

- The Type column lists the type of the partition in question. Existing window partitions generally appear with the vfat type.
- The Format column contains a check mark if the partition in question is scheduled to be formatted (erased in preparation for use) as the install process continues.
- The Size column shows the size, in megabytes, of the partition.
- The Start and End columns show the starting and ending cylinders of the partition in question. Lower numbers are nearer the beginning of the disk.

Most users have only one hard drive containing a relatively short list of partitions. If, however, you have multiple hard drives or a long list of partitions, it is important that you be able to decipher the device names in Disk Druid's Device column in order to partition safely for Linux.

Linux hard drive device names begin with either hd (for IDE hard drives) or sd (for SCSI hard drives). In SCSI systems, drives are lettered as they are found—sda being the first SCSI hard drive, sdb the second, and so on. In IDE systems, hda and hdb refer to the master and slave drives on the primary channel, respectively; hdc and hdd similarly refer to the master and slave drives on the secondary channel. The numbers at the end of the device names indicate partition numbers within a single hard drive.

Examples: The device /dev/sda1 refers to the first partition on the first SCSI hard drive. The device /dev/hdc2 refers to the second partition on the second IDE channel's master drive .

Freeing Space Created by fips

If you used the fips tool to resize an existing Windows partition in Hour 1, you likely see two partitions in your partition list now. One of these is the now smaller Windows partition; the other is an empty partition containing space that can be used by Linux. In order for Linux to be able to use the space made available by fips, however, you must delete the empty partition. Doing so will not harm your Windows partition, but it's always a good idea to have a reliable backup of any critical data before changing partitions on a disk.

The first partition in your partition list—which is shown with vfat as its type and whose size *should match closely* the size of your Windows partition after the resizing you did in Hour 1—is where Windows now resides and should not be deleted.

The second partition—which is shown with `Win95 FAT32` as its type and whose size *should match closely* the amount of space freed by `fips` during repartitioning—contains nothing but empty space, which can be used to hold Red Hat Linux.

To delete the empty partition and make this space available to Red Hat Linux, click its entry in the list, and then click the Delete button. A confirmation dialog appears, as shown in Figure 2.8.

FIGURE 2.8
The Disk Druid tool asks whether you really want to delete the partition created by `fips`.

Click the Delete button to confirm that you want to delete the free space partition created by `fips`. The partition list is updated to show the change and the amount of listed free space increases.

Before deleting either partition, *check the sizes* of the two partitions listed by Disk Druid against the sizes you selected when using `fips` to ensure that you delete the correct partition!

Calculating Needed Space

If you did not ask the Red Hat Linux installer to automatically partition for you, you will soon need to create some partitions for Red Hat Linux to use. You create at least three partitions as follows:

- A swap partition of approximately double the size of your computer's memory. If you have 256MB of memory, you need a 512-megabyte swap partition, and so on. This partition is used by the Linux virtual memory subsystem to keep memory available to applications as you work.
- A root filesystem partition to hold Red Hat Linux itself. This partition should be at least 2,000MB; 5,000MB or more is ideal.
- A 100-megabyte boot partition to hold the Linux kernel and a few related files.

Before you can create these partitions, however, you must ensure that you have enough free space for a working Red Hat Linux installation. This can be established by performing a simple test.

First, calculate the size of your swap partition by doubling the amount of RAM you have installed, and then adding 2,100 (the minimum root partition size plus the size of a boot partition). For example, if you have 512MB of memory, your total is 3,174MB. Now, check to see that you have a free space entry in your Disk Druid partition list of at least this size. If not, you don't have enough space to install Red Hat Linux. You either have to further resize or delete partitions, or you have to add an additional hard drive.

Creating a Boot Partition

After you ensure that you have enough free space to install Red Hat Linux, it is time to create the partitions where Red Hat Linux will reside. The first of these is the /boot partition, which holds the Linux kernel and a number of other files related to the kernel and booting. To create a new /boot partition, click the New button. The Add Partition dialog box appears, as shown in Figure 2.9.

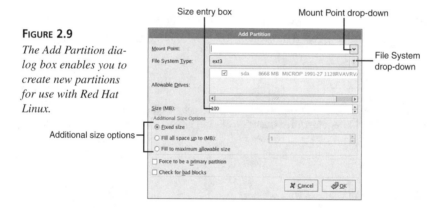

FIGURE 2.9

The Add Partition dialog box enables you to create new partitions for use with Red Hat Linux.

Fill out the dialog box as follows:

- Choose /boot from the Mount Point drop-down list to indicate that this partition is mounted on the /boot tree in the Linux filesystem. For a full explanation of what this means, see the section titled "Working with the Filesystem" in Hour 4.

- Select ext3 from the File System Type drop-down list to indicate that this partition should be formatted using the Linux ext3 filesystem.

- Enter **100** in the Size entry box to indicate that this partition should be 100MB in size.

- Check Fixed Size in the Additional Size Options area.

After you fill out the dialog, click OK to allocate space for the boot partition and return to the main Disk Druid display.

Creating a Swap Partition

Next, you must create a swap partition to allow the Linux virtual memory system to manage applications even when the system is running low on real memory. To create a new swap partition for Red Hat Linux, click the New button. The Add Partition dialog box is shown. Fill out the dialog box as follows:

- Choose Swap from the File System Type drop-down list to indicate that this partition is a swap partition.
- Enter the desired size of this partition (approximately twice the size of your installed system memory) in the Size entry box.
- Check Fixed Size in the Additional Size Options area.

Although the absence of an adequately sized swap partition hurts Linux performance significantly, swap partitions larger than twice the size of system memory do not *increase* system performance either.

After you have completed the dialog and are ready to create the swap partition, click the OK button to return to the main Disk Druid display.

Creating a Root Partition

The final partition that must be created in order to install Red Hat Linux is the root partition, which holds the bulk of the Red Hat Linux operating system and all of your data. To create the root partition, click the New button. The Add Partition dialog box is shown. Fill out the dialog box as follows:

- Choose / (the forward slash) from the Mount Point drop-down list to indicate that this partition is mounted on the root filesystem tree in the Linux filesystem. For a full explanation of what this means, see the section titled "Working with the Filesystem" in Hour 4.
- Select ext3 from the File System Type drop-down list to indicate that this partition should be formatted using the ext3 filesystem.
- Check Fill to Maximum Allowable Size in the Additional Size Options area. This gives all the remaining (contiguous) unpartitioned space on your hard drive to Red Hat Linux.

After you have completed the dialog box and are ready to create the root filesystem partition, click the OK button to return to the main Disk Druid display.

Mounting Additional Partitions

If you are installing Red Hat Linux alongside Windows and would like to be able to access your Windows hard drive from inside Linux, you need to specify a mount point for your Windows partition. To do this, click the Windows partition in the partition list and then click the Edit button.

When the Edit Partition dialog appears, enter **/mnt/win** into the Mount Point entry box, as shown in Figure 2.10. This causes the files on your Windows hard drive to appear in the /mnt/win directory in your Linux filesystem. For a full explanation of what this means, see the section titled "Working with the Filesystem" in Hour 4.

FIGURE **2.10**

Using the Edit Partition dialog box to create a mount point for an existing Windows partition.

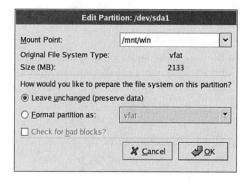

Click OK when you are done to return to the main Disk Druid display and partition list.

When editing the Windows partition, be sure to leave the Leave Unchanged (Preserve Data) option checked. Accidentally checking the Format Partition As option instead causes your Windows partition—including all your data and Windows itself—to be erased!

Checking the Partition List

At the main Disk Druid display , you should now see at least three new Linux partitions, among them a swap partition, a /boot partition, and a / (root) partition. If you are installing Linux alongside Windows, you should also still see your vfat-type Windows partition in the first position on your partition list. Figure 2.11 shows one possible Disk Druid display. If you used the installer's automatic partitioning tool, you might see many more Linux partitions in your list. This is normal.

FIGURE 2.11

The Disk Druid partition list now contains a number of partitions, several of which are used by Red Hat Linux.

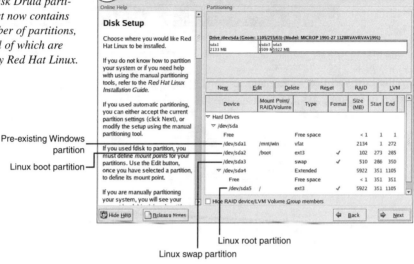

Pre-existing Windows partition

Linux boot partition

Linux swap partition

Linux root partition

You might notice partitions with the Extended type or small areas of remaining free space in your partition list. These can safely be ignored; extended partitions merely act as placeholders for compatibility with existing hardware and operating systems, and small areas of free space represent areas of the hard drive smaller than a single partition allocation unit. The important thing to understand is that neither of these types of entries represent either a significant amount of wasted space or a problem of any kind.

After you verify that all the necessary partitions appear in the list, check also to ensure that all the sizes are correct, that all the Linux partitions are marked with a check in the Format column, and that any existing Windows partitions are *not* marked with a check in the Format column.

If anything is amiss, select the partition that needs to be fixed and click the Edit button to display the partition dialog once again, where you can make changes to the selected partition.

When your list of partitions is correct as described in this section, you are finished partitioning for Red Hat Linux. Click Next to proceed with the installation process.

Boot Loader Configuration

After you finalize your partitioning, the Boot Loader Configuration screen is displayed, as shown in Figure 2.12.

Default partition checkboxes   Bootable partition list

FIGURE 2.12
The Boot Loader Configuration screen decides how your system will boot after Red Hat Linux has been installed.

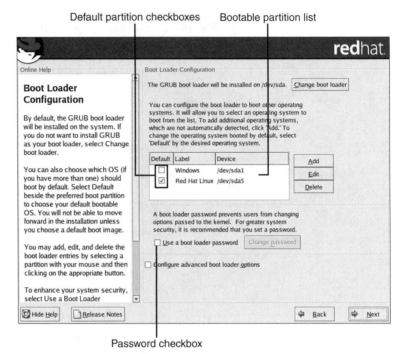

Password checkbox

A boot loader is a tool that enables you to choose which operating system you want to start when you first power on your system. For example, if you install Linux alongside Windows, a boot loader enables you to choose between Linux and Windows each time you power on.

If you have more than one bootable partition listed in the bootable partition list, you need to choose a default partition to boot. Whichever partition is checked as the default is automatically started at power on if the user fails to make a choice after a given period of time. This is a matter of convenience, but can also be very useful—for example, in cases involving unattended network servers that have been affected by power outages. To make a partition the default, click in its Default Partition check box.

If your Red Hat Linux computer will be in a public area like an office building, you also should select a password to protect your boot loader, in order to enhance system security. To do this, click in the Use a Boot Loader Password box; the Enter Boot Loader Password dialog is displayed, as shown in Figure 2.13.

Enter your password in the upper entry box. Then, enter it again in the lower entry box to ensure that you typed it correctly. Then, click OK to accept your password.

When you finish configuring your boot loader, click the Next button to proceed with installation.

FIGURE 2.13

After checking the Use a Boot Loader Password box, you are asked to enter a password.

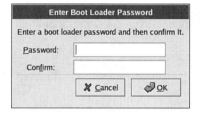

Enter Boot Loader Password

Enter a boot loader password and then confirm it.

Password: [   ]

Confirm: [   ]

✗ Cancel   ✓ OK

The GRUB boot loader is installed on Red Hat Linux systems by default. However, some experienced users might prefer the classic LILO boot loader over GRUB; other users might already be using a third-party or commercial boot loader that they don't want to replace.

To select LILO as an alternate boot loader or disable the installation of a boot loader altogether, click the Change Boot Loader button at the top of the Boot Loader Configuration screen. You are presented with a simple dialog that enables you to select GRUB, LILO, or no boot loader at all.

Be sure not to select No Bootloader unless you already have another bootloader you want to use—otherwise, you won't be able to use Linux after it's installed!

Network Configuration

Next, you are shown the Red Hat Linux Network Configuration screen, which applies only to users who will be using Red Hat Linux on a local area network or with a broadband (usually Cable or DSL) Internet service. The Network Configuration screen is shown in Figure 2.14.

The default configuration specifies that Red Hat Linux should obtain a network address and identity for your computer each time it starts by using Dynamic Host Configuration Protocol (DHCP). This is the correct configuration for personal computers on most corporate or local area networks. Users who fit into these categories can click Next and proceed to the next section.

Automatic configuration via DHCP is also the correct configuration for most home users on broadband (Cable or DSL) networks. In some cases, you need to set your computer's hostname manually for the broadband network to recognize you. If this is the case, click the Set the Hostname Manually option and enter the hostname you've been given into the entry box. Again, users who fit into this category can now click Next and proceed to the next section.

FIGURE **2.14**

The Network Configuration screen controls the way in which your Red Hat Linux computer finds its network identity.

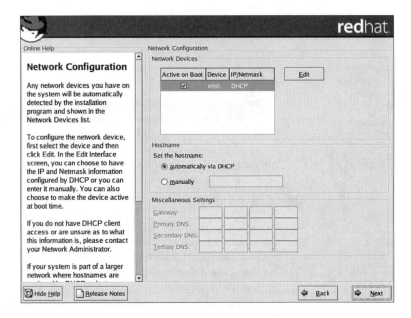

If you have been given an Internet Protocol (IP) address and Domain Name Service (DNS) information by your network administrator or broadband provider, or if this Red Hat Linux machine is a network server, automatic configuration via DHCP is likely not the correct choice for you.

To manually configure your computer for use with a static IP address, follow these steps:

1. Highlight the network interface you want to configure (if you have more than one) and click the Edit button near the top of the display. The Edit Interface dialog appears.

2. Uncheck the Configure Using DHCP option and enter your assigned IP address and netmask. If you don't know your netmask, enter **255**, **255**, **255**, and **0** in the entry boxes, from left to right, as a guess. Click OK to accept the values you entered.

3. Enter your computer's assigned hostname in the Hostname box.

4. Enter the address for your assigned Internet gateway, primary domain name server, secondary domain name server, and tertiary domain name server (if provided) in the appropriate spaces in the lower half of the screen.

After you configure your network settings according to your needs or the instructions of your network administrator, click Next to proceed to the next step in your Red Hat Linux installation.

Firewall Configuration

After your network device configuration is complete, the installer proceeds to the Firewall Configuration screen, shown in Figure 2.15.

FIGURE 2.15

The Firewall Configuration dialog enables you to set some network security parameters as Red Hat Linux is installed.

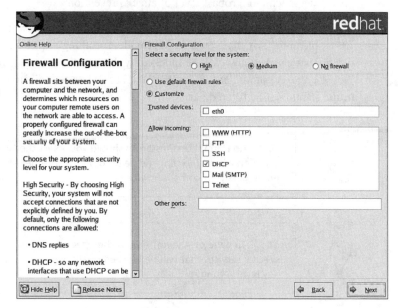

Here you can configure the basic level of security that will be maintained by Red Hat Linux on your computer system. A *firewall* is a software feature that filters incoming network traffic according to your specifications. This filter can be used to discard harmful or potentially harmful network traffic to prevent your system from being attacked by malicious network or Internet users.

The default level of security is Medium, which enables common types of Internet use, such as RealPlayer streaming and various types of chat and messaging, while still employing a basic level of protection against attacks of most kinds. This is the ideal setting for personal computing or desktop computing situations. Users who fit into this category should accept the default configuration by clicking Next to continue with the installation process.

If you opted to configure your network interface(s) using DHCP at the Network Configuration screen, DHCP is preselected in the Allow Incoming box. In such cases, DHCP should not be unchecked because DHCP—and thus the connected network interfaces—would cease to function.

If you are using your computer as a network server, especially if it is to run 24 hours a day, or if your computer has been assigned a static IP number, the High security setting should be used instead. This security setting blocks some kinds of common desktop network traffic, such as RealPlayer streaming, and some kinds of chat and messaging, but it provides a much more robust level of attack prevention.

If you are running a server, you should also check the boxes next to the services in the Allow Incoming box that you plan to provide; incoming requests for network services that are not checked now will be blocked by default. For example, if you want to run a Web server, you should check the WWW (HTTP) box to indicate that incoming Web traffic should not be filtered out.

Under no normal circumstances should you select the No Firewall option; to do so on a machine that will be used on the Internet at any time severely endangers your computer system.

The Help pane on the left side of the screen contains more details on the specific services that will be blocked or allowed by default under each security level setting.

After you finish configuring the firewall to suit your needs, click Next to continue with the Red Hat Linux installation process.

Additional Language Support

Next you are asked whether you want to install support for languages other than U.S. English, which is installed by default. The Additional Language Support list is shown in Figure 2.16.

To install support for additional languages, scroll up and down through the list and check the box next to those languages you want to install.

After you check all the languages you want to install, click the default language drop-down list at the top of the screen and select the language you would like to use as your default language while using Red Hat Linux.

When you finish configuring language support, click Next to proceed to the next step in the installation process.

FIGURE 2.16

Red Hat Linux supports an extensive list of languages in addition to the default, U.S. English.

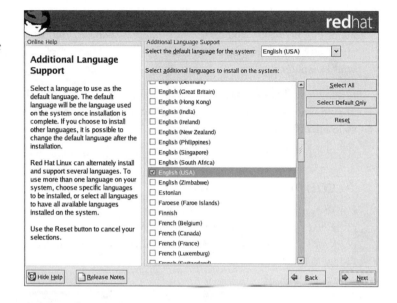

Time Zone Selection

The next screen you see contains options related to your time zone. In order to keep accurate time and communicate about your time with other users on the network and on the Internet (for example, in email headers), Red Hat Linux needs you to select a time zone. The Time Zone Selection screen is shown in Figure 2.17.

FIGURE 2.17

Select your time zone by clicking the major city nearest to you on the world map.

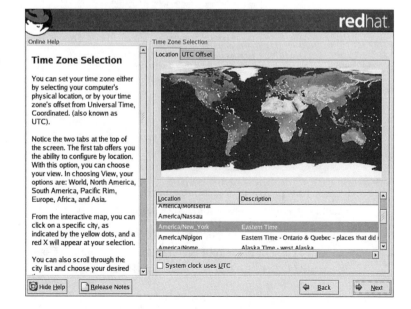

The easiest way to select your time zone is to use your pointing device to point to the major city nearest to you on the world map that shares your time zone. When the name of the city under the map is the major city nearest to you, click to set the time zone of your computer to match.

If this method is inconvenient for you, choose a location from the scrolling list under the map, or click the UTC Offset tab near the top of the screen to select your time zone as an absolute offset from universal time.

When you have chosen your time zone, click Next to continue with the installation process.

Account Configuration

For security reasons, the root (administrative) account of any Linux system must be protected by a password. The Account Configuration screen enables you to choose a password for your system's root account. The Account Configuration screen is shown in Figure 2.18.

FIGURE 2.18

You must now enter a root password to secure the administrative account on your Red Hat Linux system.

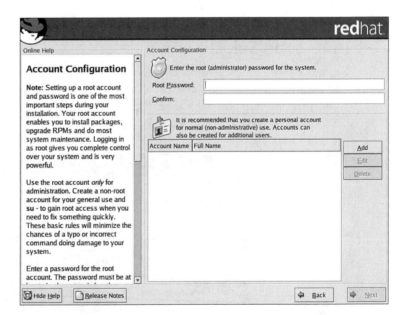

Because root password selection is mandatory, the Next button at the lower right of the screen is disabled until a suitable root password has been chosen.

To enter a root password, click in the Root Password entry box and enter the password you want to assign to the root account. Then, click in the Confirm entry box and reenter the password to ensure that you have typed it correctly.

If you see the message Root password is too short printed beneath the entry boxes, choose a longer password and enter it instead. Short passwords are easy to guess and are therefore less secure.

If, after entering the password in both boxes, you see the message Root passwords do not match, you have mistyped the password in one of the two boxes. Clear both boxes and reenter the root password.

After you enter an acceptable root password, the message Root password accepted is printed beneath the entry boxes, and the Next button at the lower right of the screen is activated.

Before you continue, you should add at least one user account to your Red Hat Linux system—the root account should be used only for the few sensitive administrative tasks that require it; all other computing should be done from user accounts. Click the Add button to add a user account. The Add a User Account dialog is displayed, as shown in Figure 2.19.

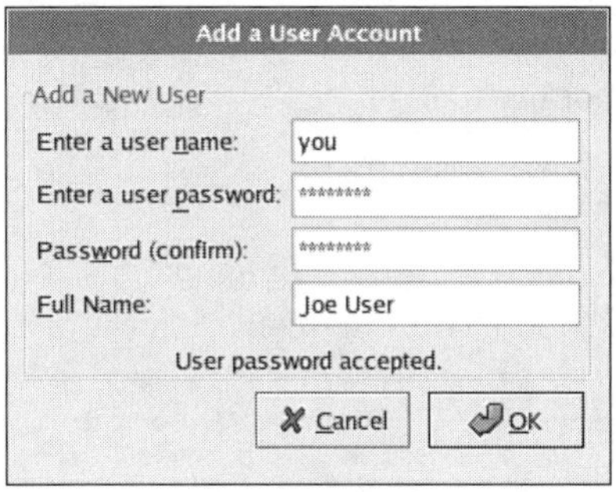

FIGURE 2.19

The Add a User Account dialog after account details have been entered. This dialog is used to add regular accounts.

Enter the username for the account you want to create into the corresponding entry box. This is the name that is entered by the user in order to log in; by convention it should be a single word entirely in lowercase letters.

After selecting a user (login) name, enter a password for this user twice, once in the Password entry box, and a second time in the Confirmation box to ensure that you haven't mistyped it.

Finally, enter the user's full name in the last entry box in the dialog; the user's full name is used for human benefit, most notably in the From: field of outgoing email messages.

After you have finished filling out the entry boxes in the Add a User Account dialog, click the OK button to create the account. Repeat the process to add additional system users if multiple users should have login accounts on this system. You learn how to add users after Red Hat Linux has been installed in Hours 18, "Command-Line System Administration," and 19, "Desktop System Administration."

After you choose a root password and create user account(s) as necessary, click Next to proceed with the installation process.

> Depending on the installation options you've selected, at some point over the next few screens you'll receive a message that says the installer is
> Reading package information...
> This process takes from a few seconds to several minutes, depending on the speed of your computer.

Authentication Configuration

If you select the Custom configuration at the Installation Type screen, you are shown the Authentication Configuration screen.

Configuration of authentication properties is beyond the scope of this book. Luckily, the default values are appropriate for most uses. Unless you have been given specific instructions by your network administrator, click Next here to accept the default configuration and proceed to the next step of installation.

Package Group Selection

If you choose to install the Server or Custom configurations at the Installation Type screen, you see the Package Group Selection screen, shown in Figure 2.20.

> If you chose to install the predefined Personal Desktop or Workstation configurations at the Installation Type screen, you don't see the Package Group Selection screen immediately. Instead, you see either the Personal Desktop Defaults screen or the Workstation Defaults screen.
>
> These screens provide a brief summary of the list of software packages that are to be installed according to your choice of either the Personal Desktop or Workstation configuration. The screen also offers you a simple choice between two options:
> - Accept the Current Package List
> - Customize the Set of Packages to Be Installed
>
> For most users, the correct answer is to click Next to accept the list of packages for the Personal Desktop or Workstation configurations as Red Hat has constructed it. If this is your choice (again, it is recommended), skip the rest of this section.
>
> If you choose to customize your package list before clicking Next, the rest of this section applies to you.

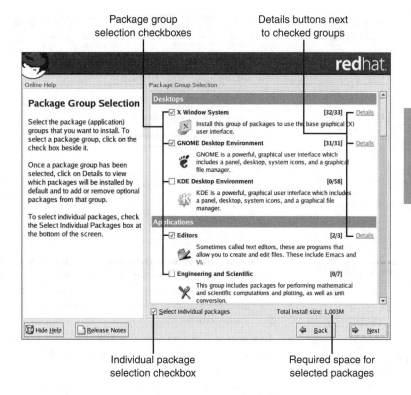

Package group
selection checkboxes

Details buttons next
to checked groups

FIGURE 2.20

*The Package Group
Selection screen
enables you to choose
which groups of soft-
ware packages you
want to install.*

Individual package
selection checkbox

Required space for
selected packages

Each item in the Package Group Selection screen represents a group of related software packages that can be selected for installation or left out of installation by checking the box at its left. Checking a box enables installation of a default selection of packages from the package group. Unchecking a box ensures that none of the packages from the group will be installed.

When a package group is checked, a Details button appears next to it (refer to Figure 2.20). Clicking the Details button provides a means by which packages from within the group can individually be marked for installation, as shown in Figure 2.21.

As you select or deselect packages and package groups for installation, the required space indicator beneath the package group selection list is updated. If this number exceeds the size of your Linux root partition, you do not have enough space to install the list of packages you have selected; you must deselect some packages before continuing with the installation process.

FIGURE 2.21

Clicking the Details button provides a way to individually select packages from a package group.

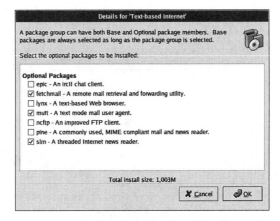

 A complete discussion of the contents of each package group is beyond the scope of this book; if you find yourself confused or unsure, consider return-ing to the Installation Type screen (use the Back button) and selecting either the Personal Desktop or Workstation options for a predefined installation that is adequate for most common computing tasks.

Also, note that it is possible to add and remove software packages later, after Linux has been installed, if you want to adjust the configuration you've chosen.

If you choose to install the Server configuration at the Installation Type screen, packages that might be useful on a Web server or Windows file server are preselected for installa-tion. You might also consider adding any of the following at the Package Group Selection screen:

- Additional network services from the Servers category, depending on the services this machine is expected to provide.

- The Text Editors group from the Applications category, to enable you to edit con-figuration files from the command line if necessary.

- The X Window System and either the GNOME Desktop Environment or the KDE Desktop Environment package groups from the Desktops category so that you can administer the server in a graphical environment (this is strongly recommended).

- The Graphical Internet package group, if you have also installed the X Window System, so you can browse the Web from this machine.

Before completing package group selection, remember that the default selection of packages for the Server installations is minimal; unless you augment it with a number of common packages from the Desktops and Applications groups, some of the information on day-to-day use of Red Hat Linux in later hours might not apply to your installation of Red Hat Linux because the necessary operating system components might not have been installed.

> Unless you are a Linux expert, you should uncheck the box labeled Select Individual Packages at the bottom of the Package Group Selection screen.
>
> If this box remains checked when you click the Next button to proceed to the next step of installation, the next screen you see breaks down package selection even further, into a list of thousands of individual software components. Even for experts, navigating this list of individual packages is a tedious and time-consuming event.

When you finish selecting the package groups and packages you want to install, click Next to proceed with the installation process.

About to Install

At this point, you have finished the bulk of the preinstall configuration that must be completed before the Red Hat Installer can begin copying software to your hard drive. The About to Install screen is displayed.

If you have any uncertainties about whether you really want to install Linux, or if you haven't yet backed up the important files in an existing Windows installation, *now is the time* to think it over, boot into Windows and back up your files, or whatever else might need to be done.

There are no options at this screen; it simply represents the last chance for the user to abort Linux installation before all the requested changes are written to your hard drive.

When you are ready to proceed, click the Next button to begin creating and formatting partitions, and then copying software to your hard drive.

Installing Packages

The first thing that occurs after installation has begun in earnest is the creation and formatting of the hard drive partitions that hold Red Hat Linux; a progress bar in the middle of the screen tracks the progress of partition creation and formatting. A few other housekeeping tasks also occur and their progress is tracked with a progress bar at the center of your screen. If your Linux partitions are very large or your computer is somewhat slow, this part of the installation process might take quite a long time.

After your Linux partitions are created and formatted and the installation image has been transferred to your hard drive, the installer begins to install the list of packages you selected for installation, as shown in Figure 2.22.

FIGURE 2.22

After creating and formatting Linux partitions, the installer begins to copy software to your hard drive.

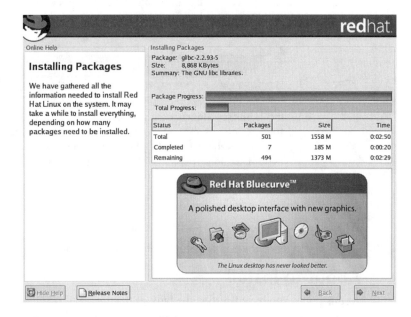

Depending on the speed of your computer and the number of packages you've selected, the installation process might take anywhere from a few minutes to several hours. You can check the time indicator in the Remaining status row (refer to Figure 2.22) for an estimate of the amount of time required for installation to finish at any given moment.

Depending on the packages you've chosen to install, the installer might at some point request that you insert additional Red Hat installation CD-ROMs. Do so when prompted and click OK to continue.

After package installation is complete, postinstall configuration begins; a progress bar in the center of the display will follow the process. After postinstall configuration, installation of packages is complete.

Boot Diskette Creation

After package installation is complete, the Boot Diskette Creation screen is displayed. This screen, shown in Figure 2.23, helps you create a floppy disk that can be used to try to start the system if the boot loader and kernel on the hard drive together are unable to load Linux correctly.

FIGURE 2.23

The Boot Diskette Creation screen enables you to create a boot floppy that can be used in some cases to access a damaged Linux installation.

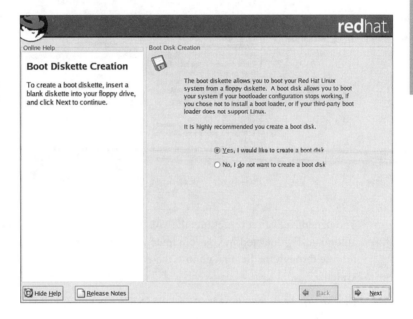

It is highly recommended that you create a boot disk and file it away for emergency situations; if at some point your Linux system should fail to start, you might be able to access it using your boot floppy.

To create the boot floppy, leave the Yes, I Would Like to Create a Boot Disk item checked and click the Next button at the lower right of the display. A dialog box appears asking you to insert a floppy disk; click the Make Boot Disk button in the dialog box to create the boot disk. A message appears in the center of the display indicating that the boot disk is being created—a process that can take several minutes.

After the boot disk has been created, the message disappears and the Graphical Interface Configuration screen is displayed.

Graphical Interface (X) Configuration

The Graphical Interface Configuration screen enables you to configure Red Hat Linux to work with your computer's graphics display hardware. You are shown a very long list of video cards and graphics chipsets, as shown in Figure 2.24.

FIGURE 2.24
The Graphical
Interface Configuration
screen presents an
extensive list of graph-
ics cards and chipsets.

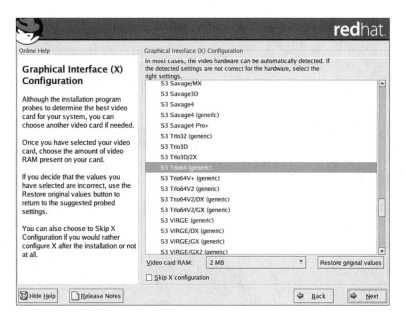

The default selection represents the video hardware that the Red Hat Linux installer has automatically detected in your computer system. If the selection is clearly inaccurate, browse through the list and choose the entry that matches the hardware in your computer system.

Be sure to check the amount of installed video memory; if it is incorrect, modify the value to reflect your configuration.

If you are unsure about what the installer has detected, leave the automatic selections in place because they are likely correct. When the correct values have been selected, click Next to continue with the postinstall configuration process.

Monitor Configuration

After configuring your video hardware, you're shown the Monitor Configuration screen, where you're able to configure Red Hat Linux to work within the capabilities of your computer's monitor. Once again you're presented with a long list, usually with one item already selected, as shown in Figure 2.25.

If the initial selection is inaccurate, or your monitor is older and can't describe itself to the Red Hat installer (in which case Unknown Monitor will be selected by default), you need to browse through the list of makes and models to select the specific monitor you own.

FIGURE 2.25

The Monitor Configuration screen enables you to select your monitor from an extensive list of makes and models.

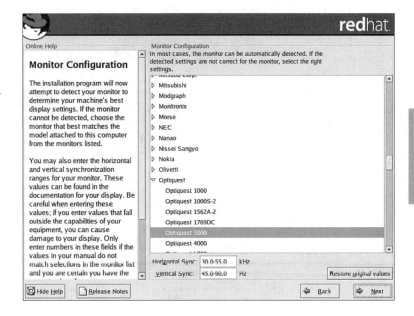

Next to each manufacturer's name in the list, you see a triangle. Click the triangle to see the list of monitors made by the manufacturer in question. When you find an entry matching your monitor, click it.

If you can't find your monitor's make and model in the list, *do not guess or select an alternate monitor*; doing so could cause Red Hat Linux to attempt to use display properties that your monitor isn't capable of supporting—something that can damage your monitor or even render it completely inoperable.

If you are unable to locate your monitor in the list, scroll to the top of the list and use an entry from the Generic make; if in doubt and Windows is installed on your system, select an entry that matches the Windows display mode you normally use.

After you select a monitor from the list, click Next to continue.

Customize Graphics Configuration

After you select a graphics adapter and a monitor type, the installer enables you to choose a default color depth and screen resolution to use in Red Hat Linux. This choice is made at the Customize Graphics Configuration screen, shown in Figure 2.26.

Default color depth   Default screen resolution

FIGURE 2.26
Select a default resolution, a default color depth, and a default login type at the Customize Graphics Configuration screen.

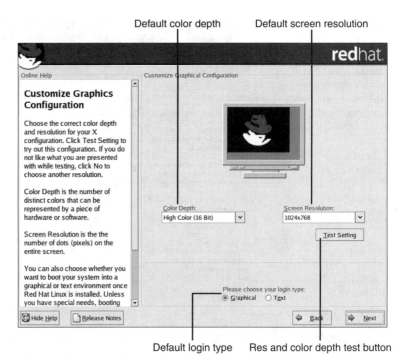

Default login type   Res and color depth test button

Select the color depth and resolution you'd like the Red Hat Linux desktop to use by default. This should be a configuration you're comfortable working in because changing resolution and color depth in Linux, although possible, is not as trivial a task as it is in other operating systems, such as Windows or Mac OS.

After you select a default color depth and resolution, you should click the Test Setting button to display a test pattern; this ensures that the combination is supported by both your graphics adapter and your monitor.

If you are unable to see the test (blank screen) or it appears garbled or flickers undesirably, you need to select a lower resolution and/or color depth and try again. If you are unable to find any working modes that pass the test, you might have selected incorrectly in the Graphical Interface Configuration or Monitor Configuration screens. Press the Back button return and verify your hardware selections.

If you find a mode that suits you and tests well, choose between graphical and text-based logins at the bottom of the Customize Graphics Configuration screen. Most users want to choose the Graphical option because this is both the most convenient and most attractive option. Select the Text login only if you plan to use the command line at the Linux console most of the time. If in doubt, choose Graphical.

When you customize your graphics selection, click Next to finish the installation.

Congratulations!

The final screen displayed by the graphical installer is the Congratulations screen, which provides a few useful World Wide Web links for new Red Hat Linux users who have successfully completed the installation.

Click the Exit button to finish the installation process and reboot the computer system. You are now ready to proceed to the next hour.

Summary

This hour, you installed the Red Hat Linux operating system to your hard drive by following these major steps:

1. You launched the Red Hat Linux installer.
2. You selected an installation typ— a list of packages to be copied to your system that will comprise the bulk of your Red Hat Linux operating system.
3. You created new hard drive partitions to hold the Linux operating system.
4. You copied Red Hat Linux to your hard drive.
5. You configured your default desktop color depth and resolution.

Assuming that you installed a boot manager this hour using the default boot manager configuration, the next time you power your computer on you should find that one of two things happens:

- If your hard drive contains only Linux, Red Hat Linux starts automatically the next time you power on.
- If your hard drive contains both Windows and Linux, you are offered a choice between starting Windows and starting Linux.

Next hour, you boot into your new Red Hat Linux system. The most difficult part of your Linux journey is now complete!

Q&A

Q What are the differences between GNOME and KDE, selectable at the Package Group Selection screen?

A In Red Hat Linux at least, GNOME is simpler, easier to use, and more closely tied to the Red Hat administration tools. KDE is more complex and difficult to use, but is also more powerful and programmable and offers a wider range of configuration options. If in doubt, both can be installed at once; you can then switch between them easily.

Q Why does the Automatic Partitioning tool create so many more partitions than you do when giving instructions for manual partitioning?

A The Automatic Partitioning tool splits the Linux filesystem into a number of much smaller filesystem areas, as is traditional for Unix-like operating systems. This kind of segmentation has a few theoretical advantages in terms of stability and security, but in practice a simpler scheme such as the one presented this hour works just as well, while offering more flexibility with regard to the use of storage space.

Workshop

The Workshop is designed to help you anticipate possible questions, review what you've learned, and begin learning how to put your knowledge into practice.

Quiz

1. True or false: If you repartitioned using the `fips` command before installing Linux, you have to delete an empty partition to free up space before Linux can be installed.

2. What Linux partitions need to be created before Linux can be installed?

3. How is the ideal size of the Linux swap partition calculated?

Answers

1. True

2. A `/boot` partition of type ext3, a root (`/`) partition of type ext3, and a swap partition

3. The ideal Linux swap partition is approximately double the size of your installed memory.

HOUR 3

Booting, Logging In, and Configuring

This hour, you start your Red Hat Linux system for the first time. You encounter the GRUB boot loader, which you use to start Linux or Windows. Then, before you can begin to use Linux for everyday tasks, there are some preliminary tasks that must be taken care of:

- You answer a few additional configuration questions that Red Hat Linux asks the first time you start your computer.
- You learn how to shut down or reboot your Red Hat Linux system.
- You configure Red Hat Linux to work with your printer.
- You configure your dial-up Internet service, if you will be connecting to the Internet using a modem.

When this hour is finished, you'll have a fully functional Red Hat Linux computer ready to perform most any common task that a Windows computer can perform.

Booting Red Hat Linux

If your computer has been a Windows-only computer thus far, you are probably used to switching on your computer and watching Windows load more or less immediately, without any intervention from you. Now that Linux has been installed on your computer, things will change a little.

Red Hat Linux has installed the GRUB boot loader to start your computer system. GRUB can start Linux or Windows; if you have both installed, it offers you a choice between the two each time you start. Switch on your computer now. If you followed along with the installation instructions in Hour 2, "Installing Red Hat Linux," and installed the GRUB boot loader, within a few moments you find yourself looking at the GRUB boot display, shown in Figure 3.1.

FIGURE 3.1
The GRUB boot display presents you with the available list of boot options. This computer has both Windows and Linux on it.

At the GRUB display, you have five seconds to select which operating system you want to start. Use your up- and down-arrow keys to move the selection bar, and press Enter to select and start an operating system in the list.

If you have Windows installed alongside Linux, you might find that Windows appears in the list of available operating systems under the DOS label. The DOS label is used by the Red Hat Linux installer to refer to most MS-DOS or MS Windows operating systems. Selecting DOS therefore starts your Windows operating system.

If you do not select an operating system yourself, GRUB automatically starts the selected operating system after five seconds.

When Red Hat Linux starts, you see a great deal of text information scrolling rapidly across your display as Linux examines and adjusts to your CPU, mainboard and memory configuration, and other hardware. Red Hat Linux then begins to start services and perform housekeeping tasks, displaying an OK message after each service is started, as shown in Figure 3.2. This process takes anywhere from a few seconds to a minute or two and is repeated each time you start Linux. It isn't important for you to remember details of the information displayed—it's intended primarily for Linux programmers who use the information for debugging purposes or experienced system administrators who have customized their configurations.

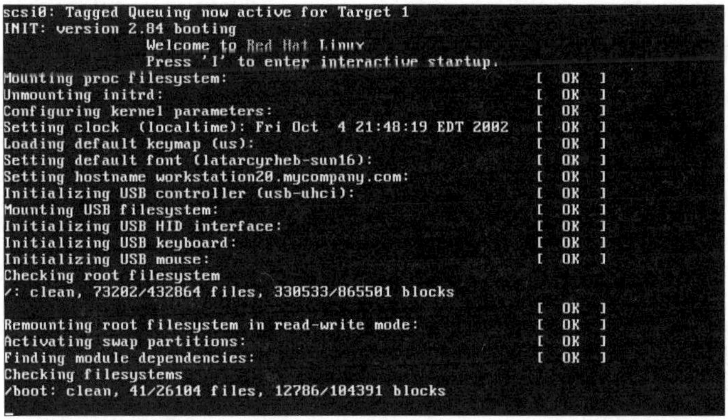

FIGURE 3.2

The Red Hat Linux boot process begins with a text mode display containing hardware information and service messages.

```
scsi0: Tagged Queuing now active for Target 1
INIT: version 2.84 booting
                Welcome to Red Hat Linux
                Press 'I' to enter interactive startup.
Mounting proc filesystem:                              [  OK  ]
Unmounting initrd:                                     [  OK  ]
Configuring kernel parameters:                         [  OK  ]
Setting clock (localtime): Fri Oct  4 21:48:19 EDT 2002 [  OK  ]
Loading default keymap (us):                           [  OK  ]
Setting default font (latarcyrheb-sun16):              [  OK  ]
Setting hostname workstation20.mycompany.com:          [  OK  ]
Initializing USB controller (usb-uhci):                [  OK  ]
Mounting USB filesystem:                               [  OK  ]
Initializing USB HID interface:                        [  OK  ]
Initializing USB keyboard:                             [  OK  ]
Initializing USB mouse:                                [  OK  ]
Checking root filesystem
/: clean, 73202/432864 files, 330533/865501 blocks
                                                       [  OK  ]
Remounting root filesystem in read-write mode:         [  OK  ]
Activating swap partitions:                            [  OK  ]
Finding module dependencies:                           [  OK  ]
Checking filesystems
/boot: clean, 41/26104 files, 12786/104391 blocks
```

For now, just enjoy the experience of watching Linux bring itself to life, piece by piece. After Red Hat Linux has started all its components, the screen clears and graphics mode starts.

Welcome to Red Hat Linux!

When your Red Hat Linux computer system is started for the first time, Red Hat automatically displays the Welcome to Red Hat Linux! screen. Beginning at this screen, you are led through a few remaining configuration steps that were not taken care of by the Red Hat Linux installer. The next section walks you through this process.

Finishing First-Run Configuration

At the Welcome to Red Hat Linux! screen, click the Forward button to proceed to the Date and Time Configuration screen, shown in Figure 3.3. Use this screen to be sure that your current date and time are correctly set.

FIGURE 3.3

The Date and Time Configuration enables you to set your current date and time.

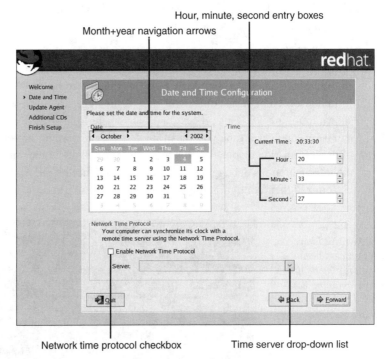

Month+year navigation arrows

Hour, minute, second entry boxes

Network time protocol checkbox

Time server drop-down list

You can choose a month and year using the navigation arrows; after the correct month and year are displayed, you can choose a day simply by clicking its number. If you need to adjust the current time (shown in 24-hour format), enter the correct values into the hour, minute, and second entry boxes. Alternatively, if your computer is connected to the Internet, you can choose to automatically set your time using network time servers by checking the Enable Network Time Protocol check box and selecting a server at random (it does not matter which server you use) from the time server drop-down list.

When you have set your date and time correctly or chosen to let the network set your date and time for you, click the Forward button to proceed to the Red Hat Update Agent screen, shown in Figure 3.4.

At the Red Hat Update Agent screen, you are given an opportunity to choose to register with Red Hat's premium update service. Because this service is an optional premium feature, we don't discuss it in this book. If you would like to sign up for the feature or learn more about it, visit http://rhn.redhat.com for details; otherwise, select the No option as shown in Figure 3.4 and click the Forward button to proceed to the Install Additional Software screen shown in Figure 3.5.

FIGURE 3.4

The Red Hat Update Agent screen enables you to sign up for Red Hat's premium update service.

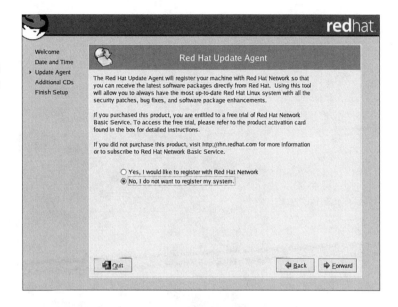

FIGURE 3.5

At the Install Additional Software screen, Red Hat gives you the option of installing more software from your CD-ROMs.

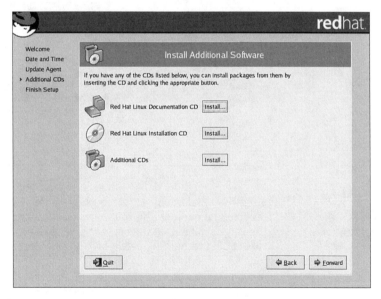

You learn how to install additional software from Red Hat CD-ROMs any time you like using desktop tools in Hour 21, "Installing Software," so there is no need to spend extra time here installing additional software. Click the Forward button to proceed to the Finished Setup! screen.

Click the Forward button to display the Red Hat login prompt.

Logging In for Configuration

After you finish the first-boot configuration discussed in the previous section, you find yourself looking at the Red Hat Linux graphical login prompt, shown in Figure 3.6. This screen is displayed every time you start Red Hat Linux.

FIGURE 3.6

Every Time you Start Red Hat Linux from now on, you will see the Red Hat Linux graphical login prompt.

Username/password entry box

Welcome to workstation20.mycompany.com

Username:

Please enter your username

> Language   > Session   > System   Fri Oct 04, 08:56 PM

Language button   System button
           Session button

If in Hour 2 you chose to perform a server installation or chose to customize your software selection and subsequently did not install the X Window system graphical environment, you will not see a graphical login prompt. Instead, you will see a text login prompt. Proceed to Hour 4, "Navigating Linux at the Console," for details on logging in and using Linux in text mode.

Identifying the Parts of the Login Screen

The Red Hat login prompt is primarily designed to enable you to log into the Red Hat desktop to use your computer. Before you log in for the first time, though, there are a few functional areas of the login screen that you need to become familiar with.

If you chose to install more than one language when you installed Linux, clicking the Language button displays a list of languages from which you can select, as shown in Figure 3.7. The language you select is the language used by Red Hat for communicating with you in the desktop environment. The default language is English.

FIGURE 3.7

Clicking the Language button enables you to select the language Red Hat will use when interfacing with you.

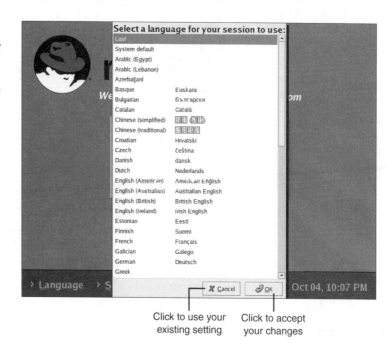

Click to use your existing setting

Click to accept your changes

If you chose the Desktop or Workstation install or chose to install the KDE and/or GNOME environments at the software customization screen as you were installing Linux, clicking the Session button at the login screen enables you to select the environment you want to use, as shown in Figure 3.8.

The GNOME and KDE options instruct Red Hat Linux to log you into the GNOME and KDE desktops, respectively. The Failsafe instructs Red Hat Linux to log you into a very basic X Window System desktop in an environment called TWM. The Last option instructs Red Hat to log you into whichever desktop environment you used last time you logged in. You can learn more about logging in to KDE and GNOME specifically in Hour 10, "Introducing the Red Hat Desktop."

The System button is perhaps the most important of the three buttons on the Red Hat Linux login screen. Clicking it presents you with options related to shutting down Red Hat Linux, as shown in Figure 3.9.

FIGURE 3.8

Clicking the Session button enables you to select the type of desktop environment you want to use.

FIGURE 3.9

Clicking the System button enables you to shut down or restart your Red Hat Linux computer.

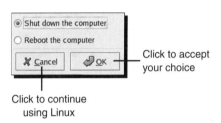

Click to accept your choice

Click to continue using Linux

Before you turn off your Linux computer, you should always remember to return to the Login screen, click the System button, and choose to shut the system down. Though it isn't *likely*, it is *possible* that not shutting down correctly could cause you to lose some of your data.

Configuring Your Printer and Internet Service

Before you begin using Linux, there are two more things that must be configured to make your Linux system fully operational if you are running a desktop or workstation system. The first of these is your printer; the second is your dial-up Internet service.

In order to configure either, you must log in to the root account and use some Red Hat configuration tools. To log into the root account, enter the word **root** into the Username box and press your Enter key. Then, enter the root password you selected when installing Linux into the same box and press Enter once more.

This hour we're going to gloss over the ins and outs of the login process and the Linux desktop—we want to dig only deep enough to configure your printer and Internet service just now; we'll get to details about the Linux desktop in later hours. If you're not comfortable entering **root** and the root password without knowing why, or if you've never worked with a graphical operating system and would like to learn about using the mouse to manipulate menus and windows, you might want to skip ahead and read Hour 10 before continuing with this hour.

Configuring Your Printer

After you enter the word **root** and the root password at the login screen, you find yourself logged into the root account's desktop environment. To configure your printer, click the GNOME Menu icon (which looks like a red colored hat) in the lower-left corner of the display, click the System Settings item in the GNOME Menu, and then the Printing item in the System Settings menu. After you click on the Printing item, the Red Hat Printer Config tool is opened.

To add a printer to your Red Hat Linux configuration, click the New button near the upper-left of the Red Hat Printer Config tool window. The Add a New Print Queue dialog appears.

Click the Forward button to display a dialog that enables you to name your printer and choose the way in which it is connected to your Red Hat Linux computer, as shown in Figure 3.10.

FIGURE 3.10

You must enter a name for your printer and select the type of connection it uses to communicate with your computer.

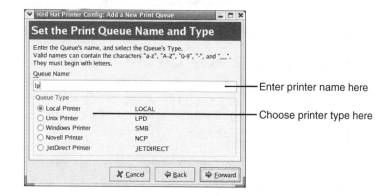

Enter printer name here

Choose printer type here

The name of your default printer in Linux should always be lp because this is what most applications expect the default printer to be called. If this is your first printer, enter **lp** into the Queue name box now. The second and subsequent printers can be called by any name you choose, though you should avoid using spaces or punctuation marks in printer names.

 The name lp stands for *line printer*, even though line-oriented printers are no longer in widespread use. This is another case in which Unix traditions can be seen in day-to-day Linux use.

If your printer is connected by USB or Parallel port, click the Local Printer type option. Through the rest of this section, let's assume that you are using a local printer—meaning a printer that is directly connected to your computer. If you need to use one of the several types of network printers listed, please contact your system administrator for further help in configuring it.

Click the Forward button to display a dialog that enables you to choose the port to which your printer is connected.

A list of common ports is shown in Table 3.1.

TABLE 3.1   Common Ports to Which Printers Might Be Connected

Port	Description
/dev/lp0	First parallel port, LPT1: or PRN: in MS-DOS
/dev/lp1	Second parallel port (if present), LPT2: in MS-DOS
/dev/usb/lp0	First discovered USB printer
/dev/usb/lp1	Second discovered USB printer

If you're using a parallel port printer, select the parallel port to which your printer is connected. If you're using a USB printer, at least one USB port should appear in the list as well—select it. After you select your printer port, click the Forward button to display the dialog that enables you to select a driver (by printer make and model) to use with your printer, as shown in Figure 3.11.

> If your printer is connected via USB and you don't see any USB printer ports listed, click Cancel to exit the Red Hat Printer Config tool, turn your printer on, and then repeat the steps in this section. Your USB printer port should now appear.

In the dialog, you see a list of printer makes. Click the triangle next to a particular make to expand a list of models. Find your printer in the list and click the triangle next to your model to show the driver for your model. Click the driver to select it. Then, click the Forward button to display the confirmation dialog box.

> For certain makes and models of printers, you will see more than one driver listed. If this is true in your case, choose the driver with an asterisk (*) next to it—this is the default driver and in nearly all cases, the best choice.

FIGURE 3.11

This dialog enables you to browse through a list of makes and models to select a driver for your printer.

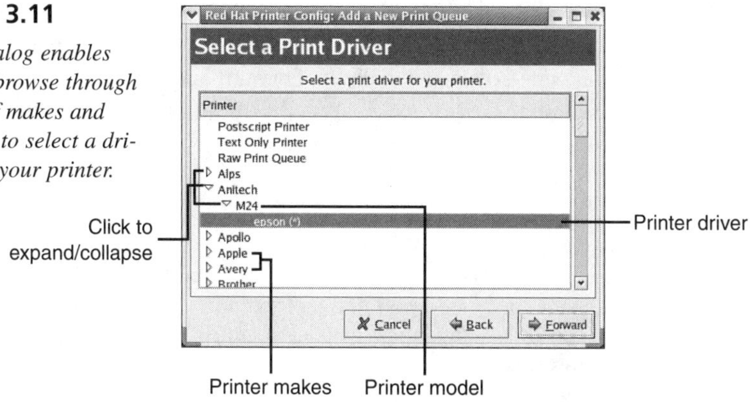

Click to expand/collapse

Printer driver

Printer makes   Printer model

Review the settings listed in the confirmation dialog; if your make and model are correctly listed, click the Apply button to save your printer configuration. If you want to add more printers, repeat the steps in this section. If you are done adding printers, click the word File at the upper left of the Red Hat Printer Config window to display the file menu, and then select Quit from the menu to exit the Red Hat Printer Config tool. You are asked whether you want to save your changes. Choose Yes to save your changes, activate the printer, and close the tool.

Configuring Your Dial-Up Internet Service

If you connect to the Internet using a dial-up service provider and a modem, you need to tell Red Hat Linux about your modem and your Internet service provider. To start the Internet Configuration wizard, click GNOME Menu, System Tools, Internet Configuration Wizard. The Internet Configuration Wizard starts, as shown in Figure 3.12.

Click on Modem connection…

FIGURE 3.12

Use the Internet Configuration Wizard to configure Red Hat Linux to connect to your Internet service provider.

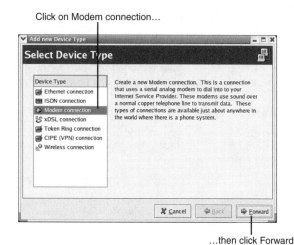

…then click Forward

In the Internet Configuration Wizard, click the Modem connection option to indicate that you connect to your Internet service provider using a modem. Then, be sure that your modem is powered on (if it is external) and click the Forward button to cause the Internet Configuration Wizard to search for your modem. When your modem is found, the settings Red Hat detected are displayed, as shown in Figure 3.13.

If your computer is directly connected to a network via Ethernet (for example, through a typical DSL or cable modem connection, or a company LAN), you have already configured your network settings when you installed Linux; if you need to change them, you learn how in Hour 19, "Desktop System Administration."

If your computer is connected to the Internet using a technology other than dial-up modem service or Ethernet, contact your network administrator or service provider for help in configuring your Internet service.

FIGURE 3.13

After your modem is found, the settings for your modem as detected by the Internet Configuration Wizard are displayed.

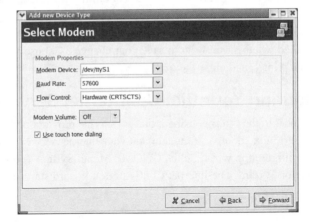

If Red Hat Linux displays a message saying that no modem can be found, check your modem to ensure that it is powered on and connected properly to your computer. If it is, or if your modem is internal and you still receive an error message, your modem is not easily supported by Red Hat Linux.

Please refer to "Communications Hardware" in Hour 1, "Preparing to Install Red Hat Linux," for details on the types of modems that are compatible with Red Hat Linux.

With the exception of the Modem Volume setting, which can be adjusted to suit your dialing volume tastes, none of the other settings should be changed from those detected by Linux. Click the Forward button to display a dialog that allows you to enter details related to your Internet service provider, as shown in Figure 3.14.

FIGURE 3.14

The Internet Configuration Wizard needs details about your Internet service provider in order to configure your connection.

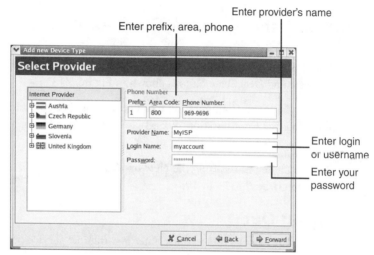

Enter provider's name

Enter prefix, area, phone

Enter login or username

Enter your password

Enter your dial-up service provider's dialing details, name, login (username), and password into the relevant entry boxes shown in Figure 3.14. When you are done, click the Forward button to display the configuration summary.

When you confirm that all the details listed are correct, click the Apply button to save your changes. The Network Configuration dialog is displayed, as shown in Figure 3.15.

FIGURE 3.15

The Network Configuration dialog enables you to activate (connect) and deactivate (disconnect) your Internet service.

Your modem's entry

Network status

Activate button

Deactivate button

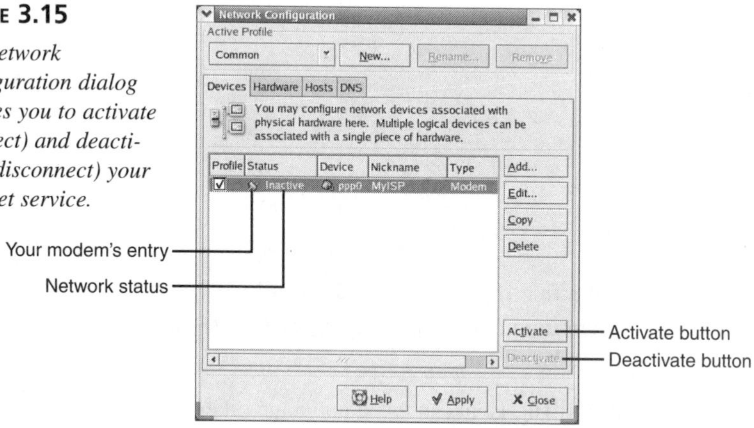

To connect to your ISP, click your modem's entry in the device list, and then the Activate button. The modem attempts to dial your ISP and connect your Red Hat computer to the Internet. While you are connected, your network status reads Active rather than Inactive, and you can browse the World Wide Web and use other Internet services. When you are ready to disconnect, click the Deactivate button.

Starting the Network Configuration Tool

In the future, you will not use the Internet Connection Wizard to start your Internet connection. Instead, you start the Network Configuration tool directly, where you can access the Activate and Deactivate buttons shown in Figure 3.18.

To start the Network Configuration tool under normal circumstances (rather than directly from the Internet Configuration Wizard), click GNOME Menu, System Settings, Network.

For additional details on using the Network Configuration tool, refer to "Managing Network Interfaces" in Hour 19.

Logging Out

When you finish configuring your printer and Internet service provider, you can exit the root account and return to the Red Hat Linux login screen by clicking the GNOME Menu and then clicking the Log Out option. A confirmation dialog appers, as shown in Figure 3.16. To confirm that you want to log out and return to the Red Hat Linux login screen, select Log Out and then click the OK button.

FIGURE 3.16

A confirmation dialog is displayed to make sure that you really want to log out.

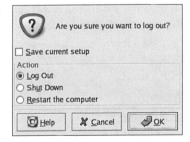

Summary

This hour, you booted for the first time into your Red Hat Linux computer system. You answered a few final configuration questions posed by Red Hat Linux, and then you did the following:

- Learned how to tell Red Hat Linux to use a language other than English when communicating with you

- Learned how to shut down or restart your system
- Added a printer to your Red Hat Linux system
- Configured Red Hat Linux to use your modem to dial your Internet service provider for Internet service
- Learned how to connect to and disconnect from your ISP

Your system is now fully configured and you are ready to begin using and learning about Linux. On to adventure!

Q&A

Q I selected the desktop or workstation install while installing Linux in Hour 2, but when I started Linux for the first time, I got a text login prompt instead of the graphical login screen. What's wrong?

A Your graphics hardware is not supported or detected properly by Red Hat Linux. Though it is sometimes possible to get initially unsupported display hardware to work, such techniques are beyond the scope of this book. You will still be able to follow the lessons but you should consider investing in an upgrade to supported graphics hardware so that you can use the Red Hat Linux desktop environment.

Q I can't find my printer in the list of makes and models in the Add New Print Queue dialog. What should I do?

A If your printer is a Postscript-compatible printer, you can select Postscript Printer at the top of the list as your printer type. If you know that your printer is fully compatible with another make and model of printer, select the driver for the other make and model. If neither of these suggestions applies to you, your only alternatives are to select Text Only Printer near the top of the list, or to invest in a supported printer. Beware that a text-only printer cannot print documents from Linux desktop applications or from the LaTeX document system discussed in Hour 7, "Working Without the Mouse."

Q I use America Online as my ISP. Can I run AOL in Red Hat Linux?

A Unfortunately, you cannot yet run AOL in Red Hat Linux.

Workshop

The Workshop is designed to help you anticipate possible questions, review what you've learned, and begin learning how to put your knowledge into practice.

Quiz

1. How do you shut down your Linux computer from the Red Hat Linux login screen?

2. What are your options if Red Hat Linux can't find your modem?

3. How do you connect to or disconnect from your ISP?

Answers

1. Click the System button near the bottom of the screen, select the shut down option from the dialog that appears, and then click the OK button.

2. Realistically, your only option is to buy a Linux-compatible modem. Details on the types of modems that are compatible with Linux can be found in Hour 1.

3. To connect, start the Network Configuration tool, select your modem and click the Activate button to activate your network connection.

   To disconnect, start the Network Configuration tool, select your modem and click the Deactivate button.

Activities

1. Restart your computer and use GRUB to start Windows to familiarize yourself with the process.

2. Try connecting to and disconnecting from your ISP several times to familiarize yourself with the process.

HOUR 4

Navigating Linux at the Console

This hour introduces you to several of the basic concepts needed to use Linux and other Unix-like systems effectively. You have installed Linux successfully; now it's time to begin to *use* Linux. Follow along and you learn to

- Switch between the desktop display and virtual consoles.
- Use basic terminology common to all Linux and Unix-like operating systems.
- Structure commands entered at the console.
- Use basic commands for file and directory manipulation.
- Understand file permissions, and thus filesystem security, at the most basic level.

Though these topics might seem mundane or obscure, they are essential building blocks of Linux skill.

Don't feel as though you need to understand everything at once; use this hour to become more familiar with Linux, but don't try to memorize the information. Just read through the text and try your hand at some of the tricks for now—the details will become clearer as you progress through future hours. You can always refer back to this hour later if necessary.

Why Learn to Use Linux at the Console?

Is it really necessary to learn to use Linux at the console?

Yes—it's necessary.

Years ago, displayed computer graphics represented a very rare, expensive, and specialized technology. Most computer systems did not ship with graphics capability because they were intended to perform office, database, and network-related tasks—tasks involving the manipulation of letters and numbers, not of pictures and colors. Unix systems, which were common long before MS-DOS or Windows systems became established in the marketplace, were among these workhorse systems. Because of this, developers didn't have graphics in mind when they built Unix.

Unix graphics did exist by the time Linux was born in the early 1990s, in the form of the X Window System still in use today. Red Hat Linux uses the X Window System to provide you, the user, with a friendly graphical user interface. When all is said and done, however, the nuts and bolts of Linux—the configuration details, much of the functional infrastructure, and the primary method of storing and retrieving data—are closely tied to text, text files, and text processing. The relationship between Linux and your data is clearest at the command line; so is the relationship between the functioning of a Linux system and the countless text-based files from which Linux is built.

After a user masters the command line, the rest of the Unix world, including the desktop, seems to fall magically into place. Only rarely do users master other Unix functions before mastering the command line.

Understanding Virtual Consoles

The term *console* refers to the combination of one input device and one output device designed to enable you to interact with your computer. In real terms, this means a keyboard and a monitor. If you have ever used an MS-DOS computer, you should already be familiar with computer use at a console.

In Linux, you'll also find the term *virtual console* in common use. This term alludes to the fact that in Linux, several *sessions* of interactive console work can be active at any time. Each session is referred to as a virtual console; you can switch between these sessions (or virtual consoles) by using special key combinations. This way, you can launch numerous full-screen applications simultaneously and switch between them easily. For example, you might want to have an editor active on one console and a Web browser active on another console. In a way, this functionality is similar to the functionality provided by a windowing system, though each virtual console occupies the entire display.

By default, when you install and boot Red Hat Linux, seven virtual consoles are configured and active. Normally, however, you see only the seventh—it is the one on which the X Window System (which represents your Linux desktop) is running. Consoles one through six are not running graphical applications, but are instead configured to allow you to log in and perform command-line work at them.

Switching Between Consoles

To display a specific console in Linux, hold down the left Ctrl and Alt keys simultaneously with one hand, and with your other hand, press F1 through F7, depending on the console you'd like to view. F1 will display console one; F2, console two; and so forth. At the moment, the first six consoles should all be identical. Holding down Ctrl and Alt and pressing F7 displays console seven, your desktop.

Logging In at a Virtual Console

To log in to a console, switch to one of the first six virtual consoles by holding down Ctrl and Alt and then pressing the matching function key. When the console appears, you see a Login prompt that looks something like this:

```
Red Hat Linux release 8.0 (Limbo)
Kernel 2.4.19 on an i686
workstation20 login:
```

To log in, enter your username and press Enter. For this hour, you should enter the name of the user account you created when you installed Red Hat Linux, rather than root; the root account should be used only for administration, never for day-to-day computing. When the Password: prompt appears, type your password and press Enter. Remember, the password characters you type do not appear on the screen. After your password is correctly entered, you are logged in:

```
workstation20 login: you
Password:
Last login: Sat Aug 3 15:06:02 on tty1
[you@workstation20 you]$
```

The last line displayed, the line ending with a dollar sign character ($), is the *command prompt*. Whenever it appears followed by a blinking underline character, the shell is ready to accept your commands.

Introducing the Shell

What exactly is a shell? A shell can be any Linux program that allows the user to give commands, and then carries out those commands using the underlying facilities of the Linux operating system . The commands in question can be anything a user might want to do, such as printing a file, starting a program, or opening a network connection. When Linux users talk about using "the shell," in everyday conversation, however, they usually mean using Linux through a command interpreter, which is a special kind of shell program that accepts words and alphanumeric characters as instructions.

The Shell's Role: Command Interpreter

The term *shell* is a metaphor; you can think of the Linux kernel, the core of Linux, as the organism that lives beneath the shell. The Linux kernel is a technical program that is not user friendly. In almost any normal circumstance, talking directly to the Linux kernel is the *hardest* way to accomplish a task. The Linux kernel is designed to communicate with electronic equipment and with other computers, rather than with humans. But at the same time, users must communicate with the Linux kernel in order to give Linux orders. As a command interpreter, the shell accepts commands that are designed to make some sort of sense to humans; the shell's job is to interpret these human-style commands and pass them on to the Linux kernel in a format that the kernel can understand.

There are several command-line shells to choose from on any Linux system; each is slightly different in terms of behavior and features, though most of the actual commands remain the same. The most common shell by far is the default shell, *bash*, which stands playfully for the Bourne-Again SHell, so named because it is a re-creation (with new features) of the old Bourne Shell, *sh*, from Unix.

Fundamentals of Using the Shell

As you work with the shell, you will soon notice that the text of every command you give the shell follows the same basic pattern. The following description of the contents of a shell command might seem obtuse at first, but hang in there. Later on, all of this will be clear to you. In general, you type the following when you give a command to the shell:

- A one-word command chosen from the massive list of available commands on your Linux system, each of which performs some specific task.

- If needed, an *option* or *flag*, which modifies the command's behavior and is usually preceded by a dash. Each command has its own list of options and flags, which enable you to adapt the behavior of the command to suit your needs.

- If needed, *arguments*, which provide data that a command needs to function, or that are needed to use a specific option.

- If needed, additional options, flags, and arguments that are accepted by the command.

This list of elements is common in the Linux and Unix world; you will see it appear each time you read the documentation for a specific command. However, in online documentation, you usually see it written like so:

```
mycommand -opt1 arg1 [-opt2 arg2 ...]
```

This line of text explains to the user precisely what you just learned: that when you use the fictional command mycommand, you should provide at least one option or flag (`-opt1`) that the command understands, followed by one argument (`arg1`). If necessary, you can enter an optional second flag (`-opt2`), followed by a second argument (`arg2`), and so on. Though it seems cryptic at first, this brief notation appears everywhere in the command-line world and will soon become second nature to you.

Working with the Filesystem

A *filesystem* is a collection of data files and the organizational details of those files, all stored somewhere inside a computer system. All modern computer operating systems use a filesystem to organize information. The Linux filesystem, however, differs in important ways from other filesystems you might have used.

Many Trees, Many Roots: The Windows File System

A Windows system's C: drive contains files of various types and file folders, each of which can hold additional files and more file folders. All these files and file folders are collectively referred to as the filesystem of the C: drive. Like most operating systems, Windows allows filesystem components to contain other filesystem components and file folders to contain other file folders. This capability creates a structure that commonly is referred to as a *tree*, as shown in Figure 4.1. At the base of the tree—in this case the C: drive itself—you can imagine a kind of *root*.

In Windows, each storage device is assigned a drive letter. Each drive letter is therefore the root of its own filesystem, and thus, of its own *filesystem tree*. An illustration of this concept can be seen in Figure 4.2.

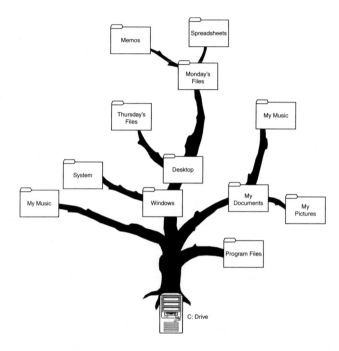

FIGURE 4.1

Any modern filesystem looks like a tree; here, the drive itself is the root of the tree in a diagram showing some of a Windows filesystem.

One Tree, One Root: The Linux File System

Linux and Unix filesystems, on the other hand, don't function like the one in Windows. Any Linux computer has only one filesystem. The most basic location within the filesystem is not a drive letter like C: or D:, but is rather the root of the filesystem, referenced with a forward slash (/). Users can access multiple storage devices in Linux; however, rather than representing a separate filesystem tree, each storage device is positioned within the single main filesystem tree, as shown in Figure 4.3. Adding a storage device to the single main filesystem tree is known as *mounting* a device on the filesystem tree.

Files and Directories

In Linux, as in Windows, most of the data you work with is stored on a hard drive somewhere in the filesystem tree in the form of *files*. Each file has a unique name and can be opened by one or several programs to access the data inside.

Where Windows has folders, Linux has *directories*. Though the names are different, the concept is precisely the same; a directory is a kind of container in the filesystem for holding files of various types or for holding other directories. The root of the Linux filesystem is commonly referred to as the *root directory* because it contains *all* other files and directories.

FIGURE 4.2

In Windows systems, each storage device has its own filesystem. The system has many trees and many roots.

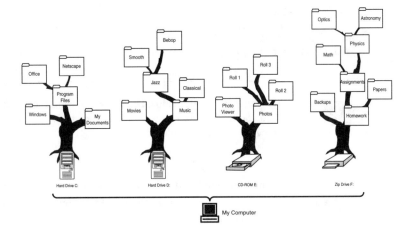

FIGURE 4.3

A Linux filesystem tree with additional storage devices mounted at /usr/X11R6, /home, /boot, /mnt/cdrom, /mnt/dvd, and /mnt/zip. Note that each device enlarges the single, unified tree, and there is still only a single root.

4

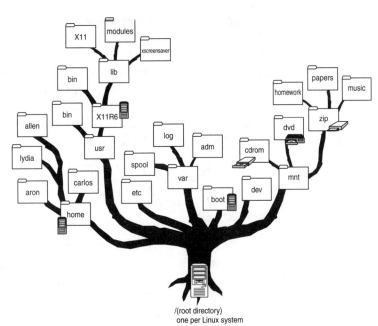

It's time to introduce your first command. The `ls` command is the command used to display the contents of a directory in the Linux filesystem. To see what is in your Linux system's root directory, enter the `ls` command now, supplying the slash (for the root directory) as an argument:

```
[you@workstation20 you]$ ls /
bin   dev  home   lib          misc  opt   root  tmp  var
boot  etc  initrd lost+found   mnt   proc  sbin  usr
[you@workstation20 you]$
```

> Note that in Red Hat Linux, the output of the ls command is color-coded to help you differentiate between files, directories, and other types of data. Directories appear in blue.

The ls command has provided you with two lines of output. Each of the names you see is stored in the root directory of your Linux system. Now list the contents of the usr directory using the same command:

```
[you@workstation20 you]$ ls /usr
bin   etc    include   lib       local  share  tmp
dict  games  kerberos  libexec   sbin   src    X11R6
[you@workstation20 you]$
```

Notice that each of the arguments to the ls command begins with a forward slash (/) and then contains one or several words separated by additional slashes. When referring to the specific location of a file or directory at the Linux command line, you begin with the root directory (/) and proceed to provide a kind of roadmap for arriving at the desired file or directory, separating each step along the way with an additional slash.

List the contents of one more directory, just for practice:

```
[you@workstation20 you]$ ls /usr/X11R6
bin   include  LessTif  lib   libexec   man   share
[you@workstation20 you]$
```

> Having trouble? If you've been faithfully trying to follow along, but are getting error messages such as "command not found" or "No such file or directory," check the capitalization of your commands.
>
> Linux, like most Unix-like operating systems, is *case-sensitive*. This means that ls is *not* the same thing as LS to Linux; similarly, x11r6 is not the same thing as X11R6.

In these commands, you listed the contents of the root directory, the directory called usr inside the root directory, and the directory called X11R6 inside the usr directory. The usr directory is inside the root directory. The road map you supplied to the ls command in each case is known as a *path*. Table 4.1 lists additional examples of paths with explanations.

TABLE 4.1   Sample Linux Paths

Path	Explanation
/	Refers to the root directory
/usr/X11R6/lib	Refers to the directory lib in the directory X11R6, in the directory usr, which is in the root directory
/usr/lib/xmms/Input	Refers to the directory Input in the directory xmms, in the directory lib, in the directory usr, which is in the root directory

It is important to familiarize yourself with the notion of a path, because many Linux commands expect you to supply a path as an argument—ls being an obvious example.

The Home Directory

You've already learned about one special directory in Linux, the root directory, which contains all other directories and files. Now it's time to learn about a second special directory, called the *home directory*. When a Linux user creates and saves files, receives email, scans an image on a flatbed scanner, or performs any number of other tasks, any data that the user needs to store on the hard drive will generally be stored in a file somewhere in the user's home directory.

Every account on a Linux system has a home directory, which is usually named after the account and located in /home. So, if you logged in as jack, your home directory is located at /home/jack. All your files and any directories you create while logged typically are contained within /home/jack. If you log out and another user logs in as jill, any files she creates after logging in typically are stored in /home/jill.

In this way, Linux allows the creation of many user accounts while keeping users' files separate from one another. This system of organization also keeps the filesystem uncluttered by assuring that most of the day-to-day files that a user creates are stored in one location owned by that user.

Most shells recognize the tilde character (~) as a special shortcut representing a user's home directory. This shortcut can be used in place of the full path when entering commands at the prompt. To the shell, for example, /home/jill and ~ are equivalent.

The Current Working Directory

Now that you've seen directories in action and are aware of the root directory and the home directory, it's time to learn to navigate the Linux system. You begin by creating a file. You can create an empty text file in Linux using the touch command and giving the filename you want as an argument. First, create a file called empty.txt:

```
[you@workstation20 you]$ touch empty.txt
[you@workstation20 you]$
```

Linux has now created for you an empty text file called empty.txt. To see that the file exists, use the ls command without arguments:

```
[you@workstation20 you]$ ls
empty.txt
[you@workstation20 you]$
```

If you're wondering exactly where the file is, you're an astute reader. Thus far, each time you used the ls command, you supplied it with an argument—the path to the directory you wanted to list. This time, however, ls lists the contents of a directory without having been told which directory you wanted to see. So what's going on? And in what directory did you just create empty.txt?

Whenever you log in to a Linux system console, the shell begins to keep track of something called your *current working directory*. At your request, your current working directory can be set to any directory in the filesystem. Linux created empty.txt in your current working directory. The ls command displays the contents of your current working directory in the preceding example. In most cases, if you provide an argument to a command without supplying a path, the command is executed as though you had actually supplied a path—the path of your current working directory.

From the previous output of ls, you can see that there is only one file in your current working directory—the file called empty.txt that you just created. To ask the shell just what your current working directory is, use the pwd (print working directory) command:

```
[you@workstation20 you]$ pwd
/home/you
[you@workstation20 you]$
```

At this point, your current working directory is your home directory—the directory in /home that belongs to your account and is intended to hold your files. When you log in, the shell always assumes that you want your current working directory to be your home directory unless you explicitly change it. To change your current working directory, use the cd command, supplying your desired current working directory as an argument. Try changing your current working directory to the root directory now:

```
[you@workstation20 you]$ cd /
[you@workstation20 /]$
```

Notice that the command prompt has changed to reflect your new current working directory. You can also use pwd to see that the change has taken effect:

```
[you@workstation20 /]$ pwd
/
[you@workstation20 /]$
```

Now using the ls command without arguments displays the contents of the root directory, rather than the contents of your home directory:

```
[you@workstation20 /]$ ls
bin   dev  home   lib          misc  opt   root  tmp  var
boot  etc  initrd  lost+found  mnt   proc  sbin  usr
[you@workstation20 /]$
```

Try making /usr/X11R6 your current working directory, using pwd to verify the change, and then using ls without arguments to list the contents of the directory:

```
[you@workstation20 /]$ cd /usr/X11R6
[you@workstation20 X11R6]$ pwd
/usr/X11R6
[you@workstation20 X11R6]$ ls
bin  include  LessTif  lib  libexec  man  share
[you@workstation20 X11R6]$
```

Because your home directory is so fundamental to day-to-day use of Linux at the command line, you can always return to it quickly by simply issuing the cd command without arguments:

```
[you@workstation20 X11R6]$ cd
[you@workstation20 you]$ pwd
/home/you
[you@workstation20 you]$
```

> You might also encounter the term *present working directory* instead of *current working directory*; these terms are identical in meaning.

Manipulating Files and Directories

Now that you're back in your home directory, assume for a moment that you want to make a copy of the file you created earlier called empty.txt. You can do this with the cp command, supplying two arguments—first the name of the source (original) file and second the name of the destination (new) file:

```
[you@workstation20 you]$ cp empty.txt notfull.txt
[you@workstation20 you]$ ls
empty.txt  notfull.txt
[you@workstation20 you]$
```

There are now two files in your home directory, `empty.txt` and `notfull.txt`, a copy of `empty.txt`. Suppose, however, that you didn't want `empty.txt` hanging around in your home directory, but instead wanted to put that particular file in its own directory called `emptyfiles`. To create a directory, use the `mkdir` command, supplying the name of the directory you want to create as an argument:

```
[you@workstation20 you]$ mkdir emptyfiles
[you@workstation20 you]$ ls
emptyfiles   empty.txt   notfull.txt
[you@workstation20 you]$
```

You have now created a directory called `emptyfiles` (which `ls` shows in blue to indicate that it is a directory) and can move `empty.txt` into it. Linux files can be moved using the `mv` command, which accepts the name of the file(s) to move as argument(s) and the destination directory as the last argument. After you are done, you can verify the effects of `mv` using the now familiar `ls` command:

```
[you@workstation20 you]$ mv empty.txt emptyfiles
[you@workstation20 you]$ ls
emptyfiles   notfull.txt
[you@workstation20 you]$ ls emptyfiles
empty.txt
[you@workstation20 you]$
```

Notice that the path arguments in the commands you've just entered don't begin with a slash character. This is because these commands were given *relative paths*, which are discussed in the next section.

Using Relative Paths

In the series of commands you just entered, you gave `ls` only a directory name, `emptyfiles`, as an argument, rather than a full path beginning with a slash. A directory name without a "roadmap" back to the root directory is called a *relative path*, so called because it doesn't begin with the root directory (/) but instead specifies that the argument is *relative to your present working directory*. Linux is smart enough to notice that the path you gave to `ls` didn't begin at the root directory; it therefore adds the path you supplied to your present working directory, which always begins with a slash. In this case, `/home/you` (the present working directory) plus `emptyfiles` (the argument given to `ls`) causes the contents of `/home/you/emptyfiles` to appear on the console, while saving you the trouble of entering a long path by hand.

To gain more practice with relative paths, try creating one more directory. This time call it `deeperfiles`. Place it "deeper" within your home directory by creating it inside the directory you created earlier called `emptyfiles`. Remember that your present working directory is still your home directory; you can use `pwd` to verify this:

```
[you@workstation20 you]$ pwd
/home/you
[you@workstation20 you]$ mkdir emptyfiles/deeperfiles
[you@workstation20 you]$ ls
emptyfiles  notfull.txt
[you@workstation20 you]$ ls emptyfiles
deeperfiles  empty.txt
[you@workstation20 you]$
```

Now, just for practice, move the file notfull.txt into the deeperfiles directory:

```
[you@workstation20 you]$ mv notfull.txt emptyfiles/deeperfiles
[you@workstation20 you]$ ls
emptyfiles
[you@workstation20 you]$ ls emptyfiles
deeperfiles  empty.txt
[you@workstation20 you]$ ls emptyfiles/deeperfiles
notfull.txt
[you@workstation20 you]$
```

If you want to review the output of the last few commands, you can scroll up or down in a virtual console by holding down your Shift key and pressing Page Up or Page Down.

4

If all of these relative paths have confused you a little, study Figure 4.4. The figure shows a diagram of the part of the Linux filesystem tree containing your home directory, as well as all the files and directories you just created within your home directory.

FIGURE 4.4

Part of a filesystem tree showing the current state of your home directory and all files and directories visible in it thus far.

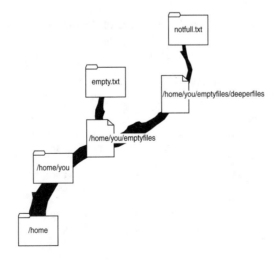

Before you finish with relative paths, you should become familiar with two special relative paths. They are a single period (.) and a double period (..), and they both can be used anywhere you would normally use the name of a directory.

The single period always refers to the present working directory. So, assuming that your present working directory is /home/you, the following three commands produce identical results:

```
[you@workstation20 you]$ ls
emptyfiles
[you@workstation20 you]$ ls /home/you
emptyfiles
[you@workstation20 you]$ ls .
emptyfiles
[you@workstation20 you]$
```

The double period always refers to the directory one branch lower in your filesystem tree, relative to your present working directory. So, assuming that your present working directory is /home/you, the following two commands produce identical results:

```
[you@workstation20 you]$ ls /home
you
[you@workstation20 you]$ ls ..
you
[you@workstation20 you]$
```

You also can use relative paths to modify your present working directory with cd:

```
[you@workstation20 you]$ cd ..
[you@workstation20 home]$ pwd
/home
[you@workstation20 home]$
```

Because the root directory is at the very base of the filesystem tree and there is no "lower" directory in the Linux filesystem, in the root directory the single period and double period are equivalent:

```
[you@workstation20 home]$ cd ..
[you@workstation20 /]$ pwd
/
@workstation20 /]$ ls
bin/dev home    lib          misc opt   root tmp var
boot etc initrd lost+found mnt   proc  sbin usr
[you@workstation20 /]$ ls .
bin   dev  home   lib          misc opt   root tmp var
boot  etc  initrd lost+found mnt   proc  sbin usr
[you@workstation20 /]$ ls ..
bin   dev  home   lib          misc opt   root tmp var
boot  etc  initrd lost+found mnt   proc  sbin usr
[you@workstation20 /]$
```

Remember that you can quickly return home by issuing the cd command without arguments:

```
[you@workstation20 /]$ cd
[you@workstation20 you]$ pwd
/home/you
[you@workstation20 you]$
```

> You will often see the double period (..) referred to as the *parent directory*. In the Linux filesystem, a file's parent directory is the directory that contains it. For example, /home is the parent directory of /home/you. You also will see the term *child directory*. In this example, /home/you is a child directory of /home.

Though beginners don't always understand just when or how the two special relative paths might be useful, routine applications do arise. For example, you can use them to move empty.txt, notfull.txt, and deeperfiles all back into your home directory:

```
[you@workstation20 you]$ mv emptyfiles/empty.txt emptyfiles/
deeperfiles deeperfiles/notfull.txt .
[you@workstation20 you]$ ls
deeperfiles emptyfiles empty.txt notfull.txt
[you@workstation20 yop]$
```

Get lost? Note that the last argument to mv in the command was the single period (.), causing mv to use the present working directory as the final destination for all the files listed:

- The first argument to mv moved the file empty.txt from the emptyfiles directory to . (the present working directory, currently your home directory).

- The second argument moved the directory deeperfiles from the emptyfiles directory to the present working directory, illustrating that mv can also be used to move directories.

- Finally, because the deeperfiles directory had already been moved to the present working directory by the processing of the second argument, the third argument moved the file notfull.txt from the deeperfiles directory to the present working directory.

To illustrate one final use of the mv command before we proceed, let's rename the file notfull.txt to alsoempty.txt and the directory deeperfiles to moreemptyfiles. There is no "rename" command in Linux, but it isn't needed because the more powerful mv command can be used to achieve the same result:

```
[you@workstation20 you]$ mv notfull.txt alsoempty.txt
[you@workstation20 you]$ mv deeperfiles moreemptyfiles
[you@workstation20 you]$ ls
alsoempty.txt  emptyfiles  empty.txt  moreemptyfiles
[you@workstation20 you]$
```

You're almost finished learning about basic navigation. But before we go on, let's take a moment to clean up the mess we made in your home directory.

Deleting Files and Directories

The command to remove files is rm; the command to remove directories is rmdir. With two quick commands and a few arguments, you can get rid of the files and directories you created and left here and there:

```
[you@workstation20 you]$ rmdir emptyfiles moreemptyfiles
[you@workstation20 you]$ rm alsoempty.txt empty.txt
[you@workstation20 you]$ ls
[you@workstation20 you]$
```

Notice that the final ls command produced no output, because there are no longer any files or directories in your home directory to list.

> The rm command can also be used to delete directories or entire sections of the filesystem tree. The rm command does this when you supply the -r (recursive) and -f (force) options, commonly shortened to -rf. One of the most commonly typed phrases in Unix is
>
> rm -rf *somedirectory*
>
> where somedirectory represents a directory full of files and other directories that are no longer needed. Although rmdir will respond with an error message if asked to delete a directory that is not empty, rm -rf will wipe it out.

> Be careful when using rm -rf! Because rm -rf simply removes files and directories (whether they are empty or not) without asking questions, you can easily wipe out vast swaths of your home directory with this command if you're not careful. When logged in as root, be doubly careful about using rm -rf, if you are brave enough to do it at all—otherwise, you could end up erasing your entire hard drive with a single command:
>
> rm -rf /

Executable Files

So far you've seen several basic text files and several directories. The /bin directory contains another type of file, called *executable* file. Executable files can be programs, commands, or scripts—tools and applications that you use, often from the command line, to get things done.

You can use the ls command to view the contents of the /bin directory:

```
[you@workstation20 you]$ ls /bin
arch          df            hostname  nisdomainname  su
ash           dmesg         igawk     pgawk          sync
[...]
date          gunzip        netstat   sort
dd            gzip          nice      stty
[you@workstation20 you]$
```

You can see that the files in this directory are coded in green and a light-blue color called cyan. Files listed in green are executable files (you learn more about the cyan files, called symbolic links, in the next section of this hour).

 You might not have noticed this when working in directories with fewer contents, but the ls command typically displays the contents of any directory in vertically arranged alphabetical order. This ordering is evident in the /bin directory.

If you look carefully, you might notice that this particular directory, /bin, contains many of the commands you've been using. The commands cp, ls, mkdir, mv, pwd, rm, rmdir, and touch are all stored in the /bin directory. All of these are started by the shell when you enter them as commands. Linux uses these commands to accomplish the work you've been requesting of the system.

Symbolic Links

The cyan files in the listing of /bin represent a very common filetype in Linux called a *symbolic link*. A symbolic link allows a given file to appear in many places or under many names at once. Symbolic links often are used to conserve disk space; other times, they're used simply for convenience. When a symbolic link points to an executable file, it enables the command to take on several identities or behaviors at once, depending on whether the user typed in the name of the original command to use it or the name of the symbolic link.

Nearly anything done to a symbolic link also affects the original file, with the notable exception of removal. Using rm with a symbolic link does not remove the original file; instead, using rm with a symbolic link removes the link itself. To get a little experience with symbolic links, let's create one now. In your home directory, create a directory called green and an empty file within it called color.txt:

```
[you@workstation20 you]$ mkdir green
[you@workstation20 you]$ touch green/color.txt
[you@workstation20 you]$ ls green
color.txt
[you@workstation20 you]$
```

Now use the file linking command, ln, commands:ln to create a symbolic link called blue that points to the green directory. To do this, supply the -s option to ln, followed by the name of the source file as the first argument and the destination link as the second:

```
[you@workstation20 you]$ ln -s green blue
[you@workstation20 you]$ ls
blue  green
[you@workstation20 you]$
```

To illustrate how the symbolic link behaves, list the files in each directory, both the original green directory and the symbolic link, blue, which points to it:

```
[you@workstation20 you]$ ls green
color.txt
[you@workstation20 you]$ ls blue
color.txt
[you@workstation20 you]$
```

You can see that the symbolic link, blue, behaves very much as the original directory, green, does. You can even make blue your present working directory:

```
[you@workstation20 you]$ cd blue
[you@workstation20 blue]$ pwd
/home/you/blue
[you@workstation20 blue]$ ls
color.txt
[you@workstation20 blue]$ cd ..
[you@workstation20 you]$
```

You won't do much more with symbolic links now, but they will come up in later hours, so it's important to be aware of them. As a final note, remember that you can also create symbolic links that point to symbolic links:

```
[you@workstation20 you]$ ln -s blue yellow
[you@workstation20 you]$ ls
blue  green  yellow
[you@workstation20 you]$ ls yellow
```

```
color.txt
[you@workstation20 you]$ cd yellow
[you@workstation20 yellow]$ pwd
/home/you/yellow
[you@workstation20 yellow]$ cd ..
[you@workstation20 you]$
```

Understanding Permissions

Every file and directory in a Linux system is governed by a set of security-related properties. These properties establish two things for each file:

- The list of owner(s) of the file or directory in question. Each file or directory must be owned by someone—in Linux there is no such thing as a file or directory without an owner.

- A list of the operations that can be performed on the file or directory, both by the owners and at times by other users as well. This list is known as the file's *permissions* and is generally represented in a particular format which will be discussed later on.

Both ownership and permissions are assigned from default values when a file or directory is created; file or directory owners can then change this information as needed.

You should be familiar with these properties when working with files and directories in Linux so you can control who is allowed to access sensitive data. You also should understand why you may not be able to access data belonging to others. The sections that follow teach you to examine and manipulate a file's ownership and permissions. Let's study some real-world examples.

Up to this point, you've created files only in your home directory, because this is where users are meant to put their files. But can you put your files somewhere else? Let's see. Visit your home directory's parent directory, /home, and try to create a file there called hello.txt:

```
[you@workstation20 you]$ cd ..
[you@workstation20 home]$ touch hello.txt
touch: creating 'hello.txt': Permission denied
[you@workstation20 home]$
```

You don't have permission to create files in the directory /home. To see why, you need to learn to use the ls command in a new way.

Long File Listings

So far you've used the ls command to get a basic listing of the *names* of the files and directories in a given directory. You can use a number of common options, however, to alter the behavior of ls so that it also lists other information, such as the creation date or size of a file or directory. Most used among these options is the -l or long listing option, which will cause ls to display a great deal of extra information about each file it lists. Try it now on your root directory:

```
[you@workstation20 home]$ ls -l /
total 196
drwxr-xr-x     2 root      root          4096 08-03 04:04 bin
drwxr-xr-x     3 root      root          4096 08-03 04:01 boot
drwxr-xr-x    19 root      root        118784 08-03 21:30 dev
drwxr-xr-x    58 root      root          4096 08-03 21:30 etc
drwxr-xr-x     3 root      root          4096 08-03 04:14 home
[...]
drwxr-x---     3 root      root          4096 08-03 18:03 root
drwxr-xr-x     2 root      root          8192 08-03 04:11 sbin
drwxrwxrwt     8 root      root          4096 08-04 04:23 tmp
drwxr-xr-x    15 root      root          4096 08-03 03:54 usr
drwxr-xr-x    18 root      root          4096 08-03 04:03 var
[you@workstation20 home]$
```

The -l option causes ls to display a wealth of new information, including (from left to right):

- The permissions (a string of characters that will be enumerated later in this hour) of the file or directory
- The number of hard links to the file or directory
- The *owning user* of the file or directory
- The *owning group* of the file or directory
- The size of the file or directory on the disk in bytes
- Creation date and time if the file or directory was created within the last six months, or creation year and date if the file or directory was created before that
- The name of the file or directory

The date, time, and size information in a long file listing is provided primarily for your convenience as a user. The hard link count provided by the long file listing is not commonly used in the course of day-to-day work, and is thus beyond the scope of a book like this one. The owning group, owning user, and permissions are all important for understanding and using Linux permissions and is your focus for the remainder of this hour.

Identity and File Ownership

In Linux, there are two basic forms of identity—the user account, which you are using right now, and the group membership. At any time, a user account may belong to one (always at least one) or several groups; groups are created by system administrators to manage security and to enhance workflow.

Every file and directory in a Linux filesystem is similarly *owned* at all times by exactly one primary user and by all the users in exactly one group. The ls command provides this ownership information in columns three and four of a long listing. As you've seen, every item in your system's root directory is owned by the root user and by the root group. For contrast, let's list the files in your home directory:

```
[you@workstation20 home]$ cd
[you@workstation20 you]$ pwd
/home/you
[you@workstation20 you]$ ls -l
total 4
lrwxrwxrwx   1 you       you              5 08-03 20:41 blue -> green
drwxrwxr-x   2 you       you           4096 08-03 20:41 green
lrwxrwxrwx   1 you       you              4 08-03 20:48 yellow -> blue
[you@workstation20 you]$
```

The files in your home directory are owned by the user you. They also belong to the group you. That group was created when your account was created, and you automatically belongs to it.

Ownership and File Permissions

What do we mean when we say that someone "has permission" to create or delete files in a given directory? In real terms, it means that the person in question owns the directory and that the permissions properties for the directory indicate that the directory's owner should be allowed to change the directory's contents. Referring back to your long listing of the root directory, you might recall the following entry for /home:

```
drwxr-xr-x   3 root     root          4096 08-03 04:14 home
```

The ownership of /home is clear; the /home directory is owned by the root user and the root group. The ten-character permissions code at the extreme left determines just what root, members of the group root, or anyone else can do to the /home directory. Each of the ten positions in the permissions code means something specific. Let's look at this code more closely, with some spaces added to separate the major parts of the code:

```
d rwx r-x r-x
```

The character in the leftmost (first) position indicates the type of file /home is. In this case, there is a d in this position to indicate that /home is a directory. The common values for file types are shown in Table 4.2.

TABLE 4.2   Common File Types from Permissions Strings

Type	Description
d	The file in question is a directory.
l	The file in question is a symbolic link.
-	The file in question is a normal file (text, data, image, and so on).

There are a few other file types, but we're not going to worry about them in this hour. Let's look at the code for /home again:

d rwx r-x r-x

Positions 2–4 of this code, rwx in the case of /home, dictate what *the* owning user of a file, in this case root, can do to it. The precise meanings of the characters in positions 2–4 are shown in Table 4.3.

TABLE 4.3   Meanings of the Characters in Positions 2–4

Position	Possible Values	Meaning
2	r = permission to read/list granted. - = permission to read/list denied.	In the case of a file, indicates whether the owning user will be allowed to read data from the file. In the case of a directory, indicates whether the owning user will be allowed to list the contents of the directory.
3	w = permission to write/create/delete granted. - = permission to write/create/delete denied.	In the case of a file, indicates whether the owning user will be allowed to write data to the file. In the case of a directory, indicates whether the owning user will be allowed to create or delete files in the directory.
4	x = permission to execute/visit granted. - = permission to execute/visit denied.	In the case of a file, indicates whether the owning user will be allowed to execute the file—to use it if it is a command or program. In the case of a directory, indicates whether the owning user will be allowed to make the directory his or her present working directory—to "visit" the directory.

In the case of /home, the owning user is allowed to list the contents of the directory, to create and delete files in the directory, and to visit the directory. Let's examine that permissions code for /home one more time:

d rwx r-x r-x

The characters in positions 5–7 (the middle group of three) have the same possible values and meanings as those shown in Table 4.3, but apply to members of the owning group, instead of to the owning user. In the case of /home, people who are not root but who happen to be members of the owning group, also called root, are allowed to list the contents of the directory and to visit the directory. They are not, however, allowed to create or delete files within the directory.

Finally, the characters in positions 8–10 (the final group of three) again have the same meanings, but they apply to all other users—users who are neither the owning user nor a member of the owning group. In this case, users who are not root and who do not belong to the root group (this includes you) will be allowed to list the contents of /home and to visit /home, but will not be allowed to create or delete files in /home. So when you tried to create a file in /home, Linux returned an error message.

More Permissions Examples

Because permissions can be a little confusing, it might help to go over some examples with brief explanations. The following are hypothetical files with owning user, owning group, and permissions codes:

-rw-r-----   1 jack   admins   16384 08-03 04:14 jacks_peppers.txt

The file jacks_peppers.txt is likely a text document containing private information that jack doesn't want anyone to edit. Here is what this long listing tells you:

- The file jacks_peppers.txt is owned by the user jack and by members of the group admins.
- [-] It is a regular file, not a directory or a symbolic link.
- [rw-] The user jack is allowed to read data from the file and to write data to the file.
- [r--] Members of the group admins are also allowed to read data from the file, but they may not write data to or make changes to the file in any way.
- [---] Users who are not jack and who do not belong to admins can't read from the file or write to the file at all.

Here's another example:

-rwxr-x---   1 root   wheel   54696 08-03 04:14 launchit

The file `launchit` is a program that likely performs an administrative task of some kind, because only `root` and members of `wheel` can run it. Here is what this long listing tells you:

- The file `launchit` is owned by the user `root` and by members of the group `wheel`.
- [-] It is a regular file, not a directory or symbolic link.
- [rwx] The user `root` is allowed to read data from the file and to write data to the file. The file `launchit` is likely a program or command because the user root is also allowed to execute it.
- [r-x] Members of the group `wheel` are allowed to read from `launchit` and to execute it, but they may not write to it.
- [---] Users who are not `root` and who do not belong to `wheel` can't read `launchit`, write to `launchit`, or execute `launchit` at all.

> When you look at the permissions of symbolic links, they will always seem to grant permission for everything to everyone. This is because a symbolic link uses the permissions of the file that it points *to*, rather than its own permissions.

Changing Permissions

There might be times when you want to change the permissions of files you own in your home directory. You might want to allow other users to modify them, for example, or to prevent other users from reading them. File permissions can be changed with the `chmod` command.

There are two ways to use `chmod`—the symbolic method and the numeric method. The *symbolic* method for changing permissions is easier to understand because it uses the same characters you've seen used for permissions codes. The *numeric* method uses numbers to assign permissions and is more commonly used by system administrators because of its brevity.

Here is the format for using `chmod` in symbolic mode:

```
chmod permcode file1 [file2 ...]
```

The `permcode` is composed of three parts:

- One letter or a combination of these letters:
  u (for owning user)
  g (for owning group)
  o (for "other")

This letter or group of letters indicates whose permissions are to be changed.

- Either a plus, minus, or equal sign, depending on whether permissions are to be added, removed, or explicitly assigned, respectively.

- One letter or a combination of these letters:

  r (for adding/removing/assigning read permission)

  w (for adding/removing/assigning write permission)

  x (for adding/removing/assigning execute permission)

  This letter or group of letters indicates how permissions are to be allocated.

Let's look at some examples to illustrate how chmod works in symbolic mode. Return to your home directory and create a new file called illustration.txt:

```
[you@workstation20 home]$ cd
[you@workstation20 you]$ touch illustration.txt
[you@workstation20 you]$ ls -l
total 4
lrwxrwxrwx   1 you      you               5 08-03 20:41 blue -> green
drwxrwxr-x   2 you      you            1096 08-03 20:41 green
-rw-rw-r--   1 you      you               0 08-04 10:01 illustration.txt
lrwxrwxrwx   1 you      you               4 08-03 20:48 yellow -> blue
[you@workstation20 you]$
```

Notice that in spite of the fact that illustration.txt is *your* file, the entire world (users who are not you and do not belong to your group) can still currently read illustration.txt. Suppose illustration.txt contained private information? You would, of course, want to remove permission for other users to read the file:

```
[you@workstation20 you]$ chmod o-r illustration.txt
[you@workstation20 you]$ ls -l illustration.txt
-rw-rw----   1 you      you               0 08-04 10:01 illustration.txt
[you@workstation20 you]$
```

You have now forbidden users who are not you and do not belong to the group you from reading illustration.txt. Other users who try to read the file will get an error message. Now suppose for a moment that you also have a twin, miniyou, who has been made a member of the group you by a system administrator. With the current file permissions of illustration.txt, miniyou would have both read and write access, assuming once again that miniyou was a member of the group you. To prevent this, you could disable access for all members of the group you:

```
[you@workstation20 you]$ chmod g-rw illustration.txt
[you@workstation20 you]$ ls -l illustration.txt
-rw-------   1 you      you               0 08-04 10:01 illustration.txt
[you@workstation20 you]$
```

Now only you have read and write access to `illustration.txt`. Users who are not you but who are members of the group you have no access. But perhaps you only wanted to prevent `miniyou` from modifying the file—not necessarily from reading it. No problem— you can restore read permission:

```
[you@workstation20 you]$ chmod g+r illustration.txt
[you@workstation20 you]$ ls -l illustration.txt
-rw-r-----   1 you      you              0 08-04 10:01 illustration.txt
[you@workstation20 you]$
```

Now you still have full read and write access; members of the group you (including `miniyou`) have read-only access. Users who are not you and not members of the group you still have no access at all. Finish by giving full read and write access to everyone in the world, just for fun:

```
[you@workstation20 you]$ chmod ugo+rw illustration.txt
[you@workstation20 you]$ ls -l illustration.txt
-rw-rw-rw-   1 you      you              0 08-04 10:01 illustration.txt
[you@workstation20 you]$
```

In practice, you'd rarely want to do this, because now anyone in any account can read at will and make any changes to `illustration.txt`. But it doesn't matter because we've reached the end of this hour and you're going to delete `illustration.txt` and the other files you've created and log out:

```
[you@workstation20 you]$ rm illustration.txt blue yellow green/color.txt
[you@workstation20 you]$ rmdir green
[you@workstation20 you]$ logout
```

Summary

This hour, you learned to switch from the dekstop on virtual console seven to one of the first six text-based consoles. You then logged in and gained experience navigating the Linux system through the shell, using a number of common commands:

You also learned about the Linux filesystem tree, special directories—such as the root directory and your home directory—and how to use full paths (which begin with a forward slash) and relative paths (which do not).

Finally, you learned about Linux permissions, sets of file or directory properties that enable you to control who can read from and write to your files while allowing other users to decide whether you will be able to read from or write to theirs.

In the next hour, you put some of your new skills to work on text files, rather than just on empty files. Until then, take a break—you've earned it!

Q&A

Q **I haven't ever created any files or directories in my home directory; yet there are already files or directories there, according to the `ls` command. Why?**

A Various Linux applications and desktop environments, such as KDE and GNOME, can create files and directories for you. Depending on the amount of work you'd already done with your Red Hat Linux system before you started this chapter, your home directory might not have been empty as you began to follow along with the examples.

Q **Is there any way to cause the `ls` command to display information one page at a time—for example, in a long file listing?**

A You can by using pipes and the `more` command, both of which are discussed in Hour 5, "Making the Console Work for You." To pause a long file listing after each page of output, enter

```
ls -l | more
```

After each page of output, press the spacebar to continue to the next page.

Q **What happens when using `mv` or `cp` if a file already exists with the same name as the destination argument I've given?**

A If the destination file already exists when using `mv` or `cp`, it is *replaced* by the new file. The existing file is deleted before the new file by the same name is created.

Workshop

The Workshop is designed to help you anticipate possible questions, review what you've learned, and begin learning how to put your knowledge into practice.

Quiz

1. What command would you use to create an empty text file called `friday.txt`?

2. What command would you use to rename `friday.txt` to `saturday.txt`?

3. What command would you use to find the ownership and permissions associated with `saturday.txt`?

4. What command would you use to change the permissions for `saturday.txt` to ensure that all users anywhere could read and write to the file?

5. What command would you use to remove (delete) `saturday.txt`?

Answers

1. `touch friday.txt`

2. `mv friday.txt saturday.txt`

3. `ls -l saturday.txt`

4. `chmod ugo+r saturday.txt`

5. `rm saturday.txt`

Activities

1. Spend some time exploring your Linux file system using `ls` and `cd` to visit directories, beginning with the root directory.

2. Practice creating, moving, and removing files, directories, and symbolic links in your home directory.

3. To familiarize yourself with virtual consoles, log in to several virtual consoles without logging out of any of them. Enter a few commands in each, and then log out of each of them one by one.

HOUR 5

Making the Console Work for You

In this hour, you gain experience with concepts that will be more useful to you the longer you use Linux. You begin the hour by exploring two ubiquitous text editors that you'll encounter over and over again in the Linux world. Then, you learn ways to make your life at the command line easier. By the end of this hour, you will be able to

- Create, edit, and save basic text files in your home directory using two common text editors.

- Manage groups of similar files more easily.

- Use the standard output path to save information in text files or to link commands.

- Locate specific files in your directory tree by filename or by content, with quick searches.

- Save time and effort by using one command's output as arguments to another command.

- Start and switch between lots of shell programs without having to exit any of them.

As in Hour 4, "Navigating Linux at the Console," this hour will help you become familiar with the shell and shell commands and techniques, rather than make you an instant pro. Try to follow along and understand what is happening, even if you don't think you can remember all of it later.

To begin this hour, you should already be logged into your account at a virtual console, ready to give commands at the shell prompt.

Creating, Editing, and Saving Text Files

In the last hour, you created a few text files using the touch command, but these were all *empty* text files—unlikely to be of much use for any common purpose. Most of the time if you're creating a text file, you need it to contain specific text that you enter.

At the Linux command line, there are two major editors commonly used to create text files—and they are polar opposites. The first is a small, classic UNIX tool called vi; the second is a large, extensible data processor called emacs. Either editor can be used to create the kinds of documents you want to create at the Red Hat Linux command line. The vi editor will be preferred by users who want a minimal, fast, no-frills editing experience, and the emacs editor is generally preferred by so-called power users. The editor you choose to use on a daily basis is ultimately a matter of personal preference and little more; some Linux administration tools integrate the vi editor as part of their functionality, however, so you should at least become moderately familiar with vi.

Although most computer users are familiar with the term *word processor*, the term *text editor* is less widely known.

A word processor includes features designed for desktop publishing, such as typeface selection, layout controls, and formatting options for the printed page. A text editor is designed to edit letters and numbers only; a text editor does not offer features for controlling the appearance or layout of text in printed output.

Using vi to Create or Edit Text Files

The vi editor is popular because, unlike emacs, it's nearly always present, even on the most minimal system. It's also popular because, unlike emacs, vi is small and fast.

Begin work on an empty document now by typing the vi command followed by the name of the file you want to create as an argument. Call this file myvifile.txt:

```
[you@workstation20 you]$ vi myvifile.txt
```

Starting vi does not always *create* a file. If you supply the name of an already existing file as the argument to vi, that file will be loaded into vi so that you can edit it.

You'll always know you're working in vi when you see the line of tilde (~) characters stretching down the left side of your console. These characters indicate that there is no text yet on any of these lines. Don't actually try to type anything yet; you won't be able to. The vi editor is line-oriented and has two modes. When you first start vi, you are in a mode not designed to allow text entry.

You are looking at the *command mode* right now. Anything you type, including normal alphabetic text, will not appear in the document; rather, it will be interpreted by vi as an attempt to demand action. In command mode, you can save your file, move your cursor around, delete phrases or lines of text, and so on.

The *insert mode* is the only mode in which you can directly enter text, and while vi is in the insert mode, text entry is nearly the only thing you *can* do. This inevitably confuses new vi users at first, but after a little practice, most people become comfortable with the two-mode system.

Let's insert some text.

Inserting Text in vi

To begin inserting text in the vi file you're working on, myvifile.txt, press the i key. Notice that the word INSERT appears at the bottom of the display, as is shown in Figure 5.1.

FIGURE 5.1

The vi editor in insert mode, waiting for you to enter text. All keyboard entry from now on will be considered text input until the Esc key is pressed.

5

Enter a few lines of text now. Follow along with the examples here, or enter your own text. Note that there is no word wrap in vi; when you come to the end of a line, you must press Enter to start a new line of text:

```
The vi editor is ubiquitous in UNIX. Because of this, it is important
that all aspiring UNIX users understand how to interact with vi.
```

 If you choose not to press Enter before you reach the right side of your display, the text on your screen will wrap around to the left side of the display in mid-word. Understand, however, that the text in vi's memory buffer will not. If you manage to fill the entire screen full of text without ever pressing Enter, the file you save will be stored as *one long line* of text.

This can have unexpected consequences when printing, emailing, or even when editing text files.

When you finish entering text, press the Esc key to exit the insert mode and return to command mode. Notice when you do so that the word INSERT disappears from the status line at the bottom of the screen.

Now you've inserted some text. But what if you want to change what you've typed so far? In vi, the methods for making changes aren't always obvious.

Editing Text in vi

You use keystroke commands to navigate and edit text in vi. Some of the most common keystrokes are shown in Table 5.1.

TABLE 5.1   Common Keystroke Commands for Editing and Navigating in vi

Keystroke	Action
l	Move cursor one character to the right.
h	Move cursor one character to the left.
j	Move cursor down one *text* line (not one display line).
k	Move cursor up one *text* line (not one display line).
x	Delete the character immediately under the cursor.
d#<Space>	Delete # characters immediately under and to the right of the cursor.
dd	Delete the current line.
i	Insert: Return to insert mode, inserting immediately under the cursor at its current position.

TABLE 5.1 continued

Keystroke	Action
a	Append: Return to insert mode, inserting immediately to the right of the cursor at its current position.
A	Append: Return to insert mode, inserting at the end of the current *text* line (not display line).
Esc	Return to command mode.

Try using the movement and editing keys in command mode to alter the text you just entered, to delete a line or a few characters of text, or to insert or append some text to the file. If you get confused or the keyboard stops responding as you expect it to while you are editing, you have likely keyed incorrectly; press Esc several times to ensure that you return to the command mode.

> If you've been following along and experimenting with vi, you've likely discovered that it's actually easier than I've made it out to be. Red Hat Linux uses an enhanced version of vi called vim. In this enhanced vi editor, you can use your arrow keys to navigate through the text, even in insert mode, so long as your terminal is properly configured (as is the case at the Linux console).
>
> This is an enhanced version of vi that isn't present on most UNIX systems, however, or even on all Linux systems—and vim might not be included in future versions of Red Hat Linux. Furthermore, some administration situations can limit you to traditional vi keys even while using Red Hat Linux. You should become familiar with the traditional vi keys and behaviors, in case you find yourself working in a traditional vi editor.

Experiment with vi for a while and try to become familiar with it; you'll encounter it often enough in Linux to make it worth your time.

Saving and Quitting, and Further Reading

Let's save the file you've just created by entering what will seem like a very cryptic command. Type a colon (:) now. Notice that a colon appears at the lower-left of the display and that the cursor has moved there; vi is now waiting for you to enter a more complex command. Type a lowercase w and press Enter. The vi editor responds with a status update at the lower-left of the display:

```
"myvifile.txt" 2L, 135C written
```

First, vi mentions the name of the file that has just been saved; you called this file myvifile.txt. Next, vi gives the number of lines in the file (2), followed by the number of individual characters in the file (135). You have now saved your first vi file.

There is also a Save As function in vi. To save your text again, this time as a new file, type a colon, and then enter **w** followed by a space and the name **mynewvifile.txt**. The vi editor responds with

```
"mynewvifile.txt" 2L, 135C written
```

You now have two copies of the file in your home directory, myvifile.txt and mynewvifile.txt. That's enough of vi for a book such as this. To exit vi, type a colon, and then type **q**. This quits vi and returns you to the command prompt.

> If you try to exit vi without first saving the file you've been working on, vi will interrupt you with an error message indicating that your file has not been saved; it will then return to command mode.
>
> If you really want to exit anyway, use :q! (with the exclamation mark added) instead of simply :q to exit; vi will then comply.

vi is powerful and worthy of some study, both because of the number of efficiency-oriented editing features it provides and because you will so often encounter it while using Linux or UNIX computers at the command line. If you're feeling adventurous, you can explore the bulky online help system in Red Hat's version of the vi editor by restarting vi and entering **:help** while in command mode. The resulting title page is shown in Figure 5.2.

> A more complete vi tutorial can also be found in *Sams Teach Yourself Unix in 24 Hours*, by Dave Taylor.

Using emacs to Create Text Files

If you found vi to be too minimal and unusual for your taste, you'll likely feel better about emacs, though emacs also has its quirks. Although vi's focus is on minimalism, basic functionality, and speed, emacs is extensible and programmable, and has over the years grown into a monster of a system. Very few people on Earth know everything that can be known about emacs; there are hundreds of modes and commands and an entire programming language (Emacs LISP) to master.

FIGURE 5.2

The title screen for the vi (vim) online help system. The help is reasonably extensive, and it is possible to become quite a vi expert simply by reading these documents.

```
*help.txt*      For Vim version 6.1.  Last change: 2001 Sep 14

                        VIM - main help file
                                                                    k
        Move around:  Use the cursor keys, or "h" to go left,      h   l
                      "j" to go down, "k" to go up, "l" to go right.    j
Close this window:  Use ":q<Enter>".
      Get out of Vim:  Use ":qa!<Enter>" (careful, all changes are lost!).

Jump to a subject:  Position the cursor on a tag between |bars| and hit CTRL-].
      With the mouse:  ":set mouse=a" to enable the mouse (in xterm or GUI).
                      Double-click the left mouse button on a tag between |bars|.
          jump back:  Type CTRL-T or CTRL-O (repeat to go further back).

Get specific help:  It is possible to go directly to whatever you want help
                    on, by giving an argument to the ":help" command |:help|.
                    It is possible to further specify the context:
                                                      *help-context*
                     WHAT                PREPEND    EXAMPLE
                  Normal mode commands    (nothing)  :help x
help.txt [help][RO]                                  1,1            Top

[No File]                                            0,0-1          All
```

For our purposes, however, emacs is going to seem friendly and simple compared to vi. You can start emacs the same way you started vi; type the emacs command followed by the name of the file you want to open or create as an argument. Use the filename myemacsfile.txt:

[you@workstation20 you]$ **emacs myemacsfile.txt**

Depending on your system configuration, it might take somewhat longer for emacs to load. This is because emacs is a much larger and more complex editor than vi. After emacs loads, you'll find yourself looking at the screen shown in Figure 5.3.

FIGURE 5.3

The emacs editor clearly has a more accessible look than vi and is designed to function in some ways that Windows users will be more accustomed to.

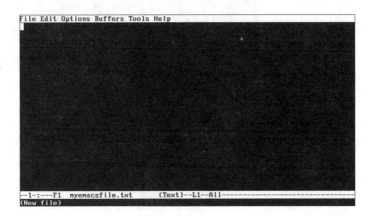

```
File Edit Options Buffers Tools Help



                              .




--1-:---F1   myemacsfile.txt       (Text)--L1--All----------------------------
(New file)
```

5

It is easy to insert text into the emacs editor; just type. You'll find that the arrow keys, Backspace and Delete keys, Page Up and Page Down keys, and Home and End keys all behave as you expect them to.

When you reach the end of the first line, you'll soon find out that like vi, emacs does not normally automatically word wrap. Remember to press Enter at the end of each line, because emacs is a line-oriented editor. If you don't press Enter at the end of each line, only one very long line of text will be written when you save your file.

The emacs Menu System

Though it might appear that there is a menu bar at the top of your emacs display in console mode, this isn't really the case. There is no way to visually activate drop-down menus at the console.

However, you can access the fairly intuitive emacs menu by pressing the F10 key at almost any time. When you press F10, your display is split in two, and the lower half of your display fills with options that can be activated with a single keypress (see Figure 5.4).

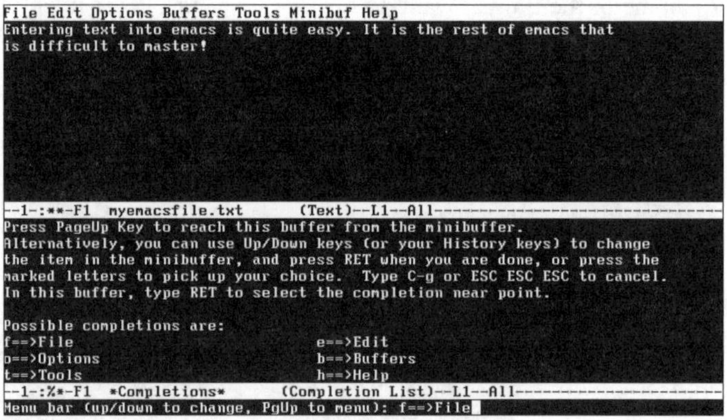

FIGURE 5.4

When you bring up the emacs *menu system at the console, each item can be activated by pressing its respective key.*

```
File Edit Options Buffers Tools Minibuf Help
Entering text into emacs is quite easy. It is the rest of emacs that
is difficult to master!




--1-:**-F1  myemacsfile.txt      (Text)--L1--All-------------------------
Press PageUp Key to reach this buffer from the minibuffer.
Alternatively, you can use Up/Down keys (or your History keys) to change
the item in the minibuffer, and press RET when you are done, or press the
marked letters to pick up your choice.  Type C-g or ESC ESC ESC to cancel.
In this buffer, type RET to select the completion near point.

Possible completions are:
f==>File                              e==>Edit
o==>Options                           b==>Buffers
t==>Tools                             h==>Help
--1-:%*-F1  *Completions*       (Completion List)--L1--All-----------------
Menu bar (up/down to change, PgUp to menu): f==>File
```

To save the file you have been working on, press f to open the file menu and then s when the file menu appears to save it. emacs displays a message in the small area at the bottom of the screen, known as the *minibuffer*, to let you know that the file has been saved:

```
wrote /home/you/myemacsfile.txt
```

You can use the F10 menu system in emacs to perform most basic editing, saving, and loading functions. For most users, the F10 menu and simpler editing style makes emacs the editor of choice over vi.

Essential emacs Keystrokes

If you aren't too ham-handed, you might be able to use emacs and the F10 menu for months or even years without getting into trouble. However, an accidental keystroke will leave most users sitting in front of a beeping emacs editor printing cryptic error messages or demands in the minibuffer.

The essential keystroke to know at times like this is written in the emacs documentation as C-g (hold down Ctrl and press g). This is the emacs abort keystroke. The emacs editor is large enough that there will be many opportunities to find yourself in an unknown state; most of the time, repeatedly pressing C-g until things return to normal is the solution to this type of confusion.

Table 5.2 lists a few other interesting emacs keystrokes—some accessible from the menu system, some not. To understand this table, you must first become familiar with the format of emacs keystrokes:

- C-x, where x is a letter, means hold down the Ctrl key and press the letter.
- C-xy, where both x and y are letters, means hold down the Ctrl key, press the first letter, release both the Ctrl key and the first letter, and then press the second letter alone.
- M-x, where x is a letter, means hold down the Alt key and press the letter.
- C-x C-y, where both x and y are letters, means hold down the Ctrl key, press the first letter, and then, without releasing the Ctrl key, press the second letter.

Note that the letters in these control combinations are case-sensitive, so be careful to press the keys indicated, rather than their uppercase or lowercase counterparts.

TABLE 5.2   Useful emacs Keystrokes

Keystroke	Explanation
C-ht	Launch the emacs tutorial, in whichmany more keystrokes are documented.
C-x C-f	Find (open or create) a file in the current editing pane—you are prompted in the minibuffer for a filename or path.
C-x C-s	Save the file you are currently working on.
C-x2	Split the current editing pane vertically.
C-x3	Split the current editing pane horizontally.
C-x1	Cause the current editing pane to fill the entire screen (hide/remove other panes).
C-xo	Select the next editing pane.
C-xk	Close (without saving) the file or buffer you are currently working in. For example, use this keystroke after you've opened the emacs tutorial to exit it again.

5

TABLE 5.2 continued

Keystroke	Explanation
C-xb	Switch to another buffer—you are prompted in the minibuffer for a buffer name; if you are unsure about the names of open buffers, press Tab for a complete list.
C-xi *file*	Insert a file at the current cursor position. You are prompted for the name of the file in the minibuffer.
C-x C-c	Exit emacs completely.
C-g	Abort the current emacs process.

One final keystroke before we finish our discussion of emacs takes you well on your way to becoming an emacs guru. To see a list of available commands in emacs, press M-x and then the Tab key. A buffer containing a list of emacs commands will appear. Press C-xo until your cursor appears in that pane; you can then use Page Up and Page Down to browse through the available commands. If you see one you'd like to try, type it into the minibuffer and press Enter.

The various emacs commands include the following:

- M-x dunnet starts a text-based adventure game.
- M-x auto-fill turns on word wrap.
- M-x calendar opens up a new pane containing a three month calendar.
- M-x ansi-term opens up a shell in the current pane. Be sure to use C-x2 or C-x3 before running this one, so that you can edit a file and work with the shell at the same time, switching between panes with C-xo, as shown in Figure 5.5.

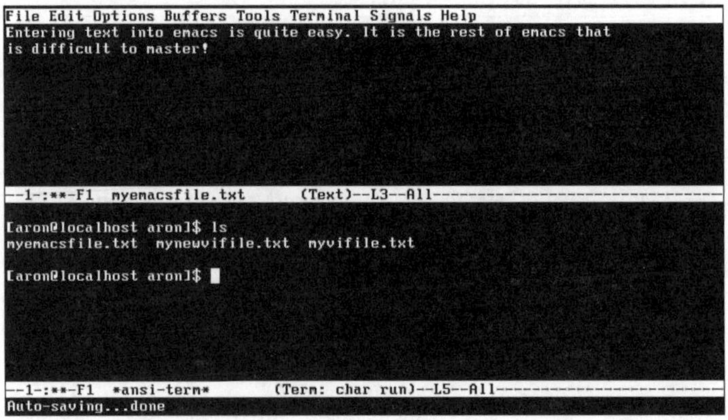

FIGURE 5.5

An emacs editor that has been split horizontally with C-x2. *A shell is started in the lower pane with* C-xo *followed by* M-x ansi-term. *Switch between the panes with* C-xo.

If you become an `emacs` user, you will soon find that, from time to time, files appear in your working directory with names similar to those of files you've been working on, but with slight additions. For example, if you've been working on a file called `myfile.txt`, you might also find `#myfile.txt#` or `myfile.txt~` in the same directory.

These are "safety" files that `emacs` creates in the interest of preserving your data.

When you exit without saving a file, `emacs` saves the file anyway, under the same name but with hash marks (#) at the front and back, in case you want to recover the changes you made later.

When you make changes to an existing file and save them, `emacs` will preserve the original (unmodified) file under the same name, but with a tilde character (~) at the end, in case you want to return to the original file later.

If you don't want to preserve the auto-save or backup files, remove them with `rm`, though you might want to load them into `emacs` first to make sure that they don't contain data that you want to save.

Grouping Files for Efficient File Management

As you begin working with larger numbers of files and editors such as `vi` and `emacs` on a regular basis, you build a library of data, reports, and files-in-progress.

Commands such as `mv`, `cp`, `rm`, and `ls` are helpful for organizing files. As your workload in Linux increases, however, you need the additional tools provided by the shell and a few more powerful commands to help you navigate your growing file collection. You can group files to make finding and accessing them faster and more efficient. The following sections explain how to group files in Red Hat Linux for more efficient file management.

Grouping Files on the Command Line

In Hour 4, you learned to perform a number of common file management tasks by entering commands and filenames, one or two at a time, at the shell prompt. Sometimes it is helpful to be able to refer to many files at once at the shell prompt, without having to type all of their names. The shell provides a tool for grouping similar filenames to save you the trouble of having to type them one by one.

To illustrate, consider the following problem. Suppose you want to store the files `myvifile.txt`, `mynewvifile.txt` and `myemacsfile.txt`, in a directory called `firstfiles`. Using the skills you learned in "Manipulating Files and Directories," in Hour 4, you first create the directory with `mkdir`, then use `mv` to move the files by name:

5

```
[you@workstation20 you]$ mkdir firstfiles
[you@workstation20 you]$ mv myvifile.txt mynewvifile.txt myemacsfile.txt
➥firstfiles
[you@workstation20 you]$
```

But that's a lot of typing just to move three text files to a more convenient location. It seems as though there should be an easier way—and there is. When used at the shell prompt, the asterisk (*) is one of a special group of characters that can be used for *filename expansion*—a way of grouping files logically so that you don't have to type all their names to manipulate all of them at once. Filename expansion is as much an art as a science; to use it, you employ specific *pattern matching tools* to try to collect files into a group and then pass that group on to the shell. It sounds complicated, but it's actually simple and powerful. Here's an example of using filename expansion to perform the task you just saw demonstrated with makedir. Try using this mv command instead:

```
[you@workstation20 you]$ mv *.txt firstfiles
```

Let's make sure that the command had the desired effect:

```
[you@workstation20 you]$ ls
firstfiles
[you@workstation20 you]$ ls firstfiles
myemacsfile.txt  mynewvifile.txt  myvifile.txt
[you@workstation20 you]$
```

Obviously, the new, simplified command produced the desired result. The phrase *.txt has grouped together all files that end with the four characters .txt.

We'll go over other examples; but first, take a look at Table 5.3, which lists the patterns commonly used for filename expansion.

TABLE 5.3 Common Pattern Matching Characters and Their Effects

Pattern	Matching Effect(s)
*	Matches all characters in any quantity, including no characters at all
?	Matches any single character
[a-b] (range)	Matches a single character in the range of characters between a and b; for example, [A-Z] would match the letter X or the letter P, but not the number 9 or the letter a
[AaBbCc] (list)	Matches a single character from the list of characters provided

Working through a few examples can help you better understand what these patterns mean and how they can help you work with groups of files in Red Hat Linux. Let's create a table of examples. Suppose you were going to rm a group of files in your home directory. Table 5.4 shows some sample `rm` arguments and files that each would (or wouldn't) match.

TABLE 5.4 Sample Commands Using Expansion and Their Effects

Command	Effect(s)
`rm *.txt`	Would remove any file with a .txt extension—for example, `a.txt`, `b.txt`, `hello.txt`, or `everybody_is_cool.txt`, but not `bicycle.gif`, `car_bills.xls`, or `myoldtxt`.
`rm a*jpg`	Would remove any file beginning with the letter a and ending with the three letters `jpg`—for example, `a.jpg`, `apple.jpg`, `answermachine.jpg`, and `anastasiajpg`, but not `boat.jpg`, `file.txt`, `monkeys.gif`, or `macaroni_list`.
`rm k*n.?if`	Would remove `kitchen.gif`, `kluckchicken.tif`, `kn.zif`, and `korn.weekday..if`, but not `korean.if`, `kasino.gif`, or `fountain.tif`.
`rm l[eou]g.*`	Would remove `leg.gif`, `log.txt`, `lug.jpg`, `log.my.hours.please`, `leg.gomyeg.go.txt`, and `lug.this`, but not `lag.gif`, `leglover.txt`, or `log`.
`rm [a-f]*`	Would remove `apple.txt`, `bacon.jpg`, `cradle.song`, `dog.walking.schedule`, `everybody.mp3`, and `fanatics_favorites`, but not `goose.txt`, `xylophone.jpg`, or `Barbie.gif`.
`rm *`	Would remove every file in the present working directory. Adding the `-rf` options would remove every file *and* every directory in the present working directory. (Remember the `-r` and `-f` options from Hour 4?)

> Be careful when grouping files using filename expansion; constructing your patterns carelessly can have unintended consequences. For example, when removing files using the methods shown in Table 5.4, Linux does not caution you or ask whether you are sure before removing *all* the files that match the pattern you supplied.

Filename expansion can be used in most circumstances to make your life at the console easier by reducing the amount of reading and typing you have to do when managing large numbers of files. As a final illustration, move the files you created with `vi` back to your home directory while leaving the file you created with `emacs` in the `firstfiles` directory:

```
[you@workstation20 you]$ mv firstfiles/*vi* .
[you@workstation20 you]$ ls
firstfiles  mynewvifile.txt  myvifile.txt
[you@workstation20 you]$ ls firstfiles
myemacsfile.txt
[you@workstation20 you]$
```

Preventing Filename Expansion

Sometimes you don't want the shell to perform filename expansion—for example, when you want to use special pattern matching characters such as the asterisk or question mark in a file's name, or as an argument to a command.

Suppose, for example, that you wanted to create a directory called *new* in your home directory to hold some new and improved files you've been working on. There is nothing illegal in Linux about having the asterisk in a file or directory name. However, when you try to create such a directory, it doesn't work:

```
[you@workstation20 you]$ mkdir *new*
mkdir: 'mynewvifile.txt' exists but is not a directory
[you@workstation20 you]$
```

Here, the shell has interpreted *new* as a pattern and tried to match it against the files in your present working directoy. As luck would have it, there is indeed a match—the pattern *new* matches the filename mynewvifile.txt, and so the shell behaved as though you had entered this:

```
[you@workstation20 you]$ mkdir mynewvifiles.txt
mkdir: 'mynewvifile.txt' exists but is not a directory
[you@workstation20 you]$
```

At times like this, you want the shell to treat the phrase you've entered as normal text, rather than as a pattern. To do this, you need to *quote* the text. This can be done with either single or double quotes (there is a difference, which we'll discuss in later hours). For now, use single quotes to create the directory *new* in your home directory:

```
[you@workstation20 you]$ mkdir '*new*'
[you@workstation20 you]$ ls
firstfiles  mynewvifile.txt  myvifile.txt  *new*
[you@workstation20 you]$
```

You have now successfully created a directory called *new* in your home directory by quoting what could otherwise have been a pattern for filename expansion.

Searching Files and Directories Quickly

You've learned how to list files with the ls command and how to change your working directory with the cd command. To find a specific file using only ls and cd, however, you must navigate your home directory tree, listing each directory, directories inside those directories, and so on, until you find the file you want. Searching with ls and cd is fine for a collection of two or three files, but how about a collection of a hundred files? A thousand? Eventually, all of those filenames will begin to look the same.

Rather than search all day by hand, you can use the `find` and `locate` commands to find the location of your stray files more quickly.

Searching for Files with `find`

You can use the `find` command to search an entire directory tree or list of directory trees for specific filenames or for filenames that match a specific pattern. The syntax for using `find` this way is

```
find tree1 [tree2 ...] -name filename
```

Calling `find` this way searches the supplied directory trees for a specific filename. For example, you can search your home directory for `myemacsfile.txt`:

```
[you@workstation20 you]$ find ~ -name myemacsfile.txt
/home/you/firstfiles/myemacsfile.txt
[you@workstation20 you]$
```

> Remember that the tilde character ( ) represents the equivalent of `/home/you` to the shell.

Find quickly locates `myemacsfile.txt` for you. It is stored in `/home/you/firstfiles`. Similarly, you can search your home directory for all files ending in `.txt` by supplying a pattern to `find` similar to the kind of pattern used for filename expansion. You need to quote the pattern you supply, however, or the shell will match the pattern to the text files in your home directory before `find` gets to see it:

```
[you@workstation20 you]$ find /home/you -name '*.txt'
/home/aron/firstfiles/myemacsfile.txt
/home/aron/myvifile.txt
/home/aron/mynewvifile.txt
[you@workstation20 you]$
```

The `find` command has searched your home directory and found three files whose names end with `.txt`. The full paths to these files have been printed for you.

Searching the Entire Filesystem with `locate`

Sometimes you want to search the *entire* Linux filesystem for a specific file. When you want to search the entire filesystem, `locate` is often a better choice than `find`. You already know how to use `find` to run a filesystem-wide search; suppose you want to find all the JPEG pictures in your Linux filesystem. You can do this by issuing a command like

```
[you@workstation20 you]$ find / -name '*.jpg'
[...]
```

5

However, you'd soon find that this kind of a search can be time-consuming, because find crawls to every corner of your hard drive, directory by directory, looking for file-names that end with .jpg. You'd also find your screen filling with error messages as find encountered place after place in the Linux filesystem that you, logged in as a normal user, don't have permission to access. For large filename searches across the entire Linux filesystem, the locate command can often be more efficient because locate consults a large database that indexes every file in your Linux system. Using locate is simple—just supply the text you want to search for as an argument:

```
[you@workstation20 you]$ locate '*.jpg'
/usr/lib/mozilla-1.0.1/res/samples/bg.jpg
/usr/lib/mozilla-1.0.1/res/samples/raptor.jpg
/usr/lib/openoffice/share/gallery/www-back/bathroom.jpg
/usr/lib/openoffice/share/gallery/www-back/aqua.jpg
[...]
/usr/share/nautilus/patterns/chalk.jpg
/usr/share/nautilus/patterns/dark-gnome.jpg
/usr/share/nautilus/patterns/gnome.jpg
/usr/share/nautilus/patterns/stucco.jpg
[you@workstation20 you]$
```

The output of the locate command will likely scroll off your screen. You can pause the output of locate or other commands by appending the text |more to the end of the command:

```
locate '*.jpg' |more
```

This displays the output of the locate command one page at a time, waiting after each screenful of information for you to press the spacebar before continuing.

This technique is known as *piping* and is discussed later this hour, in the section titled "Using Pipes to Link Commands."

Though the actual list of image files you see will vary depending on the desktop environments and other software you installed in Hour 2, "Installing Red Hat Linux," you were able to receive a long list of matching files almost instantly.

The database used by locate is rebuilt once daily when the system runs the updatedb command. This means that the data displayed by locate might at times not be current with respect to the work you've done in the last few hours. However, it also enables locate to find large numbers of files across the entire disk rapidly.

Saving a List of Found Files

Sometimes it is helpful to save the output of a search command. The shell can help you save the output of commands like find and locate by *redirecting* their output to a file. Such a text file can then be loaded into an editor such as emacs or vi for editing, perusal, or printing. To redirect the *standard output* of a command (the information it prints to the console in order to fulfill your request), use the greater than (>) symbol, followed by the name of the destination file. Save the list of JPEG files on your system to a file called myjpegs.txt:

```
[you@workstation20 you]$ locate '*.jpg' > myjpegs.txt
[you@workstation20 you]$ ls -l
total 24
drwxrwxr-x    2 aron      aron          4096 08-04 20:23 firstfiles
-rw-rw-r--    1 aron      aron          7944 08-04 21:12 myjpegs.txt
-rw-rw-r--    1 aron      aron           132 08-04 20:18 mynewvifile.txt
-rw-rw-r--    1 aron      aron           135 08-04 20:18 myvifile.txt
drwxrwxr-x    2 aron      aron          4096 08-04 20:23 *new*
[you@workstation20 you]$
```

As you can see, there is now a text file of decent size in your home directory called myjpegs.txt. This file contains the list of JPEG files in your Linux filesystem, as reported by the locate command. If you want to view the file, feel free to load it into emacs or vi.

You can redirect the output of nearly every command available at the command prompt. It is also possible to *append* the standard output of a command to an existing file by using a double greater than symbol (>>). For example, to add a list of all GIF images on your system to myjpegs.txt, use

```
[you@workstation20 you]$ locate '*.gif' >> myjpegs.txt
[you@workstation20 you]$
```

5

To avoid accidentally overwriting important contents, always be cautious when appending command output to an existing file. When you use the single greater than symbol to redirect the output of a command to a file that already exists, the content of the original file is overwritten by the new data. It is therefore important to be careful to use double greater than symbols when redirecting data so that you don't overwrite important files.

Searching Text Files for Word Patterns

You've now created a rather lengthy text file in your home directory called myjpegs.txt, which contains a list of all the JPEG images and all the GIF images stored in your Linux filesystem. But suppose you want to narrow down your list a bit further—suppose you want to find only pictures of balls.

You could load myjpegs.txt into emacs or vi and visually search for files that match your criteria, but you can find what you want more quickly by using the grep command to search myjpegs.txt. The grep command's sole purpose is to search text files for words or patterns that you supply. The grep command is called like this:

```
grep pattern file1 [file2 ...]
```

Here, pattern is the text string or pattern to search for, and file1, file2, and so on are the files that grep is to search. Lines from these files that contain the text string or match the pattern will be displayed on standard output (that is, to the console). Try searching for pictures of balls now:

```
[you@workstation20 you]$ grep ball myjpegs.txt
/var/www/icons/ball.gray.gif
/var/www/icons/ball.red.gif
/usr/lib/openoffice/share/gallery/bullets/blugall.gif
[...]
/usr/share/latex2html/icons/redball.gif
/usr/share/latex2html/icons/whiteball.gif
/usr/share/latex2html/icons/yellowball.gif
[you@workstation20 you]$
```

The grep command has found a number of filenames in myjpegs.txt that contain the word ball. Used this way, grep is a great tool for mining data from long lists. For example, find all the GIF and JPEG images that are intended to be used as icons:

```
[you@workstation20 you]$ grep icons myjpegs.txt
/var/www/icons/alert.black.gif
/var/www/icons/a.gif
/var/www/icons/apache_pb2_ani.gif
[...]
/var/www/icons/small/doc.gif
/var/www/icons/small/forward.gif
/var/www/icons/small/generic.gif
[you@workstation20 you]$
```

Searching for Text Files That Contain Specific Words

You can also use grep to help you find files that contain a certain word. For example, your home directory currently has three text files in it: myjpegs.txt, mynewvifile.txt, and myvifile.txt. Suppose you needed to find out which of these files contained the word Unix.

Using grep with the -l (list files) option, you can get results quickly and easily:

```
[you@workstation20 you]$ grep -l Unix *
mynewvifile.txt
myvifile.txt
[you@workstation20 you]$
```

In this case, grep has reported that two files in the present working directory, mynewvifile.txt and myvifile.txt, contain the word Unix.

> When you use grep -l, you perform a search that is case-sensitive—the capitalization of the word in the file must mirror the capitalization of your search term so that grep can find a match.
>
> To cause grep to perform a case-insensitive search, use the -i argument in addition to the -l argument:
>
> ```
> grep -il unix *
> ```

Using Command Output for Complex Tasks

One of the greatest advantages of the Linux command line is that it enables you to tie multiple commands and their output together in a wide variety of ways. By tying commands, you can perform complex tasks that involve multiple steps or that require refining the output for unusual situations.

The two most important techniques for tying multiple commands are the use of pipes—which enable the output of one command to act as the input for another command—and command substitution—which enables the output of one command to alter the behavior of another command.

Using Pipes to Link Commands

Sometimes it is convenient to use the output of one command as the input of another. You can use *pipes*, which are created with the vertical bar (|), to cause the shell to use the output of one command as the input or data set for another command.

For example, you have seen the list of JPEG and GIF images of balls on your system; you created this list by redirecting the output of two locate commands to a file called myjpegs.txt and then searching this file with grep for the word ball.

Suppose you now want to learn whether there are any images of balls in your Linux filesystem stored in the .png or .tif graphics formats. Wouldn't it be helpful to send the output of the locate command directly to grep so that grep could search the data on the fly?

You can do this with the help of the pipe (|):

```
[you@workstation20 you]$ locate '*.gif' '*.jpg' '*.tif' '*.png' | grep ball
/var/www/icons/ball.gray.gif
/var/www/icons/ball.red.gif
/usr/lib/openoffice/share/gallery/bullets/bluball.gif
[...]
/usr/share/latex2html/icons/redball.png
/usr/share/latex2html/icons/whiteball.png
/usr/share/latex2html/icons/yellowball.png
[you@workstation20 you]$
```

You have generated a list of all of the ball images in four formats across your entire Linux filesystem. The output of the locate command (to which you supplied four arguments) was sent directly to grep, which searched the data it received for the word ball.

A more mundane, but no less useful, application of pipes is the *paging* of command output. For example, try entering the following command:

```
[you@workstation20 you]$ ls -l /usr/bin
[...]
```

This listing is very long; the vast majority of it will scroll past the top of your console before you get a chance to see it. However, by sending the output of this command through a pipe to another command called more, the situation can be remedied. The more command is a pager—it displays a file or input data one page at a time, pausing and requiring the user to press the spacebar to continue between each screen of information. Try piping the output of ls through more now:

```
[you@workstation20 you]$ ls -l /usr/bin | more
[...]
```

There is still a great deal of information in this list, but you are now able to see *all* of it at your leisure. Don't worry if the range of applications for pipes seems murky to you now; you'll grow more accustomed to pipe use as we continue to work with the shell.

Using One Command's Answers As Another's Arguments

Another essential shell tool is known as *command substitution*. Command substitution allows the output of one command to be used as a set of command-line arguments for another command. This enables the results of a first command to alter the behavior of a second command, thereby affecting its output and *customizing* the command for the situation at hand.

Suppose you want to create a directory called jpegfiles and gather into it every JPEG image on your system for easy indexing and access. You already know how to use locate to find all the filenames that end in .jpg in the Linux filesystem. With this output, you can use command substitution to gather these files into one place:

```
[you@workstation20 you]$ mkdir jpegfiles
[you@workstation20 you]$ ln -s $(locate '*.jpg') jpegfiles
[you@workstation20 you]$
```

Enclosing the command locate '*.jpg' in parentheses preceded by a dollar sign ($) caused the output filenames from the locate command to be treated as though a user had typed them in one by one on the command line as arguments to ln -s, which is the command to create symbolic links.

Symbolic links and the ln -s command are discussed in Hour 4.

Use the ls command to get a long listing of the jpegfiles directory. You'll find that a symbolic link has been created to every file ending in .jpg on the entire system—all of the JPEG images have been collected in one place for easy access.

Command substitution in the bash shell can occur in two ways; the one shown here is to enclose the substituted command in parentheses preceded by a dollar sign:

```
$(locate myfile)
```

An alternate, more traditional way of using command substitution is to enclose the substituted command in backquotes:

```
'locate myfile'
```

The less traditional method is used in this book, because backquotes are often difficult to differentiate from forward single quotes, and can thus lead to confusion.

5

As was the case with pipes, the wide range of applications for command substitution is not likely to be immediately obvious. Don't worry, though—you'll see them again as we continue to work with the shell.

Keeping Your Shell Programs Under Control

In upcoming hours we're going to be running fairly involved applications at the console. Before we reach that point, it's important that you know about shell-based job control.

You can log in to several virtual consoles simultaneously in order to run more than one full-screen application at a time—for example an emacs on console one and a vi on console two. Switching back and forth between virtual consoles, however, can be both confusing and clumsy. Furthermore, after you learn to log into Linux systems remotely via telnet or ssh, you need to be able to use the command line without the luxury of multiple virtual consoles.

To avoid the problems associated with these situations, you can use shell-based control techniques to pause and resume multiple tasks at a single command prompt. These techniques enable you to switch between applications, move jobs to the foreground or background, and end tasks that are no longer needed. The following sections teach you how to use these and other techniques to comfortably work on multiple projects at a single Red Hat Linux console.

Moving Between Multiple Open Applications

Assume for illustrative purposes that you need to be able to start and then switch back and forth between emacs and vi without losing your place in either application. Perhaps you are working on an article comparing the two, or perhaps you are simply editing a file in vi but taking breaks every hour or so to play the dunnet game mentioned earlier when you learned about emacs.

You can use the Ctrl+Z keystroke combination to suspend work on an open application so you can open another application. You can use the job command to list all open applications.

Take a moment to load the myvifile.txt created earlier in this hour back into the vi editor:

```
[you@workstation20 you]$ vi myvifile.txt
```

When the vi editor appears on the screen, the command prompt is hidden, unavailable to you. You can now begin to edit the file, making changes as necessary. But what happens when it's time to take a dunnet break?

You can *suspend* the vi process by pressing Ctrl+Z:

```
[1]+  Stopped                 vim myvifile.txt
[you@workstation20 you]$
```

The vi process has now been suspended. Note the number 1 in brackets; this is the *job number* of the interrupted vi process. Feel free to start emacs and enter M-x dunnet to load the dunnet game if you want:

```
[you@workstation20 you]$ emacs
```

You may play the game for a while, but eventually you must return to your document in vi—you can't play forever. However, to do so you don't have to exit emacs and lose your place in the game. You can suspend the emacs process in the same way you suspended the vi process earlier—by pressing Ctrl+Z:

```
[2]+  Stopped                 emacs
[you@workstation20 you]$
```

You now have two text editors in your job list that are suspended. To see a list of your current jobs at any time, enter the jobs command:

```
[you@workstation20 you]$ jobs
[1]-  Stopped                 vim myvifile.txt
[2]+  Stopped                 emacs
[you@workstation20 you]$
```

Jobs can remain suspended indefinitely without harm; you can continue to work with the shell to perform other tasks, and vi and emacs will be ready to pick up exactly where they left off.

> You can sometimes use Ctrl+C to simply quit a running job if you don't want merely to suspend it. However, Ctrl+C won't always work. For example, it doesn't work in emacs or vi, though it will work during the output of a particularly lengthy locate job.

Resuming a Job with fg

To return to your editing work in vi, you can use the fg command, passing the percent sign (%) and the correct job number as arguments:

```
[you@workstation20 you]$ fg %1
```

As was reported by the jobs command, the vi process is shell job number 1; after you enter the fg (foreground) command supplying %1 as an argument, vi returns your editing display to exactly the same state it was in when you suspended it.

You can repeat this suspend and resume process as needed, suspending and resuming applications in any combination or order.

Running a Job in the Background with bg

Some commands in Red Hat Linux can take a long time to run, especially on older systems. At times like this, the shell can provide an ideal solution. Commands that do not require user intervention to finish can be run as *background tasks*. You can use the bg command to run jobs in the background. This command then frees you up to return to work in other open applications.

Again for purposes of illustration, assume that while you are editing with vi and playing with emacs, you decide that you also need to generate a list of all the files in your Linux filesystem that locate can tell you about. In order to save a list of this sort to a file called fileslist.txt, you must suspend whatever editor you are working in by using the Ctrl+Z keystroke and enter a command to create such a list for you:

```
[you@workstation20 you]$ locate '*' > fileslist.txt
```

The locate command is given a pattern that will match every file in its database. The output has been redirected to the file fileslist.txt. Simple enough in concept, but let's pause this job and then make it a background task. Press Ctrl+Z to interrupt the command in progress:

```
[3]+  Stopped                 locate '*' >fileslist.txt
[you@workstation20 you]$
```

Notice that the command is assigned a job number of 3 and the command prompt has returned. The command is now suspended; unless it is at some point resumed, it will never finish. To resume it in the background, use the bg (background) command:

```
[you@workstation20 you]$ bg %3
[3]+ locate '*' > fileslist.txt &
[you@workstation20 you]$
```

The command is now running in the background; Linux will continue to work on the task until it is complete. In the meantime, you are free to return to your editor or to your dunnet game by using the fg command. To see the updated list of jobs first, use the jobs command:

```
[you@workstation20 you]$ jobs
[1]-  Stopped                 vim myvifile.txt
[2]+  Stopped                 emacs
[3]   Running                 locate '*' >fileslist.txt &
[you@workstation20 you]$
```

As you continue to work with the shell, you will at some point receive a message that your background process has finished.

```
[3]   Done                    locate '*' >fileslist.txt &
```

After a process has finished, it will no longer appear in the jobs list along with the other running or suspended jobs.

Final Job Control Notes

There are two more commands related to job control that you can use to feel at home on the command line. The first is kill. The kill command can be used with a job number to forcibly terminate a job that you don't want any longer:

```
[you@workstation20 you]$ kill %2
[2]+  Stopped                 emacs
[1]-  Stopped                 vim myvifile.txt
[2]+  Terminated              emacs
[you@workstation20 you]$
```

Although kill aids in destroying jobs, the ampersand (&) aids in creating them. Rather than using Ctrl+Z and then the bg command, if you want to start a job that can run in the background from the beginning, simply follow it on the command line with an ampersand. For example, earlier you could have used

```
[you@workstation20 you]$ locate '*' > fileslist.txt &
[2] 10413
[you@workstation20 you]$
```

The first number returned after starting a job in the background is the job number, with which you are now familiar. The second number is the system process number; you learn about the system process table in more detail in Hour 4, "Navigating Linux at the Console."

Summary

This hour, you gained a collection of skills that will ultimately make you more productive at the Linux command line. You created text files with the two most common Linux editors, and you learned to group files for issuing commands and otherwise working with them efficiently. You also learned commands for finding files, file types, and specific words or word patterns in files quickly and easily. You learned two ways to hook commands together to save time, effort, and disk space. Finally, you learned to manage and switch between running shell programs without having to exit them completely or switch between consoles.

Along the way, you learned the following new commands, keystrokes, and special characters for use at the shell prompt:

- \> redirects standard output to a new file.
- \>> appends standard output to an existing file.

5

- & launches a process in the background.
- Ctrl+Z suspends a running process.
- bg, fg, and jobs, respectively, resume a job in the background, resume a job in the foreground, and list all currently existing jobs.
- find searches for files in real time.
- grep searches a file for a particular piece of text or pattern in a plain text file, or searches a set of files for a particular piece of text or pattern and returns their filenames if they contain it.
- locate searches an often-updated database of files for the file you seek.
- more pages out to the console a text file of the sort created by vi or emacs.
- sort accepts a list of items as input, arranges them into alphanumeric order, and then outputs them again.

You've now had all the shell, command, and console editor introductions you really need to be productive. Until the advanced shell topics in Hour 9, "Harnessing the Power of the Shell," you won't explore this many nuts-and-bolts type topics again; instead, it's time to proceed to information and applications.

Q&A

Q When I redirect the output of some commands to a file using the greater than symbol as described, some messages still get sent to the console. Why?

A You're seeing standard error messages, rather than standard output messages. These inform the user that something out of the ordinary has happened, and they are handled in a different way. To redirect standard error messages, append a **2>** to the end of the command, followed by the file that should hold the error messages.

Q Is there any way to simply throw the standard output or standard error messages away—for instance, if I want a command to behave "silently?"

A Yes, redirect one or both to the special device file /dev/null, which is commonly known as the "bit bucket." All data sent to /dev/null is discarded by the system.

Workshop

The Workshop is designed to help you anticipate possible questions, review what you've learned, and begin learning how to put your knowledge into practice.

Quiz

1. What pattern would you use with the `rm` command to remove the files `houseprices.txt`, `priceless.gif`, and `car.myprice`?

2. How would you search the file `shoecolors.txt` for lines containing the word `red`?

3. How would you output a list of currently running emacs jobs? (*Hint:* use a pipe.)

4. How would you quickly search your entire filesystem for a file called `RedHatLinuxNotes.txt`?

Answers

1. `*price*`

2. `grep red shoecolors.txt`

3. `jobs | grep emacs`

4. `locate RedHatLinuxNotes.txt`

Activities

1. Take some time to study both the `emacs` and `vi` tutorials and to familiarize yourself with the capabilities of each.

2. Use `locate` and `more` to get a listing of all of the files of the following types on your system, displayed one page at a time: `.txt`, `.gif`, `.jpg`, and `.gz`.

3. Start a long list of jobs, suspending each of them one by one until the output of the `jobs` command fills the entire screen. Then exit or kill each of them, one by one.

4. Start emacs and play a game of dunnet.

5

Hour 6

Getting Help at the Console

Over the course of the last two hours, you had the chance to walk through some Linux command-line and shell-use basics. You probably had a few questions that haven't been answered. This hour, you have the chance to do a little research on your own, after you learn to

- Find an online manual page for any command you might need to use at the command line.
- Ask Linux for a list of commands and manual pages that might be helpful to you in a given situation.
- Search through online text-based documentation for many console-based applications and services.
- List and save help messages generated by commands and applications themselves as you launch them.

After you have these techniques under your belt, you should feel free to spend some independent time exploring what you know thus far of the Linux console. These help tools will become staples of your console use as you become more familiar with Linux or as you encounter other Unix systems.

Introducing Manual Pages

The *manual page* is one of the most fundamental command-line tools in any Linux or Unix system. Manual pages are brief, yet complete, online documents that describe how to use a specific command or system facility.

Red Hat Linux ships with an extensive library of online manual pages. You will find that there are few commands or system files in a Red Hat filesystem that do not have an associated Red Hat manual page.

Using Manual Pages: The Basics

You can display manual pages for a given command or facility by using the man command and supplying the name of the manual page you want to read as an argument. To read the manual page for the ls command, for example, type **man ls** at the command prompt. The manual page for the command appears, as shown in Figure 6.1. To display the manual page for a facility, such as the ISO 8859-1 character set, type **man iso-8859-1**.

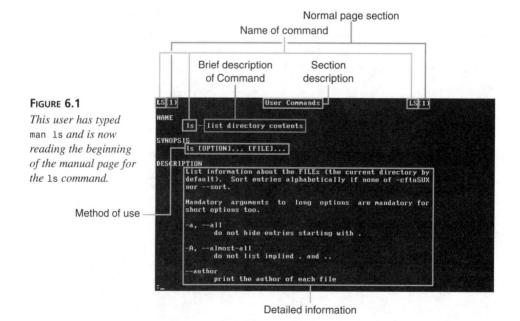

FIGURE 6.1

This user has typed man ls *and is now reading the beginning of the manual page for the* ls *command.*

Detailed information

Each manual page begins with the name of the command, the section to which it belongs, and a brief summary of the proper method for calling the command or using the facility in question. The body of the manual page, which contains detailed information, then begins.

The man command always displays a manual page using a *pager*, a command that displays one screen of text or data at a time. After reading each screen of information, you press the spacebar in order to proceed to the next screen of information. The manual pager enables you to read a manual page slowly, without losing information as it scrolls past the top of the display.

The pager used by the man command is called less; you can use less for reading other documentation, as you learn in "Reading Extra Application Documentation," later in this hour. In the meantime, practice using less now to bring up manual pages for some of the commands you already have learned. To help you navigate manual pages more effectively, some keystrokes understood by the less pager are shown in Table 6.1.

TABLE 6.1   Simple less Navigation for Reading Manual Pages

Key	Action
Space	Displays the next screen full of information
b	Displays the previous screen full of information (moves "backward" one page)
/text	Searches for the next occurrence of text in the manual page you are viewing
q	Quits (closes) this manual page and returns you to the command prompt

> Command manual pages contain useful information. As you bring up man pages with less, pay special attention to the many options for altering or enhancing the behavior of most of the commands.

Understanding Manual Page Sections

A typical Linux system holds a large number of manual pages that cover a variety of topics, from common commands, to system file formats, to various types of system programming information. Because of the number and diversity of manual pages, it is not uncommon to find that one term might represent more than one kind of item. For example, the word passwd represents both a command and a common file format; manual pages exist for both items. Because it is possible for a single word to lead to multiple manual pages, the canon of Linux manual pages is divided into numbered sections in order to help differentiate between manual pages of different types. When you use the

6

man command, you have the option of telling man to display pages from a specific section. The manual page sections are shown in Table 6.2.

TABLE 6.2   The Linux Manual Page Sections

Section	Title	Description
1	User Commands	Commands and applications that users commonly call from the Linux command line
2	System Calls	Functions used by programmers to access or control various Linux system facilities
3	Subroutines	Routines used by programmers to access various types of Linux functionality
4	Devices	Information about using various devices and device drivers of which Linux is aware
5	File Formats	Information about the formats of many of the numerous system configuration files in /etc and elsewhere that control the behavior and operation of the Linux operating system
6	Games	Manuals for installed games and entertainment-related commands
7	Miscellaneous	Documentation for various topics that don't appear to easily fit into any of the other sections
8	Administration	Information about commands and concepts related specifically to Linux system administration
L	Local	Documentation that is unique to this Linux system or this version of Linux in particular
N	New	Documentation for additional user-selected, recently installed, or as yet uncategorized commands, files, and concepts

As you might be able to see already, the sections may overlap to some extent, meaning that a command, concept, or file format may appear in a section that you don't initially expect. Each time you use the man command to display documentation, you'll notice that the section from which you are reading appears in the manual page header. For example, examine the first line of output from man ls:

```
LS(1)                              FSF                              LS(1)
```

The (1) in the first line of the manual page indicates that this manual page for ls has been taken from section one, User Commands.

The man command normally displays only the first manual page it finds for a given topic. If a topic you want to study occurs in several sections—for example, once in user commands and once in file formats—you will see only the first manual page. If you want to read *all* the manual pages for a given topic in succession, you must use the -a option:

```
[you@workstation20 you]$ man -a passwd
```

As typed, this command lists all the manual pages on file for passwd, in every section. At the end of the first manual page, after you press q to exit it, the second manual page is displayed, and so on.

If you happen to know from past experience that you want only the manual page from a particular section, you can specify the section you want to read from as an argument to man:

```
[you@workstation20 you]$ man 5 passwd
```

This command reads only the passwd manual page from section five, File Formats.

> If you want to learn more about using the man command, you can also read the manual page for man by typing **man man** at the command prompt.

Locating Manual Pages Through Topic-Based Searches

Our discussion of manual pages thus far assumes that you know which manual page(s) you want to consult for help. In the real world, this is often not the case—it is common to know that you want help with a particular *topic* but to find that there is no specific manual page anywhere under that name.

Usually when this occurs, documentation for the topic in question still exists—it is simply filed under another name or treated as a subtopic in a larger manual page. The apropos command can help you locate manual pages relevant to your topic.

For example, suppose you wanted to find manual pages that deal in detail with the concept of Linux directories. You can use the apropos command to help:

```
[you@workstation20 you]$ apropos directories
chkfontpath          (8)  - simple interface for adding, removing, and
listing➥directories in the X font server's path
cp                   (1)  - copy files and directories
mkdir                (1)  - make directories
rm                   (1)  - remove files or directories
rmdir                (1)  - remove empty directories
[you@workstation20 you]$
```

6

As you can see, apropos has supplied a list of manual pages related to the topic of directories, including manual pages for several commands you might already recognize. Note that in the second column, apropos has also provided the manual section in which the pages appear. Each manual page is also briefly summarized with a one-line description.

> A similar command to apropos, whatis might also be useful. Try typing **whatis** followed by the name of any command or system file in the /etc directory. If a manual page exists for that command or file, details about that page are displayed.

Using the GNU info System

Though the man system has been a staple in the Unix world for ages, another documentation system called info has gained some popularity in the Linux world as well. There are some cases in which you can find info pages for commands that have no associated (or no adequate) manual page. If you need more information about a command, it's a good idea to look for an info page.

The info system works in some ways like the World Wide Web. The core of the info system is the info browser. When called without arguments or options, the info browser opens to an index page listing all the topics for which info-based help can be obtained. Try starting the browser now by typing info at the command line:

```
[you@workstation20 you]$ info
```

The info display is shown in Figure 6.2.

Though the info system might seem clumsy to navigate at first, it contains a wealth of information, often in greater depth than can be found in the man pages.

Navigating the info System

Navigating inside info can be a little tricky, especially for beginners.

As in a Web browser, the info pages contain words that link to further information, such as info indexes or documents. Most of these words are followed by single or double colon characters (: or ::). To follow one of these links or open such a document, use the arrow keys to place the cursor over the linking word, and then press Enter to select it.

In info, the *node* represents the fundamental unit of documentation. Usually, when you are viewing a screen full of information, you are looking at a particular info node. Many nodes contain further links to next and previous nodes, which typically represent related information to the screen you're currently viewing, arranged in some kind of logical order. Basic keystrokes for navigating info can be found in Table 6.3.

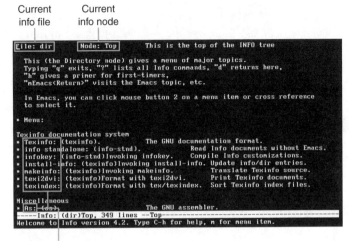

Current
info file

Current
info node

FIGURE 6.2

*When you first launch
info, you are greeted
by a screen full of
index information.*

Links to other nodes

TABLE 6.3 Basic Keystrokes for Navigating into

Key	Description
(up)	Move cursor up.
(down)	Move cursor down.
(left)	Move cursor left.
(right)	Move cursor right.
Enter	Follow the link under the cursor to the indicated node (screen full of information).
n	Proceed to the "next" logical node after this one.
p	Proceed to the "previous" logical node before this one.
u	Return "up" one node in the index, usually to the location that led you to your current node.
t	Return to the "top" node, or info index page.
q	Quit the info system.
Space	Display the next screen full of information in the current node.

6

The info system is built using the emacs editor engine. Thus, many common emacs commands, including buffer-oriented and screen-splitting commands, can be used while browsing info.

For more information on using emacs, please refer to Hour 5, "Making the Console Work for You."

Using `info` Efficiently

Though the main index page of the `info` system is useful to those not familiar with the documentation available through `info`, it can be time-consuming and bothersome to navigate for those who have used `info`.

When you are familiar with `info`, you can call it in much the same way you use the `man` command, supplying the name of the `info` document that you want to read as an argument to the command. For example, to read the `info` page for the `ls` command, you enter

```
[you@workstation20 you]$ info ls
```

Used this way, `info` functions very much like `man`; you page through the displayed document using the spacebar, then press q when you are ready to quit.

Using the `/usr/share/doc` Tree

Though the `man` and `info` documentation systems are useful, they are inadequate at times for providing complete, readable documentation about a specific software package. They are also not well-suited to situations in which documentation for a specific command is most logically spread over a collection of separate files. Often, version-specific information is also missing from `man` or `info` pages of various commands.

Many commands and applications also install separate documentation files in the `/usr/share/doc` directory tree. If you use `ls` to get a listing of this directory now, you'll find that there are quite a few subdirectories in `/usr/share/doc`, most of which contain additional documentation for the command or application.

Reading Extra Application Documentation

Most of the documentation in the `/usr/share/doc` tree is in plain text format. This means that you can read the documentation using simple pagers such as `less` and `more`. Visit the directory for the application, use `ls` to get a listing of available text files, and then call the pager to view the file you're interested in:

```
[you@workstation20 you]$ cd /usr/share/doc/zip-2.3
[you@workstation20 zip-2.3]$ ls
algorith.txt  BUGS  CHANGES  MANUAL  README  TODO  WHATSNEW  WHERE
[you@workstation20 zip-2.3]$ more MANUAL
```

> You might have noticed that we've mentioned two pagers here, less and more. Both serve the same *basic* purpose—to allow a user to page through a long document one screen at a time. There are real functional differences between the two, however. Many traditionalists use more, but the Linux man command and many other commands that page information to the user choose less instead.
>
> In practice, you'll rarely notice the difference, but if you'd like to compare features between the two, try reading the man pages for less and more.

In addition to various types of functional documentation, many of these directories contain similar types of meta-documentation—information about versioning, authorship, software licensing, and so on. Some of the more common filenames are shown in Table 6.4, though you might also find slight variations. The first page of a functional documentation file is shown in Figure 6.3, and the first page of a typical README file for the same topic is shown in Figure 6.4.

TABLE 6.4   Some Common /usr/share/doc Meta-documentation

File	Description
README	Might contain almost anything, but often contains release-specific information and information about the author or Internet addresses where the author and software can be found
BUGS	Usually contains a list of known bugs in a command or application
CHANGES	Usually contains a list of the changes since the previous release of a command or application
TODO	Usually contains a list of features or changes that are to be incorporated in future versions of a command or application
COPYING	Usually contains a copy of the software distribution license for a command or application
AUTHORS	Usually contains a list of the contributors of program code for a command or application
NEWS	Usually contains announcements, release information, and other newsworthy events related to a command or application

6

FIGURE 6.3

This is the first page of functional documenta-tion for the zip *utility from* /usr/share/doc.

```
[you@workstation20 zip-2.3]$ more algorith.txt
Zip's deflation algorithm is a variation of LZ77 (Lempel-Ziv 1977, see
reference below). It finds duplicated strings in the input data.  The
second occurrence of a string is replaced by a pointer to the previous
string, in the form of a pair (distance, length).  Distances are
limited to 32K bytes, and lengths are limited to 258 bytes. When a
string does not occur anywhere in the previous 32K bytes, it is
emitted as a sequence of literal bytes.  (In this description,
'string' must be taken as an arbitrary sequence of bytes, and is not
restricted to printable characters.)

Literals or match lengths are compressed with one Huffman tree, and
match distances are compressed with another tree. The trees are stored
in a compact form at the start of each block. The blocks can have any
size (except that the compressed data for one block must fit in
available memory). A block is terminated when zip determines that it
would be useful to start another block with fresh trees. (This is
somewhat similar to compress.)

Duplicated strings are found using a hash table. All input strings of
length 3 are inserted in the hash table. A hash index is computed for
the next 3 bytes. If the hash chain for this index is not empty, all
strings in the chain are compared with the current input string, and
the longest match is selected.
--More--(39%)
```

FIGURE 6.4

Here's the README *file for the* zip *utility from* /usr/share/doc.

```
[you@workstation20 zip-2.3]$ more README
Copyright (c) 1990-1999 Info-ZIP.  All rights reserved.

See the accompanying file LICENSE (the contents of which are also
included in unzip.h, zip.h and wiz.h) for terms of use.  If, for
some reason, all of these files are missing, the Info-ZIP license
also may be found at:  ftp://ftp.cdrom.com/pub/infozip/license.html

Zip 2.3 is a compression and file packaging utility.  It is compatible with
PKZIP 2.04g (Phil Katz ZIP) for MSDOS systems.  There is a companion to zip
called unzip (of course) which you should be able to find the same place
you got zip. See the file 'WHERE' for details on ftp sites and mail
servers.

This version of zip has been ported to a wide array of Unix and other
mainframes, minis, and micros including VMS, OS/2, Minix, MSDOS, Windows NT,
Atari, Amiga, BeOS and VM/CMS. Although highly compatible with PKware's
PKZIP and PKUNZIP utilities of MSDOS fame, our primary objective has been
one of portability and other-than-MSDOS functionality.  Features not found
in the PKWare version include creation of zip files in a pipe or on a
device, VMS, BeOS and OS/2 extended file attributes, conversion from Unix to
MSDOS text file format; and, of course, the ability to run on most of your
favorite operating systems.  And it's free.
--More--(18%)
```

Searching the /usr/share/doc Tree

Sometimes you'll find that you're looking for a particular topic in the /usr/share/doc tree, without any real ideas about which command or application documentation should be consulted.

At times like this, you can use the find and grep commands you learned in Hour 5, along with a new command called xargs. Together, these commands enable you to search all the documentation in /usr/share/doc for a particular word or string of characters. The xargs command enables you to use very large lists of output from one command as arguments to a second command (similar to the use of the command substitution shell tool you learned about in Hour 5).

In the following example, you use find to list all the files in /usr/share/doc and then grep to search each of these files for a specific string, supplying the -l option to specify that grep should print the names of files that contain the word. Let's assume that you want to find documentation about tape drives; you might search the entire /usr/share/doc tree for the word tapes:

```
[you@workstation20 zip-2.3]$ find /usr/share/doc | xargs grep -l tapes
/usr/share/doc/fileutils-4.1.9/ChangeLog
/usr/share/doc/initscripts-6.88/sysconfig.txt
/usr/share/doc/MAKEDEV-3.3.1/devices.txt
/usr/share/doc/mt-st-0.7/README.stinit
/usr/share/doc/mt-st-0.7/README
/usr/share/doc/redhat-release-7.3.93/7.2/RELEASE-NOTES-i386.fr
/usr/share/doc/dump-0.4b28/CHANGES
/usr/share/doc/specspo-7.3.93/dist.pot
/usr/share/doc/star-1.5a04/STARvsGNUTAR
/usr/share/doc/kernel-pcmcia-cs-3.1.31/PCMCIA-HOWTO
/usr/share/doc/cvs-1.11.2/FAQ
/usr/share/doc/libstdc++-devel-3.2/html/17_intro/howto.html
[you@workstaiton20 zip-2.3]$
```

You have now generated a list of all of the files in the /usr/share/doc directory tree that contain the word tapes; each of these files can be viewed using less or more.

If you're unsure about how the command you just entered works, treat this part of the hour as homework. Reacquaint yourself with Hour 5 and read the manual pages for find, xargs, and grep to learn about how each of these commands works and the arguments and options used.

Getting Help from the Commands

There is one more common and useful method for obtaining help or documentation about a specific Linux command. Nearly every command supports either -h, -help, or --help as a special option that causes the command to print a brief help message and exit. One such help message is shown in Listing 6.1.

LISTING 6.1   Output of the rm --help Command

```
Usage: rm [OPTION]... FILE...
Remove (unlink) the FILE(s).

  -d, --directory      unlink FILE, even if it is a non-empty directory
                         (super-user only)
  -f, --force          ignore nonexistent files, never prompt
  -i, --interactive    prompt before any removal
  -r, -R, --recursive  remove the contents of directories recursively
  -v, --verbose        explain what is being done
      --help        display this help and exit
      --version  output version information and exit
```

6

LISTING 6.1 continued

```
To remove a file whose name starts with a `-', for example `-foo',
use one of these commands:
  rm -- -foo
  rm ./-foo

Note that if you use rm to remove a file, it is usually possible to recover
the contents of that file.  If you want more assurance that the contents are
truly unrecoverable, consider using shred.

Report bugs to <bug-fileutils@gnu.org>.
```

Help obtained this way is often very brief, filling less than one screen and providing only the most commonly used options and arguments for a given command. Though the man or info page is almost always more exhaustive, you might find that the -h, -help, or --help options are more readily accessible in day-to-day use.

How do you know whether to use -h, -help, **or** --help?

Generally, try them in this order: --help, -h, and -help. If none of these options seems to provide a help listing for a specific command, consult the man or info page.

Because you learned how to redirect standard output to a file, you can use the same technique to save the help message from any command you care to name:

```
[you@workstation20 zip-2.3]$ ls --help >/home/you/ls.help.txt
[you@workstaiton20 zip-2.3]$
```

Help saved this way can later be treated, edited, or printed like any normal text file (we'll get to printing in an upcoming hour) .

Summary

This hour, you learned how to find online documentation for common commands, applications, file formats, concepts, and devices using one of four methods:

- The man command for viewing manual pages
- The info command for searching info-system nodes

- The `find` and `grep` commands for searching the `/usr/share/doc` tree
- The `--help`, `-help`, or `-h` options for supplying to commands given at the command line

You also learned to use `apropos` to find appropriate manual pages for a given keyword and to search more than one manual page section.

Q&A

Q I've noticed that when reading `man` pages with `less`, there are many keystrokes that seem to have some effect in addition to the ones you list in Table 6.1. Is there help inside `less` about the available keystrokes?

A Press h while reading a man page or using the `less` pager to get a list of the available keystrokes and commands.

Q Why do some commands seem to have both `man` and `info` documentation available? Isn't this redundant?

A Yes and no. Generally speaking, when both man and `info` documentation for a specific command are available, the `info` documentation is more complete; the man page has been provided simply to ensure that users who aren't familiar with `info` can still find documentation.

Workshop

The Workshop is designed to help you anticipate possible questions, review what you've learned, and begin learning how to put your knowledge into practice.

Quiz

1. When both man and `info` show documentation for a particular command, which documentation is likely to be more complete?
2. Why are there multiple man sections?
3. How do you call the man command with reference to a specific section?
4. In what directory is additional documentation, beyond man and `info`, stored?

Answers

1. The `info` documentation is usually more complete when both man and `info` cover a specific topic.
2. Because a single topic word might refer to several different commands or facilities in Linux. Multiple sections enable manual pages to be grouped logically according to function—commands with other commands, file formats with other file formats, and so on.

6

3. Include the number of the section you want to reference before the topic word or command. For example, to see the section 5 manual page for passwd, you use **man 5 passwd**.

4. Additional documentation in plain text files is provided in the /usr/share/doc directory tree.

Activities

1. Spend some time looking at the manual pages for the commands you've become familiar with in earlier hours.

2. Start the info browser and try navigating through some of the info documentation to familiarize yourself with info navigation and with the types of information available.

3. Type **ls /usr/share/doc | more** to page through a listing of the documentation directories in the /usr/share/doc tree.

4. Try using the apropos command with a few interesting words you've encountered while learning Linux, just to see whether any manual pages discuss them.

Hour 7

Working Without the Mouse

Over the last few hours, you learned to use the command line to perform basic file manipulation and data housekeeping tasks. You also learned how to get command and application documentation when you need it. In this hour, you learn to format and print documents and perform other office productivity tasks, using Red Hat Linux at the console.

This hour, you learn to

- Print text files and other information from the command line.
- Produce complex output using basic text editors such as emacs or vi in conjunction with document formatters.
- Perform and automate mathematical calculations using an editor and an arbitrary precision calculator.
- Sort formatted lists of text-based data in various ways.
- Format floppy disks for Windows or DOS and copy data to them quickly and easily.

The applications you explore in this hour represent only a fraction of the list of functional and varied applications available to Red Hat Linux console users. You can learn about other console-based applications by using the `apropos` command (see "Locating Manual Pages Through Topic-Based Searches," in Hour 6, "Getting Help at the Console").

Printing at the Command Line

While learning to work at the command line, you may have wished on several occasions that you could print the output generated by your commands. Users new to UNIX-like operating systems are often surprised to learn that nearly any kind of information can be sent to the printer directly from the command line. In fact, managing printing from the command line is quite easy after a printer has been properly configured. For details on configuring your printer, refer to Hour 3, "Booting, Logging In, and Configuring."

Printing any kind of information in Linux requires the creation of a print job. When a print job is created, the data to be printed is queued in a list of pending jobs. The print job at the top of the list is the one currently being printed; when it finishes, the system removes it from the queue in a process called *dequeueing*. The next job moves to the top of the queue, is printed, and so on, until all pending jobs have been printed.

This system enables many users to simultaneously use a Linux system for printing text and data; everyone simply waits his or her turn.

Creating Print Jobs

You create print jobs with the `lpr` command. To print an existing text file, simply supply it to `lpr` as an argument:

```
[you@workstation20 you]$ lpr myfile.txt
[you@workstation20 you]$
```

This command creates a print job containing the data from the file `myfile.txt`; when the job reaches the front of the queue, the file `myfile.txt` is printed. Data can also be queued using the `lpr` command in conjunction with pipes, which you learned about in the section "Using Pipes (|) to Link Commands" section of Hour 5, "Making the Console Work for You." For example, to print a long listing of the contents of the `/etc` directory, you pipe the output of the `ls` command to the `lpr` command:

```
[you@workstation20 you]$ ls -l /etc | lpr
[you@workstation20 you]$
```

Print jobs created with pipes behave in exactly the same manner as print jobs created from plain text files.

Listing Print Jobs

In a system where many print jobs can be queued for printing, users sometimes want to check the list of jobs that are currently in the queue, and their print order. You can use the lpq command to list print jobs. To get a listing of current jobs, enter lpq without arguments on the command line:

```
[you@workstation20 you]$ lpq
Printer: lp@workstation20
 Queue: 3 printable jobs
 Server: pid 12594 active
 Unspooler: pid 12595 active
 Status: waiting for subserver to exit at 12:14:05.406
 Rank   Owner/ID            Class Job Files                   Size Time
active you@workstation20+593    A   593 (STDIN)                1564 12:13:53
2      you@workstation20+597    A   597 (STDIN)              101781 12:13:57
3      you@workstation20+601    A   601 syslog.conf            693 12:14:05
[you@workstation20 you]$
```

In this instance, there are three print jobs in the queue, all started by you. The first two jobs contain output from commands that were piped to lpr. This is indicated by the word STDIN (for "standard input") appearing in the Files column, meaning that the lpr command is receiving the file to print through a pipe. The third job contains the text in the file syslog.conf.

Dequeueing Print Jobs

If you decide that you no longer want to print a job that's in the print queue, you can dequeue it. The system won't print a job that has been removed from the queue. To dequeue a print job, use the lprm command; the number of the print job from the Job column of lpq's output must be supplied as an argument. For example, if you want to remove the second print job from the previous example, the correct command is

```
[you@workstation20 you]$ lprm 597
Printer lp@workstation20:
  checking perms 'you@workstation20+597'
  dequeued 'you@workstation20+597'
[you@workstation20 you]$
```

Only the root user or the user who created a job can dequeue it. The root user is able to dequeue all jobs.

7

On systems with multiple printers, calling lpr, lpq, and lprm as described here affects only the default printer, usually named lp. However, all three of these commands accept an option, -P, which can be used to specify a different printer.

For example, if you have a second printer named lp2 and want to print myfile.txt to it instead of to lp, add the -P argument followed by lp2:

```
[you@workstation20 you]$ lpr -Plp2 myfile.txt
[you@workstation20 you]$
```

The identical option also can be used to affect the respective behaviors of lpq and lprm.

Creating High-Quality Documents at the Command Line

Knowing how to send data to the printer is only half the battle; being able to produce professional-quality output is also essential in the modern world. At the command line, the process of producing high-quality output occurs in two steps: *text editing*, in which the textual content of your document is entered, and *text formatting*, in which the content is arranged in a pleasing manner for printing.

This method for creating documents stands in contrast to the *WYSIWYG* method with which most users are familiar. WYSIWYG is an acronym that stands for *What You See Is What You Get*. This refers to the fact that in most word processors, which are usually graphics-based, you see fonts, styles, and document layout on the screen as they appear when printed on paper.

The WYSIWYG method of document editing has not always been the norm, however, and it has its limitations. Chief among them is the fact that it forces the user to be aware of formatting consistency at all times—you must keep track of the font size, style, spacing and indentation of each piece of text yourself, which can interfere with your stream of thought as you write. When using a text formatter, on the other hand, you only need to specify that a certain piece of text is a chapter or a title, for example, and the text formatter will take care of the details of layout and appearance for you. For many types of documents—especially lengthier ones—the text editing/formatting method of creating documents is more powerful and convenient.

In Red Hat Linux, you can use a simple text editor such as vi or emacs to create text documents, as you learned in "Creating, Editing, and Saving Text Files," in Hour 5. To use these editors, you input text in free form, without worrying too much about text formatting or consistency issues, such as centering, indentation, or typefaces. To control the appearance and layout of your text, you write the document to include *formatting codes* that will be used by a special formatting program to control the quality and layout of the output.

Though it sounds complex, with practice, you can learn to use text editors to enter and format text quickly and easily. This document-editing paradigm is a powerful one that can be used to create professional-looking layouts for large scale documents, such as books or manuals.

Introducing the LaTeX-2e Formatter

Several formatting systems are present on a typical Red Hat Linux system, including the classic UNIX formatter, `troff`. The most modern and widely used formatter today, however, is LaTeX-2e, which uses the TeX formatting engine as its core.

With LaTeX-2e it is possible to quickly produce high-quality output through a laser printer using a text editor such as `vi` or `emacs`. In fact, many professional writers, self-publishers, and educators swear by LaTeX rather than more common and widely understood WYSIWYG word processors, largely because LaTeX makes the production of high-quality output so easy.

For reasons that have faded into the obscurity of history, TeX and LaTeX are most correctly pronounced "teck" and "layteck" respectively, not "tecks" and "laytecks," though in the last few years this distinction has become less important.

Understanding LaTeX Basics

Creating a LaTeX document is easy: Start your editor of choice (usually `vi` or `emacs`) and enter text. All LaTeX documents begin as simple text files. Here are some of the important basics about the text you enter into a LaTeX document:

- **Some characters are reserved for use as formatting codes.** The backslash character (\) is reserved in LaTeX because it marks the beginning of a command; it does not show up in formatted output.

  Other special characters include the hash (#), dollar sign ($), percent sign (%), caret (^), ampersand (&), underscore (_), left and right braces ({}), and tilde (~). To insert any of these characters in your final document, you must prefix them with a backslash, or they will not appear properly. For example, to insert the text "50% of $35.00" you type `"50\% of \$35.00"` in your text editor document.

7

- **LaTeX automatically formats spacing.** LaTex always inserts a single space between words, a given amount of space between paragraphs, and so on. This means that unneeded extra spaces between words or multiple blank lines don't appear in final output unless you tell LaTeX explicitly to include them.

- **LaTeX commands begin with a backslash and then are typically followed by a single word of text.** The following is an example:

```
\command
```

Some commands require options or arguments, and in such cases you might see commands with more complex structures, usually using brackets and/or braces:

```
\command[option]
\command[option]{argument}
```

Remember, the command and the options or arguments passed to it will not appear in the final output of the document; LaTeX uses the command instead to change some aspect of the document's text layout, such as a typeface or page style.

- **LaTeX commands are case-sensitive.** Uppercase and lowercase letters matter.

Now it's time to begin your first LaTeX document.

In the computer world, it has become common to identify a file's type using a three-letter extension to the filename. For example, .gif denotes a Graphic Interchange Format file and .doc indicates a Microsoft Word file.

When you save a LaTeX document in vi or emacs, convention says that you should name it with a .tex extension to indicate that it contains TeX/LaTeX formatting commands.

Creating an Empty Latex Document

Any basic LaTeX document contains at least three commands: \documentclass{}, which tells LaTeX what sort of page layout you want to use, and then \begin{}, and \end{}, which demarcate the beginning and end of the text body, in that order.

Listing 7.1 is a simple article-style document for letter-size paper containing only one line of text. Start a text editor now and enter the listing yourself.

LISTING 7.1   A Short, Simple LaTeX Article Document

```
\documentclass[letterpaper,12pt]{article}
\begin{document}
This is a very short document. Here is my one line of text.
\end{document}
```

The first line of this document, which calls the \documentclass command, contains information about the class to which this document belongs. The information on the right in the braces specifies that this example belongs to a class of documents called article. LaTex uses classes to determine basic formatting, such as setting margins and indenting for new paragraphs. You assign a class to every LaTeX document you create. Table 7.1 lists the basic LaTex document classes.

TABLE 7.1 Basic LaTeX-2e Document Classes

Class	Description
article	This is the smallest, most basic document type and performs formatting appropriate to articles and papers just a few pages in length.
report	This is a slightly more detailed, structured document class intended to be used for papers and reports that might contain sections or chapters.
book	This is the most structured document class, intended to be used for works that will be broken into multiple chapters and might need a table of contents or index generation.

To preview the appearance of any font, type and print a small amount of text. That saves you the trouble of finding that you prefer another choice after you've printed your entire final document.

For most day-to-day uses—such as creating memos, small presentations, personal or business letters, and so forth—the article class is the best choice.

In addition to selecting a class for each LaTeX document, you may also specify several class options inside an optional pair of brackets to control additional aspects of formatting, such as paper size and column-based layouts for the entire document.

Inside the brackets that follow the \documentclass command, you can specify multiple option by separating them with commas. Table 7.2 lists the common class options.

TABLE 7.2 Common LaTeX-2e Class Options

Option	Description
a4paper	Formats output for printing on A4-sized paper
b5paper	Formats output for printing on B5-sized paper
letterpaper	Formats output for printing on letter-sized paper
legalpaper	Formats output for printing on legal-sized paper

7

TABLE 7.2 continued

Option	Description
onecolumn	Specifies that the document should be formatted into a single column as wide as the page (default)
twocolumn	Specifies that the document should be formatted into two vertical columns
oneside	Specifies that margins should be set assuming that only one side of each printed page will be used
twoside	Specifies that margins should be set assuming that two sides of each printed page will be used (different margins for even and odd pages)
openright	Specifies that for two-sided output, chapters should begin on right-side pages only
openany	Specifies that for two-sided output, chapters may begin either on left-side or right-side pages
npt	Specifies that the basic font size for text in the document should be set to n points (default is 10)

By carefully choosing a document class and document class options to suit your output medium and formatting needs, you enable LaTex to manage automatically nearly all formatting concerns. That leaves you free to concentrate on typing your document into your favorite text editor. Here are some sample uses of options, with descriptions:

- `\documentclass[a4paper,twocolumn,12pt]{article}`—Your document will be formatted as an article for A4-size paper. The text will be arranged into two vertical columns on each page. The body of the text will appear in a 12-point font.

- `\documentclass[letterpaper,twoside]{article}`—Your document will be formatted as an article for letter-size paper. The formatter will assume that you are printing on both sides of the page; the margins for even- and odd-numbered pages will therefore be different, to enable easy binding at one edge of each page.

- `\documentclass[legalpaper,14pt]{book}`—Your document will be formatted as a book for legal-size paper. The body of the text will appear in 14-point font.

Formatting and Printing Your First Document

Printing a LaTeX document is a two-step process. You first must format the document and save the formatted text in a new file. Then, you print the formatted text file. To format an existing document, you call the `latex` command, supplying the name of the LaTeX source file as an argument. Assuming that you've typed in the short document in Listing 7.1 and saved it as `myfile.tex`, you can cause LaTeX to read and format the document for printing by calling the `latex` command this way at the command line:

```
[you@workstation20 you]$ latex myfile.tex
This is TeX, Version 3.14159 (Web2C 7.3.1)
(myfile.tex
LaTeX2e <2000/06/01>
Babel <v3.7h> and hyphenation patterns for american, french, german, ngerman, i
talian, nohyphenation, loaded.
(/usr/share/texmf/tex/latex/base/article.cls
Document Class: article 2000/05/19 v1.4b Standard LaTeX document class
(/usr/share/texmf/tex/latex/base/size11.clo)) (myfile.aux) [1] (myfile.aux) )
Output written on myfile.dvi (1 page, 288 bytes).
Transcript written on myfile.log.
[you@workstation20 you]$
```

After processing the file and displaying some notes related to formatting, the latex command creates a file called myfile.dvi and then exits. The new file is called a *device-independent* file and contains the formatted output for myfile.txt. A device-independent file contains all the information necessary to create good-looking document output on any type of printing device.

To print a device-independent file such as myfile.dvi, you must convert it into the correct type of file for the printing device you plan to use. For consumer-class laser or inkjet printers, you should use the dvips program for this conversion, supplying the name of the device-independent file as an argument:

```
[you@workstation20 you]$ dvips myfile.dvi
```

The dvips command converts a device-independent file into Adobe PostScript data, which can then be used to create nicely printed output on a consumer-class printer. The dvips command generates varying amounts of output on the console display as it runs. Then, dvips creates a print job for the formatted output and sends it to the print queue. Your printer then prints the document.

> You can also use a LaTeX file to generate your own Acrobat (pdf) documents by using the pdflatex command instead of the latex command.

Selecting a Page Style

Now that you have printed a simple one-line document, it is time to begin creating more useful documents. Obviously, most documents contain more than a single line; generally, there will be a great deal of content between the \begin{} and \end{} commands in a LaTeX document.

LaTex uses *page styles* to determine the use and placement of page and chapter numbers on the printed page. Table 7.3 lists the three common page style options. The default

7

LaTex page style is plain. You can use the \pagestyle{} command to choose an alternate page style.

TABLE 7.3 Common Page Styles in LaTeX-2e

Style	Description
empty	LaTeX will not decorate pages at all; even page numbers will be omitted.
plain	LaTeX will print the page number at the bottom center of each page.
headings	LaTeX will decorate the top of each page with the page number and current chapter name.

Creating Title and Author Information

LaTeX provides an easy way to print an attractive title page for your documents, by supplying title, author, and date information in your source document and then using the \maketitle command. To define the title and author information of your document, you include several title-specific commands after the \documentclass{} command and before \begin{}. These commands are

- \title{*text*} to specify *text* as the title of the document you are creating
- \author{*text*} to name yourself as the author of the document you are creating
- \date{*text*} to specify *text* as the creation date of the document (optional)

After you have supplied a title, author, and optional date, you can insert a title page in your document at any time by issuing the \maketitle command in the text.

Controlling LaTeX Paragraphs, Line Breaks, and Pages

In LaTeX, paragraph formatting (indentation, skipping space between paragraphs, and so on) is handled automatically. The only task left to the writer is to indicate when a new paragraph should begin. You do this by inserting a blank line in the LaTeX source file using your text editor's Enter key.

The following text illustrates this technique:

```
\documentclass[letterpaper,12pt]{article}
\begin{document}
\pagestyle{empty}
This is some text in a latex document.
This is some text in the same paragraph.
This text will also appear in the first paragraph.

But this text will begin a new paragraph, because there is a
blank line before it.
\end{document}
```

Each time a blank line appears in the text file, LaTeX assumes that a new paragraph should begin. Within paragraphs, LaTeX automatically reflows text to fit the margins for the current page style. This means that the first paragraph in the example does not necessarily represent three lines of text in the final printed output; instead, LaTeX reformats and word wraps the text in these three lines as though they were typed without pressing the Enter key.

Sometimes it is the writer's intent to insert a line break. You can think of a line break as being like pressing the Enter key in the middle of a paragraph in a plain text file—the cursor moves to a new line without beginning a new paragraph, indenting, or leaving empty vertical spaces after the previous line.

To move to a new line without beginning a new paragraph, add the \newline command where you want the break to occur:

```
\documentclass[letterpaper,12pt]{article}
\begin{document}
\pagestyle{empty}
This is the first sentence in a paragraph.
This is the second sentence in the paragraph, and it doesn't
begin on a new line but is instead reflowed with the first
sentence.\newline
This sentence, however, begins on a new line.\newline
And this one.\newline And so does
this one, illustrating that commands can appear at any place
within the text.

And this is a new paragraph, of course.
\end{document}
```

One sample of output generated by this source file is shown in Figure 7.1.

FIGURE 7.1

An output page generated using a number of line breaks.

This is the first sentence in a paragraph. This is the second sentence in the paragraph, and it doesn't begin on a new line but is instead reflowed with the first sentence.
This sentence, however, begins on a new line.
And this one.
And so does this one, illustrating that commands can appear at any place within the text.
And this is a new paragraph, of course.

If it's unclear to you just how the final printed output is affected by the \newline command and blank lines for new paragraphs, experiment by printing some LaTeX text files of your own.

7

Organizing Larger Texts

To create a longer document with sections, section headers, a table of contents, or other similar structural elements, you use LaTeX sectioning commands. These commands are inserted just like the other LaTeX commands you've encountered so far—by preceding them with a backslash character anywhere in the body of your text. They are used to delineate blocks of text of the sorts you'll find in most larger documents.

Table 7.4 lists the LaTex sectioning commands.

TABLE 7.4 Common LaTeX Sectioning Commands

Command	Description
\section{*text*}	Creates a new section using the title *text* as a section header and table of contents entry
\subsection{*text*}	Creates a new subsection using the title *text* as a subsection header and table of contents entry
\subsubsection{*text*}	Creates a new sub-subsection using the title *text* as a sub-subsection header and table of contents entry
\chapter{*text*}	Starts a new chapter, using the title *text* as a chapter title and table of contents entry (report and book document classes only)
\part{*text*}	Starts a new part, using the title *text* as a part title and table of contents entry (report and book document classes only)
\appendix	Starts a new appendix using lettering rather than numbering for sequence, and makes the necessary table of contents entry
\tableofcontents	Inserts a nicely formatted table of contents at the place in the text where the command appears; the table of contents is generated automatically from information supplied by using the other commands in this table

Current versions of LaTeX contain a small bug that affects table of contents functionality. If you find that you format a .tex file only to end up with an empty table of contents, simply run LaTeX on the file a second time and the table of contents will be generated correctly.

Using these basic sectioning commands, it is a simple matter to create a well-structured document with an accurate table of contents just by adding a few extra commands. Consider the following excerpt from a LaTeX source file:

```
\documentclass[letterpaper,12pt]{article}
\begin{document}
\pagestyle{empty}
\section{Learning About Frogs}
This is the first paragraph in a section about frogs. We will have
two subsections, one about frog legs and one about frog sounds.
\subsection{Frog Legs}
Frogs often have legs. These are used for jumping, walking, and
other types of amphibian fun. Often, frog legs are green. That
is all you need to know about frog legs.
\subsection{Frog Sounds}
Frogs also make sounds. These sounds are often characterized as
'ribbits' but this word can sometimes sound silly, so we won't
talk about them any more. That is all you need to know about
frog sounds.
\section{Learing About Birds}
This is the first paragraph in a section about birds. Birds are
really not very much like frogs at all.
\end{document}
```

One sample of output generated by this source file is shown in Figure 7.2.

FIGURE 7.2

The section *and* subsection *commands have been put to good use here.*

1 Learning About Frogs

This is the first paragraph in a section about frogs. We will have two subsections, one about frog legs and one about frog sounds.

1.1 Frog Legs

Frogs often have legs. These are used for jumping, walking, and other types of amphibian fun. Often, frog legs are green. That is all you need to know about frog legs.

1.2 Frog Sounds

Frogs also make sounds. These sounds are often characterized as 'ribbits' but this word can sometimes sound silly, so we won't talk about them any more. That is all you need to know about frog sounds.

2 Learing About Birds

This is the first paragraph in a section about birds. Birds are really not very much like frogs at all.

Notice in Figure 7.2 that LaTeX has automatically numbered the sections and subsections for you. If you insert a `\tableofcontents` command before the first `\section` command, LaTeX prints a nice table of contents on the first page containing the sections and subsections and the pages on which they appear.

7

Formatting the Body of Your Text

There are times when simple page and document structure are not enough to effectively communicate in written text. In many documents, you need to emphasize certain words, or format them in a special font or size to indicate their use or meaning. LaTex uses a number of commands to center text, emphasize text, insert text in quotations, or add other formatting to printed text. You enter these commands immediately before or on either side of the text you want to format.

Here are some of the most common LaTex text formatting commands and some examples of their use:

- To emphasize a particular piece of text, usually in italics, use the \emph{} command:

  ```
  Inserting \emph{emphsized text} with LaTeX is quite easy, especially
  In the middle of a paragraph like this one, which was designed for
  \emph{your} enjoyment.
  ```

- To insert a footnote to a particular piece of text, use the \footnote{} command.

  ```
  I played football\footnote{Football is a physical contact sport and
  should only be played by well-qualified personnel with the proper
  equipment.} yesterday.
  ```

- To center text, use the \begin{center} and \end{center} commands.

  ```
  \begin{center}This is centered text.\end{center}
  ```

- To insert a quoted passage, indenting from right and left on both sides, use the \begin{quote} and \end{quote} commands.

  ```
  \begin{quote}Ladies and gentlemen, start your engines. I shall
  not warn you again; the race is about to begin! If you don't pull
  toward the line now, you will miss the gun!\end{quote}
  ```

- To create ordered (numbered) or unordered (bulleted) lists in your text, use the \begin{enumerate} and \end{enumerate} or \begin{itemize} and \end{itemize} commands, respectively, along with \item to mark the beginning of each new item.

  ```
  \begin{enumerate}
  \item This is the first numbered item.
  \item This is the second numbered item.
  \item This is the third numbered item.
  \end{enumerate}
  \begin{itemize}
  \item This is an un-numbered, bulleted item.
  \item This is another un-numbered, bulleted item.
  \end{itemize}
  ```

Figure 7.3 shows the output generated by all the commands we've just discussed.

FIGURE 7.3

Using a simple selection of commands in a plain text editor, you can add structure to printed documents using LaTeX.

Inserting *emphasized text* with LaTeX is quite easy, especially in the middle of a paragraph like this one, which was designed for *your* enjoyment.

I played football[1] yesterday.

This is centered text.

Ladies and gentlemen, start your engines. I shall not warn you again; the race is about to begin! If you don't pull toward the line now, you will miss the gun!

1. This is the first numbered item.

2. This is the second numbered item.

3. This is the third numbered item.

- This is an un-numbered, bulleted item.

- This is another un-numbered, bulleted item.

[1]Football is a physical contact sport and should only be played by well-qualified personnel with the proper equipment.

Though a wealth of other formatting commands exist, these are enough to produce most common types of documents using LaTeX. You can learn more about many of these by visiting the links provided in the section called "More Information About LaTeX" later in this chapter.

Inserting Special Characters

People who work in the publishing industry are familiar with the special characters used in printing and typesetting to insert symbols such as dashes and ellipses into text. These symbols usually can't be entered directly from a keyboard. Luckily, they can be generated in LaTeX using commands or special strings.

The most common among these can be seen in Table 7.5.

TABLE 7.5 Commonly Used Special Characters in LaTeX

Command or Sequence	Description
\ldots	Inserts a properly spaced ellipsis
--	Inserts an en-dash
---	Inserts an em-dash
``	Inserts an opening quotation mark
''	Inserts a closing quotation mark

To illustrate the use of these special characters, consider the following source line:

```
I went to the store--the bookstore, and I was there for hours\ldots
```

7

The printed output from this line would contain the indicated special characters instead:

```
I went to the store—the bookstore, and I was there for hours...
```

Putting It All Together

With the LaTex commands you've just learned, you can produce a professional-quality printing of a novel from text written with a text editor such as `emacs` or `vi`. Listing 7.2 shows the text and formatting for a document that employs several of the commands presented in this hour.

In Listing 7.2, you do the following:

- Create a new book document intended for letter-sized paper with a 12-point font, using the `\documentclass` command.
- Output a nice title page containing title and author information with the `\maketitle` command.
- Output a table of contents with the `\tableofcontents` command.
- Begin chapters called *Beginning My Novel* and *Ending My Novel* using the `\chapter` command.
- Create a bulleted shopping list using the `\begin{itemize}` and `\end{itemize}` commands, marking each item in the list with the `\item` command.

LISTING 7.2   A LaTeX Document Using Numerous Commands

```
\documentclass[letterpaper,openany,12pt]{book}
\title{My Novel}
\author{Aron Hsiao}
\begin{document}
\pagestyle{headings}
\maketitle
\chapter{Beginning My Novel}
It is in \emph{this} chapter that I begin my novel. Unfortunately,
this chapter is only two paragraphs long. Still, it promises to be
a wonderful novel, because it illustrates the formatting prowess
of LaTeX.

Furthermore, it is the first of these paragraphs which is the longest,
but not bymuch. Still, longest is longest, and to the victor go the
spoils---at least, that is what my history teacher used to tell me.
\chapter{Ending My Novel}
My novel only consists of two chapters\footnote{Though a third
is in the works} right now. The second chapter is just a mysterious
shopping list\ldots

\begin{itemize}
\item Cabbages
```

LISTING 7.2   continued

```
\item Red socks with yellow stripes
\item A green rubber washbasin
\item The latest issue of \emph{Time Magazine}
\end{itemize}

Perhaps someday, all of the items in this shopping list will be
explained. But then I suppose we will leave that bit of mystery for the
sequel.
\end{document}
```

Though this document is relatively short, you will find that if you type it, format it with
the latex command, and print it with the dvips command, the final result is quite
impressive, as shown in Figure 7.4.

Remember how to format and print? The commands, in order, are

```
latex myfile.txt
dvips myfile.dvi
```

FIGURE 7.4

*Our final impressive
sample document, cre-
ated and sent to the
printer using the
LaTeX text formatter.*

My Novel

Aron Hsiao

October 8, 2002

Chapter 1

Beginning My Novel

It is in *this* chapter that I begin my novel. Unfortunately, this chapter is
only two paragraphs long. Still, it promises to be a wonderful novel, because
it illustrates the formatting prowess of LaTeX.

Furthermore, it is the first of these paragraphs which is the longest, but
not by much. Still, longest is longest, and to the victor go the spoils—at least,
that is what my history teacher used to tell me.

Chapter 2

Ending My Novel

My novel only consists of two chapters[1] right now. The second chapter is
just a mysterious shopping list...

- Cabbages
- Red socks with yellow stripes
- A green rubber washbasin
- The latest issue of *Time Magazine*

Perhaps someday, all of the items in this shopping list will be explained.
But then I suppose we will leave that bit of mystery for the sequel.

[1] Though a third is in the works

7

More Information About LaTeX

You only scratched the surface of LaTeX and its capabilities in this brief introduction. To learn more about LaTeX or use LaTeX on serious projects, you should consult more in-depth documentation.

These sources of online documentation are a good place to start:

- `http://www.giss.nasa.gov/latex/` contains a hypertext guide to using the LaTeX formatter written by Sheldon Green.
- `http://www.maths.tcd.ie/~dwilkins/LaTeXPrimer/Index.html` contains a hypertext primer for using the LaTeX formatter written by David R. Wilkins.
- A nice, printable guide called *The Not So Short Introduction to LaTeX 2e* in portable document (.pdf) format can be downloaded at `http://people.ee.ethz.ch/~oetiker/lshort/lshort.pdf`.
- More reference material of various kinds can be found at the catchall LaTeX Web site at `http://www.latex-project.org`.

Performing Math Tasks Using the Binary Calculator

Mathematics and calculation are common daily productivity fare in any office containing computer systems. Many offices use graphic spreadsheet programs, such as Microsoft Excel or Corel Quattro Pro.

As you might have predicted, the Linux command line gives you access to a more primitive—but also more programmable—form of calculation. Though it's a powerful performer, you need relatively little training to use the Red Hat Linux binary calculator, called bc.

Starting bc and Performing Basic Calculations

To start bc, enter it at the command line without arguments. You will be dropped into the bc commmand mode:

```
[you@workstation20 you]$ bc
bc 1.06
Copyright 1991-1994, 1997, 1998, 2000 Free Software Foundation, Inc.
This is free software with ABSOLUTELY NO WARRANTY.
For details type `warranty'.
```

There is no bc prompt, but nevertheless bc patiently awaits your orders. To perform a basic calculation, just enter it naturally. For example, add a few numbers by entering digits and the plus operator as necessary, followed by the Enter key:

```
216 + 45 + 36
297
```

Notice that bc instantly prints the result. You can use other mathematical operators by typing just the characters you would expect to type. Use parentheses to specify the order of operations, as in this example, which specifies 20 + 20 as the first calculation:

```
( 1200 / ( 20 + 20 ) ) * 6
180
```

Again, the answer is instantly calculated and displayed. Use a decimal point to indicate a fractional amount, as in this example:

```
10.44 * 3.623
37.824
```

You can exit bc at any time by entering the special command quit on an empty line:

```
quit
[you@workstation20 you]$
```

The ability to perform these types of small calculations quickly, easily, and with arbitrary precision (to any number of decimal places) makes the binary calculator extremely useful.

Using Variables

Sometimes it helps to remember the results of calculations or to store numbers for later use. This can be done in bc well. To make bc remember the results of calculations or numbers you want to use later, you can assign values or the results of calculated expressions to variables:

```
a=10.1
b=6.3
c=a*b
c
63.6
```

Here, you assign the value 10.1 to the variable a, the value 6.3 to the variable b, and the result of multiplying a by b to variable c. You then display the contents of variable c by entering the name of the variable alone.

7

The results of division might at times be calculated to arbitrary levels of precision without reaching a conclusion. Use the special variable, `scale`, to determine the number of decimal places that will be calculated when dividing:

```
scale=10
3/7
.4285714285
```

Using variables and the operators shown in these examples, you can perform a relatively long and complex series of calculations with ease and accuracy.

Automating Calculations with bc

Suppose you often perform a series of calculations over and over. Rather than type the calculations repeatedly into bc using new numbers each time, you can write script to automate these types of calculations in bc. Here is an example:

1. Create a file using vi or emacs called addthree.bc, which contains the following text:

   ```
   "Number to add? "; y=read()"Adding 3 to "; y
   "produces "; y+3
   quit
   ```

2. Now, call bc from the command line and supply addthree.bc as an argument.

3. When bc prompts for a number, type a number and press Enter.

   The value of this number you enter is then stored by bc in the variable *y* and the number 3 is added to it. The result is then displayed:

```
[you@workstation20 you]$ bc addthree.bc
bc 1.06
Copyright 1991-1994, 1997, 1998, 2000 Free Software Foundation, Inc.
This is free software with ABSOLUTELY NO WARRANTY.
For details type `warranty'.
Number to add? 7
Adding 3 to 7
produces 10
[you@workstation20 you]$
```

The read() command is used in a bc script to get a number from the user and store that number in a variable. You can prompt for any number of variables using the read() command as shown previously. Text enclosed in quotes is output to the user as a prompt. Using these simple tools, relatively long and complex types of calculations can be automated.

Advanced Scripting in bc

Scripting of any kind is infinitely more powerful if flow control (if...then statements or while statements) can be used. Flow control enables sections of your script (usually certain calculations) to be repeated over and over until conditions that you specify are met. For example, if you are working on a calculus problem, you might repeat a calculation involving one variable over and over until the value of that variable approaches zero, stopping afterward to output the number of times the calculation is performed.

Though a discussion of flow control and complex scripting with bc is beyond the scope of this book, those familiar with the C computer programming language will find the flow control structures of the binary calculator familiar. More information about the advanced features of the binary calculator, including flow control statements like while() and if(), can be found in the bc main page.

Creating and Sorting Lists of Data

Database-like storage and search-oriented retrieval functions are also common day-to-day productivity uses for personal workstations. From the command line, you can accomplish these types of tasks using editors such as vi and emacs, plain text files, and a set of two simple commands: sort, which is used to sort plain text data into alphanumeric order, and grep, which is used to search text data for a specific word or phrase.

Creating Searchable or Sortable Lists

The art of creating useful plain text databases with vi or emacs revolves mainly around the ability to use spaces or tabs effectively to organize information into single lines broken into multiple single-word columns. To create a plain-text database, start your favorite text editor and follow these steps:

1. Logically (that is, in your imagination) separate the information you'd like to organize into fields a single word long. For example, for a companywide list of phone numbers, your fields might be last name, first name, area code, phone number, and department.

2. Enter your first record on a single text line, one field at a time, inserting tabs between them.

3. Enter the rest of your records the same way, one on each line, until all your records are represented in the file.

To continue with our phone number list example, let's imagine a list of phone numbers in a file called phones.txt, shown in Listing 7.4.

7

LISTING 7.4   A Simple Text-Based Database of Phone Numbers

```
Rasmussen      Jake    800    111-1111      Heating
Larsen         Eve     800    222-2222      Heating
Amberson       Laura   888    111-9999      Cooling
Swenson        Celia   800    666-6666      Operations
Wagoner        Shane   888    232-2323      Cooling
Filipanteng    Lee     800    696-9696      Heating
```

Following the format we imagined above, this list of phone numbers has five columns—last name, first name, area code, phone number, and department, in that order. The names aren't in any particular order; they've just been entered into the plain text file phones.txt using a text editor as each new person joined the company.

As simple as this file appears, it's already a database. Let's examine the ways in which we can use this data.

Displaying Specific Entries

In "Searching Text Files for Word Patterns" in Hour 5, you learned how to use the grep command to search for various kinds of text; grep is also useful for finding and displaying a specific item in a plain text database. Suppose you want a listing of all the people in our company phone list who work in the cooling department. To do that, you call the grep command, supplying the word Cooling and the name of our database file as arguments:

```
[you@workstation20 you]$ grep Cooling phones.txt
Amberson       Laura   888    111-9999      Cooling
Wagoner        Shane   888    232-2323      Cooling
[you@workstation20 you]$
```

As you can see, you easily take care of this request. Suppose, on the other hand, that you want to find the phone number for Eve Larsen and the department where she works. To search for Eve's last name, Larsen, call the grep command, supplying the word Larsen and the name of our database file as arguments:

```
[you@workstation20 you]$ grep Larsen phones.txt
Larsen         Eve     800    222-2222      Heating
[you@workstation20 you]$
```

You also accomplish this easily. Searches of this kind might not be impressive to you on a short list of six phone numbers; the same technique will work equally well, however, on a plain text database that is several thousand entries long.

Sorting List Data

Sometimes it is helpful to be able to sort data in a list. The sort command is designed for just such an occasion; sort simply accepts a plain text listing and rearranges the lines into alphanumeric order. The simplest way to call sort is to use the name of a text file to sort as an argument on the command line. Here, you sort the phone number list from previous examples:

```
[you@workstation20 you]$ sort phones.txt
Amberson        Laura   888     111-9999        Cooling
Filipanteng     Lee     800     696-9696        Heating
Larsen          Eve     800     222-2222        Heating
Rasmussen       Jake    800     111-1111        Heating
Swenson         Celia   800     666-6666        Operations
Wagoner         Shane   888     232-2323        Cooling
[you@workstation20 you]$
```

Because the surname of each individual is in the first column in your list, you now have a list displayed in alphabetical order by last name. In fact, if you were going to print a long list of phone numbers formatted this way as a phone book, the command to generate the output would be as simple as

```
[you@workstation20 you]$ sort phones.txt | lpr
```

Let's assume for a moment, however, that you want to sort based on first names, rather than last names. The sort command enables you to alter the sorting criteria—or more specifically, the column—on which it will operate by using the -k option. To use the -k option, follow the call to sort with the -k option and the number of the column you wish to use as the basis for your sort. Here, you sort the list of phone numbers based on the second column of information—the first names of the employees in the list:

```
[you@workstation20 you]$ sort -k 2 phones.txt
Swenson         Celia   800     666-6666        Operations
Larsen          Eve     800     222-2222        Heating
Rasmussen       Jake    800     111-1111        Heating
Amberson        Laura   888     111-9999        Cooling
Filipanteng     Lee     800     696-9696        Heating
Wagoner         Shane   888     232-2323        Cooling
[you@workstation20 you]$
```

Suppose you want to group employees by department, or by area code. To do that, you type the sort command, the -k option, and the number of the column that holds department names, or the area codes, followed by the name of the file to be sorted:

```
[you@workstation20 you]$ sort -k 5 phones.txt
Amberson        Laura   888     111-9999        Cooling
Wagoner         Shane   888     232-2323        Cooling
Filipanteng     Lee     800     696-9696        Heating
Larsen          Eve     800     222-2222        Heating
Rasmussen       Jake    800     111-1111        Heating
Swenson         Celia   800     666-6666        Operations
[you@workstation20 you]$ sort -k 3 phones.txt
Rasmussen       Jake    800     111-1111        Heating
Larsen          Eve     800     222-2222        Heating
Swenson         Celia   800     666-6666        Operations
```

7

```
Filipanteng    Lee     800    696-9696    Heating
Amberson       Laura   888    111-9999    Cooling
Wagoner        Shane   888    232-2323    Cooling
[you@workstation20 you]$
```

As a final example, you can get a listing of only those employees who work in Heating, sort the list alphabetically by first name, and then send the listing to the printer. This can be done by calling grep to search the file phones.txt for the word Heating, then sending that output through a pipe to the sort command with an option to sort based on the second column, and then sending that output through a pipe to the lpr command, which prints the data:

```
[you@workstation20 you]$ grep Heating phones.txt | sort -k 2 | lpr
[you@workstation20 you]$
```

More information on the sort command can be found in the man page for sort.

Summary

This hour, you learned to use the command line in everyday workflow, to produce professionally formatted, multipart documents. You've also learned to perform calculations with the Red Hat Linux binary calculator. Finally, you learned to create and sort text-based databases.

Many of the tools in this hour, most notably LaTeX and bc, are much more powerful than you might realize when you first begin using them. If you feel as though these tools might be useful to you, take time to consult the referenced documentation or the online man pages to learn more about them.

Q&A

Q Is there any way to add page numbers to text files that I create in emacs or vi without having to use a full-fledged document formatting system, such as LaTeX?

A Yes. The pr command can be used to accomplish very simple formatting tasks on basic text files, and the output can then be piped to lpr for printing. You can find out more about pr, including the options and arguments it accepts, in the man page for pr.

Q **When I try to run LaTeX, I get an error message and a prompt that looks like a question mark, from which I can't seem to exit. What's wrong?**

A This typically means you have miskeyed a LaTeX command somewhere and LaTeX has been stumped by it. Look closely at the error message; it usually displays the offending malformed command. Enter `exit` at the question mark prompt and your file will be loaded into a `vi` editor for you, where you can fix the problem.

Q **Is LaTeX a Linux- or UNIX-only tool? Is it available for Windows or for Mac OS?**

A Both Windows and Mac OS users can avail themselves of the features of the LaTeX typesetting engine. There are many versions of LaTeX for the PC, but the easiest to install and use is PCTeX, which can be found at `http://www.pctex.com`. Information on using LaTeX with Mac OS can be found at `http://www.esm.psu.edu/mac-tex/`.

Workshop

The Workshop is designed to help you anticipate possible questions, review what you've learned, and begin learning how to put your knowledge into practice.

Quiz

1. How do you send a file called `myfile.txt` to your printer?
2. How do you send a file called `myfile.tex` to your printer?
3. What three commands occur in every LaTeX file?
4. How do you start the binary calculator in interactive mode?

Answers

1. `lpr myfile.txt`
2. `latex myfile.tex`
   `dvips myfile.dvi`
3. `\documentclass{}, \begin{}, and \end{}`
4. Type **bc** at the command prompt and press Enter.

Activities

1. Try writing a letter to someone you know using LaTeX.
2. Use your favorite editor to create a text database containing your personal phone number list and perform some searches and sorts on it.

7

Hour 8

Networking Without Graphics

So far you've learned how to do many things from the console, including basic file management and housekeeping, high-quality document creation, mathematics, and simple database management. But of course the real order of the day in computing is networking, especially email and Web browsing.

This hour, you learn how to use Linux and the console to accomplish the networking tasks that are necessary to function in any office or productivity environment. These tasks include

- Web browsing, including cookie and bookmark management
- Downloading, reading, and responding to email using the `mail` command
- Managing large-volume email with Pine
- Connecting to other Linux or Unix systems through remote logins
- Transferring files between Linux and/or Unix systems

- Transferring files between Linux and Windows systems
- Printing to network printers or printers attached to other machines on the network

To make any use of this hour, your Linux system must be connected to a network or have dial-up access activated and ready for use.

If your system is connected to an Ethernet network, you configured your Ethernet settings in "Network Configuration" in Hour 2, "Installing Red Hat Linux."

If you use dial-up Internet service, use the techniques discussed in "Configuring Your Dialup Internet Service" in Hour 3, "Booting, Logging In, and Configuring," to configure and connect to your Internet service provider before continuing with this chapter.

To follow along with the Web browsing tutorial in this Hour, you need to have installed the Lynx browser. If you installed one of the basic Red Hat Linux configurations, you probably didn't install the Lynx browser. If that's the case, you can install the packages for Lynx by hand.

You first must install the indexhtml and perl-CGI packages from the second Red Hat Linux CD-ROM. You also must install the lynx package from the third Red Hat Linux CD-ROM.

Details on installing software packages under Red Hat Linux can be found in Hour 21, "Installing Software."

Browsing the Web at the Console

To many Internet users, networking seems to be an inherently graphics-centric process, largely because the World Wide Web is the primary network medium to which they've been exposed. But even the World Wide Web wasn't always so visual; in the early days of the Web, full-featured browsers such as NCSA Mosaic had only rudimentary graphics capability, and *text* was still the primary medium from which the World Wide Web was built.

Even today, though many sites are difficult to interpret without graphics, many more remain perfectly informative and useful without their graphics. When you browse the Web at the console, the text appears and is laid out more or less as the site designers intended; the graphics are simply omitted or replaced with text to indicate what the image contains.

Web browsing using a more traditional graphics-based browser and your mouse or pointing device will be discussed in Hour 13, "Networking on the Desktop."

Starting the Lynx Web Browser

For many years, the most popular of the console-based Web browsers has been Lynx. To start Lynx, simply type the word **lynx** at the command line. You will be greeted by a welcome screen, as shown in Figure 8.1.

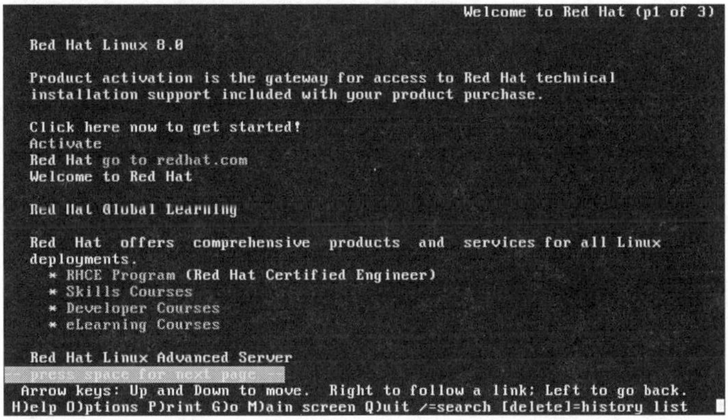

FIGURE 8.1

The Welcome screen for the Lynx browser included with Red Hat Linux.

```
                                          Welcome to Red Hat (p1 of 3)
Red Hat Linux 8.0

Product activation is the gateway for access to Red Hat technical
installation support included with your product purchase.

Click here now to get started!
Activate
Red Hat go to redhat.com
Welcome to Red Hat

Red Hat Global Learning

Red Hat offers comprehensive products and services for all Linux
deployments.
     * RHCE Program (Red Hat Certified Engineer)
     * Skills Courses
     * Developer Courses
     * eLearning Courses

Red Hat Linux Advanced Server
  press space for next page
 Arrow keys: Up and Down to move.  Right to follow a link; Left to go back.
 H)elp O)ptions P)rint G)o M)ain screen Q)uit /=search [delete]=history list
```

Using the Lynx Web Browser

Before doing anything else, let's load a Web page using Lynx, because that is what you'll do most often while using Lynx. The keystroke to go to a new URL is, not surprisingly, g. When you press the g key, a URL to open: prompt appears. Enter the URL you want to visit at the prompt, and then press Enter.

A visit to http://www.yahoo.com displays the page shown in Figure 8.2. Lynx can render most Web pages satisfactorily, although rarely you will encounter a page that is rendered so poorly that it's unusable.

You can use a number of common keystrokes to browse the Web comfortably with Lynx. These keystrokes and their actions are shown in Table 8.1.

FIGURE 8.2

The very popular Yahoo! front page, as rendered by Lynx.

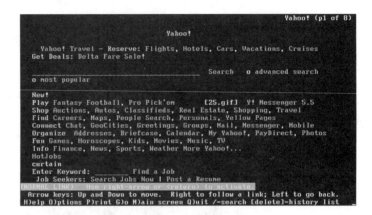

TABLE 8.1 Common Lynx Keystrokes and Their Actions

Key	Action
g	Go to a new URL (site).
Up arrow	Select previous link (highlighted link indicates selected link).
Down arrow	Select next link.
Right arrow or Enter	Follow (click) selected link.
Left arrow	Return (go back) to previously displayed page.
PgDown or +	Display next screenful (scroll down).
PgUp or -	Display previous screenful (scroll up).
Home or Ctrl+A	Display top of current page/document.
End or Ctrl+E	Display bottom of current page/document.
d	Download (save) the selected link to disk.
p	Print the currently displayed page.
/	Search for text within the currently displayed page.
a	Add a bookmark for the currently displayed page.
v	Display a list of bookmarked pages.
Ctrl+R	Reload the currently displayed page.
o	Display the Lynx options menu.
?	Display help documents for using Lynx.

These are just some of the keystroke commands you can use while browsing the Web with Lynx; for further documentation on these keystrokes, please visit the Lynx help system by pressing the ? key.

Handling Cookies with Lynx

Cookies are used by Web sites to track your activity while you visit, usually in order to tailor your experience at the site to your own personal preferences. However, cookies can at times present a security and privacy risk, and some users therefore decide not to accept them.

In its default configuration, Lynx prompts you to accept cookies from the domain (site) you are trying to visit:

```
www.about.com cookie: TMo=102987128175151412123903063  Allow? (Y/N/Always/neVer)
```

You can use these responses to control cookies in Lynx:

- Answering y accepts this cookie only, and Lynx will continue to prompt you each time this site tries to store a cookie on your machine.

- n rejects this cookie only, and Lynx will continue to prompt you each time this site tries to store a cookie on your machine.

- a accepts *all* cookies from this domain (site), with no further prompts.

- v accepts none of the cookies this site sends, now or in the future.

For normal day-to-day Web browsing, you can safely use a as your answer.

After you have accepted a cookie or chosen to accept all cookies from a given domain, you can change your preference or delete cookies inside the *cookie jar*, which can be started by pressing Ctrl+k while inside Lynx.

When you start the cookie jar, a screen similar to the one in Figure 8.3 is displayed.

FIGURE 8.3

The Lynx cookie jar enables you to delete cookies or change the cookie policy on a per-domain basis. Select the domain to change its cookie policy; to delete a cookie from a domain, select it and press the d key.

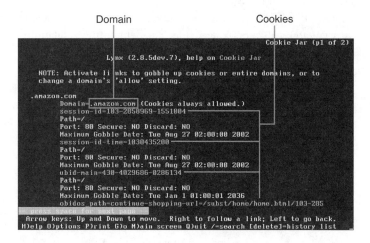

Inside the cookie jar, you can navigate upward and downward through the selections just as you would on any normal Web page. Pressing Enter on a selected domain displays this prompt, which allows you to change the policy for that domain:

```
D)elete domain's cookies, set allow A)lways/P)rompt/neV)er, or C)ancel?
```

Pressing the d key in this case deletes all the cookies associated with the given domain; pressing the a key instructs Lynx to always allow cookies from this domain, pressing the p key instructs Lynx to prompt about cookie requests from this domain, and so on.

When you press Enter after selecting an individual cookie instead of a domain within the cookie jar, you will be given the option to delete the cookie in question.

To exit the cookie jar, simply use the left arrow (back one page) or the g key (load a new URL) .

Managing Bookmarks with Lynx

One of the most important functions in any Web browser is the bookmark function, which enables you to store the addresses of specific pages or sites that were useful to you and return to them later without having to enter a complete URL by hand.

Thanks to Table 8.1, you already know that adding a bookmark in Lynx is as simple as pressing the a key. When you press the a key at a given page, you are presented with a set of options:

```
Save D)ocument or L)ink to bookmark file or C)ancel? (d,l.c):
```

This prompt asks whether you want to bookmark the currently displayed page (by pressing the d key) or the currently selected link (by pressing the l key), or to cancel entirely. After you've told Lynx whether to bookmark the current page or the current link, Lynx asks you to create a bookmark title. The default title is taken from the title of the page you're bookmarking; to use the default, press Enter.

To view your bookmarks, use the v key. Use the up and down arrows to navigate the list of bookmarks and the Enter or right-arrow key to visit a bookmarked link.

To remove a bookmark, use the r key after you have selected the bookmark you want to remove; after prompting you to confirm that you want to remove the bookmark, Lynx deletes it.

Managing Email at the Console

Though the Web drives the Internet economy, emailing remains the Internet's most-used function. It is therefore important that email be fully managable from the Linux console—and it is. The Pine program provides console users with powerful email management capabilities. In order to use Pine at the console, however, most users will need to configure Linux to retrieve mail from a remote mail server.

Fetching Post Office Protocol 3 (POP3) or Internet Message Access Protocol (IMAP) Mail

For most people who use a dial-up ISP and many who don't, managing email at the console begins with the process of bringing mail across from an SMTP-capable mail server (used by most Internet service providers) to the local workstation where their mail is saved.

Two major protocol families exist for transferring mail from an SMTP host to a local host: IMAP and POP3. The Linux program best used to fetch mail from either kind of server is called `fetchmail` and is installed by Red Hat Linux in all basic configurations.

To use `fetchmail`, you create a configuration file called `~/`**`.fetchmailrc`** (a file called .fetchmailrc stored in your home directory) that instructs `fetchmail` where to find your mail and how to go about getting it. After you have created this configuration file, you call `fetchmail` from the command line to download all your mail from your mail server to the local host (your computer), where you can use a console-based mail program to access it. The following sections walk you through each of these processes.

Creating the .fetchmailrc File

The .fetchmailrc file is a plain text file, and you can create it using either `vi` or `emacs` with methods you've already learned. The format of the file when used simply for downloading mail is relatively simple. You enter one line into the file for each mail server you want to download mail from. The format of this line is as follows:

```
poll server protocol protocol username username password password
```

The values for `server`, `protocol`, `username`, and `password` should be changed to the Internet address (domain name) of your mail server, the procotol (usually `auto` to automatically detect either POP3 or IMAP), your login, and your password, respectively. This information must be obtained from your network administrator, Internet service provder, hosting company, or Web-based email provider, depending on which you use.

You will find, after you create a ~/.fetchmailrc file, that it does not appear in the output of the `ls` command. This is because files or directories whose names begin with dots are not normally displayed by `ls`.

To cause `ls` to include files and directories beginning with dots in its output, supply the `-a` argument to the `ls` command.

For example, consider the following entry from a `.fetchmailrc` file:

```
poll mail.mycompany.com protocol auto username jackhenry password 3cheesesI8
```

This line causes `fetchmail` to download mail from a server located at `mail.mycompany.com`; `fetchmail` attempts to automatically detect the protocol that should be used. In this example, `fetchmail` attempts to log in to the mail server as `jackhenry` using the password `3cheesesI8`. If you have only one mail server account, you need only one line in your `.fetchmailrc` file; more lines should be added depending on the number of servers you will be downloading mail from.

> If you have trouble getting `fetchmail` to download mail from your server, try explicitly specifying one of the many protocols supported by `fetchmail` rather than using the `auto` protocol. The list of supported protocols can be found in the `man` page for `fetchmail`. Work with your network administrator, Internet service provider, hosting company, or Web-based email provider's technical support system until you find one that works.

After you have created a `.fetchmailrc` file, you *must* remove from it all permissions for group owner and for other users; otherwise, `fetchmail` will refuse to use the file. More importantly, if you don't protect your .fetchmailrc file by changing its permissions, your password will be vulnerable to theft. To make this change, use the `chmod` command and remove read, write, and execute permissions from group and other users (leaving them only for the owning user):

```
[you@workstation20 you]$ chmod og-rwx .fetchmailrc
[you@workstation20 you]$ ls -l .fetchmailrc
-rwx------    1 you       you           259 Oct 23  2002 .fetchmailrc
[you@workstation20 you]$
```

Now you can test out your new `fetchmail` configuration simply by entering the fetchmail command alone:

```
[you@workstation20 you]$ fetchmail
2 messages for jackhenry at mail.mycompany.com (1889 octets).
reading message 1 of 2 (933 octets)  flushed
reading message 2 of 2 (956 octets)  flushed
[you@workstation20 you]$
```

In this case, two messages are waiting to be downloaded from the mail server. They have now been downloaded and are stored on the local system where console-based mail clients can get to them.

Each time you want to check the mail server for new mail, enter the command `fetchmail`. In Hour 18, "Command-Line System Administration," you learn how to use the `cron` system to automate tasks of this kind, so that `fetchmail` can be called regularly in the background.

Using Pine to Manage Email from the Console

Without a doubt the most widely used console-based email program is Pine, based on a classic interactive mailer called Elm. Pine provides the user with a wealth of powerful email features, including support for filters, address books, and MIME attachments.

> If you find that `pine` is not available to you from the command line, it is likely that your installation choices did not result in the Pine package being installed. In order to use Pine, you need to install the Pine package from Disc 3 of the Red Hat Linux 8.0 CD-ROM set.
>
> For details on installing software, please refer to Hour 21.

Starting Pine

To start Pine, type **pine** at the command line. The first time you run Pine, you are greeted by the Pine welcome screen, which contains some information about the program, as shown in Figure 8.4.

FIGURE 8.4
The Pine Welcome screen is displayed the first time you start Pine.

```
  PINE 4.44    GREETING TEXT                                    No Messages
                    <<<This message will appear only once>>>

                Welcome to Pine ... a Program for Internet News and Email

  We hope you will explore Pine's many capabilities. From the Main Menu,
  select Setup/Config to see many of the options available to you. Also
  note that all screens have context-sensitive help text available.

  SPECIAL REQUEST: This software is made available world-wide as a public
  service of the University of Washington in Seattle. In order to justify
  continuing development, it is helpful to have an idea of how many people
  are using Pine. Are you willing to be counted as a Pine user? Pressing
  Return will send an anonymous (meaning, your real email address will not
  be revealed) message to the Pine development team at the University of
  Washington for purposes of tallying.

                Pine is a trademark of the University of Washington.

                            [ALL of greeting text]
  ? Help         E Exit this greeting      -  PrevPage Z Print
            Ret [Be Counted!]             Spc NextPage
```

Notice that a number of keys and their meanings are listed at the bottom of the display. While you are working inside Pine, the most common keystrokes used at a given screen are always displayed at the bottom for your convenience.

Pressing Enter at the Pine welcome screen sends an email to the Pine maintainers notifying them that another Pine user has gone online. You are then taken to the Pine Main Menu, which you will see whenever you start Pine, as shown in Figure 8.5.

FIGURE 8.5

The Pine Main Menu is easy to navigate; the number of messages in your INBOX is displayed at the bottom of the screen.

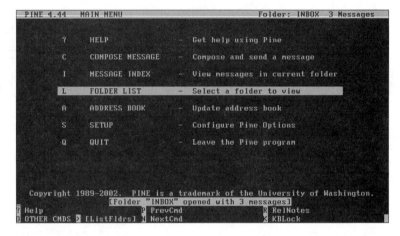

You can navigate the Pine Main Menu using the keystrokes listed at the bottom of the display or by pressing the arrow keys to select an item from the menu and Enter to select the item you want to activate.

Setting Pine Preferences

Before using Pine for sending and receiving mail, you should take a moment to configure Pine's behavior with regard to message sorting, reply quoting, and so on.

To enter Pine setup from the Main Menu, either press the s key, or use the arrow keys to navigate to the setup option and then press Enter. The general setup screen is shown in Figure 8.6.

New Pine users need only focus on the options in the Configuration area. You can enter this area by pressing the c key at the setup screen. The configuration area appears, as shown in Figure 8.7.

To change individual configuration options, use the up- and down-arrow keys to select the option you want to change, and then press Enter to select or un-select that option. Watch the lines at the bottom of the screen carefully; it is in this area that you are prompted for input when necessary. We'll change one option in this hour; leave the rest of them alone.

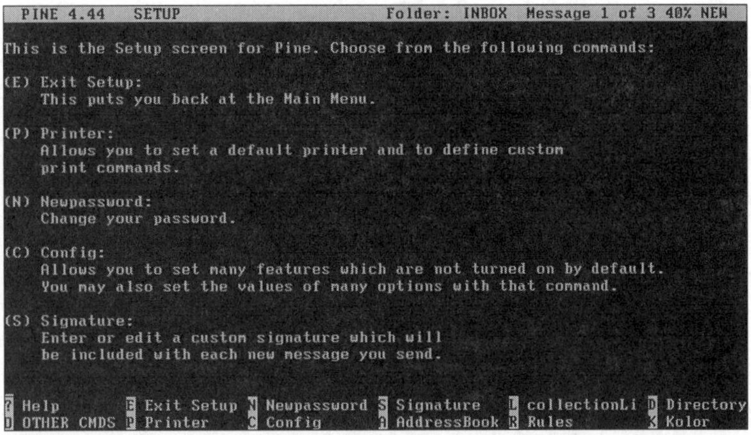

FIGURE 8.6

The general setup screen for Pine holds commands for setting printing, password, configuration, and signature preferences.

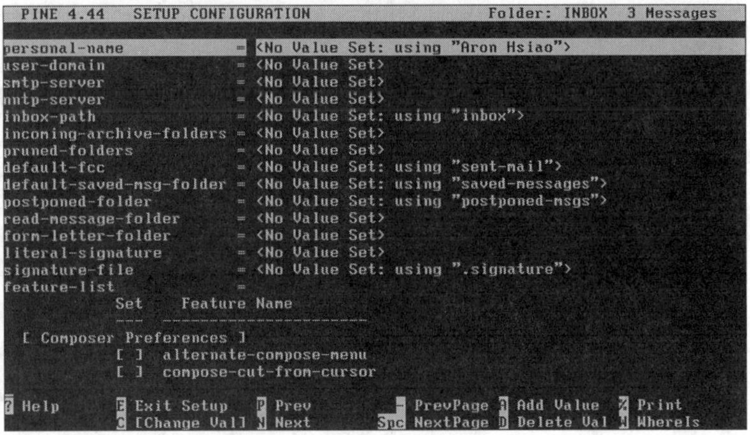

```
PINE 4.44    SETUP                        Folder: INBOX  Message 1 of 3 40% NEW

This is the Setup screen for Pine. Choose from the following commands:

(E) Exit Setup:
    This puts you back at the Main Menu.

(P) Printer:
    Allows you to set a default printer and to define custom
    print commands.

(N) Newpassword:
    Change your password.

(C) Config:
    Allows you to set many features which are not turned on by default.
    You may also set the values of many options with that command.

(S) Signature:
    Enter or edit a custom signature which will
    be included with each new message you send.

? Help          E Exit Setup N Newpassword S Signature  L collectionLi D Directory
O OTHER CMDS    P Printer     C Config      A AddressBook R Rules      K Kolor
```

FIGURE 8.7

The Pine setup configuration area contains a ponderous number of configuration options; leave most of them alone.

```
PINE 4.44    SETUP CONFIGURATION                Folder: INBOX   3 Messages

personal-name                  = <No Value Set: using "Aron Hsiao">
user-domain                    = <No Value Set>
smtp-server                    = <No Value Set>
nntp-server                    = <No Value Set>
inbox-path                     = <No Value Set: using "inbox">
incoming-archive-folders       = <No Value Set>
pruned-folders                 = <No Value Set>
default-fcc                    = <No Value Set: using "sent-mail">
default-saved-msg-folder       = <No Value Set: using "saved-messages">
postponed-folder               = <No Value Set: using "postponed-msgs">
read-message-folder            = <No Value Set>
form-letter-folder             = <No Value Set>
literal-signature              = <No Value Set>
signature-file                 = <No Value Set: using ".signature">
feature-list
                  Set      Feature Name
                  ---      ------------
   [ Composer Preferences ]
                  [ ]      alternate-compose-menu
                  [ ]      compose-cut-from-cursor

? Help          E Exit Setup  P Prev         - PrevPage A Add Value   Z Print
                C [Change Val] N Next      Spc NextPage D Delete Val   W WhereIs
```

Specifying a From Address in Pine

One option in Pine is important for users of the POP or IMAP family of protocols. Because your email address is typically not hosted on your local workstation, but rather on a mail server at a separate host, you need to explicitly tell Pine to use an email address other than the default (which is constructed using your login name and your workstation's hostname).

To specify your email address, scroll nearly all the way to the bottom of the setup configuration to the option called customized-hdrs and select it by pressing Enter. At the prompt, enter a complete From: header in the following form:

```
From: My Name <myaddr@myserver.com>
```

For example, if your name is Jack Henry and your email address is jackhenry@mycompany.com, you enter the following in the customized-hdrs option:

From: Jack Henry <jackhenry@mycompany.com>

After you have exited setup saving your changes, Pine uses this address as the default "from" address for email until it is changed.

Composing Mail Using Pine

To compose a new message from Pine's Main Menu, press the c key or use the arrow keys to navigate to Compose Message, and then press Enter (refer to Figure 8.5). You can also press the c in the message list or view screens discussed in the following sections to compose a new message. A new Compose Message screen is displayed, as shown in Figure 8.8.

FIGURE 8.8

Use the up- and down-arrow keys to navigate between the address and subject fields at the top of the Pine message composer screen.

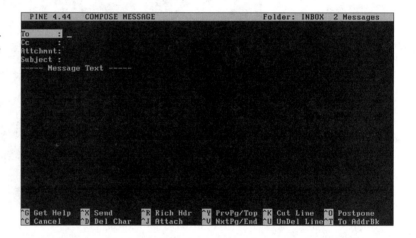

At the top of the Compose Message screen are four fields: To:, Cc:, Attchmnt:, and Subject:. Fill in each field, using the up and down arrows to switch between them. When you finish filling the fields, press the down arrow repeatedly to move the cursor into the message editor area of the screen.

You can find an expanded listing of keystroke commands in almost every screen in Pine by pressing the o key repeatedly.

You are now in the `pico` editor, a subcomponent of Pine that works like a simple text editor. Notice that `pico` automatically word-wraps your text and supports user-friendly arrow-key movement and editing keys, such as Backspace and Delete. Notice that a number of editing keystrokes are listed along the bottom of the screen; the carat (^) means that you invoke the keystroke by holding down the Ctrl key and pressing the letter indicated (see Figure 8.8).

After you have finished editing a message and are ready to send it, use the ^X keystroke (Ctrl+X) to actually send the message out across the network. To cancel a message, use the ^C (Ctrl+C) keystroke.

Reading Mail Using Pine

To use Pine to read mail from your default mailbox (the one `fetchmail` services), select the Folder List screen at the Main Menu by typing **l** or by scrolling down to the Folder List option and pressing Enter. Then, select INBOX and press Enter again. You are then at the message list display, as shown in Figure 8.9.

FIGURE 8.9

The Pine Message Index screen lists messages contained in the default INBOX folder, and it displays a list of keystroke commands you can use in this screen.

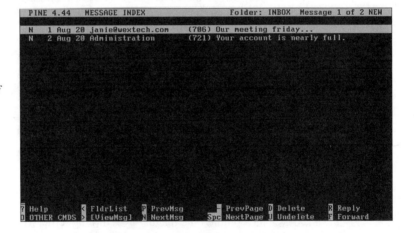

You can navigate within this list of messages, using the arrow keys to select individual messages and the Enter key to display them. Other available keys are shown at the bottom of the display (see Figure 8.9). Pressing the o letter shows still more available keystrokes. Messages marked with the letter N on the far left are messages that you haven't yet viewed.

After a message has been displayed, as shown in Figure 8.10, you have a number of choices for dealing with the message. The most common keystrokes used at the message viewer screen are shown in Table 8.2.

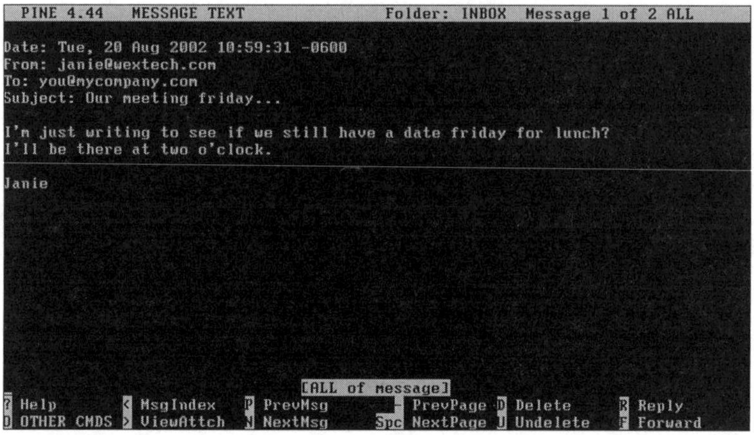

FIGURE 8.10

The Pine message viewer is more user-friendly than the message viewer in mail.

```
  PINE 4.44    MESSAGE TEXT              Folder: INBOX  Message 1 of 2 ALL
Date: Tue, 20 Aug 2002 10:59:31 -0600
From: janie@wextech.com
To: you@mycompany.com
Subject: Our meeting friday...

I'm just writing to see if we still have a date friday for lunch?
I'll be there at two o'clock.

Janie




                                    [ALL of message]
? Help            < MsgIndex  P PrevMsg       - PrevPage D Delete   R Reply
O OTHER CMDS > ViewAttch  N NextMsg     Spc NextPage U Undelete  F Forward
```

TABLE 8.2   Common Keystrokes at the Pine Message Viewer

Key	Meaning
n	Display next message in message list.
d	Mark the currently displayed message for deletion (the marked test will be purged when you exit Pine).
r	Reply to the current message (launches the message composer with either empty body or body containing quoted message, depending on your configuration).
f	Forward the current message (launches the message composer with message body containing current message and forward note).

Other keystrokes are listed at the bottom of the Message Text display; you can find still more keystrokes by repeatedly pressing the o key.

Getting Help and Quitting Pine

You can access a nice online Pine manual by returning to the Main Menu (use the m key from anywhere but inside the Compose Message screen) and pressing the ? key. Alternatively, you can select the Help menu option at the Main Menu and press Enter.

When you are ready to exit Pine, press the q key from either the Main Menu, the message list, or the message viewer. Pine prompts you to confirm that you want to exit, and then returns you to the command line, after purging all messages marked for deletion.

To read more about using Pine, please see the Pine documentation in the
`/usr/share/doc/pine-4.44` folder. Some of it is in HTML (Web) format. You
can read this documentation at the console comfortably with Lynx. To do so,
enter the following command:

`[you@workstation20 you]$ lynx /usr/share/doc/pine-4.44/index.html`

Logging In to a Remote Linux or Unix System

Remote logins are a way of accessing the command line, processor, storage, and network resources of one computer, using another computer from somewhere else on a network. They are one of the most powerful features of Unix-like operating systems, and one of the most important reasons for being able to use Linux at the console. After you have mastered the command line, you will not only be able to use workstations or servers in the same room as you without need for graphics; you will also be able to connect to nearly any machine worldwide that is running a Unix-like operating system, provided you have access to log in, and then use it to its full potential.

To illustrate, suppose you live in Chicago, but are responsible for a Red Hat Linux computer system on your company's network in San Francisco. In the past, this system was just a secretary's desktop computer, but the boss wants this computer system to be turned into a Web server. Using remote logins, you could connect to the computer in San Francisco, install a full-featured Web server program such as Apache, create Web content for the server to display, remove the old password and data files used by the secretary, and place the system online to serve Web pages to the Internet—all without ever leaving the Chicago office.

Remote logins involve two systems:

- A *client* system from which the connection originates, and on which you will be running either the `telnet` or the `ssh` command.
- A *server* system, on which a `telnet` or Secure Shell (`ssh`) server program accepts the incoming connection and provides the remote user with a command prompt. The `telnet` and `ssh` server(s) are the software systems that actually manage remote logins, providing remote login service to the connecting user.

Both `telnet` and `ssh` provide similar functionality. However, because `telnet` is not entirely secure, it is generally a good idea to use `telnet` only between two systems that lie behind the same corporate or personal firewall (that is, on the same local network), or when you absolutely must log in remotely but ssh is unavailable. The Secure Shell (ssh) system is newer than telnet, and it encrypts its communications for much better security. You will sometimes find that older systems do not accept ssh requests, however, because they only support telnet.

Logging In Remotely Using telnet

The telnet command is the oldest, least secure, but also most widely supported method of logging in remotely to Unix-like operating systems. Nearly any Linux system, Unix system, or Unix-like system connected to a network is capable of offering remote logins using the telnet command. Unfortunately, telnet does not encrypt the data it sends over the network, so anything you do or anything you type (including your password) could conceivably be intercepted by a malicious user. Because of this, it is best to use telnet behind a firewall.

To log into a remote system using telnet, enter the telnet command supplying the domain name of the system you want to log in to as an argument. For example, to log in to a computer called workstation8.mycompany.com, you enter the following command:

```
[you@workstation20 you]$ telnet workstation8.mycompany.com
Trying 192.168.242.36...
Connected to 192.168.242.36.
Escape character is '^]'.

Red Hat Linux release 8.0 (Psyche)
Kernel 2.4.18-7.80 on an i686

workstation8 login:
```

Note that after the connection has been made to the remote system in question, a ery familiar login: prompt appears. The process of logging in after connecting with telnet is exactly the same as the process of logging in at the console of your local workstation, provided you have an account on the remote machine.

After you have logged in to the remote machine, any commands you execute will affect *only that machine* rather than the machine you are logged in *from* (that is, the machine sitting in front of you). The range of commands available to you on the remote system will often seem familiar to you, given what you know about Linux so far—in many cases, they are the same commands and techniques you have been learning so far. On the other hand, you might at times find that you have logged in to a system whose commands do not seem familiar to you. In such cases, you need documentation for the operating system on the *remote* computer in order to be able to use it.

8

To log out of the remote machine again, use the `logout` command:

```
[you@workstation8 you]$ logout
Connection closed by foreign host.
[you@workstation20 you]$
```

While you are working with remote logins, pay special attention to command prompts; the hostname of the machine you are currently working on is usually displayed in your command prompt. Though this is not the case for all remote systems (especially if the remote systems in question are not running Red Hat Linux or command prompts have been specially altered), by watching the changes in command prompts you can often determine whether you are working on your local system or on a remote system at any given moment.

> Sometimes when you are logged on to a remote system, something will go awry—you'll get caught in a runaway process or task that cannot be aborted, for example. In cases such as this, use the escape keystroke, ^] (Ctrl+]) to bring up a `telnet>` prompt. At this prompt, you can then type **close** to close the connection followed by quit to exit `telnet`.

Logging In Remotely Using `ssh`

For logins that occur using the public Internet and are great physical distances apart, the ssh or *secure shell* client is a better choice, if it is offered on the system to which you must connect, because ssh encrypts all exchanged data (including passwords).

To log in to a remote host using ssh, use the following command syntax:

```
ssh -l login host
```

Here, *login* represents the name of your login account on the remote system and *host* indicates the domain name or IP address of the remote system. For example, if you had an account called jackhenry on a remote host at pc4.faraway.com, you log in with the following:

```
[you@workstation20 you]$ ssh -l jackhenry pc4.faraway.com
```

Note that ssh tries to uniquely identify each remote host by keeping track of private identification information. If this is your first time logging in to a particular remote host with ssh, you get a message stating that the remote host's identity can't be verified:

```
The authenticity of host 'pc4.faraway.com (10.4.3.3)' can't be established.
RSA key fingerprint is 48:f5:8b:d2:87:50:53:43:df:e3:10:52:17:d6:14:26.
Are you sure you want to continue connecting (yes/no)?
```

Answering yes to this question adds the remote host to the list of known identities and you will be prompted for your password.

```
Are you sure you want to continue connecting (yes/no)? yes
Warning: Permanently added '10.4.3.3' (RSA) to the list of known hosts.
jackhenry@10.4.3.3's password:
```

After you have entered your password, you are logged in and have access to the command prompt on the remote system. To log out again, you can use the logout command by typing **logout** at the command prompt and pressing Enter.

If, while logging into a familiar system, you suddenly receive an error message stating that the identity information on file doesn't match, you will know that either the remote host or the connection has been compromised—hijacked by malicious users in order to steal your data.

In such cases, always contact the network administrator of the remote system for further instruction before logging in.

Not all hosts support ssh logins. If you find that ssh doesn't work for logging into a host where you are supposed to have a remotely accessible account, you need to fall back to the telnet command, which should work for most hosts that accept remote logins and yet do not accept ssh logins. Even better, consider asking the administrator of the remote host to add support for ssh, in the interest of enhancing network security.

Exchanging Files with Linux/Unix Hosts Using ftp

At times it becomes necessary to transfer files over the network between two computer systems. The command traditionally used to transfer files between two Linux or Unix systems is ftp, which stands for *file transfer protocol*.

As with remote logins, you can use an ftp client only with systems that allow incoming ftp connections with an ftp server. If you find, while following the instructions in this section, that your connect attempts fail with an error message, it is likely that the remote system does not accept file transfer protocol connections.

Starting `ftp` and Logging In

Full use of the `ftp` command also requires that you connect to a remote system and then log in with an account and password; you will thus have to be known on the remote system before you can connect via `ftp`.

To connect to a remote system with `ftp`, enter the `ftp` command at the command prompt supplying the domain name of the system you want to connect to as an argument. You are then prompted for your account and password before being delivered to the file transfer prompt. In this example, a connection is made with a system having the hostname `archive3.mycompany.com`:

```
[you@workstation20 you]$ ftp archive3.mycompany.com
Connected to archive3.mycompany.com (10.6.2.2).
220 archive3 FTP server (Version wu-2.6.1-20) ready.
Name (10.6.2.2:you): jackhenry
331 Password required for jackhenry.
Password:
230-Please read the file README.TXT
230-  it was last modified on Fri Aug  2 15:43:13 2002 - 18 days ago
230 User jackhenry logged in.
Remote system type is UNIX.
Using binary mode to transfer files.
ftp>
```

After you log in, you are sitting at the `ftp>` transfer prompt, from which `ftp` commands can be entered to list, upload, or download files.

> Like `telnet`, `ftp` does not encrypt data as it is sent, meaning that `ftp` is best used behind a firewall.
>
> An enhanced alternative command, `sftp`, works the same way but provides encryption just as `ssh` does. Remote systems that support `ssh` also usually support `sftp`; consider using `sftp` under these circumstances.

Navigating an `ftp` Login

You will find that being logged into a remote system via `ftp` is not unlike sitting at a remote system's command prompt in some ways. As is the case with a "normal" command prompt, you can display a present working directory with `pwd`. You can list files and directories with `ls`, and you can use the `cd` command to navigate to other directories that you have permission to visit.

There is, however, one major difference between using the ftp screen and a remote system command prompt. When logged into ftp, you have not one present working directory, but *two*—the one on the local system and the one on the remote system. These dual working directories facilitate the transfer of files between the two systems; files are normally copied between the local and remote present working directories. The process of transferring files therefore involves the following steps (see the commands to implement them in Table 8.3 and a sample session in the next section):

1. Set the remote present working directory to the location where the source file lies or where the destination file is to be created.

2. Set the local present working directory to the location where the source file lies or where the destination file is to be created.

3. Copy the file from one system to another using get (to copy from the remote present working directory to the local one) or put (to copy from the local present working directory to the remote one) .

Some of the more fundamental commands that can be used in an ftp session are shown in Table 8.3.

TABLE 8.3   Common ftp Commands

Command	Meaning
ls	List files in the remote present working directory.
!ls	List files in the local present working directory.
pwd	Print the remote present working directory.
!pwd	Print the local present working directory.
cd *path*	Change the remote present working directory to *path* (may be an absolute path or a relative path).
lcd *path*	Change the local present working directory to *path* (may be an absolute path or a relative path; note the l rather than the exclamation mark!).
get *file*	Transfer *file* from the remote present working directory to the local present working directory.
put *file*	Transfer *file* from the local present working directory to the remote present working directory.
close	Close the current connection to the remote server.
open *server*	If no connection currently exists, open a new connection to *server*.
quit	If no connection currently exists, exit ftp and return to the command prompt.

Because this process and command set can seem much more complicated than it actually is, a sample session will be helpful for illustration purposes.

Sample `ftp` Session

Suppose you have just successfully logged into your account on a remote `ftp` server. In most cases, your local present working directory is the same present working directory you were using when you started `ftp`. At the same time, your remote present working directory often begins as `/home/youraccount` on the remote system (in this case, `/home/jackhenry`).

In this session, the goal is to copy files as follows:

- `/home/you/basicfile.txt` (local) -> `/home/jackhenry/basicfile.txt` (remote)
- `/home/you/textfiles/mypaper.tex` (local) -> `/home/jackhenry/documents/mypaper.tex` (remote)
- `/home/jackhenry/images/mypicture.gif` (remote) -> `/home/you/mypicture.gif` (local)

Because the first source file is located in the home directory of the local system and is to be copied to your home directory on the remote system, no changes in the present working directory need to be made. Simply put the first file:

```
ftp> put basicfile.txt
local: basicfile.txt remote: basicfile.txt
227 Entering Passive Mode (10,6,2,2,225,31)
150 Opening BINARY mode data connection for basicfile.txt.
226 Transfer complete.
115 bytes sent in 0.00075 secs (1.5e+02 Kbytes/sec)
ftp>
```

The first file has now been copied from the local system to the remote system. The next file resides in the `textfiles` directory on the local system and will be put into the `documents` directory on the remote system, so some changes to present working directories are required:

```
ftp> lcd textfiles
Local directory now /home/you/textfiles
ftp> !pwd
/home/you/textfiles
ftp> cd documents
250 CWD command successful.
ftp> pwd
257 "/home/jackhenry/documents" is current directory.
ftp>
```

Now that both present working directories are correct (as has been verified with `!pwd` and `pwd`), you can put the file:

```
ftp> put mypaper.tex
local: mypaper.tex remote: mypaper.tex
227 Entering Passive Mode (10,6,2,2,120,95)
150 Opening BINARY mode data connection for mypaper.tex.
226 Transfer complete.
101842 bytes sent in 0.014 secs (7.1e+03 Kbytes/sec)
ftp>
```

Finally, you must retrieve a file called `mypicture.gif` from a remote directory and store it in the local home directory:

```
ftp> lcd /home/you
Local directory now /home/you
ftp> !pwd
/home/you
ftp> cd ../images
250 CWD command successful.
ftp> pwd
257 "/home/jackhenry/images" is current directory.
ftp> get mypicture.gif
227 Entering Passive Mode (10,6,2,2,232,161)
150 Opening BINARY mode data connection for mypicture.gif (220376 bytes).
226 Transfer complete.
220376 bytes received in 0.179 secs (1.2e+03 Kbytes/sec)
ftp>
```

All the files in the list have now been transferred; you can close the connection:

```
ftp> close
221-You have transferred 322333 bytes in 3 files.
221-Total traffic for this session was 323337 bytes in 3 transfers.
221 Thank you for using the FTP service on archive3.
ftp> quit
[you@workstation20 you]$
```

If you find yourself transferring files that seem "broken" or corrupted afterward, you are likely not transferring in binary mode. To switch to binary mode after connecting to a server, enter the word **binary** at the ftp> prompt.

If you find that the rather verbose debugging output of the ftp client program bothers you, you can switch it off by entering the word **verbose** at the ftp> prompt.

For a list of additional ftp commands, enter **help** at the ftp> prompt; for a brief description of each command, enter **help** *command* at the ftp> prompt.

Exchanging Files with Windows Hosts Using smbclient

It is also relatively easy to browse and exchange files with Windows hosts from the Linux command line, provided you are somewhat familiar with the process of copying files from computer to computer on Windows networks and the use of the ftp command on Linux or Unix networks.

The command used for exchanging files with Windows hosts is called smbclient. Though smbclient isn't hard to use, it is important that you at least know the name of the Windows host with which you want to exchange files. If you don't know the name of the Windows host with which you want to communicate, ask your network administrator or consult the Network Neighborhood or My Network Places icons on a Windows desktop computer on your network.

Listing the Shares on a Windows Host

A *share* is a hard drive or storage area on a Windows host that has been made available to other network users. To list the shares on a Windows host using smbclient, call smbclient from the command line with the -L option and the name of the host as an argument. You are prompted for a password. If there is no password required to list the shares on a given host, press Enter. A sample result is shown in Listing 8.1.

LISTING 8.1 Sample smbclient Output

```
 1  [you@workstation20 you]$ smbclient -L newton
 2  added interface ip=192.168.1.24 bcast=192.168.1.255 nmask=255.255.255.0
 3  Got a positive name query response from 192.168.1.52 ( 192.168.1.52 )
 4  Password:
 5
 6          Sharename       Type        Comment
 7          ---------       ----        -------
 8          WinSpace1       Disk        9GB General-purpose
 9          WinSpace2       Disk        9GB General-purpose
10          MediaDrive1     Disk        30GB Fast video storage
12          MediaDrive2     Disk        45GB Fast video storage
13          Optical         Disk        1.3GB Pinnacle Sierra Optical Drive
14          lp              Printer
15
16          Server                  Comment
17          ------                  -------
18          NEWTON                  Primary video workstation
19
20          Workgroup               Master
21          ---------               ------
22          WORKGROUP               SUPERSERV
23  [you@workstation20 you]$
```

Listing 8.1 shows that the Windows host called NEWTON (line 18) in the workgroup called WORKGROUP (line 22) is sharing a number of hard drives, an optical drive, and a printer (lines 8–14). When you know the name of the share you want to access, you can connect to that share directly using smbclient.

Connecting to a Windows Share

To connect to a Windows share using smbclient, supply the full name of the share you want to connect to (including host) as an argument to smbclient in the traditional format, enclosed in quotation marks or single quotes. You are prompted for a password. If there is no password required to access the share, press Enter:

```
[you@workstation20 you]$ smbclient '\\newton\mediadrive1'
added interface ip=192.168.1.24 bcast=192.168.1.255 nmask=255.255.255.0
Got a positive name query response from 192.168.1.52 ( 192.168.1.52 )
Password:
smb: \>
```

After you have connected and entered the correct password, if necessary, you are at the smbclient prompt.

Navigating and Copying Files with smbclient

After you are familiar with ftp, you will find that using smbclient is easy; the commands are largely the same, as is the method of use.

To get a listing of smbclient commands, type **help** at the smb: \> prompt. As was the case with ftp, you can access a description of each command by typing **help** *command* at the prompt.

After you have transferred files to and/or from the Windows host as necessary, you can close the connection simply by typing **quit** at the smb: \> prompt. After typing the **quit** command, you are returned to the Linux command line.

Summary

This hour, you learned to make your way around your local area network and around the larger Internet from the Linux command line. You learned to use a number of command-line networking applications including Lynx and Pine, two mainstays of Unix command-line diehards.

Having finished this hour, you should feel comfortable doing any of the following things from the command line:

- Visiting and bookmarking a Web page
- Sending an email to a friend

- Logging into another Linux system and running several commands from its command line
- Copying files from a Windows host to your Linux workstation using the network

After this hour and the preceding hours, you should be familiar with the methods needed to accomplish most basic housekeeping, productivity, and network tasks from the command line; next hour you deal with advanced command-line use as you finish your lessons at the Linux console.

Q&A

Q I have been instructed to log in to a machine anonymously using ftp. What does this mean?

A An anonymous login can best be thought of as a guest login for public use; when you log in to a remote system anonymously, you have access only to certain restricted files and directories that the system administrator wants to make public. To log into anonymously, use either **anonymous** or **ftp** as your login name (they are functionally identical), and then enter your email address as a password. Then, log in and use ftp as usual.

Q When I use telnet or ssh to connect to a remote system, I am sometimes disconnected for no apparent reason if I am inactive for a little while. Why?

A In order to protect remote login sessions from being hijacked by malicious users, many system administrators implement a default remote login timeout—a period after which you are automatically disconnected if you haven't pressed the a key.

Workshop

The Workshop is designed to help you anticipate possible questions, review what you've learned, and begin learning how to put your knowledge into practice.

Quiz

1. What must you do to your ~/.fetchmailrc file for security reasons before you can use it to collect your email?

2. When should you use the telnet command for remote logins? When should you use ssh?

3. What is the difference between cd and lcd, pwd and !pwd, and ls and !ls?

Answers

1. You must use chmod og-rwx to remove read, write, and execute permissions for everyone but you, the file's owner.

2. You should use telnet only when ssh connection attempts are not answered by the remote system. When this is the case, you should consider asking the administrator of the remote system to add support for ssh.

3. In each case, the former command (cd, pwd, ls) operates on the local system in an ftp session, and the latter command (lcd, !pwd, !ls) operates on the remote system.

Activities

1. Try using either the ssh or telnet command to log into another Linux or Unix system on the network on which you have an account.

2. Use Pine to send an email message to someone you know.

3. Try using the smbclient command to access the public files on a nearby Windows system.

Hour 9

Harnessing the Power of the Shell

This hour represents the last of our Linux command-line training lessons. In it, you learn many of the more advanced techniques for interacting with the shell. This hour is not exhaustive by any means; the focus is on basic skills and on whetting your appetite for more, in hopes that you'll study more man pages or even read a more in-depth shell book or two.

This hour you learn how to

- Work with text, perform calculations, and do other useful tasks using some advanced commands from within shell scripts.
- Understand the basic format of a shell script.
- Use variables and variable expansion inside a shell script to allow you to perform more complex tasks or tasks involving many steps.
- Make a shell script into an executable command and accept command-line arguments and options with your script.
- Control flow with conditional statements or other techniques inside a shell script.

Because this hour is all about shell scripts, be prepared to spend a lot of time working inside a text editor, such as vi or emacs. If you've forgotten how these editors work or don't feel familiar with them any longer, you might want to review Hour 5, "Making the Console Work for You," before continuing.

Adding to Your Command Repertoire

Shell scripting is a way of building new, custom-made commands for yourself out of existing Linux tools and commands. Using shell scripts, you can shorten tasks that normally involve many steps into just one step—which you design.

Before you begin shell scripting, it will be help to become familiar with a few Linux commands that you haven't learned about in previous hours of this book. Each of these can make your life easier when you're shell scripting.

It isn't important to memorize this information; just become familiar enough with it that you have a general idea about which commands you can use for specific tasks in Red Hat Linux.

Sending Text to Standard Output with echo

The echo command is simple; it takes anything you supply as an argument and "echoes" it by printing it to standard output. echo is one of the commands that appears most often in shell scripts, largely because it enables a shell script to have output—that is, to provide information to the user. Examples seem almost silly:

```
[you@workstation20 you]$ echo "Hello, how are you?"
Hello, how are you?
[you@workstation20 you]$
```

You'll often use echo to allow commands (scripts) you create to ask questions of the user or to display the results of a calculation or operation. It is always a good idea to enclose the text you want to echo in quotes, as shown here, so that the shell doesn't try to interpret special characters, such as the asterisk (*) or question mark (?), for pattern matching.

Performing Simple Calculations with expr

The expr command provides a way of evaluating arithmetic expressions from the command line. Though expr doesn't do floating-point (fractional) math, it is nonetheless a simple, useful command. Supply the numeric and operational parts of the expression as arguments:

```
[you@workstation20 you]$ expr 3 + 4
7
[you@workstation20 you]$ expr 144 + 13666 / 10
1510
[you@workstation20 you]$ expr 10 - 10
0
[you@workstation20 you]$
```

> The common operator for multiplication on a computer is the asterisk (*).
> Recall that at the command prompt, this is also a character that performs
> filename expansion. Because you want to provide expr with mathematical
> operators and not with a list of matching filenames, always remember to
> enclose the asterisk in quotes when using expr:
>
> ```
> [you@workstation20 you]$ expr 3 '*' 36
> 108
> [you@workstation20 you]$
> ```

Because each number and operator in the computation is a separate argument, you should
always take care to separate the numbers and operators with spaces.

Displaying Text File Beginnings or Endings with `head` and `tail`

Sometimes it is useful to be able to display only the first few lines or only the last few
lines of a text file. The head and tail commands can be used to accomplish this. Usually
head and tail are used with one option, a dash followed by the number of lines to display:

```
[you@workstation20 you]$ head -4 myfile.txt
This is line 1 in a file called myfile.txt that is 16 lines long.
This is line 2 in a file called myfile.txt that is 16 lines long.
This is line 3 in a file called myfile.txt that is 16 lines long.
This is line 4 in a file called myfile.txt that is 16 lines long.
[you@workstation20 you]$ tail -2 myfile.txt
This is line 15 in a file called myfile.txt that is 16 lines long.
This is line 16 in a file called myfile.txt that is 16 lines long.
[you@workstation20 you]$
```

For example, suppose you want to find the document class details of a LaTeX file called
mylatexfile.tex. Rather than loading the entire file into an editor such as vi or emacs,
you could use the head command to display the first line of the file:

```
[you@workstation20 you]$ head -1 mylatexfile.tex
\documentclass[letterpaper,12pt]{article}
[you@workstation20 you]$
```

Editing Streams of Data with `sed`

Sometimes it is also useful to be able to edit streams of data on-the-fly before outputting them. The command used to do this is the *stream editor*, `sed`, one of the most widely used commands in the Unix world.

The most common way to use `sed` is to have it accept a stream of data through a pipe, providing as an argument a command on how the data `sed` receives should be changed. Though there are many `sed` commands, only one of them, the most common one, is covered in this hour. It is the s (substitute) command, and works in either of two ways:

```
sed 's/search/replace/'
```

```
sed 's/search/replace/g'
```

In both cases, `search` is a string of text that is to be searched for and `replace` is the text that should replace it. If a g is appended to the end of the argument, all occurrences of `search` will be replaced with the text in `replace`; if there is no g, only the first occurrence will be replaced. Note that nearly any character can be substituted for the slash / if necessary (allowing you to use the slash in the `search` or `replace` strings when you need to do so). Note that you also can provide multiple commands to `sed` by separating them with semicolons inside the quote.

Here are some examples of `sed` used in combination with `head`, which provides input to `sed` through a pipe:

```
[you@workstation20 you]$ head -4 myfile.txt | sed 's/file/stupid file/'
This is line 1 in a stupid file called myfile.txt that is 16 lines long.
This is line 2 in a stupid file called myfile.txt that is 16 lines long.
This is line 3 in a stupid file called myfile.txt that is 16 lines long.
This is line 4 in a stupid file called myfile.txt that is 16 lines long.
[you@workstation20 you]$ head -4 myfile.txt | sed 's/file/silly file/g'
This is line 1 in a silly file called mysilly file.txt that is 16 lines long.
This is line 2 in a silly file called mysilly file.txt that is 16 lines long.
This is line 3 in a silly file called mysilly file.txt that is 16 lines long.
This is line 4 in a silly file called mysilly file.txt that is 16 lines long.
[you@workstation20 you]$ head -4 myfile.txt | sed 's!line 2!line 2 2/3!'
This is line 1 in a file called myfile.txt that is 16 lines long.
This is line 2 2/3 in a file called myfile.txt that is 16 lines long.
This is line 3 in a file called myfile.txt that is 16 lines long.
This is line 4 in a file called myfile.txt that is 16 lines long.
[you@workstation20 you]$ head -4 myfile.txt | sed 's/e 2/e 5/;s/e 4/e 7/'
This is line 1 in a file called myfile.txt that is 16 lines long.
This is line 5 in a file called myfile.txt that is 16 lines long.
This is line 3 in a file called myfile.txt that is 16 lines long.
This is line 7 in a file called myfile.txt that is 16 lines long.
[you@workstation20 you]$
```

In the last command, two commands were used—data was piped through sed to change the number 2 to the number 5 in the first command (before the semicolon), and the number 4 to the number 7 in the second command (after the semicolon).

For a more real-world example, consider what most people would call a search-and-replace function. Suppose you had written a long novel using LaTeX in which you'd named the main character Evan—and now you want to change his name to Sebastian. Rather than load the long LaTeX file into a text editor and use the search-and-replace functionality, you could simply use sed and output redirection:

```
[you@workstation20 you]$ sed 's/Evan/Sebastian/g' MyNovel.tex > MyNewNovel.tex
[you@workstation20 you]$
```

Just like that, you have created a new copy of your novel, MyNewNovel.tex, in which the main character's name appears as Sebastian—no additional work needed.

You can use the dollar sign ($) and carat (^) in a sed command to match the end or beginning of a line, respectively. For example, to substitute the text goodbye with farewall *only when goodbye occurs at the end of a line*, use the following sed command:

```
s/goodbye$/farewell/'
```

Similarly, to substitute the text Hello with Greetings *only when Hello occurs at the beginning of a line*, use the following sed command:

```
s/^Hello/Greetings/'
```

The sed command is a staple in the Unix world because it is much more powerful than the few examples here have demonstrated. sed is especially powerful when its pattern matching capabilities are used.

To learn more about sed, please take time to study the sed manual page at your leisure; it will likely prove helpful to you as you use the shell on an ongoing basis.

Using Shell Variables and Quoting

Before you begin to create scripts, let's look at two concepts that will become increasingly important as you deal with the complexity of the tasks at hand. These concepts are shell variables (and variable substitution) and quoting.

Variables are special words that, when expanded, are replaced by values that you've assigned to them. The shell provides a built-in process for creating and keeping track of variables, known as *variable substitution*. Variable substitution enables you to generalize commands that are included in shell scripts, making it possible for you to change the way a script acts (for example, the files it will affect) simply by changing the values of the variables it uses.

The use of variables in shell scripts involves three basic steps:

1. The creation of a variable, usually by simply assigning a value to a word using the equals sign.

   Usually, this also involves using quotation marks to enclose the assigned value, to ensure that you're not misinterpreted by the shell.

2. Later in your script, indicating to the shell that you want the value of the variable to be substituted for the variable's name exactly where it appears.

   This is done by prefixing the name of your variable with a dollar sign ($).

3. Enclosing (when expanding a variable in the midst of other text) the name of the variable in braces ({}), to clarify to the shell the name of the variable you are trying to expand.

For example, through the use of variables, you can write a script that performs a specific set of operations on a file without having to explicitly name the file in the script—thus allowing the *user* to name the file that should be affected each time the script is run.

Creating and Substituting Variables

To understand how to create variables, assume for a moment that in your work on a day-to-day basis, you often encounter people stopping by your desk to request printouts of these documents—`newempl.txt`, `hours.txt`, and `phonebook.txt`—all of which are stored in `/home/you/textfiles`. The command you know to print these files from any present working directory is

```
[you@workstation20 you]$ lpr /home/you/textfiles/newempl.txt /home/you/textfiles/
➥hours.txt /home/you/textfiles/phonebook.txt
[you@owrkstation20 you]$
```

One way to reduce the amount of typing you have to do is to use a variable. You can create a variable to hold the names and paths of the files you need to repeatedly print, saving yourself the trouble of typing all the names and path information:

```
[you@workstation20 you]$ PRINTFILES="/home/you/textfiles/newempl.txt /home/you/
➥textfiles/hours.txt /home/you/textfiles/phonebook.txt"
[you@workstation20 you]$
```

You have now created a variable called PRINTFILES, which holds the list of filenames you so often need to print. To use the variable, substitute it for the file and pathname information in a command line. From now on, whenever you want to print these three files from this shell session, you can simply type

```
[you@workstation20 you]$ lpr $PRINTFILES
[you@workstation20 you]$
```

This command is much shorter! But how does it work? The shell is replacing the word PRINTFILES by the contents of the variable PRINTFILES. To see this effect with a command that makes it more clearly visible, try using the echo command to display the value of PRINTFILES:

```
[you@workstation20 you]$ echo $PRINTFILES
/home/you/textfiles/newempl.txt /home/you/textfiles/hours.txt /home/you/
➥textfiles/phonebook.txt
[you@workstation20 you]$
```

Because the shell replaced PRINTFILES with the value you assigned to it before calling the echo command, echo outputs the value you assigned to PRINTFILES.

After you have created a variable, you can substitute the value of the variable anywhere at the command line or in a script by preceding the name of the variable with a dollar sign ($).

When variable names are ambiguous, you can also enclose the name of a variable in braces ({}) to indicate to the shell exactly where the variable name begins and ends.

For example, assume that you want to use the contents of the variable WORD immediately before the number 2000 in a script—the shell might mistakenly assume that you are referring to a variable called WORD2000:

```
[you@workstation20 you]$ WORD=YEAR
[you@workstation20 you]$ echo $WORD2000

[you@workstation20 you]$ echo ${WORD}2000
YEAR2000
[you@workstation20 you]$
```

By enclosing the name of your variable, WORD, in braces, you show the shell which variable name should be expanded—WORD, the variable you created, rather than a variable called WORD2000 that you did not intend to create.

Quoting Carefully

When you create variables, it is usually a good idea to enclose the value you want to assign in quotation marks. This tells the shell that you want to assign *exactly* the value inside the quotes, rather than expanding patterns or other variables or treating values separated by spaces as arguments or commands. There are several types of quoting that can be done at the command line; variables can be created or assigned using any of them:

```
VARIABLE=value
```

```
VARIABLE="value"
```

```
VARIABLE='value'
```

Each of these is subtly different. The first method (no quoting) is the simplest. However, because the shell normally uses a number of characters in special ways, such as the space to separate arguments or the vertical bar (|) to create a pipe, quoting is necessary if you want to assign these characters to a variable:

```
[you@workstation20 you]$ MYNAME=Horace Walpole
bash: Walpole: command not found
[you@workstation20 you]$ MYNAME="Horace Walpole"
[you@workstation20 you]$
```

In this case, quoting is needed to prevent the shell from using the space as a separation value. Among the other characters that must be enclosed in quotes if assigned to variables are parentheses (( )), braces ({ }), and brackets ([ ]). There is also a difference between the result of enclosing data in single quotes and the result of enclosing data in double quotes. In double quotes, although most special characters are ignored, command and variable subsitution are still performed; in single quotes, they are not. This difference is subtle and perhaps best illustrated by example. Consider the following sequence:

```
[you@workstation20 you]$ QUOTEA="My name is $MYNAME."
[you@workstation20 you]$ QUOTEB='My name is $MYNAME.'
[you@workstation20 you]$ echo $QUOTEA
My name is Horace Walpole.
[you@workstation20 you]$ echo $QUOTEB
My name is $MYNAME.
[you@workstation20 you]$
```

As you can see here, when a phrase is placed within single quotes, the dollar sign ($) ceases to be a special character. When a phrase is placed within double quotes, the dollar sign retains its special meaning and variables will be substituted as necessary, though other special characters will lose their unique functionality. Here is an example using the date command and command substitution which simply prints the current date to standard output:

```
[you@workstation20 you]$ date
Thu Aug 21 14:34:02 MDT 2002
```

```
[you@workstation20 you]$ TIMEA="The time right now is $(date)."
[you@workstation20 you]$ TIMEB='The time right now is $(date).'
[you@workstation20 you]$ echo $TIMEA
The time right now is Thu Aug 21 14:34:14 MDT 2002.
[you@workstation20 you]$ echo $TIMEB
The time right now is $(date).
[you@workstation20 you]$
```

Because quoting can so radically affect the behavior of shell variable substitution and shell command substitution, it's important to gain an understanding of the way it works. Feel free to experiment a little longer with variables and quoting until you feel comfortable using them.

Environment Variables

Before you finish looking at variables and quoting, it is important to learn about a special class of variables known as *environment variables*. These are variables that tell the shell how to behave as you work at the command line or in scripts; changing the value of these variables changes some behavioral aspect of the shell.

The single most important environment variable is PATH. The PATH variable contains a list of all the directories that are known to hold commands. When you type a command at the command line, the shell searches through all the directories listed in PATH until it finds a program by that name. The shell loads and runs the program (in reality, a command) and passes on to it any arguments you have supplied. Try printing the contents of PATH now:

```
[you@workstation20 you]$ echo $PATH
/usr/local/bin:/bin:/usr/bin:/usr/X11R6/bin:/home/you/bin
[you@workstation20 you]$
```

In this case, the shell searches for commands in /usr/local/bin, /bin, /usr/bin, /usr/X11R6/bin, and /home/you/bin, in that order. To see where the shell eventually finds any given command, you can use the which command:

```
[you@workstation20 you]$ which emacs
/usr/bin/emacs
[you@workstation20 you]$
```

This means that when you type emacs at the command line, the shell uses the PATH variable to search in /usr/local/bin and /bin before finally finding emacs in /usr/bin. If you add to the PATH variable, you can cause the shell to search in more places:

```
[you@workstation20 you]$ PATH="/usr/sbin:$PATH"
[you@workstation20 you]$ echo $PATH
/usr/sbin:/usr/local/bin:/bin:/usr/bin:/usr/X11R6/bin:/home/you/bin
[you@workstation20 you]$
```

You have now added an additional directory, /usr/sbin, to the PATH; /usr/sbin will be searched first for the remainder of this shell session whenever a command is entered.

Perhaps the most important thing to notice about the default value of PATH in Red Hat Linux is the fact that /home/you/bin appears in it. This means that as you create shell scripts throughout the rest of this hour, you will be able to place them in the bin directory in your home directory and then use them like any other command.

For more information on the available environment variables and their functions, please see the manual page for bash.

Creating Your Own Commands Using Shell Scripting

Now that you've acquired a sizable amount of experience using the console and the shell, have learned a number of common commands, and are familiar with concepts such as pipes, command substitution, variable substitution, and quoting, it's time to begin creating shell scripts.

A shell script is really a way of automating complex tasks or repetitive sequences of commands that you often carry out at the shell so that you don't have to type these commands over and over each time you want to repeat the task. Often, the sequences of commands in shell scripts are complex enough that your shell scripts really become new commands, tailor-made to your productivity needs.

Structurally, a shell script is a plain text file that contains normal commands just as you might type them at the command line, in the order in which you want them to be executed when the script is run. In more complex shell scripts, you might also find various special control statements that are interpreted and acted upon by the shell. These can cause the shell to call extra commands or to ignore some commands in the script, depending on user input or testable environmental conditions—such as the existence (or nonexistence) of a particular file or directory.

Beginning a Shell Script

To create a shell script, launch your favorite editor (generally vi or emacs) and create a new file called myscript. On the very first line of this file, enter the following:

```
#!/bin/sh
```

This line indicates to Linux that the file you are creating is a shell script. When you call myscript from the command line, Linux checks the first line of the file, realizes that it is a shell script, and then calls the shell, /bin/sh, to execute your list of commands.

Processing Command-Line Arguments

The simplest use of shell scripting is to automate a series of commands you often use, in order to avoid always having to type them.

Recall that in Hour 7, "Working Without the Mouse," you learned that printing a LaTeX file in Linux is a two-step process. First, you must run your input file through the formatter with the `latex` command to produce a `dvi` file. Then, you must use `dvips` to print the file. You can use shell scripting to create a command that automates this process. The goal for our first script is to create a command that enables the user to pass one argument—the name of a `.tex` file—and have the file both formatted and printed without needing to enter further commands.

You create this command using a special set of variables that hold command-line arguments. Within a shell script, the shell creates a special set of variables called 1, 2, 3, and so on to hold the command-line arguments entered by the user when the shell script was called. Using `$1`, `$2`, `$3`, and so on therefore substitutes the value(s) of the argument(s) the user provided.

Consider the script in Listing 9.1. In this script, you are creating a variable named `LATEXFILE` and assigning to it the value of the special variable `$1`. That means that the the first argument passed to `myscript` will end up in the variable `LATEXFILE` as the script is running.

> Notice that nearly everything in `myscript` is enclosed in double quotes. In Linux, filenames may contain spaces. To access filenames that contain spaces, the filename needs to be quoted. By quoting every place where a file is accessed in `myscript`, you guarantee that the script will work if it is ever called with a filename containing one or more spaces as an argument.

LISTING 9.1 A Shell Script Called `myscript`

```
#!/bin/sh
LATEXFILE="$1"
DVIFILE="$(echo "$LATEXFILE" | sed 's/tex$/dvi/')"
latex "$LATEXFILE"
dvips "$DVIFILE"
```

The second variable assignment in `myscript` is considerably more involved than the first, but it is manageable. The entire value of the variable is enclosed in `$()`, meaning that the value of `DVIFILE` will be obtained through command substitution—in other

words, the output of the commands inside the parentheses becomes the value of
DVIFILE.

Inside the parentheses, you do two things. First, the echo command echoes the value of
LATEXFILE. Remember that this value is the name of a .tex file that was passed to
your script by the user. You then use the vertical bar to pipe the output of echo to the sed
command, where you change the .tex to .dvi. Thus, if the value of LATEXFILE is
myfile.tex, the assigned value of DVIFILE is myfile.dvi. If you want to see this at
work outside a script, try typing it at the command line:

```
[you@workstation20 you]$ echo myfile.tex | sed 's/tex$/dvi/'
myfile.dvi
[you@workstation20 you]$
```

The rest of the script in Listing 9.1 is simply a list of commands the shell is to execute.
The script calls LaTeX with the name of the .tex file supplied by the user. You already
know that when LaTeX formats this .tex file, the result is a .dvi file by the same name
in the same directory as the original file.

Because a .dvi file can be printed with the dvips command, your script then performs
this second step, calling dvips and supplying as an argument the .dvi file by the same
name. This command prints the file.

Making myscript Easily Executable

After saving myscript, you have a file called myscript in /home/you which contains all
the commands necessary to allow the shell to automate the printing of .tex files for you.
Naturally, you want to try the script out to see if it works. However, you can't do that
just yet.

Recall that the shell maintains an environment variable called PATH that contains the list
of directories in which commands are found. Before this script can be used like other
commands, you must move it into one of the directories listed in the PATH variable so
that the shell can find it, and then give it executable permissions so that the shell can
execute it. Because /home/you/bin appears in the PATH environment variable, you can
prepare the script for execution by making sure that /home/you/bin exists (using mkdir
to create it if it doesn't), then using mv to move the script there and chmod to set executable permissions:

```
[you@workstation20 you]$ mkdir ~/bin
[you@workstation20 you]$ mv myscript ~/bin
[you@workstation20 you]$ chmod u+x ~/bin/myscript
[you@workstation20 you]$ ls -l ~/bin
total 4
-rwxrw-r--    1 you       you            115 Oct  1 13:52 myscript
[you@workstation20 you]$
```

Let's try it out:

```
[you@workstation20 you]$ myscript myfile.tex
[...loads of output...]
```

If you tried this experiment on a real LaTeX file, you should have enjoyed success—the file was formatted and printed. You have created a new command! The name myscript is a little generic, so let's rename it:

```
[you@workstation20 you]$ mv ~/bin/myscript ~/bin/lxprint
[you@workstation20 you]$
```

The new command myscript has now been renamed lxprint and its calling syntax is as follows:

```
lxprint filename.tex
```

Here, *filename.tex* represents the name of the .tex file that should be printed.

Using Conditional Statements

Sometimes in a shell script it is helpful to execute part of the script if some condition is true, or a variable holds some specific value. Perhaps you want a particular script to generate printed output only if the user calls the script with the -print option, or perhaps you want a script to create a new file only if a file by the same name doesn't already exist. This technique of omitting or including certain parts or behaviors of a script depending on current cicumstances or user input is called *conditional execution*.

The most basic form of conditional execution in shell scripts is used with the following syntax. Here, the first set of commands is executed only if *test expression* is true. The optional word else precedes a second set of commands that will be executed only if *test expression* is not true.

```
if [ test expression ]; then
    command
    command
    ...
else
    command
    command
    ...
fi
```

The term *test expression* refers to one of a number of different kinds of tests and comparisons that can be performed. The most common of these are shown in Table 9.1; many more can be found in the manual page for test.

TABLE 9.1 Common Test Expressions

Expression	Meaning
val1 = *val2*	True if the word or quoted text item *val1* is identical to the word or quoted text item *val2*
val1 != *val2*	True if the word or quoted text item *val1* is not identical to the word or quoted text item *val2*
val1 -gt *val2*	True if the numeric value of item *val1* is greater than the numeric value of item *val2*
val1 -lt *val2*	True if the numeric value of item *val1* is less than the numeric value of item *val2*
val1 -eq *val2*	True if the numeric value of item *val1* and the numeric value of item *val2* are equal
-e *file*	True if *file* is the name of an existing file of any kind
-f *file*	True if *file* is the name of an existing regular file (not a device or a directory)
-d *directory*	True if *directory* is the name of an existing directory
-x *command*	True if *command* is the name of an existing file that is marked as executable

To illustrate conditional execution, let's modify lxprint in two ways. First, let's add a few lines so that if the user supplies the classic --help as an option, lxprint prints a help message. Then, let's force lxprint to verify that a file actually exists before it tries to call latex or dvips. If the file doesn't exist, lxprint should display an error message.

The new and improved lxprint is shown in Listing 9.2.

LISTING 9.2 The New and Improved lxprint

```
1  #!/bin/sh
2
3  if [ "$1" = --help ]; then
4      echo "Use lxprint to print out LaTeX files in one easy step."
5      echo "Just supply the name of a .tex file as an argument!"
6      exit
7  fi
8
9  LATEXFILE="$1"
10
11 if [ -f "$LATEXFILE" ]; then
12     DVIFILE="$(echo "$LATEXFILE" | sed 's/tex$/dvi/')"
13
14     latex "$LATEXFILE"
15     dvips "$DVIFILE"
```

LISTING 9.2   continued

```
16 else
17      echo "There doesn't seem to be a file called $LATEXFILE."
18      exit
19 fi
```

This listing includes two conditional statements. The first one, which begins on line 2 and ends on line 7, checks to see whether the argument supplied by the user is really actually the word --help. If it is, a help message is displayed. The second conditional statement, which begins on line 11 and continues through line 19, checks for the existence of the file the user has asked to be formatted and printed. If the file exists, formatting and printing commence. If the file does not exist, an error message is printed.

> It's traditional to indent four spaces for each new level of nesting in a script. Indenting commands within if...then conditional statements is not mandatory. However, in complex scripts in which if...then statements can occur within other if...then statements, indentation can make it much easier to visually understand how a script works.

Notice that one final command has also been introduced here. The exit command can be used to exit a shell script and return to the command prompt.

Let's try the two new conditional chunks of our script, first by calling lxprint with the argument --help, and then by calling it with a nonexisting filename:

```
[you@workstation20 you]$ lxprint --help
Use lxprint to print out LaTeX files in one easy step.
Just supply the name of a .tex file as an argument!
[you@workstation20 you]$ lxprint nosuchfile.tex
There doesn't seem to be a file called nosuchfile.tex.
[you@workstation20 you]$
```

The changes are functional and the lxprint command has been further improved.

Testing Over and Over Again

The types of tests shown in Table 9.1 aren't only for use with if...then statements. They can also be used with another type of statement, known as the while...do statement, which follows this format:

```
while [ test expression ]; do
    command
    command
    ...
done
```

The difference between if...then and while...do is that in the former case, commands are executed a single time if the test condition is true and in the latter case, they are executed again and again and again as fast as the computer can execute them until the condition is false.

Let's continue to use lxprint as our test case. When working with publishing projects involving multiple documents, it isn't uncommon to have multiple source files. For example, a large project called 02projections might be split across several files ending in sequence numbers:

```
02projections1.tex
02projections2.tex
02projectison3.tex
```

It would be nice if lxprint could accept a base name like 02projections and then be smart enough to print all the files in the set in sequence. Using a while loop and some more conditional statements, this can be done easily. The result is shown in Listing 9.3. This script includes comments—lines that begin with a hash mark (#)—and are inserted for the benefit of humans only. The shell ignores comments.

LISTING 9.3   The New lxprint Command Incorporating Sequence Printing

```
 1 #!/bin/sh
 2
 3 # If the user uses '--help' as an argument,
 4 # we want to display a help message.
 5
 6 if [ "$1" = --help ]; then
 7     echo "Use lxprint to print out LaTeX files in one easy step."
 8     echo "Just supply the name of a .tex file as an argument!"
 9     echo "  * or the base name of a numbered sequence of .tex files"
10     echo "    to print them all!"
11     exit
12 fi
13
14 LATEXFILE="$1"
15
16 # If the filename supplied as an argument exists,
17 # then print it out.
18 if [ -f "$LATEXFILE" ]; then
19     DVIFILE="$(echo "$LATEXFILE" | sed 's/tex$/dvi/')"
20
```

LISTING 9.3   continued

```
21      latex "$LATEXFILE"
22      dvips "$DVIFILE"
23 else
24
25      # If the filename doesn't exist as supplied, see if
26      # it's a base filename -- for example, if the user
27      # supplied '02projections' as an argument and the file
28      # '02projections1.tex' exists, then the user wants to
29      # print the entire sequence.
30
31      if [ -f "${LATEXFILE}1.tex" ]; then
32
          # The variable COUNTER will hold the current number
33          # in the sequence we're printing. We'll start at
34          # 1 and use expr to add one to it each time we
35          # print another file.
36
37          COUNTER=1
38
39          while [ -f "$LATEXFILE$COUNTER.tex" ]; do
40              echo "Printing $LATESFILE$COUNTER.tex"
41              latex "$LATEXFILE$COUNTER.tex"
42              dvips "$LATEXFILE$COUNTER.dvi"
43              COUNTER=$(expr $COUNTER + 1)
44          done
45
46      else
47
48          echo "There doesn't seem to be a file called $LATEXFILE."
49          exit
50
51      fi
52 fi
```

9

The execution of lxprint is gradually getting more complex. Now when lxprint starts, it first checks to see whether the user has sent --help as an argument in lines 6–12. If this isn't the case, it checks to see whether the user has supplied a valid filename in line 18; if the user has, the file is formatted and printed in lines 19–22. If the argument isn't a valid filename, lxprint checks to see whether it might be a base filename by adding a number and the .tex extension to it in line 31. If it is, lxprint formats and prints all the files in the set, in sequence, by using a while..do loop and the COUNTER variable, which holds the number of times the commands in the loop have been executed so far; this happens in lines 37–44. So long as another file in the sequence seems to exist, the loop is executed again and the value of COUNTER increases by 1.

Take a moment to study the script, the use of `expr`, and command and variable substitution as they appear here. It might seem daunting at first, but you should eventually be able to follow the flow of the script as it is written.

Repeatedly Executing for a Predefined Set

Although the `if..then` and `while..do` statements both work by performing a test and making a decision based on the result, another statement, the `for..do` statement, simply executes a set of commands for every element in a list. For example, the `for..do` loop provides ideal functionality for performing the same set of operations on each file in a long list of files. The syntax is

```
for var in item1 item2 item3 ...; do
    command
    command
    ...
done
```

The `for..do` statement first assigns the value *item1* to the shell variable *var* and then executes the commands inside the statement. After it reaches `done`, it assigns the value *item2* to the shell variable *var* and executes the commands inside the statement again. This continues until there are no more *item*s.

Let's illustrate the use of the `for..do` loop by giving the `lxprint` command one more capability—to print *every* `.tex` file in a user's current working directory if the user supplies `--all` as an argument or option. This can easily be done with a well-placed `for..do` statement. The updated and final `lxprint` is shown in Listing 9.4.

LISTING 9.4   The `lxprint` Command with the `--all` Capability Added

```
 1  #! /bin/sh
 2
 3  # If the user uses '--help' as an argument,
 4  # we want to display a help message.
 5
 6  if [ "$1" = --help ]; then
 7      echo "Use lxprint to print out LaTeX files in one easy step."
 8      echo "Just supply the name of a .tex file as an argument!"
 9      echo "  * or the base name of a numbered sequence of .tex files"
10      echo "    to print them all!"
11      echo "  * or --all to print every .tex file in the pwd!"
12      exit
13  fi
14
15  # If the user supplies --all as an argument, then use
16  # filename expansion and a for..do statement to print
17  # every .tex file in the present working directory, one
```

LISTING 9.4   continued

```
18 # by one. Then exit.
19
20 if [ "$1" = --all ]; then
21    for LATEXFILE in *.tex; do
22        echo "Printing $LATEXFILE"
23        DVIFILE="$(echo "$LATEXFILE" | sed 's/tex$/dvi/')"
24
25        latex "$LATEXFILE"
26        dvips "$DVIFILE"
27    done
28    exit
29 fi
30
31 LATEXFILE="$1"
32
33 # If the filename supplied as an argument exists,
34 # then print it out.
35 if [ -f "$LATEXFILE" ]; then
36    DVIFILE="$(echo "$LATEXFILE" | sed 's/tex$/dvi/')"
37
38    latex "$LATEXFILE"
39    dvips "$DVIFILE"
40 else
41
42    # If the filename doesn't exist as supplied, see if
43    # it's a base filename -- for example, if the user
44    # supplied '02projections' as an argument and the file
45    # '02projections1.tex' exists, then the user wants to
46    # print the entire sequence.
47
48    if [ -f "${LATEXFILE}1.tex" ]; then
49
50        # The variable COUNTER will hold the current number
51        # in the sequence we're printing. We'll start at
52        # 1 and use expr to add one to it each time we
53        # print another file.
54
55        COUNTER=1
56
57        while [ -f "$LATEXFILE$COUNTER.tex" ]; do
58            echo "Printing $LATEXFILE$COUNTER.tex"
59            latex "$LATEXFILE$COUNTER.tex"
60            dvips "$LATEXFILE$COUNTER.dvi"
61            COUNTER=$(expr $COUNTER + 1)
62        done
63
64    else
65
66        echo "There doesn't seem to be a file called $LATEXFILE."
```

LISTING 9.4   continued

```
67          exit
68
69    fi
70 fi
```

The change in Listing 9.4 is relatively small, but potentially confusing because `*.tex`
looks like a single item. Remember, though, that the shell uses the `*` if it is not enclosed
in quotes to "expand" to a list of matching filenames. So in this case, `*.tex` is replaced
by a space-separated list of `.tex` files, as if you'd typed them yourself. The `for..do`
statement then uses this list as the basis for the value of the `LATEXFILE` variable as it executes the commands between the `do` and the `done` in lines 21–27. At the end of the
`for..do` statement, `exit` in line 28 returns the user to the command prompt.

Beyond Shell Scripting

Believe it or not, all the techniques we've documented so far this hour can be used
directly at the command line as well as from within shell script files. Though `if..then`
has limited utility when entered directly at the command line, `while..do` and especially
`for..do` can have incredible utility on a day-to-day basis.

To use one of these structures at the command line, enter it as you would in a script.
After you begin a loop or conditional statement, the shell prompt changes and remains
altered in appearance until you reach the closing `fi` or `done`; then the commands in the
loop are executed. For example, you can use a similar `for..do` loop to the one in Listing
9.4 to print all the .txt files in your home directory to the printer; use the `*.txt` pattern
as your `for..do` list and the lpr command inside the loop:

```
[you@workstation20 you]$ for GONNAPRINT in *.txt; do
> lpr "$GONNAPRINT"
> done
[you@workstation20 you]$
```

Notice how the prompt changed after you entered the `for..do` line and remained different until you entered the word `done`. After entering `done`, the shell sends every file ending with .txt in the current working directory to the printer with the `lpr` command.
Over time, you'll find unexpected uses for `for..do` and to a lesser extent, `while..do` and
`if..then` everywhere you look—sometimes when you least expect them.

Shell scripting is a very powerful application development tool; there are a large number
of techniques, statements, structures, commands, and facilities offered by the shell that
are not discussed in this book. For more in-depth information on shell scripting and shell
programming, I recommend the following two books, which cover shell scripting and the
`bash` shell commonly used with Linux in detail:

- *Sams Teach Yourself Shell Programming in 24 Hours* by Sriranga Veeraraghaven
- *Learning the bash Shell* by Cameron Newham and Bill Rosenblatt

Summary

This hour, you learned to harness the power of the Linux shell to create your own power-ful, functional commands in just a few minutes using shell scripting. Specific topics you learned about in this hour include

- Creating, assigning values to, and substituting variables
- The different types of quoting and how to use them for variable and command sub-stitution
- The PATH environment variable and its implications for commands and shell scripts
- Assigning execute permissions to your script and moving it to a directory listed in PATH so that it can be easily called
- The if..then conditional statement structure
- The while..do conditional statement structure
- The for..do conditional statement structure

After you've spent some time practicing the techniques you learned in this hour, you will be able to use techniques such as command substitution and filename expansion, along with the wide variety of shell commands you learned earlier to employ the shell effi-ciently.

Though use of the console and the shell prompt might seem like a blur to you after these few short hours, as you refer back to them while using Linux, you'll gradually become more familiar with the command-line personality of Linux and other Unix-like operating systems. In time, you'll come to feel at home on the command line to the same extent that you do at a graphical desktop.

Q&A

Q I'm trying to write a long shell script and it's not working like I expect it to. Are there any tools to help me see exactly what the shell is doing when my script is running?

A Yes. Inserting the special command set -x into your shell script causes the shell to display everything it does afterward, one line at a time, as your script is running. Inserting the special command set +x later in your script turns this debugging fea-ture off again.

Q **When I try to use quotes at the command line, I often end up trapped by a strange prompt that doesn't seem to accept any commands. Why?**

A If you're stuck at a prompt that looks like a greater-than symbol, it means you've used unbalanced quotes somewhere in your command. These can take the form of mismatched quotation marks (one single and one double) or an uneven number of quotes (meaning that you've forgotten to close a set of quotes somewhere). The shell is waiting for a matching close quote for an opening quote that you've entered. Try entering a single quote or a double quote; one of these should return you to the command prompt.

Q **I'm trying to experiment with shell scripts, but my script `test` doesn't seem to do anything at all, no matter what I put in it! Why?**

A There is actually a `test` command at `/usr/bin/test` that the shell is likely finding before it finds your `test` script. Thus, `/usr/bin/test` is being executed instead. The easiest solution is to rename your script to something else using the `mv` command.

Workshop

The Workshop is designed to help you anticipate possible questions, review what you've learned, and begin learning how to put your knowledge into practice.

Quiz

1. What is the functional difference between single quotes and double quotes when assigning values to variables?

2. What special character causes the value of a variable to be substituted?

3. How do you test for the existence of a directory in an `if..then` statement?

4. In the statement `for MYVAR in a b c d e; do`, which begins a `for..do` loop, what values will the variable `MYVAR` hold?

5. What do the carat (`^`) and dollar sign (`$`) characters do when used in a `sed` command?

Answers

1. When a value is assigned in single quotes (`'`), variable and command substitution are not performed even if a dollar sign (`$`) appears in the value. When a value is assigned in double quotes (`"`), variable and command substitution are performed before the value is assigned the variable.

2. The dollar sign ($).

3. `if [ -d directory ]; then`, where *directory* is the name or path of the directory you want to test for.

4. The commands inside the loop will be executed five times. The values of MYVAR each time through the loop will be `"a"`, `"b"`, `"c"`, `"d"`, and `"e"`, in that order.

5. The carat matches the beginning of a line; the dollar sign matches the end of a line.

Activities

1. Experiment with quoting and assigning values to variables, and then expand them using the echo command. Do this until you feel familiar with the way variable assignment and substitution works.

2. Study the final listing of the lxprint command until you feel confident that you understand how every line in it works.

3. Try modifying the lxprint script to make sure that when the user passes a file-name as an argument, it is a .tex file and not some other kind of file. (*Hint:* there are at least two ways to do this, both using command subsitution and an if..then statement; one uses the grep command and the other uses sed.)

9

HOUR 10

Introducing the Red Hat Desktop

Although you spent a great deal of time getting to know the Linux console in earlier chapters, most of the work you do with Red Hat Linux will take place through a graphical user interface (GUI). By the time you finish this hour, you will be comfortable enough with the Linux desktop to do some exploring on your own.

In this hour, you learn how to manage all of the Red Hat Linux desktop basics, including

- Logging in and identifying the basic parts of the Red Hat Linux desktop
- Selecting an alternate desktop environment
- Launching applications through the desktop menu
- Manipulating application windows
- Working with virtual desktops
- Logging out

The Linux GUI, unlike the GUI used by Windows or Mac OS, is highly modular. Because of this, there are a number of different graphical working environments commonly used by Linux users, each of which provides its own system of menus, icons, behaviors, and benefits. Red Hat Linux includes two of these, the GNU Network Object Model Environment (GNOME) and the K Desktop Environment (KDE). Both are powerful, integrated working environments that should seem familiar to Windows users, at least superficially.

Notes on GNOME and KDE in Red Hat Linux 8

Unless you chose to customize your Linux installation in Hour 2, "Installing Red Hat Linux," you have installed the GNOME environment on your computer system. Red Hat Linux installs GNOME by default, because its development is supported by Red Hat and because most of the Red Hat administration tools are integrated with (that is, share an appearance and set of behaviors with) the GNOME environment, though they also function in the KDE environment.

In other Linux operating systems, there are significant differences between the GNOME and KDE environments, which are obvious even to casual users. The most important difference is that in other Linux operating systems, the GNOME and KDE environments offer different sets of applications—different Web browsers, different office productivity applications, and so on. In Red Hat Linux 8, however, the GNOME and KDE environments have been retooled to be very close to one another in terms of appearance and functionality; they also share a common set of applications. Only experienced Linux users are therefore likely to see the difference between the two in Red Hat Linux 8.

Because of these changes, the next several chapters of this book focus primarily on accomplishing various desktop tasks using GNOME, because it is Red Hat's default environment of choice for new users. Thanks to Red Hat's modifications to KDE, in most cases the tasks discussed in these chapters can be performed in exactly the same way in the KDE environment, though the examples and illustrations show the GNOME environment. You can use these hours to work through either environment. Where significant differences exist, KDE-specific sections appear in the chapters to help you accomplish equivalent tasks in the KDE environment.

Logging In to the Desktop

The Linux security model requires that all users must log in to the system before they can use applications, create files, and so on. This requirement also applies to the Red Hat Linux desktop. When you boot Red Hat Linux, you eventually find yourself face to face with the desktop login prompt, shown in Figure 10.1.

FIGURE 10.1

The Red Hat Linux desktop login prompt appears after you boot the system.

To log in, simply enter your account name, press Enter, and then enter your password. If you enter your information correctly, you are soon greeted by the Red Hat GNOME desktop, as shown in Figure 10.2.

The components of the GNOME desktop shown in Figure 10.2 include

- The taskbar lies at the bottom of the screen and provides menus and icons to launch applications, a visual representation of already running applications, and a clock to show the time.

- Application launchers are icons that start Linux applications when they are clicked.

- The GNOME Menu (a picture of a red hat) shows a list of menus and additional applications when clicked; in the KDE environment, this is known as the KDE menu, though its appearance is the same.

- Desktop icons provide a graphical way to open storage devices or browse through or discard your files.

- The desktop selector enables you to switch between virtual desktops—the GUI equivalent of virtual consoles.

- The system clock shows the current time.

Desktop icons

FIGURE 10.2

The default Red Hat GNOME desktop holds the tools you need to start working with applications.

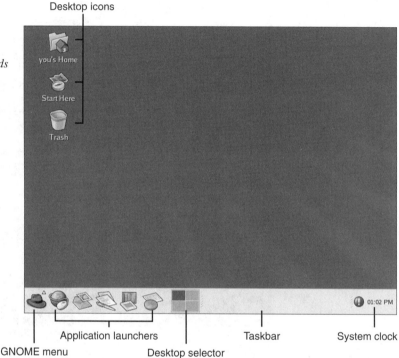

GNOME menu   Application launchers   Taskbar   System clock

Desktop selector

You can also choose to log in to KDE from the login prompt. After entering your username at the Red Hat Linux login prompt, click the word Session at the bottom of the login display. You are presented with a menu enabling you to select an environment. Select KDE and a dialog appears, explaining that your default setting is Default. This means that if you don't specify otherwise, Red Hat logs you in to the environment you most recently used. If you want to make KDE your default desktop environment, select Yes.

When you choose KDE as your default desktop environment, you open it each time you log in to begin a new session on the desktop. You can change this default setting later by clicking the Session button at the bottom of the login screen.

When you log into the KDE environment for the first time, you are presented with a configuration dialog that asks for your current location and language of preference. After you select your preference and click Next, KDE starts for the first time. The components of the KDE desktop match those of the GNOME desktop and appear in the same positions; refer to Figure 10.2 for details.

Navigating the Desktop

If you use Windows, Macintosh, or any GUI operating system, you should feel right at home in the Red Hat Linux graphical interface. Most of the components of the Red Hat desktop should seem familiar to you, regardless of the computing platform you're accustomed to.

Across the bottom of the display is the taskbar, containing a number of icons. The taskbar is designed to give you immediate access to frequently used processes and information. You click its icons to open menus, launch programs, or select a desktop format. Starting at the left, here's what the taskbar contains:

- The icon marked with a Red Hat is the GNOME Menu button (or in the KDE environment, the KDE Menu button), which gives you access to all the major applications, tools, and tasks you can perform in the desktop, including logging out.

- The icon marked with a rocket circling earth launches the Web browser.

- The icon that looks like a letter and envelope launches the email program.

- The "document and pen" icon launches the OpenOffice Writer word processor.

- The "bar chart and slide" icon launches the OpenOffice Impress presentations manager, a program you can use to prepare slide shows and other format business presentations.

- The final icon launches the OpenOffice Calc spreadsheet program, used for preparing calculations and formatting them as graphs.

To the right of these icons is the desktop selector, which looks like a quartered rectangle; you learn more about using the desktop selector later this hour. At the far right of the taskbar is the system clock.

Down the left side of the desktop display are other icons. These icons, too, give you one-click access to frequently used tools and folders. You learn how to add your own icons to the desktop later, but the icons that appear there by default are

- The Home icon opens a folder that contains your home directory (similar to My Documents in Windows). After you double-click the icon to open your directory, you can open documents listed in the directory by double-clicking on them.

10

- The Start Here icon duplicates most of the functionality of the GNOME Menu (or KDE Menu) but allows you to double-click on icons to perform these tasks.
- The Trash icon is a clickable shortcut to a folder that contains all your deleted files. You can drag files and drop them in this folder.

Icons for any removable media (such as a CD-ROM) will also appear on your desktop below these icons, when you insert a disk or CD.

Launching Applications

Click the GNOME Menu icon at the lower left of the display. Here you'll find a listing of the most commonly used system commands and submenus of utilities, tools, and applications, organized by category. Hover your mouse cursor over any submenu to open it; Figure 10.3 shows the Accessories submenu opened. Clicking the entry for a specific application launches that application in a new window.

Take a moment to familiarize yourself with the menu, and then move the mouse over the Text Editor entry in the Accessories submenu and click to launch the Text Editor application.

FIGURE 10.3

The GNOME Menu icon enables you to launch a wide variety of applications.

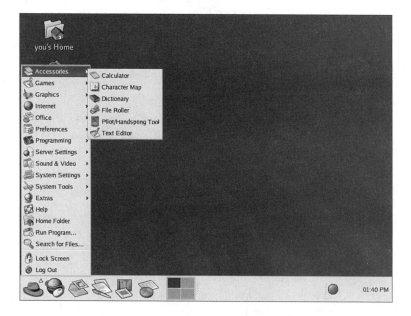

Throughout the rest of the text, when you are to choose a series of menu items or commands, you'll see each choice separated by a comma. So, for example, instructions for clicking the GNOME Menu icon to open the GNOME Menu, hovering over the Accessories submenu listing to open that menu, and then clicking the Text Editor listing to open the text editor, would read

Choose GNOME Menu, Accessories, Text Editor.

When you click Text Editor, the text editor opens in its own application window. Figure 10.4 shows the GNOME text editor, gedit, along with callouts to its window control icons.

When you open an application in the Red Hat Linux desktop, an icon representing that application appears in the taskbar (in Figure 10.4, this button is labeled Untitled 1 - gedit). You can click these buttons to move between open application windows.

10

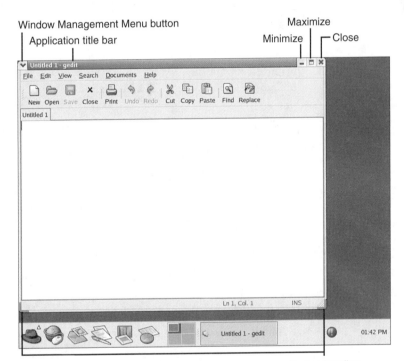

FIGURE 10.4

The text editor opens in its own window, with a toolbar of icons for common text editing tasks, including Cut, Paste, Print, and others.

Using Window Controls

The application window of the text editor in the Red Hat Linux graphical interface works much like the Windows version you might be accustomed to. Here is a list of the window controls and their use:

- **The Window Management menu button.** Click this button to display a list of actions relevant to the application window.
- **The Application title bar.** This area displays the name of the application and in some cases the current file open in that application.
- **The Minimize Window button.** Click to hide the application window (you can click the application's taskbar button to restore it).
- **The Maximize Window button.** Click to expand the application window to fill the desktop.
- **The Close Window button.** Click to close the window and the application.

> You can click and drag elements in the Red Hat Linux graphical interface windows, just as you can in a Windows interface. Click and drag by clicking the element and holding the mouse button down as you move the cursor to drag the element to the desired position.

Moving, Resizing, Minimizing, and Maximizing Windows

By clicking or clicking and dragging elements of application windows, you can change their size, shape, and position to suit your needs and to enhance your workflow. This small collection of standard controls enables the user to manipulate the work environment to suit his or her needs.

Try these operations on the gedit window you started earlier:

- To move a window, click on the application title bar and drag the window to the new position.
- The lower corners of the application window are marked with colored edges called Resize Handles; click and drag these handles to resize the application window.
- To cause a window to fill the entire screen, click the Maximize Window button; the application window fills the screen. When you've maximized the window, the Maximize button changes to a Restore Window button.

- To restore a maximized window to its original size, click the Restore Window button.

- To minimize (hide) a window, click the Minimize Window button; the window disappears from the desktop but its taskbar still appears. Brackets around the button indicate that the application is open, but its window has been minimized.

- To display a minimized application window again, click the application's taskbar button; the window reappears on the desktop and the brackets disappear from the window's taskbar button.

- To close (quit) an application, click the Close Window button in the upper-right corner of the window. If you made no changes since last saving the current file, the application closes immediately. If you've made changes since last saving the file, you're asked whether you want to save the changes. Click Yes to save changes and exit the application.

10

Generally speaking, you will find that the window management menu (the window decoration at the upper left) contains little more than a list of items that perform the same tasks as other window decorations, such as minimize, maximize, and close—though there is one important additional use for this menu that will be discussed later this hour in the context of virtual desktops.

Application Menus

Another important set of application controls lies near the top of each application window in the Application menu bar. In gedit, these controls include File, Edit, View, Search, Documents, and Help. Though the items may vary among applications, nearly every application has an application menu bar.

Clicking any item in the Application menu bar displays a menu of relevant options or controls. File and Help appear in most application windows. Though you learn how to use the Help menu in Hour 14, "Getting Help on the Desktop," you might want to take some time now to experiment with this menu and its contents.

Working with Multiple Windows

The true power of any graphical desktop environment lies in its enabling users to quickly and easily work in several open applications at once. The GNOME applications you use with Red Hat Linux offer this capability. To see this capability in action, you can try launching several applications now.

If you don't already have a gedit (text editor) window running, launch one now choosing GNOME Menu, Accessories, Text Editor. So that you have several applications to work with, also choose GNOME Menu, Games, Same GNOME and GNOME Menu, Accessories, Calculator. Each of these applications opens in its own window, and an icon for each appears in the taskbar, as shown in Figure 10.5.

Changing the Active Application

When you have multiple windows open on the Linux desktop, each window's status is indicated in the appearance of its application title bar and taskbar icon. You can enter commands and perform tasks in an active window; in the Linux world, this window is said to be *focused*. Inactive or *unfocused* windows are idle until you click them or their taskbar icon. An unfocused window has a greyed-out application title bar. A focused window's title bar is in color, and its taskbar button appears to be pushed in. When you press a key on your keyboard, only the application that is currently focused will respond to your keypress and act on what you have entered. Applications that do not have focus do not respond.

FIGURE 10.5

The GNOME desktop with three running applications: the gedit text editor, the GNOME Calculator, and the Same GNOME game. The active application is the topmost window (here, the GNOME Calculator). Note that there are now three taskbar buttons.

To change focus, click the target application's taskbar icon or an exposed area of its window. When you do so, the window you select is raised to the top of the stack of windows on your desktop and becomes the new focused window. Figure 10.6 shows the same set of open applications you saw on the desktop in Figure 10.5, but with a new focused application.

If you want to focus a window that's completely covered on the desktop, you can click the window's taskbar icon; this makes the window active, just as though you'd clicked its application title bar.

Minimizing and Restoring with the Taskbar

You can use the taskbar icons to minimize and restore application windows and to switch between active applications. When you click the taskbar icon of the *currently active* window, the window is minimized, as if you had clicked on the Minimize Window button. You can then restore the window by clicking again on the window's taskbar icon.

FIGURE 10.6

After clicking the Same Gnome *application title bar, the* Same Gnome *application window is made active. Notice that other windows are still present and the applications are open; they are simply inactive.*

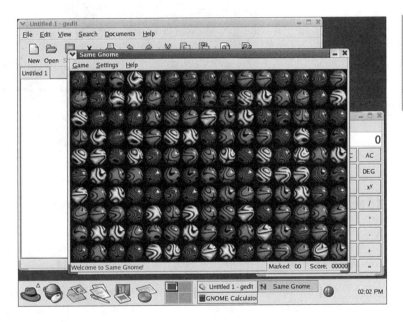

10

Shading a Window

There is one final window operation that can be helpful on crowded desktops. This operation is known as *window shading* and can be accomplished by *double-clicking* (clicking twice in rapid succession) on an application window's title bar. When a window is shaded, only its title bar appears; the rest of the window is hidden. The title bar itself can then be moved or minimized like any application window. Some users find that they are more easily able to navigate the desktop using shaded windows when running out of space than minimized windows; it is a matter of personal preference.

Try shading every running application on your desktop. A desktop with all applications shaded is shown in Figure 10.7.

To restore a shaded window, double-click the title bar once more. The window is restored to its previous size and shape.

FIGURE 10.7

*All application win-
dows on this desktop
have been shaded.
Note that one of the
windows, in this case
the GNOME
Calculator, remains
active; all keypresses
will continue to be sent
to the active window!*

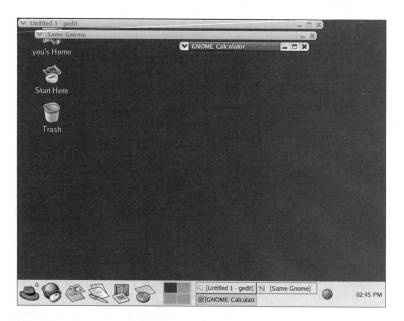

Understanding Virtual Desktops

Many of the window management techniques discussed so far will seem familiar to users of Windows and Mac OS. However, Linux desktops typically offer one function with which converts from other operating systems are generally less familiar.

Virtual desktops are similar in some ways to the *virtual consoles* you used in earlier chapters. Each virtual desktop is a complete desktop, with its own sense of desktop space, its own applications, its own desktop wallpaper, and so on. When you start an application on a Linux desktop, the window for the application you've started appears on a virtual desktop. If you then swith to another virtual desktop, that window is no longer visible, though it is still active; it's invisible because the desktop on which it resides is no longer visible.

Virtual desktops can be used to minimize desktop crowding when you are using many applications at the same time; by starting a few applications on each desktop, you can avoid having to manage a taskbar crammed full of window buttons. Many users also use virtual desktops to categorize their running applications by starting all the Internet-related applications on one desktop, the word-processing applications on another desk-top, and so on.

Knowing Which Desktop Is Active

Earlier in this hour, you saw a reference to a taskbar element called the desktop selector; it's the quartered, rectangular block that appears between the taskbar's program and application window icons. The desktop selector shows which of the virtual desktops is currently active. The virtual desktops themselves are laid out in a kind of side-by-side grid, just as the desktop selector shows.

The default GNOME environment contains four virtual desktops, arranged in a 2×2 grid. The darkened square in the desktop selector is the currently active desktop. Each of the small desktop icons contains a miniature diagram of the windows that currently are displayed.

Selecting a New Desktop

To switch between virtual desktops, click in the desktop selector on the desktop that you want to make active. That desktop is then displayed and the new active desktop is highlighted in the desktop selector.

Figure 10.8 shows the GNOME environment with a new desktop selected. All the applications launched earlier are still running and can be seen in the small icon for the first desktop in the desktop selector.

FIGURE 10.8
The GNOME environment with a fresh virtual desktop selected. Note that the applications started in the other virtual desktop are all still running, as represented by the open window images in that virtual desktop's quarter of the desktop selector.

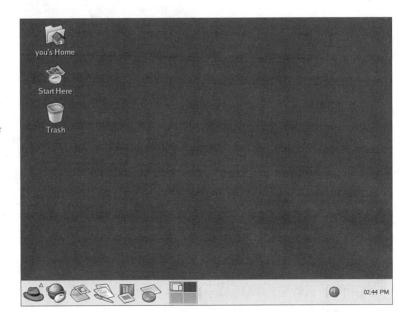

10

Moving a Running Application to a New Desktop

To move a running application window from its current virtual desktop to the same physical position on a different virtual desktop, use the Window Management menu (the button at the extreme upper left of any application window).

In this menu, you find options to move the application in question to any of the four virtual desktops or workspaces. A fifth option, put on all workspaces, causes the application to appear at the same location on the screen no matter which virtual desktop is currently active; as a matter of convenience, this enables you quick access to application windows you use often. When an application is set to appear this way, it is said to be *sticky*. The Window Management menu is shown in Figure 10.9.

FIGURE 10.9

Use the Window Management menu to put running applications on other desktops or to make them sticky.

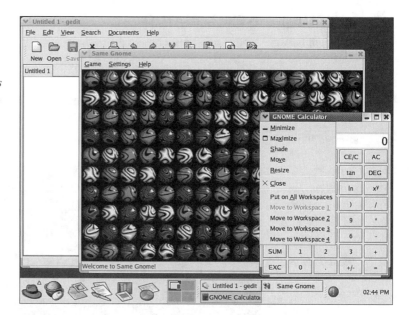

Using the KDE Window Management Menu

The window management menu displayed when clicking at the upper left of any KDE application window is slightly different from the one displayed in the GNOME environment.

With the KDE window management menu, applications are moved between virtual desktops by selecting the To Desktop submenu and then selecting either a specific virtual desktop or the All desktops option to force the application window to be sticky.

An additional option, Always on Top, causes the application window in question to always appear to lie on top of other application windows. After this option is selected, it is not possible to cover the window in question with another application window until the option is selected again. For example, suppose you are using a number of applications on your desktop, but would like the Calculator application to always be visible so that you can quickly and easily access it without having to click on a taskbar button. You might choose to always keep the Calculator on top; this way, it could never be obscured by other application windows.

Logging Out of the GNOME Desktop

To log out of the desktop environment, choose GNOME Menu, Log Out. A dialog with several options is presented, as shown in Figure 10.10. The default selection, Log Out, returns you to the desktop login prompt. Checking the Save Current Setup option causes GNOME to remember the list and positions of your currently running application windows and restore them when you next log in. This dialog also offers two system options: Click Shut Down to shut down the Red Hat Linux system, or choose Restart the computer to shut down and restart the system.

FIGURE 10.10

Logging out of the GNOME desktop environment. Note that you can save your current setup for restoration at your next login.

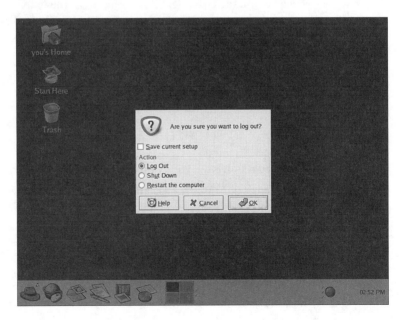

10

Summary

This hour, you logged into the Linux desktop environment of your choice for the first time. For most users, this means logging into the GNOME environment, though for a few users who customized their Red Hat installations, this might mean logging into the similarly configured KDE environment.

In your environment of choice, you learned to identify and use the components of an application window, including

- The application title bar, which indicates focus and provides a convenient way to move or activate a window
- The Minimize Window and Maximize Window buttons, which provide ways to hide a window or cause it to fill the entire display
- The Close Window button, which enables you to exit an application and remove its window
- The Resize Handles, which appear at the bottom of an application window and enable you to change its size

You also began to use the GNOME Menu or the KDE Menu to launch applications and gained some experience using the desktop selector to switch between the four virtual desktops that come configured in the default Red Hat desktop environment.

Finally, you logged back out again, learning how to save the list of running application windows and their locations if you want to have them automatically restored the next time you log back into your Red Hat Linux desktop.

Q&A

Q I do not seem to have KDE available on my system. Why?

A The KDE environment is not installed by default in Red Hat Linux 8.0; the easiest way to install KDE is to choose to customize your list of applications while you are installing Linux and select KDE there.

Because Red Hat has taken care to ensure that the default GNOME and KDE environments do not differ significantly, most novice users will gain little from installing KDE in addition to GNOME.

Q What are the advantages of KDE over GNOME or vice versa?

A The KDE environment provides the advanced user with the opportunity to select a different set of applications (Web browser, email program, and so on) that are more closely integrated than those in the GNOME environment.

Some users also prefer some of the behavioral quirks of the KDE environment (such as the busy mouse cursor while launching applications) over the GNOME environment.

Q When I launch applications, they appear in different places or at different sizes from those shown here. Why?

A Most likely, your desktop is set to display at a different screen resolution (number of horizontal and vertical pixels) than the desktop that was used to make the illustrations for this book. This might cause application windows to appear either larger or smaller relative to our illutrations and can cause new application windows to appear in different positions.

Workshop

The Workshop is designed to help you anticipate possible questions, review what you've learned, and begin learning how to put your knowledge into practice.

Quiz

1. Where can the GNOME Menu and KDE Menu be found?

2. When multiple application windows are present, how do you change the active (focused) application window?

3. When a window is minimized (hidden), how can you restore it to its previous position and appearance?

4. How do you log out of the desktop?

Answers

1. The GNOME Menu appears at the lower left of the GNOME desktop. The KDE Menu appears at the lower left of the KDE desktop. In either case, the menu icon looks like a red hat.

2. Click on a window's title bar or anywhere inside the window to focus it.

3. A minimized window can be restored by clicking on its button in the taskbar.

4. By clicking GNOME Menu, Log Out or KDE Menu, Log Out.

Activities

1. Try starting a number of applications to fill your desktop. Then, experiment by moving them around, minimizing them, and focusing them one by one.

2. Put a running application on another virtual desktop. Then, switch to that desktop to display it.

3. Start a few applications, and then log out, choosing to save your session. Log in again and notice how your applications have been restarted and placed for you.

HOUR 11

Working with Files on the Desktop

In previous hours, you learned about the Linux desktop; you know how to access the desktop and open, move, and close application windows. In this hour, you learn how to use the Linux desktop file management system. You learn how to use the file manager to find, manipulate and display files in Red Hat Linux. You also learn how to use context menus to open, edit, copy, move, or otherwise change the files you've created. You learn a number of specific important skills in this hour, including how to

- Create a new text file with the text editor, and then use the file dialog box to name it.
- Open a file manager window displaying the files contained in your home directory.
- Open an existing file using the file manager, edit it, and save the changes.
- Navigate within a file manager window to other directories in the Linux filesystem.

- Copy or move a file from one directory to another directory using the file manager.
- Change file permissions using the file manager.
- Use the context menu to perform common file management tasks.

Though most of the illustrations and examples in this hour refer to the GNOME desktop and its components, KDE users should be able to follow along as well—both desktop environments support the same types of file management tools and techniques. Important differences between the two are noted wherever they exist.

Creating a New Text File Using the Text Editor

You already know how to create a text file using vi or emacs from the Red Hat Linux command line. While working in a graphical environment, you can use a different, more user-friendly tool to create text files. You learned how to launch a Text Editor window in Hour 10, "Introducing the Red Hat Desktop," by choosing Main Menu, Accessories, Text Editor. Launch a text editor now and enter several lines of text.

 After you have started the text editor, you might notice that the application title bar actually displays the name gedit (if you are working in the GNOME environment). This is the *real* name of the text editor program.

In order to create a new text file containing the lines of text you've entered, you must save the file. To do so, open the File menu and choose Save, as shown in Figure 11.1.

After you have clicked on Save, the Save As file dialog appears. A *file dialog* is a special dialog box that enables you to save or load files into an application by navigating the filesystem graphically, as shown in Figure 11.2.

You'll use the file dialog frequently as you work in Red Hat Linux. Here are its major components and how they're used:

- The *directory navigation pane* contains a list of directories in the application's present working directory. Double-clicking any directory in the list makes it the application's working directory.

FIGURE 11.1

Save your work by choosing File, Save.

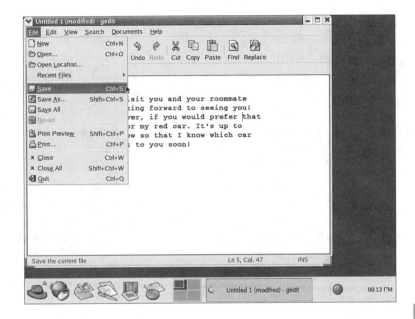

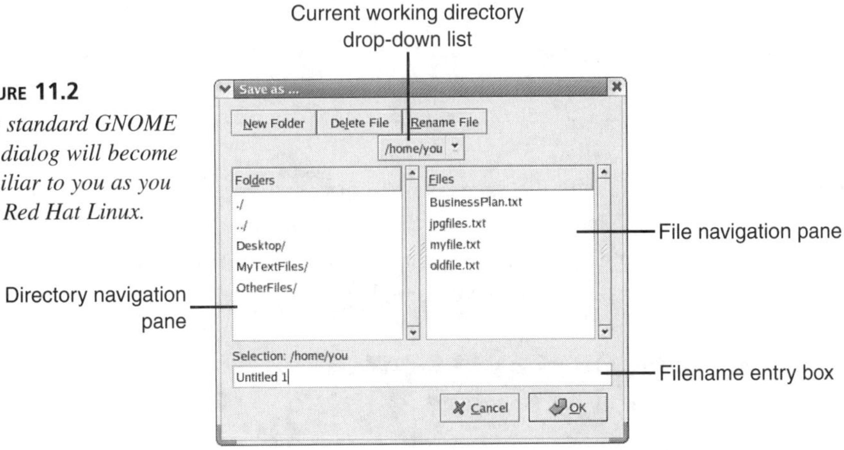

Current working directory
drop-down list

FIGURE 11.2

The standard GNOME file dialog will become familiar to you as you use Red Hat Linux.

Directory navigation pane

File navigation pane

Filename entry box

Notice that the special . and .. directories also are listed and are used in the same way. Recall that . always refers to the current directory, and .. refers to the directory that contains the current directory. For more information on . and .., see "Using Relative Paths" in Hour 4, "Navigating Linux at the Console."

11

- The *file navigation pane* contains a list of all of the non-directory files in the current directory. Double-clicking a filename has the effect of selecting and/or saving the file in question.

- Use the *filename entry box* to enter a filename or full file path for loading or saving. If you enter only a filename, the filename you enter is appended to the application's current working directory to create a full path. For example, if the application is working in the /home/you directory, and you enter `myfile.txt` in the filename entry box when saving, your file will be saved to /home/you/myfile.txt.

- The *current directory drop-down* shows the name of the current directory; all the files and directories shown are stored in this directory. Click the drop-down arrow to see a list of parent directories, beginning with the current directory and ending with the root directory (/). Click any directory in the drop-down list to make it the current directory.

 If the file dialog box seems confusing to you, take a few moments to navigate around the filesystem using the dialog box and becoming comfortable with it. Use the present working directory drop-down to visit the root directory of the Linux filesystem, and then double-click your way back to /home/you using the directory navigation pane.

When you feel comfortable with the Save As file dialog and have navigated back to /home/you, enter a suitable name for the text file in the filename text box; for this example, name the file **anotherfile.txt**, as shown in Figure 11.3. After you've named the file, click OK to save it and close the Save As dialog.

FIGURE 11.3

Here, text is being saved in a file named anotherfile.txt *in the* /home/you *directory.*

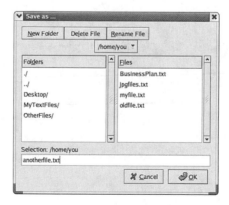

After you've saved the file under its new name, the filename appears in the application window's title bar. From now on, choosing File, Save while you work in this file saves your changes in `anotherfile.txt`.

> You might notice that the Text Editor's File menu has two save options, Save and Save As. Choosing Save saves your changes in the current file; choosing Save As opens the Save As dialog box, enabling you to save the file under a different name or in a different directory. Each time you use Save As and enter a new filename for a file you're working on, a new file will be created.

After you have saved `anotherfile.txt`, choose File, Quit to exit the text editor; once again, you have an empty desktop.

Using the File Manager

At the command line, you used commands such as `ls`, `cd`, `mv`, and `cp` to manipulate files and folders in your home directory and throughout the entire Linux filesystem. To open an existing text file, you used either the `emacs` or `vi` commands, supplying the name of the file you wanted to open as an argument.

On the desktop in a graphical environment, you use your pointing device to perform these tasks onscreen in a program called a file manager. In GNOME, the file manager is called Nautilus; in KDE, the file manager is called Konqueror.

Using the file manager and your pointing device, you can perform all the basic file manipulation tasks in Linux:

- List the files in a directory.
- Move, rename, copy, and delete files.
- Create directories and symbolic links.
- Duplicate existing files or directories.
- Change permissions.
- Delete files, directories, and symbolic links.

Although the file manager does not offer a set of powerful programming tools like those introduced in Hour 9, "Harnessing the Power of the Shell," its easy-to-use, mouse-driven interface often compensates for its comparative lack of flexibility.

11

Opening a File Manager Window

The file manager is always active so long as you are logged in; even when you have no open windows, the icons on your desktop are being managed by the file manager.

You create directories, copy files, and execute other desktop file management tasks by opening a file manager window. Double-click the Home icon at the upper left of your desktop to open the file manager (in Nautilus, this icon carries the name of the account you're logged into). A file manager window appears, displaying the files in your home directory, as shown in Figure 11.4.

Users of the KDE desktop can access the KDE file manager, known as Konqueror, by double-clicking the Home icon on the KDE desktop. A Konqueror window with /home/you as the displayed location will be started, as shown in Figure 11.5.

For basic file management operations of the kind you're exploring in this hour, Konqueror is similar to Nautilus in nearly every way. KDE users should therefore follow along, referring to Figure 11.5 as necessary to identify Konqueror components.

FIGURE 11.4

A folder icon designates a directory in the Nautilus file manager window. The file manager labels each file icon with the file's name and size, and each directory with a name and the number of items it contains.

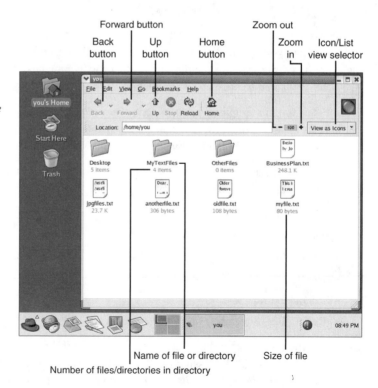

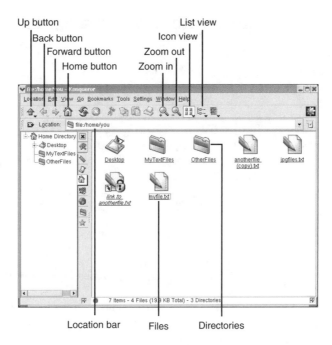

FIGURE 11.5

Though much of the functionality is the same, a Konqueror window is somewhat different in appearance from a Nautilus window.

Up button
Back button
Forward button
Home button
List view
Icon view
Zoom out
Zoom in

Location bar   Files   Directories

 Depending on the amount of work you've already done with your Red Hat Linux system, you might see a different list of files when you open a file manager window. In any case, the list of files that you see represents the files that are present in your home directory. If you see an empty window, it means that no files are present in your home directory.

11

Navigating the Directory Tree

To make use of the file manager, you need to know how to navigate through it to access specific files and directories. A file manager window contains two navigation tools, the most important of which is the location bar, shown in Figures 11.5 and 11.6. The location bar lists the path containing the files currently displayed in the Nautilus window. You can type a path in this bar to display the files the directory contains.

To use the location bar, click in the location bar, delete the existing location, and enter the path to the root directory (/). The window then displays the root directory's contents, as shown in Figure 11.6.

FIGURE 11.6

After entering the path to the root directory (/), the contents of the root directory are displayed. Each of the folder icons represents a directory that resides in the root directory.

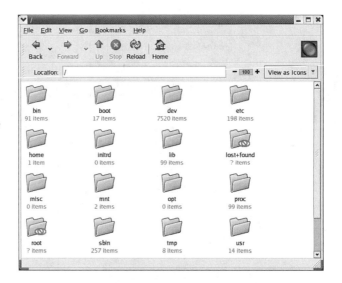

You can also double-click any of the icons in the Nautilus file manager window to display or open (depending on the file type) the file or directory that the icon represents. In the listing for the root directory shown in Figure 11.6, for example, double-clicking a folder icon for any of the directories opens the directory and changes the location bar to reflect the new path. The results of double-clicking the Home icon are shown in Figure 11.7.

FIGURE 11.7

After double-clicking the Home icon, the contents of /home are displayed in the Nautilus window.

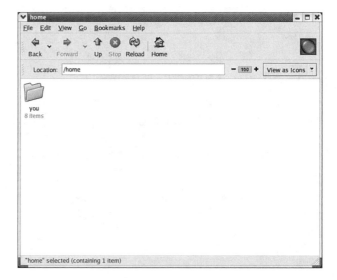

To return to /home/you, simply double-click the you icon. The location bar updates and the files in /home/you are once again displayed.

> You can move quickly through the Nautilus directories using the icons in the Nautilus window's toolbar. Most of these buttons work like their counterparts in a Web browser. Use the Back and Forward buttons to return to directories you've visited since you opened the window. Click Home to return Nautilus to your home directory. The Up button moves you up one directory level, which is similar to visiting the .. directory at the command line. If you are in the /home/you directory, for example, clicking Up causes /home to become the active directory. Clicking Up again displays the root (/) directory.

Working with Files and Directories

You've learned your way around the file manager; now it's time to get to work. To open, copy, cut, move, or otherwise work with files in a Red Hat Linux graphical user interface, you use the *context menu*. To do that, right-click the file's icon (position your cursor over the icon and click the button on the right of the mouse or trackball) and choose an option in the menu that appears near your cursor. A context menu displays a list of actions you can perform on the associated file; if you right-click a text file, for example, you see options associated with the text editor. To see the context menu in action, right-click `anotherfile.txt` to display the menu shown in Figure 11.8.

FIGURE 11.8

The context menu for text files is displayed when right-clicking the file anotherfile.txt.

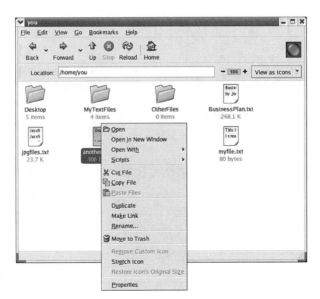

You can choose any option in a context menu by clicking it. Here's what the options in the context menu do:

- Open displays the file in the file manager window, without opening the text editor.
- Open in New Window creates a new file manager window and displays the file there.
- Open With shows a submenu of text editors that you can select to open the file in order to edit it and save your changes.
- Cut File clips the file from the current directory so you can move it to another using the Paste Files command.
- Paste Files becomes active after you use the Cut File command to remove an item from a directory; move to a new directory and click Paste Files to place the cut item in the new location.
- Duplicate copies the selected item.
- Make Link creates a symbolic link to the file.
- Rename allows you to change an item's name.
- Move to Trash puts the file in the desktop trash can, effectively throwing it away (deleting it).
- Remove Custom Icon, Stretch Icon, and Restore Icon's Original Size alter the appearance of the selected icon.
- Properties displays properties such as file size, date last edited, and so on, for the selected item.

You learn more about using these and other menu options in the sections that follow.

Though you work with context menus for files in this hour, you can access context menus for many items on the Linux desktop. Context menu options provide a quick, intuitive method for managing or manipulating most desktop items in Red Hat Linux.

Opening, Editing, and Closing an Existing File

To open the anotherfile.txt file for editing, right-click its icon and select Open With from the context menu. A submenu containing a list of applications and other options appears, as shown in Figure 11.9.

FIGURE 11.9

You can choose a text editor from the Open With submenu; the selected file opens in that text editor so you can change the file's contents and save your changes.

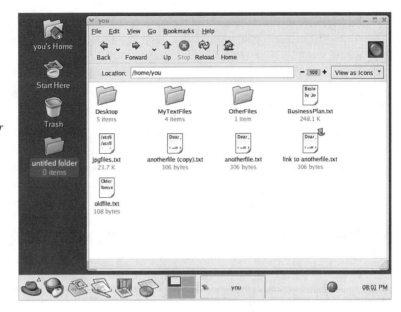

Generally, the first option in the submenu is the one most commonly associated with the type of file in question. In this case, the listed program, gedit, is actually the name of the program file for the GNOME text editor you've been using all along. Selecting gedit loads the file into the GNOME editor you've become familiar with.

After a file has been loaded into an application, you can edit and save the file.

The Open With submenu also lists other programs with which you can open the file. In the case of anotherfile.txt, these include the vi editor and the OpenOffice applications suite; you learn more about OpenOffice in Hour 12, "Introducing OpenOffice."

Two final entries in the submenu, Text Viewer and Other Viewer, display the file in Nautilus or in another file manager application. After a file has been opened in a text editor, you can use the editor window to make changes to your file and save the file just as you normally would.

Cutting, Copying, and Pasting Files

If you have worked in Word, WordPerfect, or other common word processing programs, you are familiar with the cut, copy, and paste functions. If not, you won't have any trouble using these functions; they provide a simple way to move text in a document, but you can also use them to move files from one directory or location to another in the Red Hat Linux file manager.

11

You can use the Copy File command to copy a file to another directory without removing the file from its original location. To duplicate a file, right-click it to produce the context menu, and then choose Copy File. Navigate to the directory where you want the file's duplicate to appear, and right-click empty space in the directory window. In the context menu that appears, choose Paste Files. A duplicate of the file will be created in the currently displayed directory using the same filename.

You also can use the context menu to remove a file from its current location and place it in a new directory. To move a file, right-click its icon and then choose Cut File. The file disappears (is deleted) from the current directory. Navigate to the directory where you want to place the file, right-click empty window space, and choose Paste Files from the context menu. The file is recreated in the currently displayed directory.

Duplicating a File in the Current Directory

If you want to create a copy of a file within the same directory, you can use the Duplicate context menu command. Duplicate places a copy of the selected file in the current directory and adds "(copy)" to the filename. The results of a duplicate operation can be seen in Figure 11.10.

FIGURE 11.10

The original file, anotherfile.txt, *sitting alongside its newly created duplicate,* anotherfile (copy).txt.

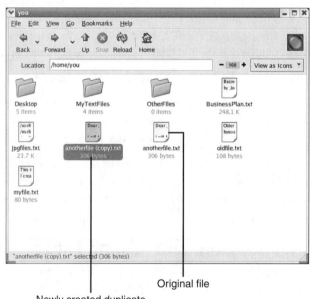

Newly created duplicate

Original file

It is important to understand that the copy you have created is a new file in its own right; subsequent changes you make to the original file will not appear in the copy. Duplicate files are therefore a convenient way for mantaining several different revisions of the same file.

Selecting Multiple Files

Many of the context menu and drag-and-drop operations discussed here can be performed on a number of files simultaneously. Select more than one file at a time and then perform the operation just as you would for a single file.

There are two ways of selecting multiple files at once. The first and easiest, commonly referred to as using a *rubber band*, is accomplished by clicking the left button on your pointing device in an empty area of the file manager window, dragging the pointer and enlarging the rubber band to enclose a number of files, and then releasing the button. Selected files are highlighted to show that they have been selected. This process is shown in Figure 11.11.

FIGURE 11.11

Using the rubber band to select four files simultaneously in /home/you. The selected files are highlighted.

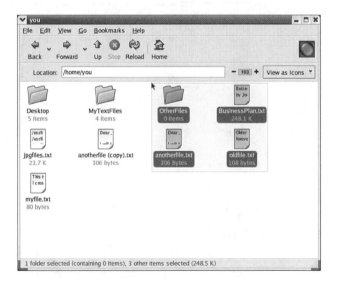

The other way to select multiple files is to hold down the Ctrl key while single-clicking each file you want to select, one-by-one. This enables the selection of noncontinguous groups of icons.

Creating a Symbolic Link

A symbolic link is a kind of alias for a file; it allows one file listed and opened from two different places or directories for convenience. For example, by using a symbolic link, a file called budget-2000.txt could be listed both in the directory budgets and in the directory year2000files; the file could then be displayed or edited from either place.

To create a symbolic link to an existing file or directory, choose Make Link from the context menu. A symbolic link to the original item is created, with the text "link to" prepended to the original filename. The results of selecting the Make Link item can be seen in Figure 11.12.

Original file   Newly created symbolic link

FIGURE 11.12
The original file,
anotherfile.txt, *and*
a newly created sym-
bolic link that points to
it, link to another-
file.txt.

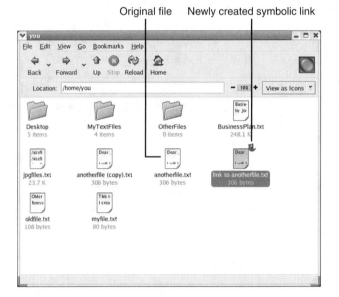

Renaming an Item

You can use the Rename command in the context menu to change a file, directory, or symbolic link's filename. After selecting Rename from the menu, the icon's filename appears in a text box, as shown in Figure 11.13; type a new name for the file and press Enter to save the name and exit the text box.

> When renaming a file, be sure not to change the file's three-letter extension, if it has one, because doing so might change the way Red Hat Linux or other operating systems identify the file's type!

FIGURE 11.13
The file anotherfile
(copy).txt *is ready to
be renamed; when the
filename text box is
active, as shown here,
you can type to replace
the current name.
Press Enter to save the
new name.*

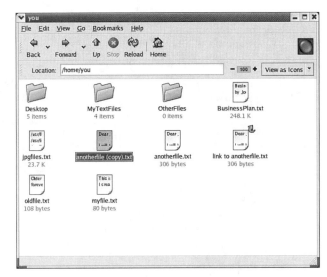

Deleting Items

To delete a file or directory, select the Move to Trash option from the context menu. The selected item disappears from the currently displayed directory and is moved to the trash can. Double-click the Trash icon to view, restore, or permanently delete trashed items (see "Working with Trash Contents," later in this hour).

Changing File Permissions

To change the permissions for a file or directory, select the Properties item in the context menu. A dialog box appears, as shown in Figure 11.14.

After the Properties dialog box has been displayed, select the third tab, Permissions to display a pane containing permissions options, as shown in Figure 11.15.

The group ownership selector in this dialog can be used to change the group ownership for the file or directory in question. Click the selector; a drop-down appears listing groups to whom ownership of this file can be given. Select a new owner by clicking the desired group.

For a refresher on file permissions and user and group ownership, refer to "Understanding Permissions" in Hour 4.

To learn more about using groups in Red Hat Linux, refer to Hour 18, "Command-Line System Administration."

FIGURE 11.14

Selecting Properties from the another-file.txt *context menu causes a properties dialog box to be displayed.*

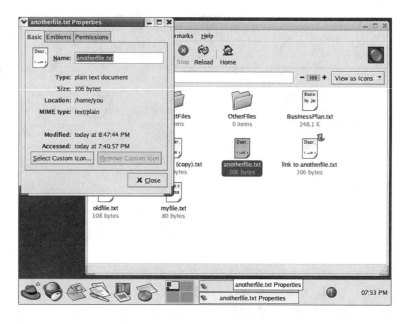

FIGURE 11.15

The Permissions pane allows the file or directory permissions to be altered. The equivalent permissions string from ls -l *output is shown after the Text view label.*

Permissions toggles

Group ownership selector

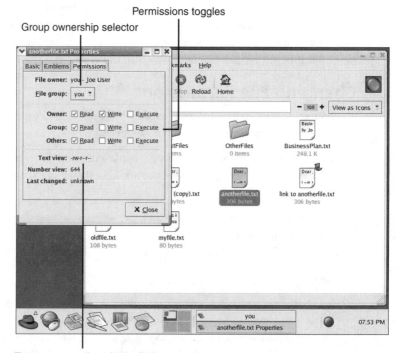

Text representation of permissions

The permissions toggles can be checked or unchecked to allow or disallow read, write, or execute permission for any of the various types of file or directory ownership. As you change the permissions for the file or directory, the equivalent output from the `ls -l` command is shown after the `Text view` label.

Creating a New Directory

To create a new directory in the currently displayed directory, right-click an area of empty space within the file manager window. A context menu for the currently displayed directory appears.

Select the New Folder item in the context menu to create a new directory in the currently displayed directory, as shown in Figure 11.16. The new directory appears with the name `untitled folder`, in a selected text box; type a new name and press Enter to name your new folder.

FIGURE 11.16

The newly created directory is given the name untitled folder. *Type a new name to name your folder, or simply press Enter to accept the default name.*

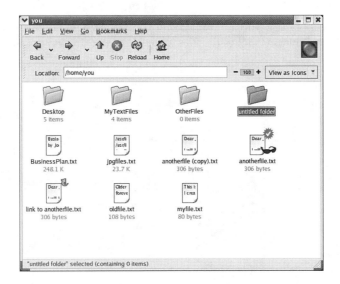

 Don't be confused by the terms *folder* and *directory*—for our purposes, these terms can be used interchangably. Typically, when accessed from the command line, they are known as *directories,* and on the desktop they are called *folders.*

Rearranging or Sorting Icons

One last set of tasks is most easily performed via the current directory context menu. The icons in the currently displayed directory can be rearranged and resorted by right-clicking an empty area of the current directory to display the current directory context menu, and then selecting Arrange Items. The submenu shown in Figure 11.17 will be displayed.

Depending on how you want the current directory to be displayed, you select from the following:

- By Name sorts the files in ascending alphabetical order (from A-Z).
- By Size sorts the files in descending order, from largest to smallest, beginning with directories, which are sorted by the number of items each contains.
- By Type groups the files by type (usually indicated by a file's three letter extension), sorting alphabetically (from A–Z) within each type.
- By Modification Date sorts the files in order from the files or directories most recently edited to those least recently edited.
- By Emblems groups the files by the emblems that have been assigned to them.
- Compact Layout causes the icons to be spaced more closely together, as shown in Figure 11.18.
- Reverse Order causes the the ordering of the sorting methods listed above to be reversed.
- Manually allows you to position the icons as you choose.

FIGURE 11.17

The Arrange Items submenu enables you to dictate the way in which Nautilus organizes the display of files and directories in the current directory.

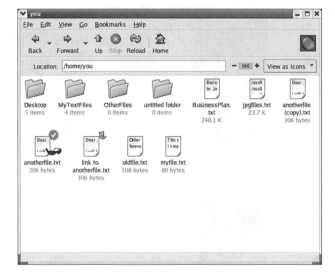

FIGURE 11.18

When Compact Layout is enabled, the icons for the files in the directory are spaced more closely.

Manipulating Files Using Drag and Drop

Nearly all of the file and directory operations you've learned to perform so far are accomplished using context menus. Although the context menu is certainly a powerful tool, another technique known as *drag and drop* is often more convenient.

To drag and drop, place your cursor over the icon of the file or directory you want to move, and then click the mouse or trackball button and hold it down as you drag the pointer and icon to the new location. Release the button to "drop" the item into its new location. The following sections show you how to use drag and drop in some simple file management tasks.

Moving a File into a Directory or to the Desktop

In order to perform a drag-and-drop operation, both the file you want to affect and its destination must be visible on the screen. To move a file into a directory using drag and drop, use the left button to drag the file's icon onto the icon of the directory you want to move the file into. When that directory's icon is selected, release the button to drop the file into the new location.

You also can use drag and drop to move files and directories to the desktop. Using the file manager, navigate until the icon for a file or directory that you want to move is visible, and then click it and drag it out of the file manager window and onto the desktop. Release the mouse button to drop the file. Figure 11.19 shows the results of dragging and dropping untitled folder from /home/you to the desktop. You can use the same drag-and-drop process to move files and directories from the desktop back into a file manager window or into directories displayed there.

11

FIGURE **11.19**

The directory untitled folder *has been dragged and dropped onto the desktop. Files can be stored in it as in any other directory.*

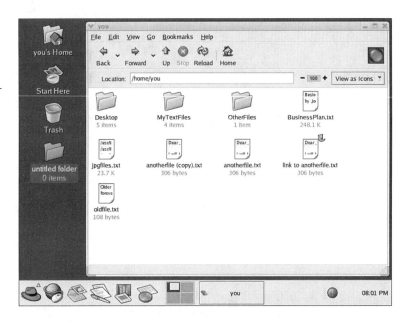

 Files or directories can also be moved into the Trash (thrown away) using this technique. Simply drag the file you want to throw away onto the Trash icon. When the Trash icon is highlighted, release the button and the file in question will be placed in the Trash.

Moving a File Between Two Directory Windows

Sometimes you need to have two file manager windows open in order to perform certain file or directory operations. To move a file from /home/you/MyTextFiles into /home/you/OtherFiles, for example, you must have open windows for both directories.

In an open file manager window, navigate to /home/you/OtherFiles. Then, open a second file manager window by double-clicking the you's Home icon once again. Another file manager window opens; in this one, navigate to /home/you/MyTextFiles, as shown in Figure 11.20.

 Note that you might need to move or resize one or both file manager windows before you are able to see both of them and work between them effectively. Refer to Hour 10 for a refresher course on moving and resizing windows, if necessary.

FIGURE 11.20

Two file manager windows are visible here. One is currently displaying /home/you/ MyTextFiles, and the other is displaying /home/you/OtherFiles. Looking at the two location bars makes this clear.

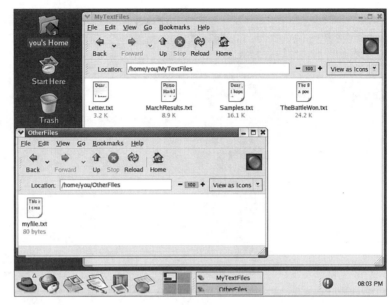

After you have both windows open and two separate directories displayed, you can drag and drop files between the two directory windows. The moved files disappear from the first window (directory) and appear in the new location.

Context Drag and Drop

You also can use an operation called *context drag* to move, copy, and link files in the file manager. To use this feature, you drag and drop using the *right* pointer button rather than the left one. When you release the right button, a context menu appears for the drag-and-drop operation. You can choose options from this menu to perform several different operations.

Try the context-drag operation by dragging a file to the desktop using the right button instead of the left button of your pointing device. When you release the button, a menu similar to the one shown in Figure 11.21 appears.

When you choose an option in the context menu, the selection action is performed. Here are the choices:

- Move Here moves the file or the directory and all of its contents from its original location to the location where you released the button.
- Copy Here copies the file or the directory and all of its contents from its original location to the location where you released the button.
- Link Here creates a symbolic link in the location where you released the button pointing to the file's original location.

11

Figure **11.21**

*The context drag has
been used between the
file* /home/you/jpg-
files.txt *and the
desktop. The context
menu enables you to
choose the action you
want the file manager
to perform with the file
in question.*

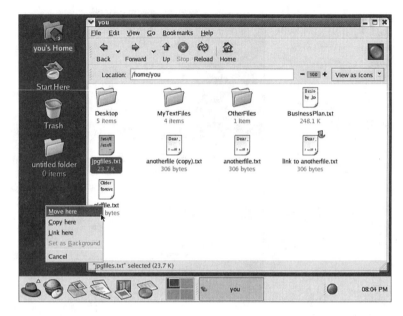

Figure **11.21**

*The context drag has
been used between the
file* /home/you/jpg-
files.txt *and the
desktop. The context
menu enables you to
choose the action you
want the file manager
to perform with the file
in question.*

Working with Trash Contents

The Trash icon represents a special directory used to temporarily hold items you have
deleted using the file manager. This directory gives your files a second chance—allowing
you to be certain that you no longer want to access or edit a deleted item. After you send
an item to the Trash by deleting it, you can do two things with it: You can restore the
item or you can permanently delete it. The following sections describe these operations
in detail.

Restoring Files That Have Been Thrown Away

If you decide you want to save an item that you've previously sent to the Trash, you can
restore it to the desktop or a directory. To do this, double-click the Trash icon to open a
new file manager window listing the Trash contents, as shown in Figure 11.22. Then,
drag and drop or cut/copy and paste files from Trash to other storage areas, such as
/home/you.

Emptying the Trash

If you know you don't want to save any of the files and directories you've thrown in the
Trash, you can permanently delete them from the Trash folder. Emptying the Trash folder
removes the deleted items from your hard drive forever. To empty the Trash, follow these
steps:

1. Right-click the Trash icon on the desktop to produce the context menu.
2. Select Empty Trash; a dialog appears, asking you to confirm that you want to empty the Trash.
3. Select the Empty option to permanently delete all items currently in the Trash folder; select Cancel to abort the operation.

FIGURE 11.22

Double-click Trash to open a file manager window listing its contents. To restore a file or directory from Trash, drag and drop or cut/copy and paste items to the location where you want to store them.

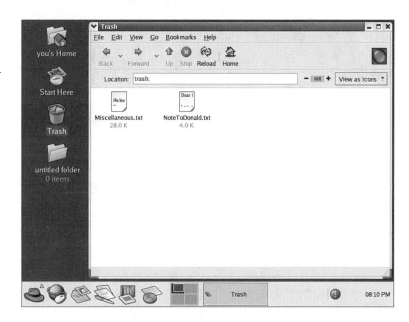

11

When you empty the Trash, any files or folders it contains are erased forever and cannot be recovered.

Summary

This hour, you learned to use the desktop file manager to move, copy, modify, and delete files and directories. Along the way, you gained practice launching graphical applications and using the standard file manager dialog boxes to browse the filesystem and choose filenames. You gained practice with basic cut, copy, and paste procedures, and you learned how to create symbolic links and duplicates using the file manager window menu bar and context menus.

You also learned to take advantage of some convenience features, such as emblems for icon classification, zooming to make file management easier on the eyes, and using the Trash to restore or permanently delete files and folders.

Q&A

Q **I notice that the file manager displays letters or words in some icons but not in others, and they often don't make sense. Why?**

A If a file is human-readable (that is, not a program or an image file or something composed mostly of data), the file manager will attempt to use the first few letters or words from the document as part of the icon to help you identify files without having to open them.

Workshop

The Workshop is designed to help you anticipate possible questions, review what you've learned, and begin learning how to put your knowledge into practice.

Quiz

1. How do you open a file manager window?

2. How do you copy a file from your home directory to your desktop using drag-and-drop?

3. How do you create a new directory?

4. How do you open an existing file for editing?

Answers

1. Double-click the Home icon on your desktop.

2. Open a file manager window, and then use the right button on your pointing device to drag the file's icon to your desktop. When you release the button and the context menu appears, select Copy Here to copy the file.

3. Right-click inside the file manager window. Choose New Folder from the context menu that appears.

4. Right-click the icon for the file you want to edit. Choose Open With from the context menu that appears, and then choose the application you want to use for editing from the Open With submenu.

Activities

1. Spend some time navigating your filesystem using the file manager, the location bar, and directory icons.

2. For practice, create a new text file and then change the permissions using the file manager so that only the owning user can read the file.

3. For practice, try copying some of the text files in /etc to your home directory using the file manager.

4. Insert a CD-ROM and double-click the CD-ROM icon on your desktop. Spend some time browsing the contents of the CD-ROM disc using the file manager.

11

HOUR **12**

Introducing OpenOffice

In this hour, you learn to create documents and spreadsheets in the Linux desktop environment using OpenOffice 6.0, a full-featured office applications suite, which is included with Red Hat Linux and is similar to Microsoft Office. The tasks you learn to perform include

- How to launch the OpenOffice applications
- How to create a new word processing document using the OpenOffice Writer application
- How to control basic formatting and layout in OpenOffice Writer documents
- How to create a new spreadsheet using the OpenOffice Calc application
- How to perform basic calculations in OpenOffice Calc spreadsheets

By the end of the hour, you should have mastered basic office productivity skills on the Linux desktop.

The OpenOffice Applications

OpenOffice 6 is the latestversion of a suite of productivity applications for use with Red Hat Linux. The OpenOffice suite is very similar to Microsoft Office, Corel WordPerfect Office, or other "office" suites you might be familiar with. Because OpenOffice is open-source software (like Linux itself), it is a favorite among Linux users. OpenOffice is also available for use with the Windows OS. Because OpenOffice is capable of opening and saving in MS Office file formats, it is possible to exchange files with users of Windows and MS Office using OpenOffice.

Like most suites of office productivity applications, OpenOffice contains a series of distinct applications, each of which performs a specific task:

- OpenOffice Writer, a full-featured word processing and document layout application similar to Microsoft Word or Corel WordPerfect. OpenOffice Writer enables you to create memos, letters, articles, reports, and books.
- OpenOffice Calc, a powerful spreadsheet and calculation application similar to Microsoft Excel or Corel Quattro Pro. OpenOffice Calc enables you to perform math-oriented tasks, such as budgeting, engineering calculations, physics calculations, and statistics.
- OpenOffice Impress, a presentations manager similar to Microsoft PowerPoint or Corel Presentations. OpenOffice Impress allows you to create visual slide shows with illustrations, charts and graphs to help you to present information to others.
- OpenOffice Draw, a drawing and image manipulation program which allows you to create clean, well-structured sketches and diagrams as well as to edit photos and other types of raster graphics.
- OpenOffice Math, an equation editor, for editing and inserting complex mathematical equations into your documents for output.

In this hour, you explore Writer and Calc; these are the most commonly used application in the OpenOffice suite. For a full treatment of the OpenOffice suite, refer to the following books on StarOffice, which is based on OpenOffice technology:

- *StarOffice 6.0 Office Suite Companion*, by Solveig Haugland and Floyd Jones
- *Special Editing Using StarOffice 6.0*, by Michael Koch

Online documentation for OpenOffice and all of its features can also be found by selecting Help, Contents from any OpenOffice application. Every dialog box in OpenOffice also contains a help button; clicking it displays documentation about that dialog in particular.

Launching an OpenOffice Application

Because office productivity functionality is so essential to the role of any computer system in nearly any environment, the OpenOffice applications figure prominently in both the default GNOME and KDE layouts in Red Hat Linux.

Launch icons for the three most commonly used OpenOffice component applications (Writer, Calc, and Impress) appear side-by-side on the desktop taskbar, as shown in Figure 12.1.

FIGURE 12.1
Clicking one of these icons launches one of the most commonly used OpenOffice component applications.

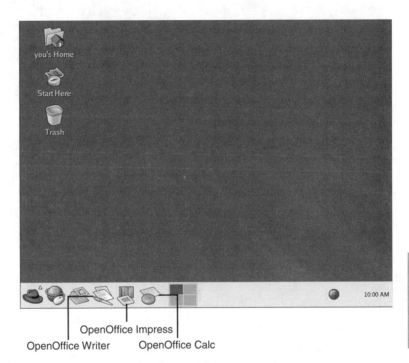

OpenOffice Impress
OpenOffice Writer   OpenOffice Calc

Creating and Formatting an OpenOffice Writer Document

The OpenOffice Writer application is used to create professional-looking letters, reports, memos, books, and other types of text-based documents that are commonly used in business and academia. In OpenOffice Writer, you enter and format lines and paragraphs of text, usually with the eventual goal of outputting them to a printer in an easy-to-read format.

Launching OpenOffice Writer

Click the OpenOffice Writer icon to launch the application. Click the taskbar icon; the splash logo appears as the application loads. When the program is loaded, a new Writer application window containing an untitled document appears, as shown in Figure 12.2.

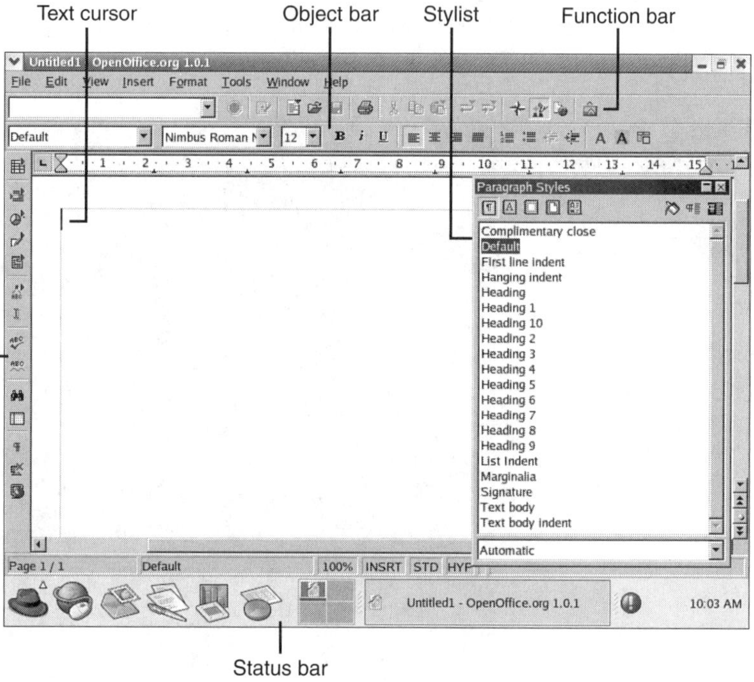

FIGURE 12.2

A new OpenOffice Writer window. Because no document has been loaded by the user a new document Untitled1 *appears in the application window.*

Text cursor   Object bar   Stylist   Function bar

Main toolbar

Status bar

If this is the first time you have launched an OpenOffice application, you are shown a dialog box called the Address Data Source AutoPilot. This dialog enables you to tell OpenOffice where your contacts information is stored, so that you can easily send documents to your contacts without having to manually find their names and addresses. Because you won't be working with addresses in this hour you can safely click Cancel to dismiss this dialog and leave the OpenOffice address book unconfigured; OpenOffice includes tools to configure your address book at any time.

The following are components that make up the OpenOffice Writer window:

- The toolbars contain function buttons that, when clicked, perform common tasks, such as saving or printing a file, changing text alignment, or inserting a table.

- The text body looks like a piece of paper or several pieces of paper and is where you enter text as you create documents. This element contains the *text cursor*, a blinking line that indicates where new text appears as you enter it. The faint gray line near the edge of the text body area indicates the position of the text margins.

- The status bar displays information about the size of your document, the position of your cursor and other mundane but useful data.

- The stylist window enables you to use prebuilt or custom styles to format your document (the stylist is an advanced word processing topic and is discussed in this book). Move this window out of the way by clicking and dragging its title bar; close it by clicking the close button at its upper-right corner (or press the F11 key). You can restore a closed stylist window by choosing Format, Stylist or by pressing the F11 key.

Entering Text

To enter text in OpenOffice Writer, position the text cursor where you want to enter new text, and then begin typing. Any text you type is inserted at that position. Words automatically *wrap* to the next line when you reach the right margin, so you do not have to press Enter at the end of each line to remain within the right margin and avoid splitting a word across two lines.

Enter a line or two of text now so that you have a non-empty document to work with for the rest of the section. The OpenOffice Writer application with a few lines of text entered is shown in Figure 12.3.

FIGURE 12.3

The cursor moves from left to right and from the top of the screen toward the bottom as you type text into OpenOffice Writer.

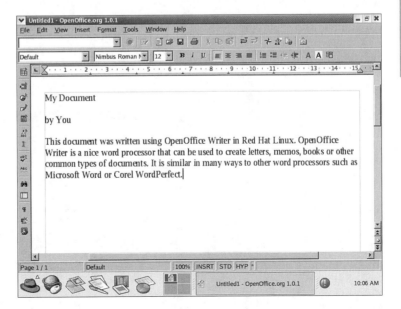

12

Editing Text

One of the greatest advantages inherent in using a word processing application such as OpenOffice Writer is that you easily can change text after you've entered it. Here are some of the most common editing techniques:

- You can remove individual letters or words using Backspace and Delete editing keys; Backspace deletes characters to the left of the insertion point, and Delete deletes characters to the right of the insertion point.

- You can edit blocks of text by selecting the block and then choosing an editing key or command. Click at the beginning of the block of text you want to edit, and then drag your cursor to the end of the text (see Figure 12.4). Selected text appears highlighted onscreen. Click Cut to remove the text from the document. Cut text can remain deleted from the document or moved to a new location (see the steps that follow this list). Click Copy to copy the selected text, and then position your cursor where you want to place a copy of the text and click Paste; a copy of the selected text appears at the insertion point.

- By selecting blocks of text, you can also type new text to replace existing text. Select a letter or word, and then begin typing to replace it with new text.

FIGURE 12.4

By selecting blocks of text, you can issue a single editing command to apply changes to the entire block.

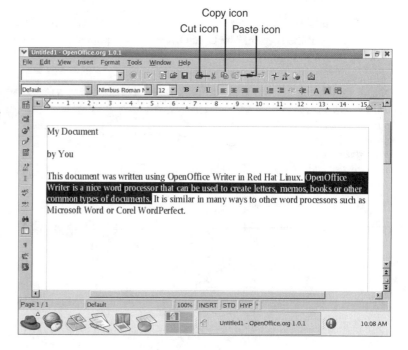

To move a selected block of text to another location within a document, follow these steps:

1. Click the Cut button (the scissors icon) to remove the selected text (or choose Edit, Cut); the text disappears from the document.

2. Position the cursor at the location in the document where you want the moved text to appear.

3. Click the Paste icon or choose Edit, Paste; the text appears in the new location.

You can also select text using your keyboard. Position the text cursor before the block of text you want to select. Press and hold your Shift key as you use the navigation keys to move the text cursor to the end of the block of text you want to select. When you have selected the block of text you want, release the Shift key.

The Insert command key on your keyboard enables you to toggle between Insert and Overwrite mode. In Insert mode, new text you enter pushes text to the right. In Overwrite mode, new text overwrites text to the right of the cursor, letter for letter. Press the key to toggle between the two modes.

Changing the Appearance of Text

12

You can apply different font sizes, typefaces, and text effects to change the appearance of text within your OpenOffice Writer documents. These changes can make your document look more professional and add emphasis to important words or phrases.

To change the appearance of text in your document, select a block of text and then click one of the following Object bar items (see Figure 12.5):

- The typeface drop-down list changes the fundamental style of your text; for example, you might choose to use a sans-serif font like Helvetica rather than a serif font like Thorndale.

- The font size drop-down changes the physical size of your text on the printed page; larger numbers indicate larger text.

- The bold button causes text to appear in **boldface**.

- The italic button causes text to appear in *italics.*

- The underline button causes your text to be <u>underlined</u>.

- The font color selector enables you to choose a new color for your text.
- The font highlight selector enables you to choose a new background color for your text (to make it appear highlighted onscreen or in a color printout).

The bold, italic, underline, color, and highlight buttons work as toggles; click them again to toggle them off.

FIGURE 12.5

Object bar items have been used to change the appearance of the text in the first line of this document. The title text is now in Helvetica typeface, size 24, boldface.

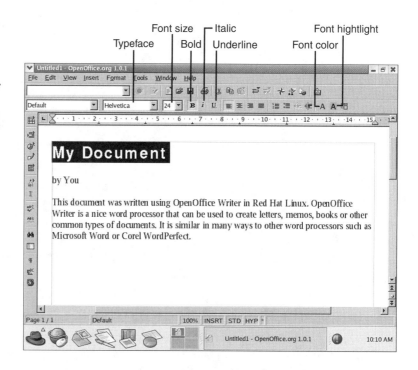

To apply font styles before you begin typing, position the text cursor where you'd like your text to be inserted, and then use the font size, bold, italic, and other appearance-editing tools to set your choices. The text you enter reflects your settings.

You can align text along the right or left margins, or you can center text on the page. You also can *justify* the text to create straight margins on both the right and left sides. Click in a paragraph then choose one of the four alignment buttons located to the right of the Underline button in the formatting Object bar. Each button face shows the alignment it provides. Select multiple paragraphs, and then click a button to align all of them. You also can choose text alignment before you enter text; choose an alignment option, and then type. The text you enter is aligned with that style until you choose another option.

Changing Paragraph Formatting

You can format text in single-spaced, double-spaced, or 1.5-line–spaced paragraphs. You also can indent paragraphs as you type, or apply indentation to paragraphs of existing text. You choose line spacing and indentation options within the Indents & Spacing tab of the Paragraph dialog box.

To change the line spacing or indentation properties of an existing block of text, select the block of text you want to modify, and then choose Format, Paragraph; the Paragraph dialog box shown in Figure 12.6 appears.

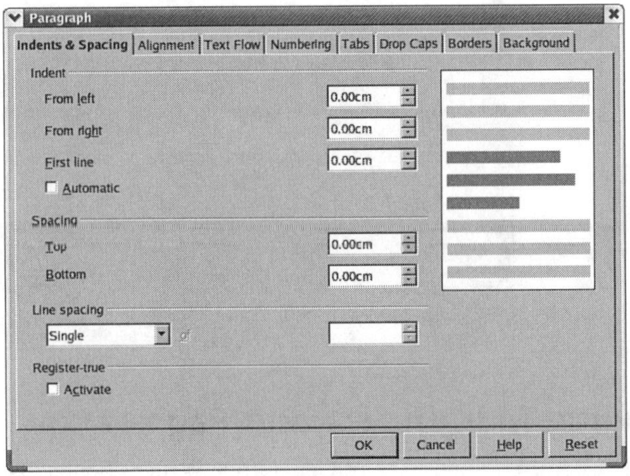

FIGURE 12.6

The indentation and spacing values are given in centimeters; enter a value or use the arrows to increase or decrease the value. The preview pane on the right shows the effect of your changes.

By changing the values of the settings in this dialog box, you can alter the spacing or margins of a selected block of text or set values for new text before you enter it:

- Use the From Left and From Right settings in the Indent area of the tab to indent paragraphs from the page margins; the higher the values, the greater the indentation.

- Use the First Line setting in the Indent area to cause the first line in each selected paragraph to automatically be indented some additional distance relative to the left margin. Check the Automatic check box to make this the default behavior.

- Use the Top and Bottom spacing settings to force OpenOffice Writer to leave some amount of empty space above and/or below each paragraph.

- Use the Line Spacing drop-down box to choose the single, double, or 1.5 line spacing.

- Use the Register True setting to cause all printed lines in your document to use the same baseline so that you can't see gray smudges between the lines on the current page caused by text lines on the next page.

12

Figure 12.7 shows the paragraph in our sample document altered to double-spaced and automatically indented from the left margin on the first line.

FIGURE **12.7**

Double-spacing and first-line indent are common uses for the Paragraph formatting dialog box.

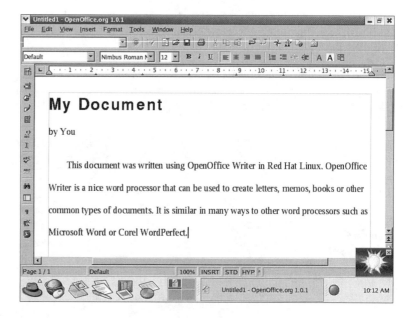

Changing Margin Size and Page Layout

You can customize the margins of OpenOffice Writer documents, and you can change the size and orientation of their printed format. To edit these settings, use the Page tab of the Page Style dialog box, shown in Figure 12.8. Open this dialog box by choosing Format, Page.

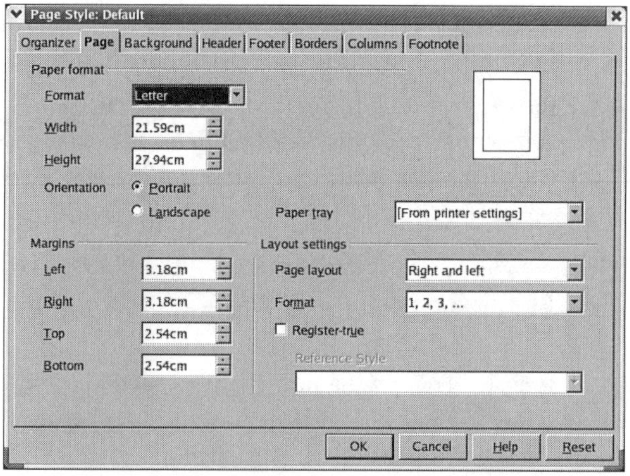

FIGURE **12.8**

Use the Page Style dialog box to change document page margins, paper size, and paper orientation.

Here's how to use the settings in the Page Style dialog box to change the layout of your document:

- Use the settings in the Paper Format area to choose a printed format (such as Letter, Legal, Envelope, and so on), the paper size, and orientation. The Paper Tray setting enables you to choose which paper tray the print job should feed from.

- The settings in the Margins area enable you to set specific Left, Right, Top, and Bottom margin sizes, as measured in centimeters. Type in a size or use the arrows to raise or lower the default settings.

- The Page Layout setting in the Layout area enables you to apply the current settings to all pages (right and left), to only odd pages (right), to even pages (left), or to apply the current settings in anticipation of two-sided printing, to allow for easy binding (mirrored).

- The Format setting in the Layout area enables you to specify the type of page numbering that should be used if you have chosen to insert page numbers in your document.

When you have made the changes you want, click OK to accept them. The changes you make in the Page Style dialog box affect the entire document you're working on.

Saving a File

When you finish entering, editing, and formatting a document, you can save the file for later retrieval or use.

Save the document by clicking the Save button (floppy disk icon) in the Function bar (or by choosing File, Save). If you have made changes to or entered text in a file that has not yet been saved, the Save As dialog box appears, as shown in Figure 12.9.

Here's how to use the options in the Save As dialog box:

- Select a directory and folder in the file and directory list box. Double-click a directory or folder to open or select it; that's where your file will be saved. Use the Up One Level button to move to the next-higher-level directory; use the Default Directory button to store the saved file in the default (your home) directory. Click the Create a New Directory button to create a new directory that will be stored in the currently listed directory.

- Type a name for your file in the File Name text box.

- To save your file in a format other than the OpenOffice Writer format, click the File type selector and choose a new file type, such as RichText or Microsoft Word format. This enables you to exchange the file you're creating with users of other office software, such as MS Office.

- The Automatic file name extension box should always be checked; this allows StarOffice to automatically choose the correct three-letter extension for your file based on the file type you have selected.

FIGURE 12.9

The Save As dialog enables you to select a location and a name under which to store the document you have created. The files and directories in the current directory are shown in the file and directory list box.

Create new directory

Default directory

Up one level

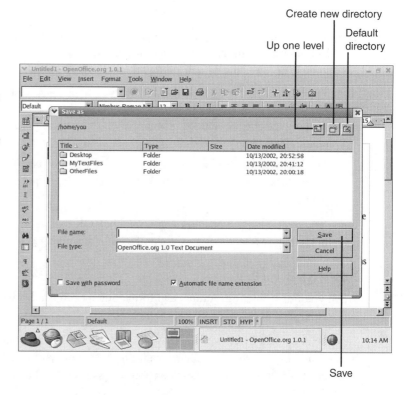

Save

 If you would like to protect your file with a password, check the Save with password box. When you do so, you are prompted to enter a password which will be used to protect the file. When anyone tries to open the file later on, OpenOffice asks them for the password; if they are unable to provide it, the file is not opened.

When you have chosen the file name, format, and directory, click Save to apply your choices. Each time you save this file in the future, changes are stored under the same filename.

You can use the Save As option in the File menu to select a new name for an existing document. This enables you to create a copy of the original file under a new name, so you can make changes to the copy while preserving the original file's content.

Opening a File

To edit or print an existing saved document, you must first open it. You can open a document by clicking the Open icon (looks like an open folder) in the Function bar; alternatively, you can choose File, Open from the menu bar.

After either action, the Open dialog box appears, as shown in Figure 12.10.

FIGURE 12.10

The list box in the Open dialog box lists all the files and directories contained in the current directory (here, /home/you); double-click a file to open it.

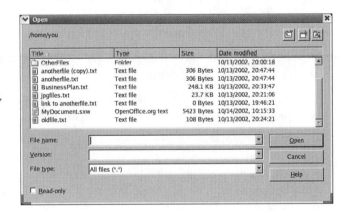

Scroll until you see the file in the file and directory list box and double-click the filename or enter the filename into the Filename entry box, and then click Open.

If your file isn't in the current directory, here's how to use the other controls in the Open dialog box to find the file:

- To open another directory, double-click the name of the directory in the file and directory list box. You can double-click the Default directory button at any time to return to your home directory.
- Use the Up One Level button to open the parent directory of one currently listed.

If you need to narrow down a long list of directory contents in order to find a specific file, you can do so by limiting the display to only files of the type you're looking for. Use the File Type selection box in the Open dialog box to select the type of files you want to be listed; only those files from the current directory that match your chosen file type are displayed.

Printing a File

Printing a document is a simple process in OpenOffice Writer. Begin by opening the document you want to print. If you want to print the entire document, click the Print button (marked with a printer icon) in the Function bar. The document is sent to the printer.

If you want to print only a portion of the document, print multiple copies, or change any of the page layout settings (such as orientation, paper size, and so on); begin the print process by choosing File, Print. The Print dialog box opens.

The highlighted controls in the Print dialog box can be used to alter several aspects of the OpenOffice Writer printing behavior:

- The Number of copies entry box enables you to determine how many copies of the output OpenOffice Writer will cause your printer to generate.

- The Print to file checkbox enables you to output the printer data to a file, rather than to your printer. OpenOffice prompts you for the name of the file if you select this option. Because data that would normally have been sent to your printer is in a language suited to printers rather than to humans, you will rarely, if ever, use this option.

- If you have chosen to print more than one copy of your file, selecting the Collate option causes the entire document to be printed in sequence multiple times (pages 1, 2, 3, 1, 2, 3). If you do not check the Collate option, each page is output several times in a row (pages 1, 1, 2, 2, 3, 3).

- The Print range options enable you to choose to print only a segment of the document rather than all of it; to do so, enter a page number or range of numbers that you want to print. If you want to print only a paragraph or other block of text from the document, select the block with your mouse, open the Print dialog box, and click the Selection button in the Page Range area.

When you've made your choices in the Print dialog box, click OK to begin printing.

Working with OpenOffice Calc

The OpenOffice Calc application is an electronic spreadsheet similar in form and function to Microsoft Excel or Corel Quattro Pro. OpenOffice Calc can be used to perform mathematical calculations of all kinds. For example, a homeowner can use OpenOffice Calc to amortize a loan or maintain a personal budget, an engineer might use OpenOffice Calc for load calculations, and a pollster might use OpenOffice calc to maintain lists of statistics.

To use an electronic spreadsheet, the user provides lists of numbers to OpenOffice Calc along with the formulas and calculations that should be used with the numbers. OpenOffice Calc documents consist of rows and columns of *cells*, each of which can contain one of four things:

- Empty space
- Text for the purposes of labeling numbers or groups of numbers for human eyes, according to their meaning or use
- A number
- A formula that will be used to perform calculations using the numbers in one or several other cells

Though electronic spreadsheet applications often seem awkward to users at first, they are an extremely powerful and commonplace tool in office environments. Because OpenOffice Calc can read and save files in Microsoft Excel format, users of OpenOffice Calc can exchange files with MS Office users everywhere.

Familiarizing Yourself with Calc

To start the OpenOffice Calc application, click its icon on the taskbar. If no other OpenOffice applications are running, the splash logo appears while the program loads, and then a new Calc application window opens, containing an untitled electronic spreadsheet (see Figure 12.11).

Before entering any data, familiarize yourself with the parts of the OpenOffice Calc window. The Calc window demonstrates what a rich feature list this application offers. Here's how to use the Calc onscreen tools and components:

- Click buttons in the toolbars to perform common tasks, such as saving or printing a file, changing text alignment, or formatting numeric data within a cell in a specific way based on the type of data—for example, two decimal places for currency.
- Click a cell within the spreadsheet to make it active and display its contents in the input line. Cells can contain text and numeric data, as well as formulas that calculate values in one or more other cells. The currently selected cell is surrounded by a bold black line that forms the cell boundary.

12

- Use the status bar to find your current cell position in a spreadsheet and to perform quick calculations on the right side of the status bar by highlighting blocks of cells.

- Enter cell contents (text, numeric data, formulas) in the input line. The data you enter here appears in the active or selected cell.

- Use the scrollbars to change the viewing area of the spreadsheet display. Cells are identified by a row number and column letter.

- Use the worksheet tabs to switch between open worksheets; each worksheet is like a separate sheet of paper containing its own rows and columns of cells. You add data to a cell by selecting a cell to make it active, and then entering the numbers, text, or formula for the cell into the cell input text box at the top of the Calc screen. You learn how to enter each type of data into cells in the following sections. Active cells are surrounded by a thick black outline, called the *selection box*. You can move the box around the spreadsheet using the arrow and Page Up/Page Down keys, or by positioning the text cursor over a cell and clicking the mouse. Cells are identified by row number and column letter; in Figure 12.12, cell H14 is selected.

FIGURE 12.11

A new OpenOffice Calc window. Because no spreadsheet has been loaded by the user yet, a new document called Untitled1 *appears in the application window.*

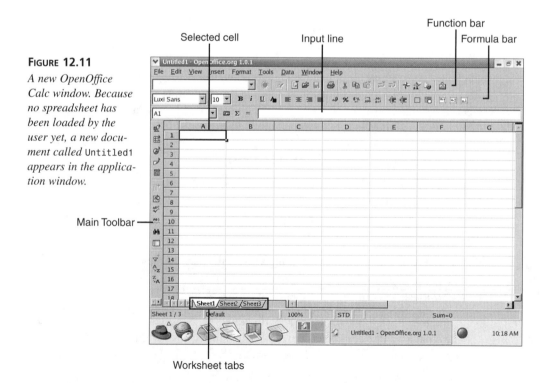

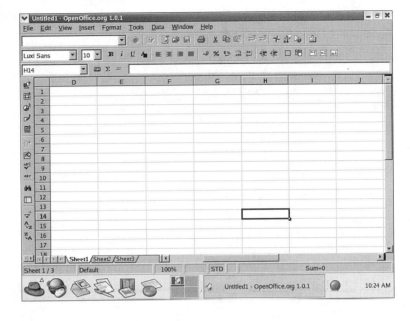

FIGURE 12.12

*Each cell in a spread-
sheet can be refer-
enced with a unique
combination of letters
and numbers. Here,
cell H14 is selected.*

Though you're now visually familiar with Calc, the best way to learn to use a spreadsheet is to start a spreadsheet application and create one. You step through that process in
this section and the sections which follow.

Entering Text Labels

For our sample spreadsheet, let's create a simple sheet that helps keep track of the
amount of money you've found laying around while walking down the street lately.
Though this scenario is a little wishful thinking, it will help illustrate the use of spreadsheets. We start with some text labels to show what our spreadsheet is to be used for.

Text labels are essential in an electronic spreadsheet because they enable those studying
the spreadsheet to understand what the numeric data represents. For example, by entering
the words "Race Times" next to a list of race results or "Monthly Income" next to a
series of numbers representing income on a month-by-month basis, you make the
spreadsheet easier for readers to understand. In our sample spreadsheet, we create a title
for the sheet, along with enough labels for days and weeks to represent one month of
money-finding.

To enter a text label in a cell, select the cell where the text label should start and begin
typing. The text you enter appears both in the cell and on the input line, as shown in
Figure 12.13. When you are done, press Enter to accept the text label you entered.

FIGURE **12.13**

Entering a text label is easy; select the cell where the label should start and begin typing. Here, a label has been entered in B2.

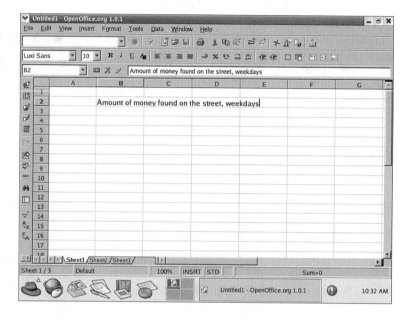

You can change the appearance of the text label text to differentiate it from other entries in the worksheet. You can use a different typeface; alter the font size; apply bold, italic, and underlining; and change the color of the text. To change the appearance of a text label, select the cell containing the label, and then use the tools and selection boxes in the Object bar to apply changes. All these tools appear in the same place in OpenOffice Calc that they did in OpenOffice Writer, with one exception; in Calc, the text color button is immediately to the right of the underline button in the Object bar.

Row size is automatically adjusted for the size of text contained within the cells in a given row. Figure 12.14 shows the same text label as in Figure 12.13, now enlarged slightly and made boldface. A number of additional text labels have been entered as well, in anticipation of the numeric data that is to be entered next.

Entering and Formatting Numeric Data in Cells

To enter numeric data in the spreadsheet, navigate to the cell you want and type in the numbers. When you finish entering a number, press the Enter key to accept the numeric data as the value for the cell.

Figure 12.15 shows the spreadsheet from Figures 12.13 and 12.14 with numeric data filled in.

The numeric values in Figure 12.15 are clearly intended to be currency; however, OpenOffice Calc is dropping trailing zeroes in decimals in some cells (C5, F5, D6, E6, and D8).

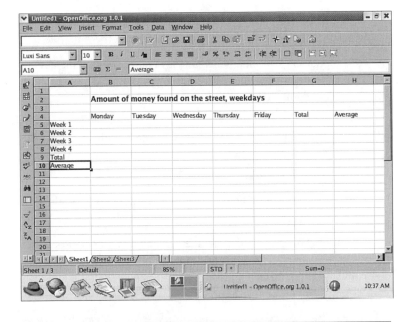

FIGURE **12.14**

The title of the spread-sheet has been made large and boldfaced; a number of additional text labels have been entered in B4 through H4 and A5 through A10.

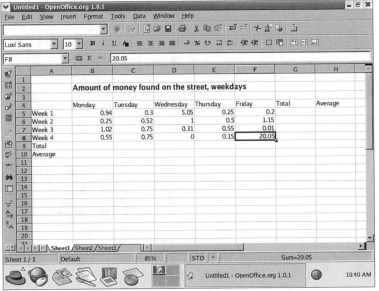

FIGURE **12.15**

The numeric data for this spreadsheet have been filled in by hand, from B5 through F8.

An electronic spreadsheet provides structured formatting of numeric data, to display numbers as a dollar value, percentage, or with a specific number of decimal places. The default numeric format in OpenOffice is the Standard format, in which trailing zeroes after a decimal point are dropped and numbers are otherwise displayed as they were entered. The following are the most common other numeric formats:

- Currency format, which displays numbers with the assumption that they are dollar values—with a leading currency symbol and two digits of precision after the decimal point

- Percentage format, which displays numbers multiplied by 100, with two digits of precision after the decimal point and a trailing percent sign

- Fixed-precision formats, which display numbers with a fixed number of digits of precision after the decimal point

All these types of numeric formats can be applied using the Object bar buttons shown in Figure 12.16.

To format a single cell, select the cell and click the appropriate Object bar button. To format a group of cells, click the upper-left cell with your pointing device and drag to the lower-left cell before releasing. This selects an entire range of cells. Then, click the appropriate Object bar button.

FIGURE 12.16

The Object bar buttons for numeric formatting have been used to alter the appearance of the data in the cells in B5 through H10.

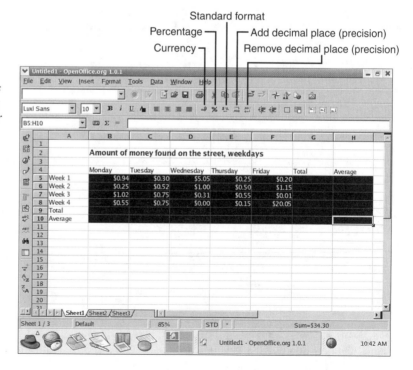

Figure 12.16 shows the sample worksheet with a large range of cells selected and formatting applied. The Object bar button for currency format has already been clicked; all the numeric data has been reformatted to appear as currency. Any numeric data that later appears in the empty selected cells will also appear as currency.

Entering Formulas

Formulas are the essence of the electronic spreadsheet; though formulas may be as simple as an addition or subtraction expression, they may also be extremely complex.

Typical uses for formulas in spreadsheets include finding sums or averages of long lists of numbers or calculating percentages based on known quantities, such as the number of respondents in a survey. Users with more specific needs can perform physics, engineering, or calculus computations in a spreadsheet.

In our sample worksheet, formulas must be used in several places. A number of cells have been reserved to hold column or row totals; these totals will be calculated using formulas. The same is true for the cells left for averages. For example, the total findings for week one are to be displayed in G5. Thus, the number that should eventually appear in G5 should be the result of B5 plus C5 plus D5 plus E5 plus F5.

To enter a formula that performs a series of simple calculations, select the cell in which the result should be displayed. Then, follow these steps:

1. Type an equal sign (=) to indicate to OpenOffice Calc that you are about to enter a formula.

2. Enter a formula consisting of cell references (the letter and number that refer to a cell) and operators such as +, -, /, and *. A cell reference can be entered either by typing the letter and number of a cell or by clicking on the cell in question.

3. After you type the complete formula, press Enter to accept the formula and calculate the result.

The process of entering a simple formula to perform a basic calculation is shown in Figure 12.17.

12

Though the formula entered in G5 is no longer visible in the cell on the spreadsheet, the formula can still be viewed and edited. When G5 is selected, the formula appears in the Input line.

Even though hidden, formulas are always active. If you change the numeric data in a cell used in a formula calculation, the displayed result of the formula calculation is automatically updated to reflect the new numeric data you've entered.

FIGURE 12.17

Entering a formula. G5 displays the results of this calculation, rather than the formula, after Enter is pressed.

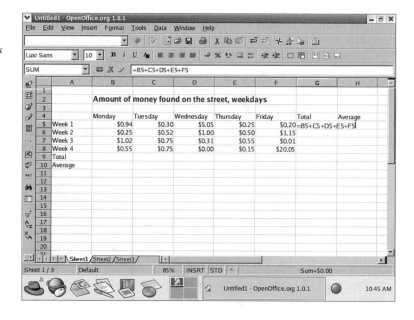

Using Functions in Formulas

Though the formula in G5 works, the method of entering cell references one at a time can become clunky when many cells are involved in a calculation. For many types of common calculations, predefined *functions* are built in to OpenOffice Calc, which can operate on ranges of cells. For example, there is a simpler way to sum several cells and display the result. This simpler formula uses the sum() function, which totals the values in a range of cells. Some functions also provide the ability to perform calculations that have no operator like + or -; the trigonometric functions are examples of these—sin() represents the trigonometric Sine function, cos() the Cosine function, sinh() the Hyperbolic Sine, and cosh() the Hyperbolic Cosine.

A spreadsheet program such as OpenOffice Calc includes hundreds of functions that can be used to perform many different types of calculations in user formulas. You can get a listing of the available functions in OpenOffice Calc and some information on how to use each of them by clicking Insert, Function List and then choosing All from the drop-down list that appears, as shown in Figure 12.18.

To use a function like sum() within a formula, follow these steps:

1. Type an equal sign (=) to indicate to OpenOffice Calc that you are about to enter a formula.

2. Enter the name of the function and a left parenthesis. Then, select a cell or a range of cells upon which the function is to act by clicking or clicking and dragging, as shown in Figure 12.19.

3. Close the function by entering a closing parenthesis.

4. After you type the complete formula, press Enter to accept the formula and calculate the result.

FIGURE 12.18

The Functions dialog enables you to search through and find descriptions of each function in the list of OpenOffice functions.

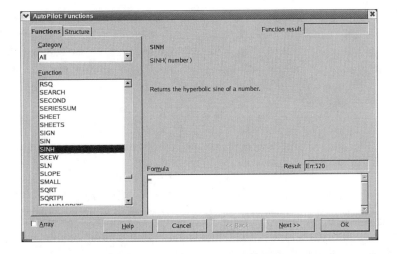

FIGURE 12.19

Entering a function as part of a formula. Enter the name of the function, in this case, sum(, and then select a range of cells using the pointing device.

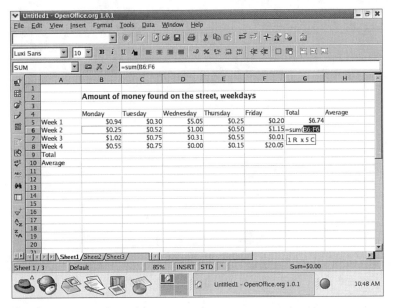

Our sample spreadsheet also includes a number of cells that are designed to hold an average of the amount of found money for a specific day of the week, or a specific week of the month. The average() function, which calculates an average over a range of cells,

can be used to fill these cells. Figure 12.20 shows the spreadsheet with a few more formulas entered.

Copying Formulas

It is quite common for a single formula to be used over and over, needing to be adjusted
only to account for differences in the position of its cell in the spreadsheet. This is the
case in our sample sheet—most of the total and average cells use the same basic calculations (sum or average) over and over again. In cases like this, a formula can be copied
from one cell to another and OpenOffice Calc automatically adjusts the cell references to
compensate.

In our sample spreadsheet, for example, the formula in C9 is essentially the same formula used in B9, except that Calc adds values in column C instead of column B. This is
an ideal candidate for formula copying.

FIGURE 12.20

*The sample spread-
sheet with a few more
formulas filled in.*

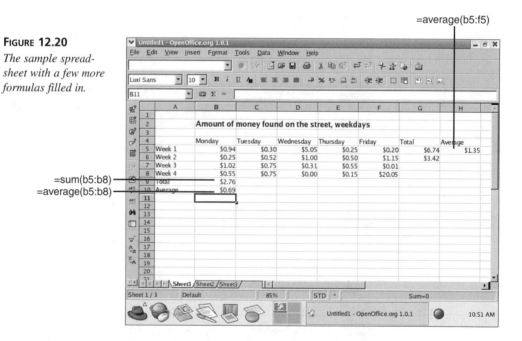

To copy a formula, follow these steps:

1. Select the cell containing the formula you want to copy.

2. Choose Edit, Copy to copy the selected formula.

3. Select the cell or range of cells where you'd like to use the same formula.

4. Choose Edit, Paste to copy the formula to the cells; the same formula appears in each destination cell, but with adjustments for position in the spreadsheet.

Figure 12.21 shows the result of copying the formula in B9 and pasting it into a selected range of cells from C9 through F9. Each cell contains the correct calculation for its column.

Figure 12.22 shows the sample spreadsheet completed, by following these steps:

1. The average formula in B10 was copied to the range of cells from C10 through F10.

2. The total formula in G6 was copied to the range of cells from G7 through G8.

3. The average formula in H5 was copied to the range of cells from H6 through H8.

FIGURE 12.21

The formula from B9 has been copied to cells C9 through F9.

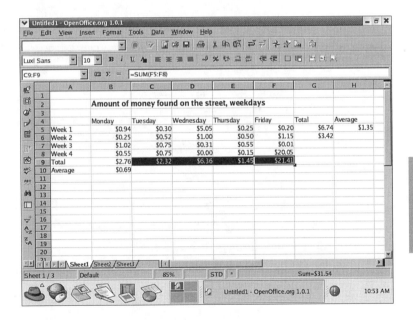

Printing, Saving, and Opening Spreadsheets

Printing, saving, and loading spreadsheets in OpenOffice Calc is nearly identical to printing, saving, and loading word processing documents in OpenOffice Writer.

To save a spreadsheet, follow these steps:

1. Click on File, Save.

2. When the Save as dialog is displayed, select a location and enter a name for your file.

3. If you want to be able to exchange the file with users of MS Office, be sure to select one of the Microsoft Excel formats from the File type drop-down list. If you want to protect your file with a password, check the Save with password box.

4. Click the Save button to save your file.

FIGURE 12.22

The sample spread-sheet is now complete; average money find-ings and total money findings have been computed by day and by week.

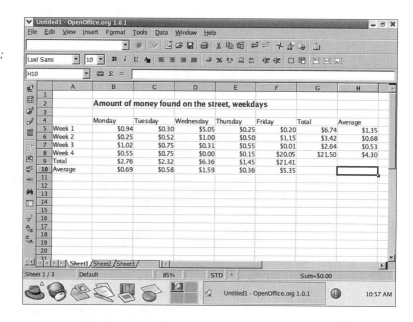

To print a spreadsheet, click on File, Print and click the OK button in the Print dialog. To print only a range of cells that you select, follow these steps:

1. Select the range of cells that you want to print.

2. Click on File, Print to display the Print dialog.

3. Choose the Selection option in the Print range area of the dialog.

4. Click on the Ok button to print your selection.

Summary

This hour, you learned to use the basic features of the two most commonly used OpenOffice applications—OpenOffice Writer, a full-featured word processing application, and OpenOffice Calc, a powerful electronic spreadsheet.

In OpenOffice Writer, you learned to do the following:

- Enter and edit text using your pointing device and the Writer text cursor.

- Select blocks of text in order to move them around or copy them within a document.

- Alter the appearance, size, or style of existing text or newly entered text.
- Change the alignment of text paragraphs to left alignment, right alignment, center alignment, or full justification.
- Change the margins, indentation, and spacing properties of paragraphs within your document.

In OpenOffice Calc, you learned to do the following:

- Navigate an electronic spreadsheet and identify and select specific cells.
- Enter text labels into cells and adjust their appearance.
- Enter numeric values into cells and change their format for more attractive output.
- Enter formulas to perform calculations based on numeric data in other cells in the spreadsheet.
- Find and use functions within your formulas.
- Copy formulas from one cell to another cell or a range of cells to save time and effort.

In both applications, you learned to save your work, load existing files, and print the documents you create.

Q&A

Q Is there a spell check in OpenOffice Writer?

A Yes. You can access the spell check feature by clicking Tools, Spellcheck, Check. This displays a spell check dialog; as each misspelled word is found, you can replace it with a word from a list of possible corrections or enter a new correction on your own.

Q In Microsoft Word or Corel WordPerfect, when I misspell a word as I type, the word processor underlines that word in red so that I know it's been misspelled. Does Writer have similar functionality?

A Yes. On the Main Toolbar down the left side of the Writer window, you'll see a small button containing the letters ABC over a wavy red line. Clicking this button enables the spell-as-you-go feature.

Q Can I mix numbers, cell references, operators like + and -, and functions in a single formula in Calc?

A Yes. In formulas, you can mix numeric elements, operators, and functions in any order. For example, the following formula is valid and works as expected:

=sin(F26/100+G26*1.1)+10

12

Workshop

The Workshop is designed to help you anticipate possible questions, review what you've learned, and begin learning how to put your knowledge into practice.

Quiz

1. How do you italicize a block of text in Writer?

2. How do you change to double-spacing in Writer?

3. How do you begin a formula in Calc?

4. How do you format a range of numeric data cells as currency in Calc?

5. How do you use a simple function such as `sum()` or `average()` within a formula in Calc?

Answers

1. Select the block of text with your pointing device, and then click the italic button in the Object bar.

2. Choose Format, Paragraph to open the Paragraph dialog box, and then choose Double Spacing in the line spacing drop-down list.

3. Click the cell you want, and then type the equal sign.

4. Select the range of cells with your pointing device, and then click the currency format button in the Object bar.

5. Enter the name of the function by hand followed by the left parenthesis. Then, select the range of cells to include in the function's calculation using your pointing device. Finally, close the function by entering a right parenthesis.

Activities

1. Create a new Writer document, save it, exit Writer, and then restart Writer and open the document again to become familiar with saving and opening files.

2. Explore the different fonts, sizes, and styles available to you while creating documents in Writer.

3. Try using Calc for a practical calculation of some sort, such as a budget or balancing a checkbook.

4. See what happens when negative numbers are entered into Calc cells.

Hour 13

Networking on the Desktop

This hour is designed to help you become proficient in using networks on the Linux desktop. The most important network of all, the Internet—and by extension the World Wide Web—figures prominently, but you also explore some interaction on local area networks. By the time you're done, you'll learn

- How to launch and use the Mozilla Web browser to access your favorite sites on the World Wide Web

- How to configure and use the Evolution email and calendar client to send and receive Internet email

- How to browse a Windows-based local area network and access files on Windows hosts using the file manager

- How to transfer files to and from a file transfer protocol server using desktop tools

If you are already familiar with use of the Mozilla Web browser, either with Linux or another platform such as Windows or Mac OS, you will find that you already know most of what is presented in the browsing-oriented section of this hour. If you find this to be true in your case, feel free to skip ahead to the sections on email or file exchange.

Introducing Mozilla

By far the most visible use for computer networking technology worldwide is for access to the many sites and pages of the World Wide Web. It is widely known that the most common platform for accessing the World Wide Web is the Internet Explorer Web browser. Although Internet Explorer is available for both Windows and Mac OS, Microsoft has chosen not to produce a version of Internet Explorer for Linux.

Linux World Wide Web users have always been supported instead by Netscape Corporation and the Netscape Web browser. In 1998, Netscape Corporation made the Netscape Web browser an open-source product and the Mozilla project was born. Mozilla is a modern, feature-full, standards-compliant Web browser and is now the primary platform for browsing the Web on the Linux desktop.

Launching the Mozilla Browser

The Mozilla Web browser can be launched by clicking the Web Browser icon on the toolbar. The icon appears as a picture of a computer mouse circling the globe.

Browsing the Web with Mozilla

After the Mozilla Web browser is loaded, a new Mozilla browser application window appears on your desktop showing the default Welcome to Red Hat Linux page, as shown in Figure 13.1.

Each of the items shown in Figure 13.1 performs an important function while you are using Mozilla:

- The URL bar shows the address of the currently displayed Web site and enables you to enter addresses for new Web sites that are to be displayed.
- The Status bar shows the progress Mozilla is making in loading a new Web page.
- The Personal toolbar contains a list of folders and bookmarks to enable you to more easily collect and visit your favorite Web sites.
- The Application launchers are used to start Mozilla components, such as the Mail & Newsgroups client.

- The sidebar provides centralized access to many of Mozilla's functions.
- The currently displayed Web page is the large area of the application window, in which you can interact with the site you're currently visiting.

FIGURE 13.1

Clicking the Web Browser icon causes the Mozilla Web browser to appear on the desktop.

URL bar   Personal toolbar

Web Browser   Status bar
icon

Visiting a Web Site

To visit a new Web site, move your pointer so that it is inside the URL bar and double-click. The currently displayed URL address is highlighted. After the current URL has been highlighted, begin typing the URL you want to visit; the original URL disappears as you enter the new address. Press Enter when you finish typing the URL. Figure 13.2 shows Mozilla displaying the URL `http://www.yahoo.com/`, otherwise known as Yahoo!, one of the most popular destinations on the World Wide Web.

> *URL* stands for *Uniform Resource Locator*; a URL is more commonly known simply as an *address*. You know an Internet address or URL because it begins with a word followed by a colon and two slashes, like `http://` for Web sites or `ftp://` for file transfer protocol archives that hold downloadable files.

13

The browser window in Figure 13.2 has been maximized so that it occupies the entire screen. To maximize your browser window, click the maximize window decoration near the upper right of the window's title bar.

Because the sidebar uses valuable screen real estate and because the sidebar is a little-used feature that we won't be discussing in this hour, the sidebar has been disabled as well. To disable your sidebar, click View, Show/Hide, Sidebar.

FIGURE 13.2

A new URL, http:// www.yahoo.com, *has been entered and Mozilla has loaded and displayed the page.*

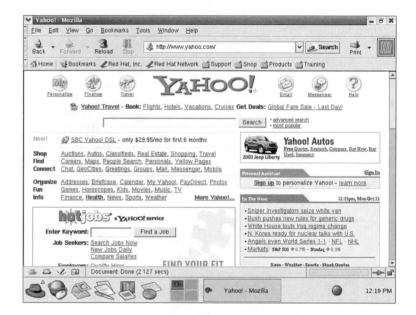

Like most Web sites, Yahoo! is too long to be displayed within a single screen of information. You can scroll upward and downward by clicking and dragging on the scrollbar at the right edge of the Mozilla window. For pages that are also too wide to fit into the Mozilla window horizontally, you can scroll left and right by clicking and dragging on the scrollbar at the bottom edge of the Mozilla window.

Navigating Web Sites

Browsing the Web is not simply a matter of entering new URLs into the URL bar; central to the life of the World Wide Web is the *hyperlink*, a word or image displayed in the browser window that, when clicked, automatically loads and displays a new URL. As you move your mouse around the browser window, you know that you have encountered a hyperlink when the appearance of the mouse pointer changes from an arrow to a hand.

Figure 13.3 shows the result of clicking the words `Yahoo Health` shown in Figure 13.2. Notice that the URL in the URL bar has been updated to reflect the address of the page that is now being displayed.

Back button
Forward button

FIGURE 13.3

Clicking a hyperlink at `http://www.yahoo.com` *has caused this site,* `http://health.yahoo.com,` *to be displayed. The new URL is reflected in the URL bar. The Back button has become active.*

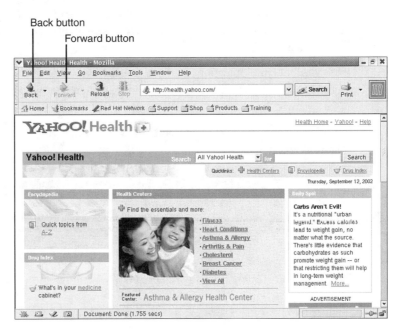

After you view at least two sites in succession, either by entering new URLs yourself or by clicking hyperlinks, you see the Back button become active. The Back button enables you to return to the URL you were viewing immediately before the URL currently being displayed.

Similarly, after you click the Back button, you see the Forward button become active. After you click the Back button to return to an earlier URL, you can use the Forward button to return again to the later URL. Both the Back and Forward buttons are shown clearly in Figure 13.3.

13

Sometimes it is helpful to be able to return to a URL you visited several sites ago. Rather than clicking the Back button repeatedly, try clicking the small downward arrow to the right of the Back button. This displays a drop-down containing your *history*—a list of the most recent few URLs you loaded—and you can then choose to return to any of them by clicking its entry in the list.

The small downward arrow to the right of the Forward button provides similar functionality, but moves you forward through the list instead.

Remembering URLs You Like

Sometimes as you're clicking hyperlinks, visiting page after page on the World Wide Web, you encounter a Web page whose address you'd like to save so that you can return directly to it at some later time. Rather than try to remember the URL displayed in the URL bar or write the URL down somewhere, you can use the Mozilla *bookmarks* function to remember the address for you.

A browser bookmark functions in much the same way that a real bookmark does. It saves your place so that you can return to the same location later without a lot of extra searching or legwork. Remembering a URL this way is known as *bookmarking* it.

To bookmark any site you are currently viewing, click Bookmarks, Bookmark This Page, as shown in Figure 13.4.

FIGURE 13.4

Choosing to bookmark the current page causes its address to be remembered for easy access later.

Bookmarks that you create this way are added as clickable options to the bottom of the Bookmarks menu. After you create a bookmark, you can reload the page at any time by clicking Bookmarks and then the entry for the URL you want to visit.

Browsing with Tabs

Whether for the purpose of comparing two Web sites or for some other reason, it is often helpful to be able to load two Web pages at the same time and then switch between them quickly. Rather than use two browser windows to accomplish this task, Mozilla offers another solution: tabbed browsing.

Tabbed browsing is a method of keeping two or more Web pages loaded at the same time and allowing the user to switch between them with a single click. To create a new tab, press Ctrl+T. A tab index appears and a second tab is created, as shown in Figure 13.5.

FIGURE 13.5

A new tab is created; it is currently blank because no URL has been entered yet. The original Web page is still in Mozilla's memory; it can be displayed by clicking its tab.

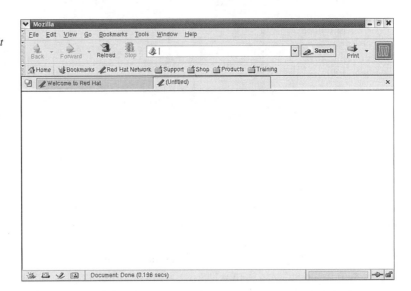

Each tab can hold its own Web page; to load a Web page into a tab, click the tab you want to use, and then enter the desired URL into the URL box and press Enter. The title of the Web page loaded into a given tab is always displayed on the tab's label. Each time you want to create an additional tab, press Ctrl+T.

To delete a tab, click it. After the tab in question has been displayed, either click the X to the extreme right of the tabs index or right-click the tab in question and choose Close Tab in the pop-up context menu that appears.

Disabling Pop-up Windows

Though the default Mozilla configuration is functional and adequate for many purposes, you might want to alter one preference. Mozilla can be configured to prevent the appearance of various types of pop-up windows. Some pop-up windows are desirable—for example, when a site opens a window that contains specific functionality or information in response to your click. Most pop-up windows, however, are displayed automatically. These types typically contain advertisements and annoy most users.

To disable nonrequested pop-up windows, click Edit, Preferences to display the Mozilla preferences dialog, as shown in Figure 13.6.

13

Uncheck to disable pop-ups

FIGURE 13.6

*In the Scripts &
Plugins window in the
Preferences dialog,
you can prevent most
types of unwanted
pop-ups.*

Click to expand

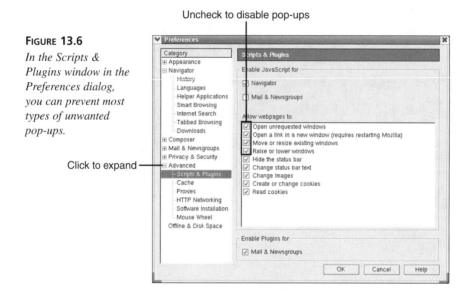

In the list of categories on the left, expand the Advanced category by clicking the plus sign to the left, and then select the Scripts & Plugins item. Unchecking the first four options disables nearly all forms of pop-up advertising currently used on the World Wide Web.

After you make the necessary changes, click OK to save them and dismiss the Preferences dialog.

Exiting Mozilla

To exit Mozilla at any time, click File, Quit or use the application close button at the extreme upper right of the application window.

Reading and Writing Email

Many users of the Internet today read and respond to their email using Web-based mail services such as Yahoo! Mail or Hotmail. If you access your mail this way, the previous section on Web browsing with Mozilla also provided you with the necessary skills to access your email within Linux.

If on the other hand you are accustomed to accessing your mail with a standalone mail program such as Microsoft Outlook or your Internet Service Provider (ISP) has given you an email account that you want to use, this section is where you'll get email up and running.

In Red Hat Linux, the email program many people prefer is a GUI-based mail and calendar program called Evolution that in many ways is similar to Microsoft Outlook.

Launching Evolution

To launch Evolution, click the email icon on the taskbar. The icon looks like a postage stamp hovering above an envelope.

When you click the icon, a splash window showcasing the logo for Ximian, the developer responsible for Evolution, is displayed for a few moments before the application starts.

Configuring Evolution

After a brief period of time, the splash window is replaced by the Evolution Setup Assistant dialog box, containing a greeting message. Click the Next button to continue with Evolution configuration. The Identity configuration pane is displayed, as shown in Figure 13.7.

Enter your full name as you want it to appear to others and your email address as supplied by your Internet Service Provider or network administrator. If you want to associate yourself with a particular organization (often your company name), enter that in the Organization box.

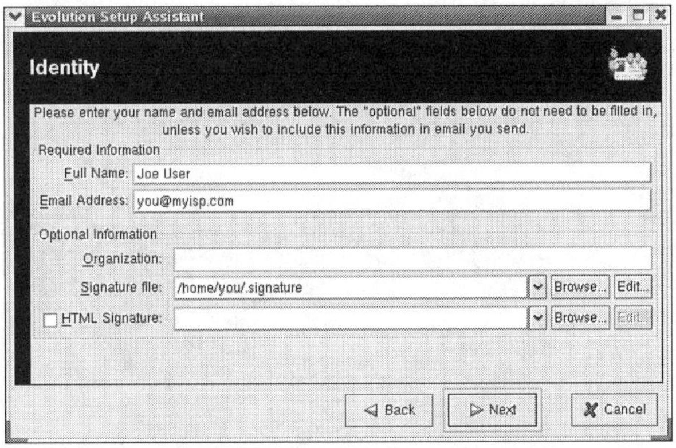

FIGURE 13.7

In the Identity configuration pane, you can enter your full name, your email address, an optional organization, and signature files to be added to the end of each message.

The two signature boxes are for entering the names of text files that are automatically added to the end of any email that you send as a kind of signature. For example, if you have created a file called /home/you/myaddress that contains your address and contact information in a few short lines and you'd like to add this to the end of each email you send, enter **/home/you/myaddress** into the Signature file box.

Click Next when you finish entering information in the Identity pane. The Receiving Email pane is displayed, containing a drop-down list that enables you to choose an email server type. The type of server you should select depends on how your mail delivery is configured and the type of service you use to access the Internet.

- Select POP if you connect to the Internet through an ISP who uses a POP server or your mail is delivered to a host that employs a POP server. Most dial-up Internet users choose this option.

- Select IMAP if you connect to the Internet through an ISP who uses an IMAP server or your mail is delivered to a host that employs an IMAP server. Most users of corporate networks choose this option.

- Select Local Delivery if your computer is a server or workstation connected directly to the Internet with its own domain name that is also your email address; also select this option if you plan to use the `fetchmail` program to retrieve your mail from POP or IMAP servers, as was described in Hour 8, "Networking Without Graphics."

- The other options, Standard Unix mbox spools, Maildir-format mail directories, and None are for unusual situations and should not normally be used.

If you select Local delivery, a text box is displayed containing a pre-entered spool name, /var/spool/mail/you. This is the path to your Linux mail spool and should not be changed. Click Next to continue with configuration.

If you select POP or IMAP, the Receiving Email pane changes to include a series of entry boxes designed to enable you to enter details about the mail server from which your mail should be collected, as shown in Figure 13.8.

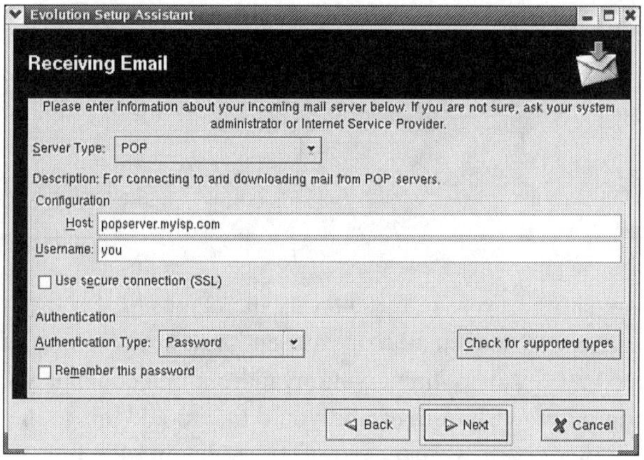

FIGURE 13.8

When POP or IMAP delivery is selected, you are asked to provide information about the mail server that hosts your email.

Enter the name of your POP or IMAP server into the box labeled Host and the name of your login account on that server into the box labeled Username. This information should have been provided to you by your ISP, network administrator, or hosting company. If you have been instructed to enable a secure connection via SSL, check the Use secure connection box.

Leave the password type set to Password unless you were instructed to do otherwise by your network administrator, mail host, or ISP. If you want Evolution to remember your password rather than asking you for a password each time you read your mail, check the Remember this password box.

After you enter the necessary information about your IMAP or POP server, click the Next button to continue with configuration. Whether you select Local delivery, POP, or IMAP as your delivery type, after clicking Next you should see a second Receiving Email pane containing additional options, as shown in Figures 13.9 and 13.10.

FIGURE **13.9**

The Receiving Email pane in the Evolution Setup Assistant for users who select POP delivery.

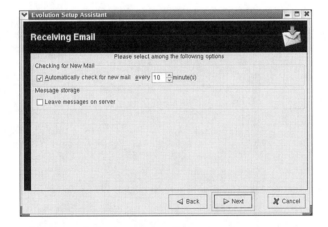

FIGURE **13.10**

The second Receiving Email pane in the Evolution Setup Assistant for users who select IMAP delivery.

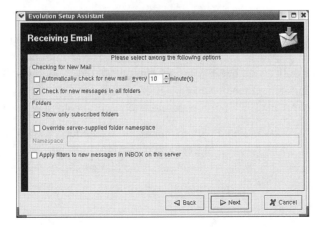

13

If you want Evolution to automatically check your email on a periodic basis whenever it is running, check Automatically check for new mail and adjust the timer to reflect the number of minutes you'd like Evolution to wait between each mail query. Be sure not to check too often or you might use more than your fair share of network resources, thereby annoying the administrators responsible for your mail server.

If you use IMAP delivery and want to apply mail filters you create to messages on the server, check the Apply filters to new messages box. (If you don't know what filters are or don't plan to use them, leave this setting as it is.)

Unless you have been instructed to do otherwise by your network administrator, ISP, or mail host, leave any other settings on the second Receiving Email pane as they appear by default. After you adjust the options in the second Receiving Email pane to suit your needs, click Next to proceed to the Sending Email configuration pane, shown in Figure 13.11.

FIGURE 13.11
The Sending Email pane enables you to configure your out-bound mail service according to your needs.

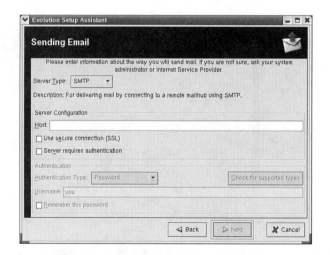

If you have not been provided with the name of an outbound mail server by your ISP or network administrator, select Sendmail as your Server Type now. The Sendmail option generally works well, but if your computer is not directly connected to the Internet with a Fully Qualified Domain Name (FQDN), you might find that a few systems refuse to accept your mail. There are no additional options to configure for Sendmail delivery.

If you have been provided with the name of an outbound SMTP mail server by your ISP or network administrator, select SMTP as your Server Type and adjust the items in the rest of the Sending Email pane to match the outbound mail server information you've been given:

- Enter the domain name of the outbound mail server in the Host box.

- Check Use secure connection if your ISP supports secure SMTP, or if you have been instructed to do so by the administrator of the outbound mail server.

- If you have been assigned an account and password to use with your outbound mail server, check the Server requires authentication box and enter your account information.

- If you have been assigned an account and password to use with your outbound mail server and want the password to be remembered rather than having to type a password each time you send an email, check Remember this password.

After you finish configuring the items in the Sending Email pane, click Next. The Account Management pane is displayed. The options on the Account Management pane should not be changed if this is your first time using Evolution. Because you have only one account configured so far, it should be treated as the default account. The Name of the account is chosen based on the settings you entered in earlier panes. Click Next to proceed to the Timezone configuration pane, as shown in Figure 13.12.

FIGURE 13.12

The Timezone configuration pane enables you to select your time zone so that your all email messages are dated correctly.

The Timezone configuration panel contains a number of small pink dots; as you move over each dot, the name of the city or location the dot represents is displayed at the bottom of the panel. Click the dot closest to you to select the correct time zone. If none of the dots represents a location you know to be in your time zone, the drop-down list at the bottom of the display contains a much longer list of place names. Select one that shares your time zone.

13

After you choose your time zone, click Next. If you have used another email program—such as Pine—Evolution asks whether you want to import your email from the other program. If you choose to do so, your email is copied into Evolution's mailbox. After all configuration is done, the Evolution Setup Assistant displays a message indicating that you successfully configured Evolution. Click Finish to launch and begin using the main Evolution application now.

Composing a New Email

The main Evolution window appears and the summary page is displayed after you finish Evolution configuration. The maximized main window is shown in Figure 13.13.

Inbox (email) button   Mail summary

FIGURE 13.13

The Evolution Summary page presents an Outlook-like layout; among the many functions available is the Inbox (email) button.

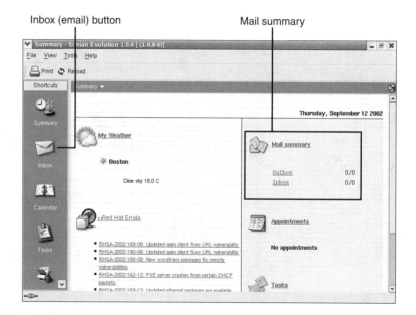

To prepare to send a new email message, click the Inbox button at the left of the application window to start the email component of Evolution; the email component appears, as shown in Figure 13.14.

To send a new email message, click the New Message button near the upper left of the Evolution email application. The message composer is displayed, as shown in Figure 13.15.

Enter the email address of the person for whom this message is destined in the To: box and a subject for this email message in the Subject: box. If you want to send this email message to more than one person, enter additional email addresses, separated by spaces, in the Cc: (carbon copy) box.

New message
(compose) button

FIGURE 13.14

The Evolution email component is displayed after you click the Inbox button down the left side of the Evolution application window.

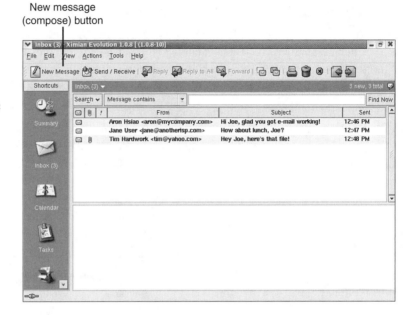

FIGURE 13.15

Use the Evolution message composer window to create and send new email messages.

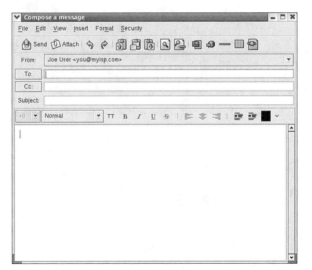

13

After you fill out the header (destination and subject) of your message, click in the message entry area and begin to type your message.

Using HTML Formatting in Your Message

If you want to enable HTML (Web-style) formatting for the message you're writing, click Format, HTML. The text editing toolbar, shown in Figure 13.16, is activated. This enables you to alter the appearance, size, or alignment of parts of your message to suit your tastes.

The buttons in the text editing toolbar work very much like the formatting buttons you encountered in OpenOffice Writer in Hour 12, "Introducing OpenOffice." Either select text you want to alter and click buttons to perform the alterations you want to make, or position your cursor, click a button, and enter new text with the property you've selected.

FIGURE 13.16

Use the buttons in the text editing toolbar to change the appearance, size, or alignment of your text.

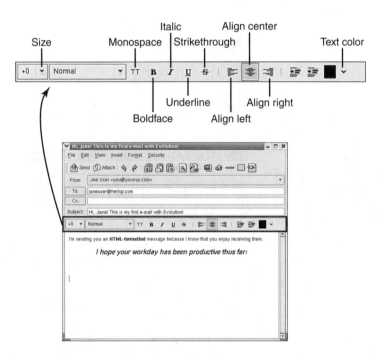

Although most users at Web-based mail services such as Yahoo! mail or Hotmail are able to receive HTML formatting in their email, many other email users across the Internet are not able (or don't want) to receive HTML-formatted messages.

Because not everyone is prepared to receive HTML-formatted messages, some people consider it annoying to receive them. Before you send these specially formatted messages make sure your intended recipient does not object to receiving HTML mail.

Attaching a File to Your Message

It is often helpful to be able to attach files to your messages in order to share your work with others across the Internet. To attach a file to an outbound message in the Evolution message composer, click the Attach button. The Attach a file dialog appears, as shown in Figure 13.17.

Browse to the file you want to attach, click the file's name in the file dialog, and click OK. The file is attached to the email message, as shown in Figure 13.18.

FIGURE 13.17

When you click Attach in the composer window, a file dialog appears to enable you to select a file to attach to your email message.

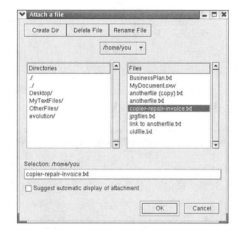

FIGURE 13.18

An attached file is given an icon at the bottom of the composer window. The attached file's name appears beneath the icon.

Icon for attached file

13

If you change your mind about a file you've attached and want to remove it again, right-click the attached file's icon at the bottom of the Evolution composer window and choose Remove from the pop-up context menu that appears. The file, and the icon that represents it, will be removed from your message.

Sending Your Message

After you finish composing your message, addressed it, given it a subject, and attached any files you want to send along with it, you are ready to send the message across the network to your intended recipient.

To send your message, click the Send button at the upper left of the composer window. Evolution displays a message near the bottom of the window indicating that it is attempting to send the message, as shown in Figure 13.19.

FIGURE 13.19

Evolution indicates that it is attempting to send the message you've composed.

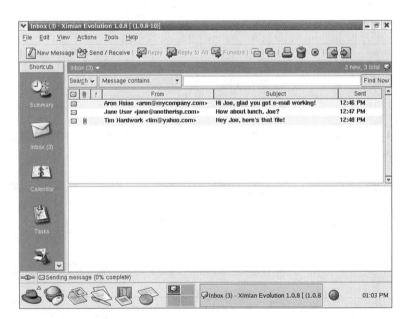

Downloading New Mail

Before you can read your email messages using Evolution, you must collect them, either from your mail server or from your Linux mail storage if you receive mail directly to your system. Click the Send/Receive button to initiate mail downloading. A progress dialog appears, indicating that mail is in transit, as shown in Figure 13.20. If you are connecting to a mail server, you are asked to provide your password before mail can be exchanged.

After communication with the mail server about new messages is complete, any new mail waiting for you is listed in the index in your default mail folder, as shown in Figure 13.21. The number of unread messages waiting in your inbox is shown in parentheses in the application title bar. To display a message, click it and it is displayed in the lower pane.

Send/Receive button

FIGURE 13.20

A progress dialog indicates that mail is being transferred.

Replying To or Forwarding a Message

To reply to a message you're viewing, click the reply button at the top of the Evolution mail window. A new message composer window is opened with the To: and Subject: boxes already filled out to reflect the fact that you are sending a reply.

Enter your message as you normally would and finally click the Send button in the composer window to send your reply. To forward a message you're viewing to another user, click the Forward button at the top of the Evolution mail window. A new message composer window is opened containing the contents of the message and a small header indicating that it's been forwarded. Enter a destination address in the To: box and click the Send button in the composer window to send your reply.

13

FIGURE 13.21
New mail is indexed in the upper pane of the Evolution window. When you click a message, the body of the message is displayed in the lower pane.

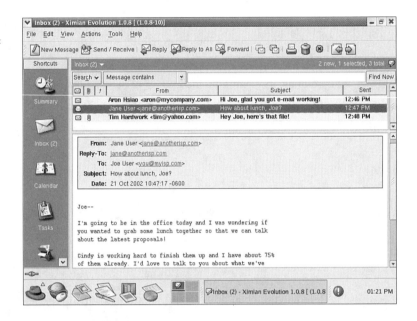

Accessing an Attachment

Incoming messages with attached files are marked with a paper clip icon in their index entry. At the bottom of the displayed message, an attachment icon and the attached file's name also appear, as shown in Figure 13.22.

To access the attachment, click the down arrow next to the attached file icon. A pop-up menu appears asking whether you want to save the file or open it in one of several applications.

If you want to save the file to your account, click Save to Disk. A file dialog appears, enabling you to name and save the file as desired.

The other actions listed in the pop-up menu list various applications that can be used to open the attached file for viewing or for editing. If you select one of these, the application you select is launched and the attached file is automatically loaded for you.

Printing and Deleting

To print a message, click the print message button. The Print Message dialog box appears, enabling you to print more than one copy of the message if desired. Click the Print button in the dialog to send the job to the printer after you enter the number of copies you want to print.

Paperclip icon

FIGURE **13.22**

Attachments in email messages are indicated in the index by a paper clip icon and in the message body by an icon and filename at the bottom of the message.

Attached file

To delete a message, click the delete message button. The message is marked for deletion, indicated by a strikeout line through the message's entry in the index, as shown in Figure 13.23.

FIGURE **13.23**

The first message in the index is marked for deletion, as is indicated by the line through the message entry.

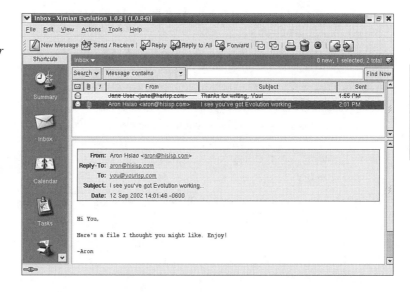

13

To purge (completely erase) messages that have been marked for deletion, click Actions, Empty Trash. A warning is displayed asking you to confirm your request before the messages are finally deleted.

If you have marked a message for deletion but want to restore it so that it won't be deleted next time you empty the trash, click your right mouse button on the message's entry in the index and choose Undelete from the pop-up context menu that appears. The horizontal line through the message disappears, showing that the message is no longer marked for deletion.

Exiting Evolution

To exit Evolution at time, click File, Quit or use the application close button at the extreme upper right of the application window.

Accessing Windows Networks

Most local networks today are Windows networks. To be useful, a Linux workstation must be able to access files and directories on Windows servers around the local area network.

The Red Hat Linux desktop does not ship with a My Network Places or Network Neighborhood icon. However, using the desktop file manager, it is possible to access files and folders across the local Windows network.

Accessing Files on Windows Machines in GNOME

To access the files on a Windows host on the local network using Nautilus, the GNOME file manager, open a file manager window by double-clicking the Home icon on your desktop. The familiar file manager window from Hour 10, "Introducing the Red Hat Desktop," appears. Initially, the files in /home/you are displayed; this is reflected in the Location bar.

Click in the Location bar and backspace over /home/you. In place of /home/you, enter the URL smb://*windowshost* where *windowshost* is the name of a Windows host or server on the local network whose resources you want to browse. The contents of a Windows host called newton are shown in Figure 13.24. Note the contents of the Location bar.

While browsing a Windows host using the file manager, you can navigate the remote file system just as you would local files in the file manager window.

FIGURE 13.24

Browsing the contents of a Windows host called newton *on the local area network by entering an* **smb://** *URL into the file manager window.*

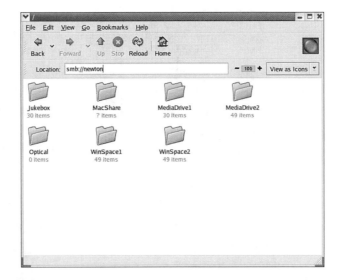

Using File Transfer Protocol (FTP) on the Desktop

Many networks continue to use file transfer protocol (FTP) to distribute files internally, and many of the best download sites on the Internet still use FTP as their primary method of file exchange.

In Hour 8, you learned to use the classic Unix ftp client at the command line. However, a more user-friendly application for FTP file exchange exists for use on the desktop. To start the desktop FTP client, click GNOME Menu, Extras, Internet, gFTP. A similar menu path can be used to start gFTP in the KDE: KDE Menu, Extras, Internet, gFTP.

After clicking gFTP, the gFTP application is displayed, as shown in Figure 13.25.

Connecting to a Remote System

To connect to a remote system using gFTP, open a gFTP application window and then follow these steps:

1. Click in the Host address box and enter the name of the remote host you'd like to connect to.
2. Click in the Login box and enter your login account name on the remote system.
3. Click in the Password box and enter your password on the remote system.
4. Click the Connect button.

13

FIGURE 13.25

The gFTP application (shown maximized) can be used to transfer files via file transfer protocol.

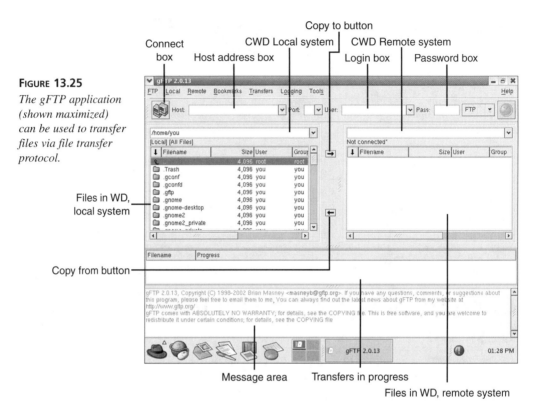

Your system then attempts to connect to the remote system using the information you've entered. Information on the progress of the connection attempt is displayed in the Message area. When the connection is established, you see a list of the files in the current location on the remote system in the files list for the remote system (on the right side of the gFTP window). Figure 13.26 shows a gFTP window connected to a remote system.

Copying Files to a Remote System

To upload or copy files to a remote system you're connected to using gFTP, follow these steps:

1. In the panel on the left side of the gFTP window (the local panel), navigate to the directory containing the files you want to copy from the local system. This can be done either by double-clicking successive directory icons until you reach the correct working directory, or by simply entering a path, such as **/home/you/myfiles**, into the current working directory bar.

2. In the panel on the right side of the gFTP window (the remote panel), navigate using the same techniques to the directory you want to copy the files to.

FIGURE 13.26

*The gFTP window
after a connection has
been made. Now the
panel on the right is no
longer empty; it lists
the files in the current
working directory on
the remote system.*

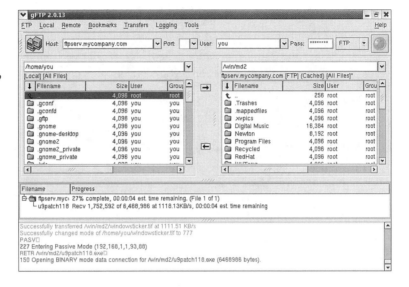

3. In the local panel, click the name of a file you want to transfer so that it is high-lighted.

4. Click the Copy-to button. As the file is being transferred, details about the transfer appear in the Filename Progress box. When the transfer is complete, the file also appears in the remote directory listing on the right.

5. Repeat steps 3 and 4 for each file you want to copy.

If you want to copy many files at once, you can select a range of files by clicking and highlighting the first file, and then holding down the Shift key and clicking the last file. An entire range of files are highlighted, and any copy operations then act on the entire list of files you've selected.

You can also select multiple files individually by holding down the Ctrl key as you click each file.

13

Copying Files from a Remote System

To download or copy files from a remote system you're connected to using gFTP, follow these steps:

1. In the panel on the right side of the gFTP window (the remote panel), navigate to the directory containing the files you want to copy to the local system.

2. In the panel on the left side of the gFTP window (the local panel), navigate to the directory you'd like to copy the remote files to.

3. In the remote panel, click the name of a file you want to transfer so that it is highlighted.

4. Click the Copy-from button. The file is transferred from the remote system to your system. When the transfer is complete, the file also appears in the local directory listing on the left.

5. Repeat steps 3 and 4 for each file you want to copy.

Closing an FTP Connection

To close an open gFTP connection, click the Connect button. The connection is closed and the list of files in the remote panel is cleared.

To exit gFTP, click FTP, Quit.

Summary

This hour, you learned to use several desktop networking tools to accomplish common networking tasks on the Red Hat Linux desktop.

You learned to do the following while using the Mozilla Web browser:

- Load and display a new Web page.
- Create and destroy tabs to hold multiple Web pages.
- Create bookmarks to your favorite Web sites and manage your personal toolbar.
- Disable pop-up ads while browsing the Web.

You learned to do the following while using the Evolution email and calendar client:

- Configure a new email account on a POP or IMAP server or using a local Linux mail spool.
- Create and send email messages in plain text or HTML format, attaching files to your messages as needed.
- Read and reply to incoming mail addressed to you.

You also learned to use the GNOME and KDE file managers to browse files on Windows hosts using the smb:// URL, and to connect to and exchange files with file transfer protocol servers using the gFTP application.

Q&A

Q Doesn't the Mozilla application also contain an email client?

A Yes. If you are more comfortable using Mozilla email than Evolution, feel free to use it instead. Evolution was discussed here because it is the tool preferred (and used by default) by Red Hat Linux.

Q Is there any way to browse windows workgroups or domains, similar to what happens when I double-click Network Neighborhood or My Network Places on a Windows host?

A The Red Hat Linux desktop and GNOME and KDE file managers do not provide functionality that reliably duplicates this type of browsing on Windows hosts. It is therefore necessary to know the name of the Windows host you want to access and to use the `smb://` URL to do so.

Workshop

The Workshop is designed to help you anticipate possible questions, review what you've learned, and begin learning how to put your knowledge into practice.

Quiz

1. How do you know whether a message in Evolution has been marked for deletion?

2. How do you enable the HTML editing mode in the Evolution message composer?

3. How do you list the volumes on a Windows host called `winstation10` using a Linux file manager?

Answers

1. Deleted messages appear to have a line drawn through them in the message index.

2. In the message composer, click Format, HTML.

3. Enter `smb://winstation10` into the Location box of the file manager (this works identically in either KDE or GNOME).

Activities

1. Browse to all your favorite Web sites in the Mozilla Web browser and add them to your list of bookmarks.

2. Spend some time exploring the other features and areas of the Evolution email and calendar client.

13

3. Send an email to a friend using Evolution and ask him or her to send a reply in order to test your Evolution email configuration.

4. Try browsing a few nearby Windows hosts using your file manager.

HOUR 14

Getting Help on the Desktop

When you work with Red Hat Linux, you have a number of Help tools and resources available to you. Both KDE and GNOME offer their own help resources, and you also can access systemwide help through menus in individual applications. This hour, you learn how to use desktop tools to find these and other help and documentation materials for assistance with applications and commands commonly used in Red Hat Linux systems. By the end of the hour, you'll know how to do the following:

- Find help information on a per-application basis using desktop application menus.
- Use the GNOME Help Browser to read comprehensive documentation for the GNOME environment.
- Use the KDE HelpCenter to read comprehensive documentation for the KDE.
- Take advantage of user-friendly desktop tools to read manual pages and info pages.

After you learn these techniques for finding and using desktop help, you can reference nearly any kind of online documentation available in a Red Hat Linux installation.

Using Application Help

The most natural place to find help or documentation information for an application is within the application itself. Nearly every desktop application you use in Linux includes some form of online help that you can open from within the application.

Documentation of this sort is most useful, because it is written by the authors of the application in question. This documentation typically assumes that readers are actually *using* the application while reading the help information. As a result, you should be able to use the documentation to work through your problem step-by-step, often with alternative suggestions and other information to assist you with snags you might encounter.

Finding and Launching Application Help

When an application includes its own online help or documentation file(s), it is generally accessible through the Help menu found in the application menu bar (by convention, the Help menu is the rightmost menu on the menu bar).

In any application, the Help menu contains a list of help and documentation-related options. In GNOME applications, the Help menu contains (at least) the Contents option, which launches application documentation, and the About option, which displays the application version, copyright, authors, and other miscellaneous information.

A typical GNOME application help menu is shown in Figure 14.1.

In KDE applications, the Help menu is typically more extensive, commonly containing several options, including

- Handbook, which contains application documentation
- What's This?, which provides context-sensitive help for various parts of the application window
- Report a Bug, which enables the user to report problems encountered while using the application
- About, which displays the application version, copyright, authors, and other miscellaneous information

You might also find additional options to supplemental documentation; the absence or presence of such supplemental documentation varies on an application-by-application basis. A typical KDE Help menu is shown in Figure 14.2.

FIGURE 14.1

Opening the Help menu in a GNOME application will generally reveal at least a Contents option and an About option.

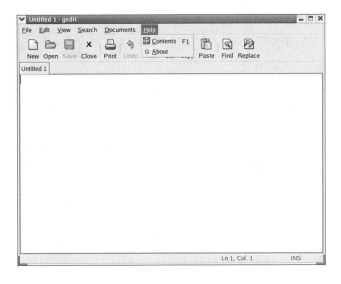

FIGURE 14.2

A typical KDE Help menu contains a number of options.

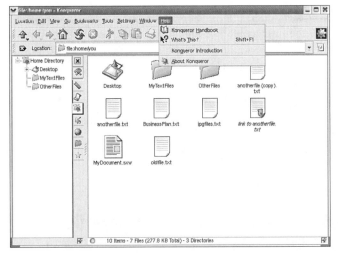

Using the About Option in Help Menus

When you need to learn version, licensing, or other information about your KDE or GNOME application, choose Help, About to open the About information screen. Licensing information provides details about the ways in which you are allowed to use and distribute the application. Version information can be helpful to the application's author if you need to submit a bug report, and can be useful to know in cases where separate applications are meant to work together, but only in certain version combinations.

14

In a GNOME application, the About information includes email addresses for the program's authors (click the Credits button to see it). If you have a bug report, feature request, or specific question about an application not covered in the application's online documentation, you can use the email contact information in the About dialogs to write the authors of the application and ask them directly. When submitting a bug report about an application or asking a question about an application of the application's author, be sure to include the following information:

- The version of the Linux operating system you're using (Red Hat Linux 8)
- The name of the application in question
- The version of the application in which you've encountered a problem or about which you have a question
- A complete, in-depth description of the problem you're experiencing or the question you need answered, including details about what other applications are typically running and the circumstances surrounding the incident. Bug reports or help requests for KDE applications must follow the same format. The KDE About information window has tabs for copyright, authors, and license agreement information of the same types available in GNOME application About dialogs. When you finish using the About information, click the OK (GNOME) or Close (KDE) button to close the About window.

> Be sure to check the other types of online documentation that you learn about in this hour before you contact an application's author with questions about using the application—application authors don't like to receive questions they've already answered in online documentation.

Using What's This? in KDE Applications

The What's This? item in KDE application Help menus can be used to get context-sensitive help for parts of a KDE application window. When you select the What's This? option in a KDE help menu, the mouse pointer changes to a question mark; you can then click a part of the application window to get help information about it (see Figure 14.3). Not all parts of every window have help information available, but you should always check here first if you need to know what a screen element is or does.

Figure 14.3

Clicking an application element with the special mouse pointer displays help for that element; after you click for help, the mouse pointer returns to normal. To view further context-sensitive help, select What's This? again.

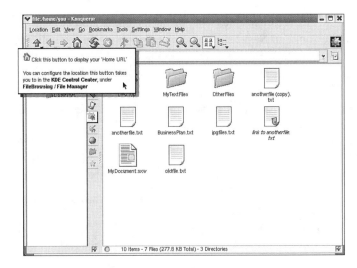

Viewing Help Contents in GNOME Applications

In GNOME applications, the application manual or other use-oriented documentation can be displayed by selecting Help, Contents. The GNOME Help Browser opens and displays the table of contents for the available application help; in Figure 14.4, GNOME Help displays the table of contents for gedit version 2.1 help.

Figure 14.4

Clicking the Contents option in the Help menu displays the table of contents for the application's help. Click a section listing to view that section's contents.

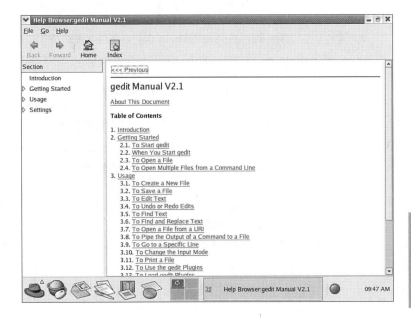

14

To read any section of the Help contents, click its title in the table of contents; use
the Previous and Next buttons to move through Help contents pages, as shown in
Figure 14.5. In this example of the online GNOME manual, the Contents link takes you
back to the table of contents.

FIGURE 14.5

*Use the Previous and
Next buttons to move
back and forth through
the Help contents
pages. The Contents
link returns you to the
table of contents.
Clicking a listing in
the Section pane opens
a list of subsections
within that topic.*

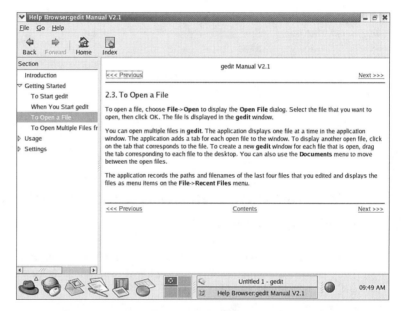

You can click Help contents listings in the Section pane (on the left side of the window)
to open a list of subsections; click a subsection to display its contents in the right pane of
the window. Choose File, Close or click the application close button (X in the upper-
right corner) to close the application's online help.

Viewing KDE Application Handbooks

To view a KDE application's handbook, open the application's Help menu and choose
Handbook; the KDE HelpCenter application opens and displays the handbook's front
page.

Some handbooks contain graphics or title information near the top of the front page; if
the table of contents isn't immediately visible in the handbook's front page, scroll down
to display it, as shown in Figure 14.6.

FIGURE **14.6**

Scrolling down the front page reveals the table of contents for the Konqueror handbook. Click a heading or subheading to display the page in question.

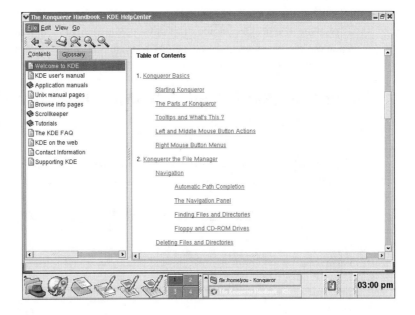

Most KDE application help handbooks work like the GNOME Help Browser. You can click the related heading or subheading in the table of contents and use Next and Prev buttons to move back and forth through the material. Clicking the Home link at the bottom of the page returns you to the front page of the handbook you're viewing.

Unlike the GNOME Help Browser, however, the left pane of the KDE HelpCenter window doesn't hold a clickable index for the application's handbook. Instead, this pane contains help for other parts of the KDE system (you learn more about using these help resources in "Launching and Using KDE's HelpCenter," later in this hour).

To close a KDE Handbook, choose File, Quit or click the application close button.

In the KDE HelpCenter, you can always print the currently displayed handbook or help page by selecting File, Print.

Using Systemwide Help in GNOME and KDE

Though application-specific manuals or handbooks are certainly useful for understanding how to use a particular application, often you need more general help for the desktop environment you're using. Both KDE and GNOME provide general help systems that document the fundamentals of the desktop environment and the aspects of operation that lie outside the bounds of any particular application.

In these help systems you're likely to find FAQs (frequently asked questions), fundamentals on using the desktop, some discussion of the environment's intended use, and some idea about the basic structure of the environment and the way in which its components work together to provide you with a comprehensive desktop environment.

Launching and Using GNOME's Help Browser

To launch the GNOME Help Browser from the desktop, click the GNOME menu (the Red Hat icon), and then choose Help.

The GNOME Help Browser window opens to display the systemwide help table of contents for the GNOME environment, as shown in Figure 14.7.

FIGURE 14.7

The GNOME Help Browser gives you access to help documentation for GNOME applications, utilities, graphics, and game packages, as well as system help, man *pages, and* info *pages.*

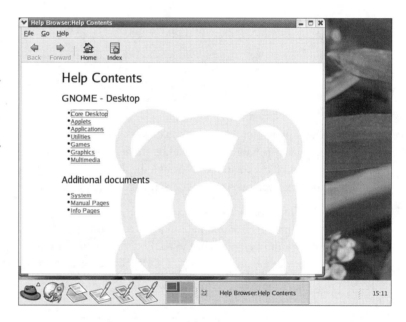

Each of the links in the GNOME Help Contents leads you to a list of documents for that category; each document within a category represents an online manual. For example, clicking the Core Desktop link leads to the list of documents and online manuals shown in Figure 14.8.

FIGURE 14.8

The list of documents in the Core Desktop section of the systemwide GNOME help documentation.

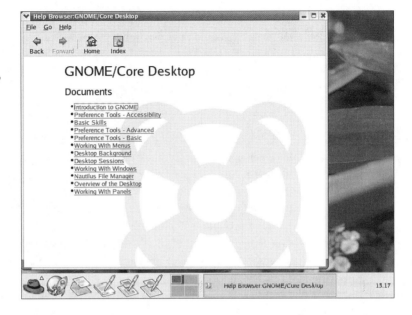

Documents in the Core Desktop section are likely to be especially helpful when you're new to Red Hat Linux or the GNOME environment. Topics covered include configuration techniques; basic methods of using the mouse to accomplish file and window management tasks; and efficient use of the file manager, taskbar, and desktop. Other help sections include the following:

- Applets, which discuss several small applications that can be launched to reside in the taskbar
- Applications and Utilities sections, which include manuals for applications and utilities you encounter while working in GNOME
- Games, which contains the manuals for all the game applications in the Game submenu of the GNOME Menu
- Graphics and Multimedia sections, which include additional manuals for graphics-oriented or multimedia-oriented applications you encounter while working in GNOME
- Additional Documents sections, which contain Manual and Info pages of the type you're familiar with (discussed later this hour)

When you finish reading manuals and documentation in the GNOME Help Browser, click File, Close Window to exit.

14

Launching and Using KDE's HelpCenter

The KDE HelpCenter is a comprehensive help system with a number of features not available in the GNOME Help Browser. Although you won't learn all of them in this hour (feel free to explore the HelpCenter yourself), take a moment to learn about some of the more essential KDE HelpCenter features.

Open the HelpCenter by clicking the KDE Menu (Red Hat icon) at the lower left of your desktop and choosing Help.

When the HelpCenter opens, you see the Welcome to KDE index in the right pane; in this index, you can click links to access some good beginner's guides to the KDE. The left pane of the HelpCenter window contains the KDE systemwide help contents list. You can return to the Welcome to KDE index at any time by double-clicking the Welcome to KDE listing in this pane. Double-clicking the KDE on the Web or Contact Information listings in this pane displays a list of links to KDE Web sites with additional documentation or email addresses for KDE developers to contact for specific types of problems, respectively.

If you're new to KDE, you'll especially appreciate the information available in two of the KDE HelpCenter handbooks—*A Quick Start Guide to the Desktop* and *KDE User's Guide*. These guides give you a quick overview of the KDE user essentials, and the information is always just a few clicks away in the Welcome to KDE HelpCenter index.

You do not need to launch a specific KDE application and access its Help menu in order to view its handbook. To view the handbook for any KDE application from within the KDE HelpCenter, double-click the Application Manuals icon on the left side of the HelpCenter window. A collapsible list of application categories will be displayed, as shown in Figure 14.9.

Clicking the plus or minus signs to the left of a category expands or collapses the category, respectively. Double-clicking an application icon displays the handbook for the related program—as if you'd selected Help, Handbook from within the application itself.

A very comprehensive KDE glossary, which provides brief definitions for many KDE terms and components, can be accessed by clicking the Glossary tab in the left pane of the HelpCenter window. You then have the choice of browsing terms alphabetically or by topic, as shown in Figure 14.10. Double-clicking any of the terms displays the definition for the term in question.

FIGURE **14.9**

To read application handbooks, double-click the Application manuals icon.

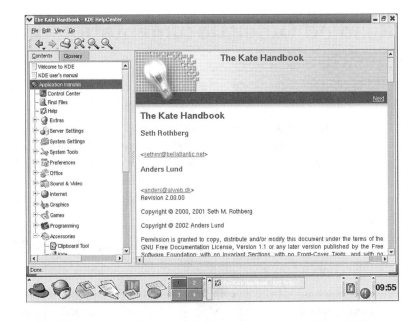

FIGURE **14.10**

The HelpCenter glossary can help you identify and recognize KDE components and concepts.

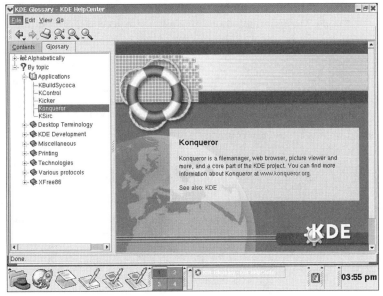

To close the KDE HelpCenter, choose File, Quit.

14

Reading Other Documentation on the Desktop

In Hour 6, "Getting Help at the Console," you learned to obtain online help for Linux commands and other topics using the man and info commands.

These types of documentation can be accessed using desktop tools as well, something that will come in handy when you reach Hour 16, "Advanced Linux Desktop Use." In that hour, you begin to use the command line and Linux commands while working on the desktop, and you will appreciate fast, more user-friendly desktop access to man and info pages. The following sections explain how to access this information from both GNOME and KDE.

Reading man and info Pages Using the GNOME Help Browser

As you learned in "Launching and Using GNOME's Help Browser," links to the man and info pages are listed in the Additional Documents list on the Help Contents screen (refer to Figure 14.3). Clicking the Manual Pages link leads to a list of the manual page sections. Manual pages are available in these sections:

- Applications (man command section 1)
- Development (man command sections 2 and 3)
- Hardware Devices (man command section 4)
- Configuration Files (man command section 5)
- Games (man command section 6)
- Overviews (man command section 7)
- System Administration (man command section 8)

More information on the division of system manual pages into sections and the meanings of each section number can be found in "Understanding Manual Page Sections" in Hour 6.

Click any section in the list to open a list of manual pages offered for that section; Figure 14.11 shows a portion of the list of man pages available in the Applications section.

When you locate the manual page you want to read, click its link to display it, as shown in Figure 14.12.

Figure 14.11

FIGURE **14.11**

The alphabetical list of manual pages in each section is quite long. The number in parentheses is the section you are browsing.

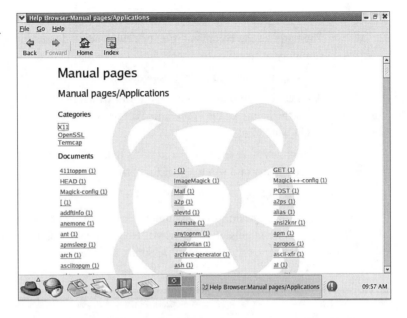

FIGURE **14.12**

Displaying the manual page for the ls command.

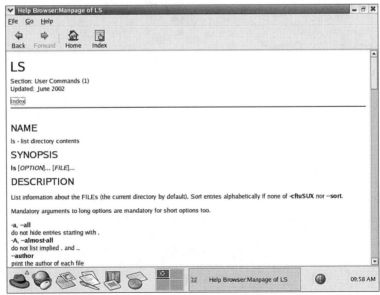

Manual pages you read in the GNOME Help browser are formatted according to the same guidelines used by the man command. Each manual page contains the following information:

14

- The man command section from which the manual page has been taken
- The name of the command, file, or device being documented and a brief (one-line) summary of its purpose
- A synopsis of how to use the command, file, or device
- A longer description in paragraph form, which provides more detailed information about the nature of the command, file, or device and the situations in which you might want to use it
- A summary of options and arguments that can be provided to alter the behavior of the command or a summary of the format of the configuration file in question
- Author, bug reporting, and copyright information

The process for browsing info documents is similar; click the Info Pages link in the default table of contents of the GNOME Help Browser. An index of available info pages is displayed, as shown in Figure 14.13; click a listing to display the page, as shown in Figure 14.14.

FIGURE 14.13

Clicking Info Pages displays a list of info *pages that the GNOME Help Browser can display.*

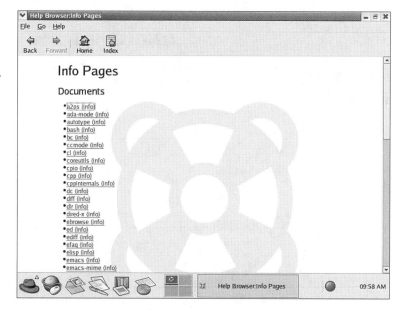

Remember that info pages are much more complex and free-form than system manual pages. An info page may be only a single, scrollable page of documentation, or you may find that a single info page about a given topic leads to a number of informative subpages that are accessed by clicking on links within the document. If you are willing to adapt to the free-form, almost World Wide Web–like nature of the info system, you will find a great deal of useful help in info documents.

Figure 14.14

Displaying the info *page for the* emacs *editor using the GNOME Help Browser.*

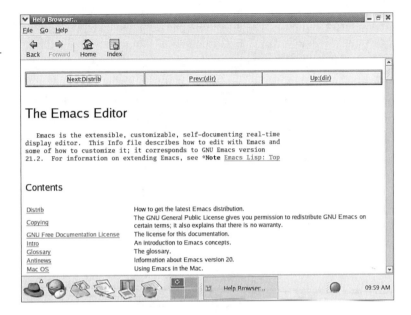

Reading man and info Pages Using KDE's Konqueror

Accessing man and info pages in the KDE is somewhat easier than accessing similar documentation in the GNOME environment.

To read a man page in KDE, start a File Manager window by double-clicking the Home icon on your desktop. In the Location bar of the File Manager window, type **man:command**, where **command** is the name of the topic or command whose manual page you want to read. Figure 14.15 shows the Konqueror file manager displaying the manual page for the ls command. For more information on using the file manager, refer to Hour 11, "Working with Files on the Desktop."

To display an info page in KDE, enter **info:command** into the Location bar of the File Manager window (again, substituting the topic or command you want for **command**). Figure 14.16 shows the Konqueror file manager displaying the info page for the emacs editor. Note the text that has been entered into the location bar.

Using Konqueror, you can print nicely formatted man or info pages by displaying the page in question and then clicking File, Print.

14

Figure 14.15

Open a File Manager window in KDE, and then type **man:** *followed by a command or topic name to display the associated* man *page. Here, the Konqueror file manager displays the manual page for the* ls *command.*

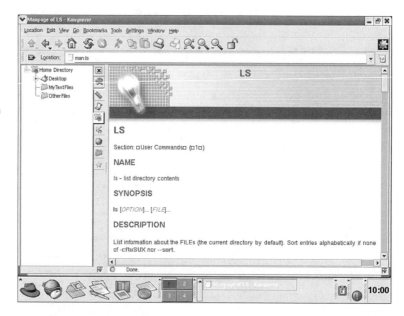

Figure 14.16

The Konqueror file manager displaying the info *page for the* emacs editor.

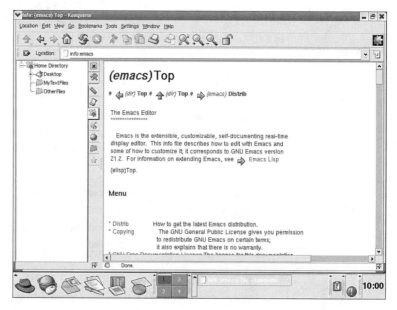

Summary

This hour, you learned to access several types of help and documentation at the Linux desktop by employing different techniques and tools.

You learned to access application-specific manuals or handbooks in both the GNOME and KDEs using the application Help menus.

You also learned to access a more general, systemwide set of documents and tutorial information using either the GNOME Help Browser or the KDE HelpCenter. This documentation is intended for new users to the environment in question and often covers basic topics that apply to all applications. You also learned to access some types of help unique to the KDE HelpCenter, such as the systemwide glossary and the master list of email contact information for KDE developers.

Finally, you learned to read man and info pages, useful for using commands at the command prompt, using desktop tools. In the KDE, you learned to print man and info pages as well.

Q&A

Q **Access to man and info pages is clear to me. How can I access the /usr/share/doc information discussed in Hour 6 at the desktop?**

A Because the files in /usr/share/doc are plain text files, you can open a file manager, visit /usr/share/doc, and double-click icons for the files you want to read. If you need further help, refer to Hour 11.

Q **Is there a way to print from the GNOME Help Browser?**

A Unfortunately, the GNOME Help Browser does not support an easy way to print. If you have a compelling need to print man or info pages, consider doing so using the KDE desktop environment.

Workshop

The Workshop is designed to help you anticipate possible questions, review what you've learned, and begin learning how to put your knowledge into practice.

Quiz

1. How do you open the manual or handbook for a running application?
2. How do you launch the systemwide help application?
3. How do you read a man page in GNOME? In KDE?
4. What information should be submitted with an application bug report?

14

Answers

1. Click Help, Contents in GNOME applications, or click Help, Handbook in KDE applications.

2. Click the GNOME Menu or KDE Menu (located at the lower right of the desktop), and then click Help.

3. To read a manual page in GNOME, open the Help Browser, click Manual Pages, choose a section, and then click the manual page you want to view. In KDE, open a Konqueror window and type **man:command** into the location bar.

4. You should always include the name of the application, the version of the application, the specific problem you encountered, a list of other applications that were running at the time, and a detailed description of the context in which the problem occurred—what you did to cause the problem, what you were trying to accomplish, and so on.

Activities

1. Read some of the introductory material in the Core Desktop (for GNOME) or Welcome to KDE sections of the online documentation.

2. Try launching a few applications in the desktop of your choice and browsing the related manual or handbook.

3. Read some `man` and `info` pages for your favorite console commands in the desktop environment of your choice.

HOUR 15

Customizing the Desktop

You already learned to find your way around the Linux desktop in day-to-day work. This hour, you learn how to modify your Linux desktop's behavior and appear3ance to suit your needs, preferences, and working habits. By the end of this hour, you'll know

- How to change the default settings related to mouse movement
- How to change the color and appearance of the elements on your Linux desktop
- How to change your desktop wallpaper and screensaver
- How to edit the contents of the taskbar to aid in launching your favorite applications more quickly

Making these kinds of changes can enhance your productivity and comfort at the desktop significantly. Furthermore, customizing your desktop can also be fun!

Using the GNOME Control Center

The GNOME Control Center is the primary tool used for customizing the appearance and behavior of the GNOME desktop environment. The GNOME Control Center is simply a large list of settings that can be clicked on and changed; each of these settings has some effect on desktop behavior or appearance.

To launch the GNOME Control Center, click GNOME Menu, Preferences, Control Center. After you select Control Center from the Preferences menu, the GNOME Control Center appears in a file manager window containing a number of icons related to various aspects of configuration, as shown in Figure 15.1.

FIGURE **15.1**

The GNOME Control Center contains a number of configuration-related icons.

Changing Mouse Behavior

Depending on the type of pointing device you're using and whether you're left-handed or right-handed, you might find that you're not comfortable with the speed of the pointer on your display or the configuration of click and double-click behavior.

To launch the Mouse Preferences dialog used to configure mouse behavior, double-click the icon in the Control Center labeled Mouse. The Mouse Preferences dialog appears, as shown in Figure 15.2.

FIGURE 15.2

The Mouse Preferences dialog can be used to change the behavioral properties of the mouse. The default view is shown here.

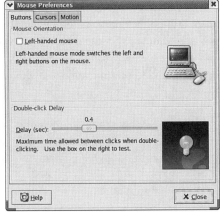

15

 The Mouse Properties dialog is used to configure your pointing device even if you use a trackball, touchpad, trackpoint, or similar device instead of a Mouse.

The default view in the Mouse Preferences dialog, shown in Figure 15.2, is of the Buttons tab, which contains the following options:

- Mouse Orientation reverses the order of the buttons on your pointing devices. Left-handed users should check this option to allow the button under their index finger to act as the first mouse button.

- Double-click Delay changes the speed at which you must double-click in order for the double-click to be recognized by the Linux desktop. If you often find that your double-clicks seem to be ignored by the Linux desktop, you should click the slider and increase the allowable delay between clicks.

The second view in the Mouse Preferences dialog can be displayed by clicking the Cursors tab, as shown in Figure 15.3.

This view enables you to change the appearance of the mouse pointer, or cursor, on the screen. It contains the following options:

- Cursor Theme controls the appearance of the mouse pointer on the desktop. If you find that your mouse pointer is difficult to see, you might want to choose another default appearance for the pointer by clicking it.

- Locate Pointer makes it easier to find a "lost" mouse pointer on the desktop by drawing a large square around the mouse pointer when the control key is pressed. If you often find yourself searching for the mouse pointer, consider enabling this option. This option may be especially useful to owners of laptop computers and flat-panel displays, which tend to blur movement and thus make a lost mouse pointer more likely.

FIGURE 15.3

The Cursors tab contains options related to the appearance of the mouse pointer on the screen.

The third and final view in the Mouse Preferences dialog can be displayed by clicking the Motion tab, as shown in Figure 15.4.

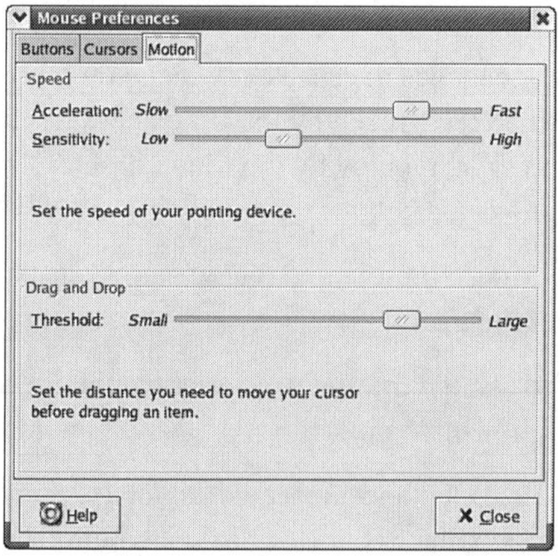

FIGURE 15.4

The Motion tab contains options related to the speed of the mouse pointer on your desktop while moving the mouse.

This view enables you to change both the sensitivity and the speed with which the mouse pointer responds to your input and moves around on the desktop. It contains the following options:

- Speed contains options related to the speed of the mouse on the desktop. It contains two sliders, labeled Acceleration and Sensitivity. Acceleration controls the absolute speed of the pointer on your desktop. Sensitivity controls the distance the mouse must be moved before mouse acceleration takes effect.

- Drag and Drop controls the distance the mouse must be moved while clicking an icon before the desktop assumes that you want to drag the icon, rather than click it. If you have unsteady hands, you should increase the Drag and Drop value.

After you configure the options in the Mouse Properties dialog box to suit your needs, click Close to close the dialog box.

Changing Window Appearance

If you find the default appearance of the application windows on your desktop to be ugly or difficult to use, you can alter the colors and decorations used to draw application windows using the Theme Preferences dialog box.

To launch the Theme Preferences dialog used to configure window appearance, double-click the icon in the Control Center labeled Theme. The Theme Preferences dialog box appears, as shown in Figure 15.5.

FIGURE 15.5

The Theme Preferences dialog box can be used to change the physical appearance and colors of application windows.

The first tab in the Theme Preferences Dialog is the Application tab. This tab controls the appearance of the parts of application windows inside the border and title bar. By default, the Bluecurve theme is selected. To change the appearance of all application windows, click one of the other themes. The appearance of all windows changes, as shown in Figure 15.6.

FIGURE 15.6

Clicking a theme changes the appearance of all existing and future windows. The Redmond95 theme creates a Windows-like appearance.

The second tab in the Theme Preferences Dialog is the Window Border tab, shown in Figure 15.7. This tab controls the appearance of application window borders and title bars. By default, the Bluecurve theme is also selected in this dialog. To change the appearance of all application window borders and title bars, click one of the other themes. The appearance of all window borders and title bars changes, as shown in Figure 15.8.

FIGURE 15.7

The Window Border tab is used to change the physical appearance and colors of application window borders and title bars.

FIGURE 15.8

Selecting the Gorilla theme creates a very different title bar appearance from the default Bluecurve theme.

Ambitious users can download and install their own themes from the Web
site http://themes.org.

To download a theme, visit http://themes.org using your Web browser. The
themes in the GTK 2.0 section of the Web site can be installed in the Red
Hat Linux GNOME desktop.

To install a theme, follow the directions on the Web site to save the theme
of your choosing to your home directory. Then, click the Install New Theme
button in the Theme Preferences dialog and enter the downloaded
theme's filename when prompted, or use the Browse button to choose the
theme from a list of files in your home directory.

The theme you downloaded will then appear in the themes list and can be
selected like any other theme.

Any appearance changes you make using the GNOME Control Center affect
your GNOME desktop environment only. If you have Installed KDE and want
to change the appearance of the KDE, refer to the section called "Using the
KDE Control Center" later this hour.

When the appearance of application windows and their borders and title bars is acceptable to you, click the Close button to close the Theme Preferences dialog.

Changing Your Desktop Wallpaper

Desktop wallpaper is an image or pattern that appears on the desktop "beneath" icons
and application windows. To change your desktop wallpaper, double-click the
Background icon in the GNOME Control Center. The Background Preferences dialog
appears, as shown in Figure 15.9.

To change the picture used as your desktop wallpaper, click the image button below the
words Select Picture in the Background Preferences dialog. A standard file dialog
appears, showing a list of images included with Red Hat Linux that are stored in
/usr/share/backgrounds/images. Select one of these attractive images or enter the filename of or browse to one of your own images and select it instead.

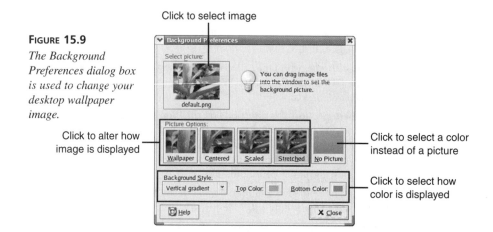

FIGURE **15.9**

*The Background
Preferences dialog box
is used to change your
desktop wallpaper
image.*

After you select the image you want to use, click one of the four buttons to the left under the words Picture Options to decide how the picture is displayed. The following are the available options:

- Wallpaper should be used if the image is smaller than your desktop to cause the image to be "tiled" over and over again across your display.

- Centered causes the image to be centered with respect to the desktop. If the image is smaller than the desktop, the edges of the display show a solid color. If the image is larger than the desktop, some of the image's edges may be cut off.

- Scaled causes the image to be enlarged or shrunk as necessary to fit the size of your desktop as closely as possible without changing the shape of the image.

- Stretched causes the image to be enlarged or shrunk, changing the shape of the image as necessary to fit the size of your desktop exactly from edge to edge, both horizontally and vertically.

If you don't want to use a picture as your desktop wallpaper image, but instead would prefer a solid color or blend of colors, click the rightmost icon under the text Picture Options. This forces the desktop to use a color or pair of colors as the background rather than a desktop wallpaper image. You can click the Top Color and Bottom Color buttons (see Figure 15.13) to change the colors. The Background Style drop-down list enables you to select one of three options for painting the desktop with the colors you've selected:

- Solid color uses only the first color you've selected, painting the entire desktop.

- Horizontal gradient blends the two colors together from left to right.

- Vertical gradient blends the two colors together from top to bottom.

After you configure your desktop wallpaper to suit your tastes, click the Close button in the Background Properties dialog to close it.

Changing Your Screensaver

A screensaver is a special program that takes over your computer display when you haven't used your computer for a period of time. The screensaver paints patterns or animations on the screen until you return and press a key or move the mouse. To change your screensaver, double-click the Screensaver icon in the GNOME Control Center window. The Screensaver Preferences dialog appears, as shown in Figure 15.10.

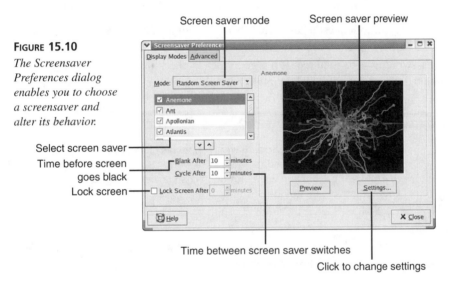

FIGURE 15.10
The Screensaver Preferences dialog enables you to choose a screensaver and alter its behavior.

To select the way in which screensavers are used on your system, use the Mode drop-down box. There you can choose among the following options:

- Disable Screen Saver turns the screensaver feature off. Your desktop remains visible no matter how long it has been inactive.

- Blank Screen Only causes the screen to go black after a period of inactivity, rather than displaying graphics or animations for your amusement.

- Only One Screen Saver causes the screensaver that has been selected in the selection box to become active after a period of inactivity.

- Random Screen Saver causes the desktop to cycle through the list of screensavers at random, displaying one after another in turn, after a period of inactivity.

You can click any of the screensavers in the screensaver selection box to see a preview of the screensaver in the right side of the window. If you select the Only One Screen Saver mode, this also selects the screensaver that is used after a period of inactivity.

After a screensaver has been selected, you can alter its settings (usually things such as color and speed of animation) by clicking the Settings button.

The number in the Blank After box determines how long a screensaver is allowed to run on an inactive system before the screen goes completely blank.

The number in the Cycle After box determines how long a screensaver is allowed to run before a new screensaver starts if you have selected the Random Screen Saver mode.

To cause the system to request a password when you return from a period of inactivity, check the Lock Screen After box and select the number of minutes of inactivity after which a password is to be required. It is a good idea to check this option if you work in an environment in which other people might have physical access to your computer system.

> The Advanced tab in the Screensaver Preferences dialog contains options that most users won't need to alter, so we won't discuss them here. Feel free to explore the tab if you want, but don't change any settings unless you know what you are doing!

When you configure your screensaver according to your own preferences, click the Close button to close the Screensaver Preferences dialog.

Changing Other Desktop Preferences

Because of the limited amount of space in a book like this one, you can explore only the most commonly changed GNOME desktop preferences—preferences related to mouse movement, application window appearance, desktop wallpaper, and screensavers. Many other aspects of the GNOME desktop can be altered through the GNOME Control Center, however:

- Use the Password icon to change your password and personal information available to other Red Hat Linux users on your computer system.

- Use the Accessibility icon to change various aspects of GNOME behavior to better suit disabled or differently abled individuals.

- Use the File Types and Programs icon to change icons and programs used by the file manager to handle various types of files in day-to-day use.

- Use the Font icon to fine tune the fonts used by GNOME to be as clear and visible as possible on your computer system. Special options exist for Laptop computers or for those who find the default fonts to be too fuzzy.

- Use the Keyboard icon to change the key repeat speed and the default text cursor's appearance, and to enable or disable the keyboard bell.

- Use the Keyboard Shortcuts icon to tie Ctrl, Alt, and Function keystrokes of your choosing to various common GNOME functions, such as closing or maximizing windows.

- Use the Menus & Toolbars icon to show or hide text beneath toolbar icons and to show or hide icons in application drop-down menus.

- Use the Sound icon to change the sounds you hear when performing common tasks, such as hiding or closing windows, or to disable sound altogether.

- Use the Window Focus icon to change how windows are selected; choose either the default mode in which you must click a window to make it active, or an alternate mode in which any window the mouse is pointing to will become active.

Feel free to explore the rest of the GNOME Control Center and to experiment with various settings until your desktop behaves exactly as you'd like it to.

Using the KDE Control Center

The KDE Control Center is the primary tool used for customizing the appearance and behavior of the KDE. The KDE Control Center is simply a large list of settings that can be clicked and changed; each of these settings has some effect on desktop behavior or appearance.

To launch the KDE Control Center, click KDE Menu, Control Center. After you select Control Center from the KDE Menu, the KDE Control Center appears, as shown in Figure 15.11.

While using the KDE Control Center, you find that clicking the little plus or minus icons in the Index tab expands or collapses lists of settings dialogs. Clicking the Help tab when any settings dialog is displayed displays extensive help for the dialog in question.

Changing Mouse Behavior

To change the mouse movement, button, and drag-and-drop properties in KDE, expand the Peripherals list in the KDE Control Center and double-click the Mouse icon. The Mouse dialog is shown in the right side of the Control Center window, as shown in Figure 15.12.

FIGURE 15.11

The KDE Control Center contains an extensive list of user-configurable settings to alter the behavior of the desktop.

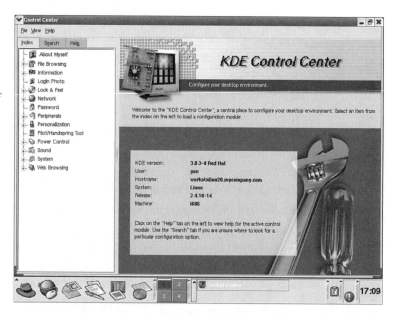

FIGURE 15.12

The Mouse dialog in the KDE Control Center enables you to change mouse behavior properties.

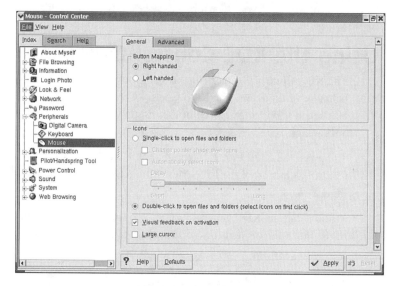

By default, the General tab of the Mouse configuration dialog is shown. The General tab contains several configuration options:

• The Button Mapping option enables left-handed users to reverse the order of the mouse buttons for more intuitive mouse functionality.

- The top half of the Icons option enables you to choose whether you want KDE to activate icons only after a double-click or whether a single-click should activate icons. If you select single-click, several additional options are activated. These are fully documented in the Help tab while viewing the Mouse dialog.

- The Visual Feedback on Activation check box enables you to decide whether the "throbber" (small animation) will appear each time you try to launch a program in KDE. The throbber is used to indicate that a program is currently being loaded from the hard drive.

- The Large Cursor check box enables a larger mouse pointer to be used instead of the default pointer.

Mouse movement and drag-and-drop properties for the KDE desktop can be changed by clicking the Advanced tab, which is shown in Figure 15.13.

FIGURF 15.13

The Advanced tab of the Mouse dialog enables you to change movement and drag-and-drop properties.

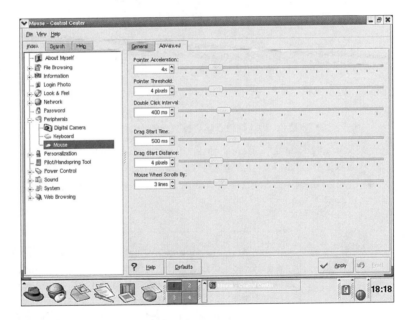

There are six settings in the Advanced tab of the Mouse dialog, each of which alters a different aspect of mouse behavior with respect to pointer movement or drag-and-drop movement. The settings have the following effects:

- Pointer Acceleration controls the absolute speed of the mouse pointer across your desktop when the mouse is moved rapidly.

- Pointer Threshold controls the distance the mouse must be moved before pointer acceleration is engaged.

- Double Click Interval changes the speed at which you must double-click in order for the double-click to be recognized by the Linux desktop.
- Drag Start Time controls how long the mouse pointer must pause after a click in order for subsequent pointer movement to be considered a drag, rather than a simple click.
- Drag Start Distance controls the distance the mouse must be moved during a click before the movement is considered a drag, rather than a simple click.
- Mouse Wheel Scrolls By controls the sensitivity of the scroll wheel on your pointing device, if it is so equipped.

When you configure the mouse properties to suit your tastes, click the Apply button at the lower right of the window to cause the changes to take effect.

> Sometimes when you click Apply, you receive a message saying that you must restart KDE in order for the changes you've made to take effect.
>
> When this occurs, simply log out and then log back in; this has the effect of restarting KDE and causing your changes to become active.

Changing Window Style

To change the appearance of the interior of application windows on your KDE desktop, expand the Look & Feel list in the left side of the Control Center window and double-click the Style icon. You will be presented with the Style dialog, as shown in Figure 15.14.

> If you try to open a new configuration dialog in the KDE Control Center and are shown a dialog asking whether you want to Apply or Forget your changes or Cancel, you have changed a setting in the current dialog that hasn't been made active yet.
>
> To make the new setting active before the new dialog is displayed, click Apply. To discard any changes you've made, click Forget. To stop loading the new dialog and return to the dialog currently being shown, click Cancel.

To choose a style, click one of the styles in the Widget Style list box. The preview area in the lower half of the dialog shows you what the style in question looks like, if you apply it. When you have found a style that suits you, click Apply to apply the appearance to existing windows.

Widget Style listbox

FIGURE 15.14

The Style dialog enables you to extensively modify the appearance and behavior of application windows.

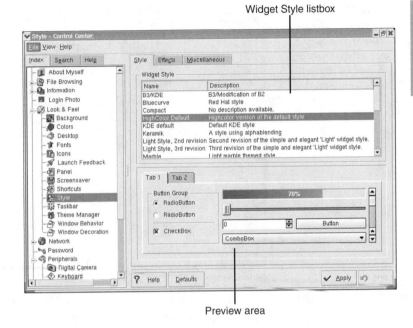

Preview area

The Effects tab of the Style dialog contains a single check box labeled Enable GUI Effects. When checked, a number of additional options are made active; using them, you can choose to enable various types of animation or visual enhancement for KDE desktop tasks.

The Miscellaneous tab of the Style dialog, shown in Figure 15.15, contains a number of options related to the behavior of application window components.

The check boxes that appear in the Miscellaneous tab control the following aspects of application window behavior:

- Highlight Buttons Under Mouse determines whether buttons within applications change in appearance as the mouse pointer passes over them, to indicate that they can be clicked.

- Transparent Toolbars When Moving determines whether detachable application toolbars are shown only as an outline when you drag them around the desktop.

- The Toolbar Icons drop-down list controls how buttons appear in application toolbars—as buttons without text, or with text labels in various positions relative to the matching icon.

- Show Icons on Buttons determines whether little graphic icons are shown on dialog box buttons.

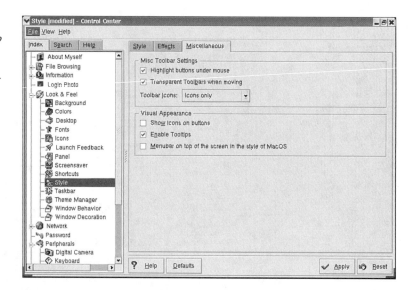

FIGURE 15.15
The Miscellaneous tab of the Style dialog enables you to configure various aspects of application behavior.

- Enable Tooltips determines whether tooltips (small labels that appear when you leave the mouse pointer over a button) are displayed or not.

- Menubar on Top of the Screen in the Style of MacOS controls whether application menu bars appear at the top of each application window, or whether a single menu bar is drawn across the top of the entire display, its contents changing depending on which window is active at a given moment.

When you configure the items in the Miscellaneous tab to suit your preferences, click the Apply button to save the changes and make them active.

Changing Application Colors

To change the colors used by the KDE desktop for application windows and application text, double-click the Colors icon in the Look & Feel list on the left side of the Control Center window. The Colors dialog appears, as shown in Figure 15.16.

Alter the current color scheme by clicking a color scheme you'd like to try in the Color Scheme list box. The preview area is updated to show what that color scheme looks like in a running application. If you find a color scheme you'd like to use, click Apply to activate and save the change.

Scheme edit area

Color Scheme listbox   Color Scheme preview area

FIGURE 15.16

The Colors dialog enables you to select the color scheme that will be used by KDE when drawing application windows and text.

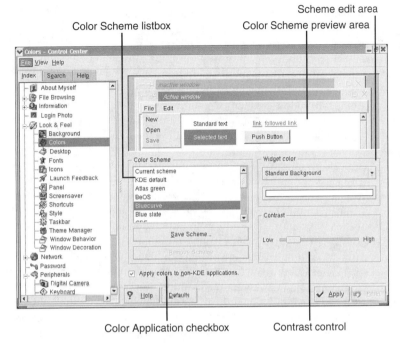

Color Application checkbox   Contrast control

The other items in the Colors dialog are used as follows:

- The Widget Color edit area can be used to create your own color scheme. The drop-down box contains a list of the various components from which application windows are built. Select the components one by one, and then click the color button to select a color for the component in question.

- The Contrast control is used to alter the intensity of the highlights and shadows on buttons and other window decorations.

- The Color Application check box controls whether applications from outside the KDE (such as GNOME applications) should be colored in the same way that KDE applications are colored.

If you alter any of these settings in addition to selecting a new color scheme, click Apply to save and activate the changes.

Changing Window Borders and Title Bars

To change the borders and title bars of application windows, double-click the Window Decoration button in the Look & Feel list in the left side of the Control Center window. The Window Decoration dialog is displayed, as shown in Figure 15.17.

FIGURE 15.17

*Use the Window
Decoration dialog box
to alter the appearance
of window borders and
title bars.*

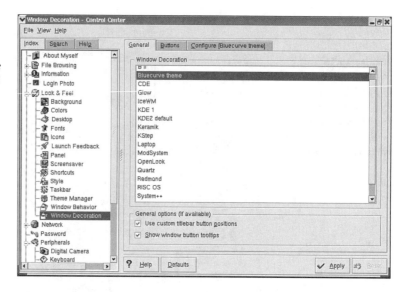

To select a new title bar theme, click a theme in the Window Decoration list box, and
then click the Apply button to see how the theme looks on existing windows. If you don't
like the change, select the original title bar theme and click Apply again to return to your
previous setting.

For certain title bar themes, the Configure tab contains additional options
to alter the appearance of the title bar further. For other themes, this tab is
empty.

Changing Desktop Wallpaper

To change your desktop wallpaper image or use solid colors instead of an image for
your KDE desktop, double-click the Background icon in the Look & Feel list on the left
side of the Control Center window. The Background dialog is displayed, as shown in
Figure 15.18.

FIGURE 15.18

The Background dialog enables you to change the desktop wallpaper for each of your virtual desktops.

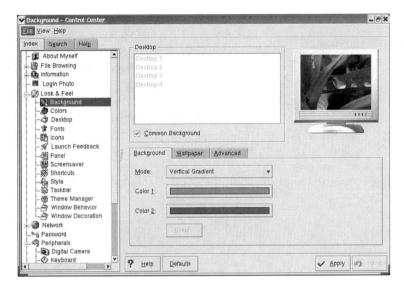

15

The default tab in the Background dialog controls the colors that are used for the desktop if no image is selected as a desktop wallpaper image. Two colors can be selected by clicking the Color 1 and Color 2 buttons; the blending between these two colors is then selected in the Mode drop-down list:

- The Flat mode creates a desktop using only a single solid color, Color 1, as its image.

- The Pattern mode alternates Color 1 and Color 2 in a pattern chosen by clicking the Setup button.

- The various gradient modes blend the two colors across the entire desktop. Try each of them to see what they do if the idea of a gradient appeals to you.

The second tab in the Background dialog is the Wallpaper tab, shown in Figure 15.19. In KDE, wallpaper refers to an image file that is used as the background for your desktop.

At the top of the Wallpaper tab, you're given a choice between three modes of wallpaper operation:

- No Wallpaper disables wallpaper images altogether and as a result, causes the colors chosen on the Background tab (see earlier discussion) to be used for the desktop image.

- Single Wallpaper uses a single wallpaper image for your desktop. You can select the image that is used by using the Wallpaper drop-down list.

• Multiple Wallpapers enables you to create a list of wallpaper images that will be rotated periodically as you work. When you check this option, the Setup Multiple button becomes active. Click this button to bring up a dialog where you can choose a list of images by clicking them, as well as the frequency with which they should be rotated.

FIGURE 15.19

Use the Wallpaper tab to select a wallpaper image for your desktop, or to disable image wallpaper altogether.

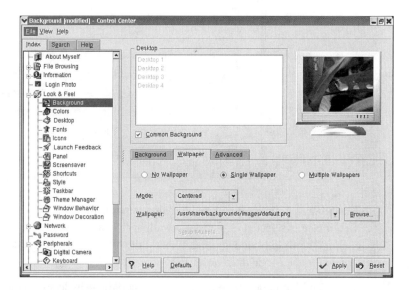

If you chose to use one or several wallpaper images on your desktop, you can use the Mode drop-down list in the Wallpaper tab to control how the image is displayed. Choose from one of the following:

• Centered causes the image to be centered with respect to the desktop. If the image is smaller than the desktop, the edges of the display show a solid color. If the image is larger than the desktop, some of the image's edges may be cut off.

• Tiled should be used if the image is smaller than your desktop to cause the image to be tiled over and over again across your display.

• Center Tiled creates an effect similar to Tiled, but places the first tile in the center of the display.

• Centered Maxpect causes the image to be enlarged or shrunk as necessary to fit the size of your desktop as closely as possible without changing the shape of the image.

• Tiled Maxpect works like Centered Maxpect but causes any unfilled space to be tiled with the image.

- Scaled causes the image to be enlarged or shrunk, changing the shape of the image as necessary, to fit the size of your desktop exactly from edge to edge, both horizontally and vertically.

- Centered Auto Fit causes the image to be enlarged or shrunk in such a way as to fill the entire screen, without changing its shape. Rather than leaving empty space at the edges if necessary, some of the image may be cut off to ensure that the screen is filled.

After you configure the Background dialog to suit your tastes, click the Apply button to save and activate the changes you've made.

> If you want to use a different wallpaper configuration for each virtual desktop, uncheck the box labeled Common Background near the middle of the Background dialog.
>
> If you want to blend a wallpaper image with a solid color, explore the Advanced tab of the Background dialog.

Changing Your Screensaver

To change your screensaver in the KDE, double-click the Screensaver icon in the Look & Feel list on the left side of the Control Center window. The Screensaver dialog is displayed, as shown in Figure 15.20.

To use screensavers, make sure that the Enable Screensaver check box is checked. After the box has been checked, click any of the screensavers in the Screen Saver list box to see a preview of the screensaver in the preview area. The other settings in the Screensaver dialog control the following:

- The Delay Before Activation (Wait For) box enables you to control how long the system must be inactive before a screensaver takes control of the desktop.

- The Require Password check box determines whether your password is required to return to the desktop after a screensaver has taken effect.

- The screensaver Priority control enables you to decide how much system time is dedicated to running the screensaver; the more time you dedicate to the screensaver, the faster it runs, but the slower any existing applications run while the screensaver is active.

After you configure your screensaver settings according to your preferences, click the Apply button to save and activate the changes you made.

Screen saver listbox

Enable screen saver checkbox   Start delay

FIGURE 15.20

*The Screensaver dia-
log box enables you to
change the screensaver
used when you are
logged into KDE.*

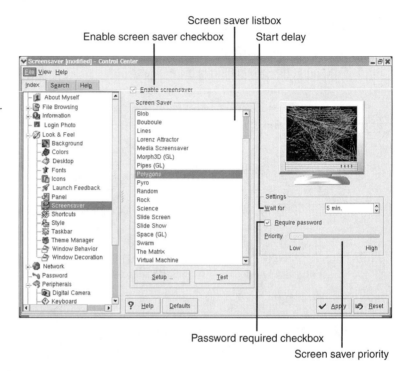

Password required checkbox

Screen saver priority

Configuring the Desktop Taskbar

In addition to changing the simple look, feel, and mouse behavior of your desktop environment, it is important to be able to change the way in which you access the applications you most commonly use.

Specifically, you should be able to launch the applications you most commonly use from
the taskbar, where they can be accessed easily without having to look for them in several
levels of menus.

Adding an Icon to the Taskbar in GNOME

To add an icon to the taskbar in GNOME, right-click in an empty area of the taskbar and
select Add to Panel, Launcher from Menu from the pop-up context menu that appears. A
facsimile of the main GNOME menu appears, as shown in Figure 15.21.

Browse through this facsimile of the GNOME menu until you find the application whose
icon you want to add to the taskbar. Click the icon. Instead of launching the application,
the new application icon appears on your taskbar. Clicking the new icon launches the
related application, as expected.

FIGURE **15.21**

Preparing to add an application icon to the taskbar in GNOME.

Adding an Icon or Menu to the Taskbar in KDE

To add an icon to the taskbar in KDE, click KDE Menu, Configure Panel, Add, Button. You see a facsimile of the main KDE menu appear, as shown in Figure 15.22.

FIGURE **15.22**

Preparing to add an application icon to the taskbar in KDE.

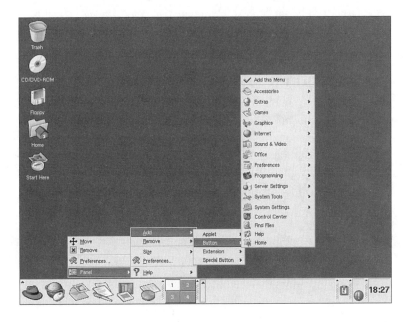

Browse through this facsimile of the KDE menu until you find the application whose icon you want to add to the taskbar. Click the icon. Instead of launching the application, the new application icon appears on your taskbar. Clicking the new icon launches the related application, as expected.

To add a menu to the taskbar in KDE, follow the same process, but select Add This Menu at the top of the menu you want to add to the taskbar. Adding a menu results in an icon with a small arrow above it.

Moving an Icon on the Taskbar

To move an icon to the left or right on the taskbar in either KDE or GNOME, right-click the icon you'd like to move and select Move from the pop-up context menu that appears. After you select Move from the context menu, you find that your mouse pointer has changed in appearance to indicate that you are moving an icon, and that moving your pointing device to the left or right causes the icon on the taskbar to move to the left or right, displacing existing icons as necessary. When you position the icon where you want it, click any mouse button to release the icon; it remains in that position unless you move it again.

Removing an Icon from the Taskbar

To remove an item from the taskbar in either KDE or GNOME, right-click the icon you'd like to remove and select either Remove (KDE) or Remove from Panel (GNOME) from the pop-up context menu that appears. After you select Remove from the context menu, the icon is removed from the taskbar permanently, or until you decide to add it again.

Additional Taskbar Configuration

There are a number of additional types of taskbar configuration that can be fun to explore, though we won't cover them in detail here. In both GNOME and KDE, these types of configuration can be immediately found in the same menus used to add icons to the taskbar, namely KDE Menu, Configure Panel, Add in KDE, or by right-clicking the taskbar and choosing Add to Panel in GNOME.

Among the additions that can be made to the taskbar this way are the following:

- Applets are small programs that perform useful tasks, such as clocks, system monitors, or volume controls. These can generally be moved and removed in the same manner as taskbar icons—by right-clicking them and choosing either Move or Remove.

- Child Panels are like second (or third, fourth, and so on) taskbars that can be positioned around the screen and can contain additional icons or applets if you run out of space on the primary taskbar.
- Drawers (in GNOME) are similar in some ways to menus; icons can be added to them and clicking them produces a menu listing the icons they contain.

More help on using the GNOME or KDE taskbars can be found in the following locations:

- In GNOME, start the GNOME Help Browser and visit Core Desktop, Working with Panels to view the manual for the GNOME panel (taskbar) application.
- In KDE, start the KDE HelpCenter. Scroll down on the default Welcome to KDE page until you see the Desktop Panel document. Click the link to view the handbook for the KDE kicker (taskbar) application.

Summary

This hour, you learned how to change the most commonly changed desktop properties in both GNOMEs and KDEs. In GNOME, this is accomplished through the GNOME Control Center. In KDE, this is accomplished through the KDE Control Center. Among the desktop properties you learned to change are the behavior of your mouse (including suitability for left- or right-handed use), the color and appearance of application windows, and your desktop wallpaper and screensaver.

You also learned to add icons for your favorite applications to the GNOME or KDE taskbars so that you can launch them without having to access lengthy menus. Finally, you learned to move items on your taskbar around so that they appear in convenient logical order for you, and to remove items from your taskbar that you no longer want to appear there.

Q&A

Q You've explained how to install new themes in GNOME. Is it also possible to add themes in KDE?

A Yes, but KDE doesn't make the process as simple or intuitive as GNOME does. If you are feeling ambitious, you can visit http://www.kde-look.org for a collection of KDE themes. On the left side of the home page, you'll find a Howto link that contains documentation for installing KDE themes.

Q I've accidentally removed my GNOME menu or my KDE menu! How do I get it back?

A In GNOME, right-click an empty area of the taskbar and choose Add to Panel, GNOME Menu. In KDE, right-click an empty area of the taskbar and choose Add, Special Button, KDE Menu.

Workshop

The Workshop is designed to help you anticipate possible questions, review what you've learned, and begin learning how to put your knowledge into practice.

Quiz

1. How do you launch the GNOME Control Center? The KDE Control Center?

2. What is a gradient? How do you enable a gradient?

3. How do you move an icon on the taskbar?

4. How do you remove an icon from the taskbar?

Answers

1. In GNOME, click Gnome Menu, Preferences, Control Center; in KDE, click KDE Menu, Control Center.

2. A gradient is a gradual blending from one color to another color. To enable a gradient, disable the use of wallpaper images, and then select your colors and gradient from the Background dialog.

3. Right-click the icon you want to move and select Move from the context menu.

4. Right-click the icon you want to remove and select Remove from the context menu.

Activities

1. Explore some of the areas of the Control Center for your desktop that we didn't discuss. See what the settings do.

2. Change the appearance and colors of your desktop applications and wallpaper to suit your tastes.

3. Add a few application icons to your taskbar and arrange them as you prefer them to appear.

4. Try adding some applets or child panels to your taskbar.

HOUR **16**

Advanced Linux Desktop Use

In previous hours, you learned the ins and outs of using Red Hat Linux at the command line; you also learned how to use the most popular applications on the desktop. This hour, you learn to integrate the two—to launch a selection of desktop applications directly from the command line and to write shell scripts that can take advantage of the desktop environment. By the end of this hour, you'll have learned

- How to start a terminal application window to access the Linux command line on the desktop
- How to launch graphical applications via the command line
- How to write shell scripts that interact with users via the windowing environment
- How to write scripts for Nautilus file manager

By combining the power of the command line with the productivity enhancements of the desktop, you increase both your workflow and the complexity of tasks you are able to accomplish using Linux.

Introducing the Desktop Terminal Application

So far in your Linux experience, all the time you've spent using the command line has also been spent at a grey-and-white text console. The console is the purest form of command-line use, and being able to use the command line in such a minimal environment is an important skill for Linux users. You draw upon this skill to perform rescue and administration tasks, should your system experience problems.

However, it is also possible to use the command line from within the relative security and flexibility of the Desktop environment using a tool called a *terminal*. The terminal is a software application that behaves like a small console-in-a-window, in which you can type commands and interact with the shell just as you do at a full-screen console. Though this combination of command line and desktop window might at first seem incongruous, it is in fact quite natural; the command line can be integrated closely with the Desktop experience, and most of the skilled Linux users of the world always keep the command line near at hand when working at the Linux desktop.

Starting the Terminal Application

The terminal application can be started in either the GNOME or KDEs by clicking Menu, System Tools, Terminal. Doing this starts the terminal application, shown in the GNOME environment in Figure 16.1.

FIGURE 16.1

The terminal application gives you access to the Linux command line and the shell on the desktop.

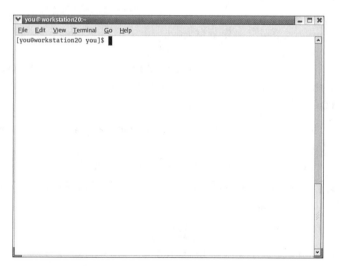

Though the colors are unfamiliar, the command prompt itself should by now seem very familiar to you. The command prompt you see in the terminal window is a full-fledged Linux command prompt; at it, you can use any of the Linux commands you learned so far.

You might remember that while using the command line at the console, multiple virtual consoles are provided so that you can enjoy the benefits of running many command-line applications at once. You can enjoy similar benefits by launching multiple instances of the terminal application at once *or* by creating multiple *tabs* inside the terminal application, each of which contains a command line of its own. A new command line can be opened in a new tab by clicking File, New Tab, Default. A terminal window with three running command prompts, each in its own tab, is shown in Figure 16.2.

16

FIGURE 16.2

The terminal application with three running command prompts, each in its own tab.

First tab   Second tab   Third tab

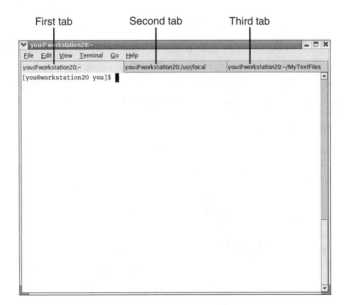

In the KDE's terminal application, a new tab can be opened with Session, New Shell.

The command lines in each tab are completely autonomous; each has its own current working directory and its own list of jobs, and all can be busy simultaneously if you run particularly involved commands in them that take some time to complete.

To close a tab and exit the command line (shell) that is running in it, click the tab to make it active and enter the word **exit** at the command line. The tab disappears.

Launching Desktop Applications with the Terminal

It is both possible and common to launch desktop applications from the command line in a terminal window. Though the KDE and GNOME menus and the icons on the taskbar are usually convenient ways to launch desktop applications, it is at times more convenient to be able to type the name of an application at the command line to start it—for example, if you want to be able to supply a command-line argument, as you'll shortly see.

To use the command line to launch an application whose name you already know, enter its name at the command line. For example, recall the GNOME `gedit` text editor that you learned to use in Hour 11, "Working with Files on the Desktop." To launch `gedit` from a terminal window, enter **gedit** at the command prompt:

```
[you@workstation20 you]$ gedit
```

In fact, you can also supply the name of the file you want to edit as an argument to the command, as was the case with command-line editors such as `emacs` and `vi`. For example, to load the file `myfile.tex` into the `gedit` text editor, type **gedit** followed by the name of the file you want to load into the editor:

```
[you@workstation20 you]$ gedit myfile.tex
```

Entering a command like this one causes the `gedit` editor to start and load the file you have supplied as an argument, as shown in Figure 16.3.

FIGURE 16.3

The gedit *editor was launched at the command line in the terminal window;* myfile.tex *was given as an argument.*

Job Control at the Terminal Command Line

You might notice that as you start application windows like gedit using the command line in this way, you are unable to enter further commands in the terminal window. This is because gedit acts as the foreground job in the terminal window. Only after you exit gedit does the command prompt return.

> For a command-line refresher, including such concepts as foreground jobs and background jobs, return to Hour 5, "Making the Console Work for You."

16

In fact, you can start an application like gedit in the background, so that you instantly have access to the command line again when gedit starts, by appending the ampersand (&) to the end of the command:

```
[you@workstation20 you]$ gedit myfile.tex &
[1] 9770
[you@workstation20 you]$
```

Calling gedit as a background job this way instantly displays a job number (in this case, 1) and a process id number (in this case, 9779) and then returns you to the command prompt. Though the gedit window opens and you can edit myfile.tex, you also have access to the command line in the terminal window because gedit is running in the background.

All the command line job control techniques that you learned in "Keeping Your Shell Programs Under Control" in Hour 5 can be used from a command line in a terminal window as well, including the following:

- The Ctrl+Z keystroke in the terminal window to suspend a foreground job and restore the command prompt

- The bg and fg commands in the terminal window to move existing jobs to the foreground or background

- The kill command in the terminal window to end a running job

- The ampersand (&) at the end of a command to start the command in the background, keeping the command prompt available for additional work while the command you have called runs and finishes

The only difference between job control at the command line in a terminal window and job control at a console command line is that in a terminal window, many of your running jobs are application windows, meaning that you can interact with them even while they are in the background by clicking your mouse pointer within their borders.

Using nohup to Keep Jobs Running

If you start a number of jobs in a terminal window and then close the window or exit the shell, all the jobs in that shell exit as well. This can be an undesired side effect—often when you start a desktop application in the background, you want the desktop application to remain even if the shell where it was started exits.

The nohup command enables you to indicate that a command should not exit if the shell in which it was started exits or is closed. For example, to launch a gedit window in the background, which remains open even if you close the terminal window used to start it, enter the following:

```
[you@workstation20 you]$ nohup gedit &
```

The nohup command can also be used with job control numbers on existing background or suspended jobs:

```
[you@workstation20 you]$ nohup %1
```

When you use nohup, a file called nohup.out is created in your home directory. This file is a plain text file that displays any error messages or warnings that the application normally displays to the terminal window from which it was started. You can safely delete this file after your applications have been closed.

Accessing Desktop Files from the Command Line

Because some users find themselves storing or copying the documents they often work with to the actual desktop, it is helpful to know how to access those files using the command line as well. Specifically, it is important to know the path to files that are stored on the desktop.

In the GNOME environment, files on the desktop are stored in ~/.gnome-desktop; in the KDE, files on the desktop are stored in ~/Desktop. To access files on your desktop using commands in a terminal window, refer to these locations when performing operations. For example, to create an empty file on your GNOME desktop called emptyfile.txt using the touch command you learned in Hour 4, "Navigating Linux at the Console" enter the following at a command line:

```
[you@workstation20 you]$ touch ~/.gnome-desktop/emptyfile.txt
[you@workstation20 you]$
```

Entering this command creates a file on your desktop called emptyfile.txt, as shown in Figure 16.4.

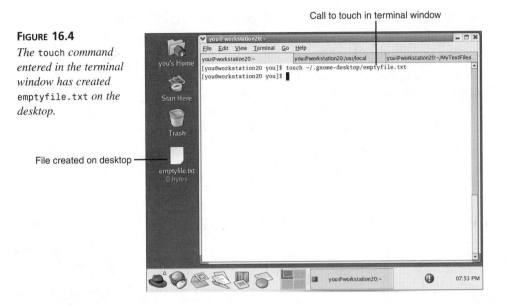

FIGURE 16.4

The touch *command entered in the terminal window has created* emptyfile.txt *on the desktop.*

Call to touch in terminal window

File created on desktop

Files and directories that are stored on the desktop can be accessed using any of the command-line file management techniques you learned in earlier chapters.

Using Basic X Window System Applications

The GNOME and KDE desktop applications that are included with Red Hat Linux are always easily accessible from the application menus at the lower-left of your display; however, Red Hat Linux also installs a set of desktop applications that are not accessible via the menus and must be launched via the command line. These are the applications that are included with the X Window System itself, which forms the basis of GNOME and KDE but can be used without them.

X Window System applications are not a part of the GNOME or KDEs, but are desktop applications with wider compatibility—they can usually be found on any Linux or Unix computer with a graphical desktop environment of any kind, regardless of whether a user-friendly environment such as GNOME or KDE has been installed.

If you performed a "server" or "custom" installation of Red Hat Linux in Hour 2, "Installing Red Hat Linux," and opted not to install the GNOME and KDEs, the basic set of X Window System applications might be the only applications available to you at the desktop; it is therefore important that you be familiar with a few of them.

Using a Desktop Terminal Without GNOME or KDE

If, when you installed Red Hat Linux, you chose to install the X Window System but not the GNOME or KDE, the desktop you experience appears somewhat different from the GNOME and KDE desktops shown so far in this book. Furthermore, you won't have a menu at the lower left of your display that contains a Terminal application. Instead, you find yourself in a desktop environment called TWM when you log in, facing the X Window System's more basic terminal application, xterm.

The TWM environment does have a menu; you can access it by clicking the root window—any area of the desktop not covered by an application window. You can launch a new terminal application in TWM at any time using this menu, as shown in Figure 16.5.

FIGURE 16.5

The default X Window System desktop is quite plain; here, the TWM root menu is used to launch a new xterm terminal application.

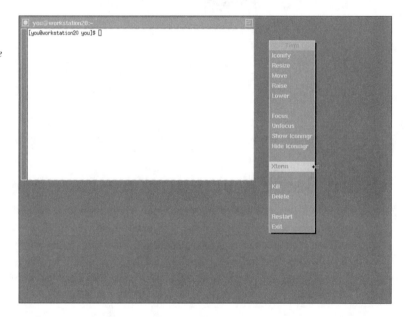

The applications in the rest of this section can be started from the command line in GNOME, KDE, or in TWM. Because most users have installed GNOME, the figures are shown in the GNOME environment; however, you launch these applications from your terminal no matter which environment you are working in.

The TWM environment can also be accessed by logging in using the Failsafe option at the Red Hat login screen, and then entering the command **twm** at the single terminal on the failsafe desktop.

Using Emacs on the Desktop

You will find that a few of the applications that can be used at the Linux console actually have enhanced X Window System functionality when you call them from the desktop. The emacs editor is one such application; this is one of the reasons for its enduring popularity—it is equally at home either at the console or on the desktop—even desktops without GNOME or KDE. Try calling the emacs command in an open terminal window now:

```
[you@workstation20 you]$ emacs myfile.tex &
[1] 10037
[you@workstation20 you]$
```

Instead of a bland text editor that fills the terminal window, a fully desktop-enabled emacs application window appears, as shown in Figure 16.6.

FIGURE 16.6

The emacs *editor looks different in the desktop environment and is quite user-friendly.*

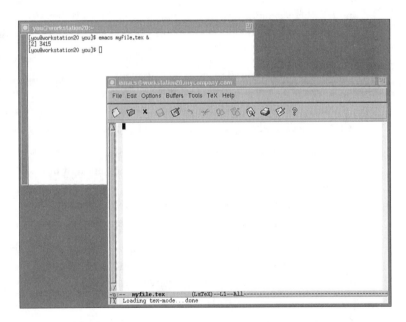

When working on the desktop, the emacs application is fully mouse-driven and somewhat easier to use and learn about. For example, to start the emacs tutorial, click Help, Emacs Tutorial. To save a file and exit, click File, Save and then File Exit Emacs.

Using X Window System Convenience Applications

The basic X Window System applications include a number of small convenience applications that when used together create a more pleasant user experience.

The xclock application provides a nice-looking desktop clock. Entering **xclock &** at the command line in a terminal window displays a clock, running the clock application in the background.

The xcalc application provides a functional calculator that can be used to perform most simple types of calculations. Entering **xcalc &** at the command line in a terminal window displays the calculator, running the calculator application in the background.

The xbiff application displays a picture of a mailbox that changes appearance depending on whether a user has unread mail waiting in his or her system mailbox. Entering **xbiff &** at the command line in a terminal window displays the mailbox checker, running the application in the background.

The xeyes application displays a pair of eyes that "watch" your mouse as it moves across the screen. This helps you find your mouse pointer if you have a very large (in terms of resolution) or very busy desktop. Entering **xeyes &** at the command line in a terminal window displays the eyes, running the application in the background.

The xload application displays a graph of the workload on your system's processor over time. On busy systems, this can provide an indication of how slowly your system might be responding to incoming network requests. The harder the processor is working, the higher the graph goes. Entering **xload &** at the command line in a terminal window displays the load graph, running the load application in the background.

The xmag application magnifies a small area of the screen by enabling you to click the area you'd like enlarged. When you enter **xmag &** at the command line in a terminal window, the mouse pointer changes. Wherever your next mouse click occurs on the display, a 64×64 pixel area is magnified and displayed in an application window.

Figure 16.7 shows all these convenience applications being used on the Linux desktop.

The xman enables you to read manual pages in an easily scrollable application window. When you enter **xman &** at the command line in a terminal window, the manual page reader is displayed. Clicking the Manual Page button brings up the Manual Page window, as shown in Figure 16.8.

FIGURE 16.7

All these X Window System applications were started from the same terminal window.

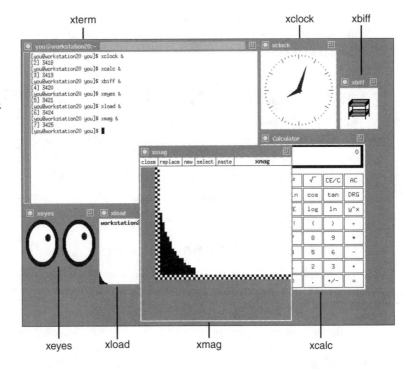

FIGURE 16.8

The xman application reads manual pages in an easily scrollable application window.

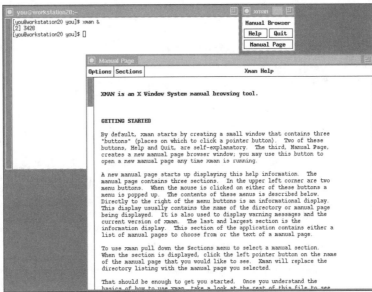

In the Manual Page window, choose a manual page section by clicking the Section button near the top of the window, and then select the manual page you want to read from the resultant list.

Interacting with the User in Shell Scripts

In Hour 9, "Harnessing the Power of the Shell," you learned to write shell scripts to perform sequences of commands without user intervention. Sometimes it is also helpful to be able to get user input as a shell script is running—to allow the user of the script to make choices about how tasks will be performed, for example.

The xmessage command can be used in shell scripts to enable the scripts to interact easily with the user via the mouse.

Using xmessage in Shell Scripts

To use xmessage in your shell scripts, it must be called from within a script with the -buttons option and two arguments—a comma-separated list of buttons and the message that should be displayed to the user above the buttons. The format looks like this:

```
xmessage -buttons "button1,button2,button3" "My Message"
```

This causes a dialog box with buttons labeled button1, button2, and button3 to appear below the message My Message. For example, the following call to xmessage displays the dialog box shown in Figure 16.9:

```
xmessage -buttons "Yes,No" "Would you like some ice cream?"
```

FIGURE 16.9

A dialog box created by calling the xmessage *command.*

When the user clicks one of the buttons beneath the message, the dialog disappears and returns a value to the script, which is assigned to the special shell variable $?. If the first button was clicked, the value 101 is assigned to the variable. If the second button is clicked, the value 102 is assigned to the variable, and so on.

Sample xmessage Script

In order to illustrate the use of xmessage, it might help to study some sample scripts. These samples use techniques learned in Hour 9, so if you find yourself confused by the explanations, you should review Hour 9 before continuing.

Suppose you want to create your own replacement for the rm command (used to remove files) that prompts the user with a confirmation dialog box before actually deleting a file. Listing 16.1 shows what a script called myrm, which does just this, might look like. Start an editor and create a file called ~/bin/myrm. Enter the listing, look at the listing, and then you go over it line by line to see how it works.

LISTING 16.1   Sample Script for myrm Command

```
1  #!/bin/sh
2
3  xmessage -buttons "Yes,No" "Remove file $1?"
4  RESULT=$?
5
6  if [ $RESULT -eq 101 ]; then
7      rm "$1"
8  fi
```

This is a short shell script, which performs a simple function, so it's fairly easy to dissect:

- Line 1 begins with the standard header for a shell script file. This is required in order for a shell script to work.

- Line 3 uses xmessage to display a dialog box with Yes and No buttons. The message is simply the words Remove file followed by the first argument supplied by the user, which is substituted for $1.

- Line 4 saves the value of the special variable $?, which contains the exit status of xmessage, to the variable RESULT. If the first button is clicked, the value of RESULT is 101. If the second button is clicked, its value is 102.

- Lines 6–8 check to see whether the value of RESULT is 101. If so, it means that the user clicked Yes, so the file is deleted. If not, no action is performed—the script simply reaches its end, so it exits without deleting the file.

To try out this script, use the chmod command to make myrm executable:

```
[you@workstation20 you]$ chmod u+x ~/bin/myrm
[you@workstation20 you]$
```

Then, try using the script to delete a file like myfile.tex. Entering the following command causes the dialog shown in Figure 16.10 to be displayed:

```
[you@workstation20 you]$ myrm myfile.tex
```

Clicking the Yes button at this point causes the file to be deleted. Clicking the No button leaves the file intact.

16

FIGURE **16.10**

The myrm *command displays a dialog to ask whether you really want to delete the file you've supplied as an argument.*

Second Sample xmessage Script

One more example might help illustrate a more dynamic use of the xmessage command. Suppose you have a set of LaTeX files in your home directory. If you don't, create some empty LaTeX files now for purposes of illustration using the touch command:

```
[you@workstation20 you]$ touch myfile.tex yourfile.tex oldfile.tex newfile.tex
[you@workstation20 you]$
```

Now suppose you want to create a shell script that enables you to edit any one of your LaTeX files in an emacs window by typing texedit and selecting the name of your file using an xmessage dialog. Start a text editor window and enter the Listing 16.2 as ~/bin/texedit, and then you'll go over it line by line.

LISTING 16.2 Sample Script for texedit Command

```
 1  #!/bin/sh
 2
 3  xmessage -buttons "$(ls -m *.tex)" "Which LaTeX file?"
 4  RESULT=$?
 5
 6  INDEX=100
 7  for TEXFILE in *.tex; do
 8      INDEX=$(expr $INDEX + 1)
 9      if [ $RESULT = $INDEX ]; then
10          emacs $TEXFILE &
11      fi
12  done
```

This script is also relatively short, but its operation is somewhat more complex than the script in the first sample:

- Line 1 begins with the standard header for a shell script file. Again—it is required in order for a shell script to work as expected.

- Line 3 uses xmessage and command substitution to display a dialog box with one button listing each .tex file in the current working directory. This is done with a call to the ls command using the -m option, which causes listed files to be separated by commas (see the ls manual page for details).

- Line 4 saves the value of the special variable $?, which contains the exit status of xmessage, to the variable RESULT. If the first button is clicked, the value of RESULT is 101. If the second button is clicked, its value is 102.
- Line 6 creates a variable that our script uses to count through the buttons one by one. Because clicking the first button results in the value 101, our counter begins at 100.
- Lines 7–12 create a for..do loop; the commands between for and done are executed once for each .tex file in the current working directory; each time through, the variable TEXFILE contains the name of a .tex filename in the current directory.
- Line 8 adds 1 to the value of INDEX for each time through the loop, meaning that for the first value of TEXFILE, the value of INDEX is 101; when the value of TEXFILE changes the second time through the loop, the value of INDEX changes once more to 102, and so on.
- Lines 9–11 watch the value of INDEX. When it is the same as the value of RESULT, meaning that the value of TEXFILE is the same as the button the user clicked, the emacs editor is started using TEXFILE as an argument.

Let's see the script in action. After you save the file ~/bin/texedit, remember to use the chmod command to mark it as executable so that you can call it at the command line:

```
[you@workstation20 you]$ chmod u+x ~/bin/texedit
[you@workstation20 you]$
```

The dialog box in Figure 16.11 is shown when you enter the texedit command at the command prompt:

```
[you@workstation20 you]$ texedit
```

FIGURE 16.11

The xmessage *dialog enables the user to choose between all the* .tex *files in the current working directory.*

Clicking one of the filename buttons causes the file in question to be loaded into a new emacs editor application window.

Scripting the Nautilus File Manager

You can access shell scripts through the Nautilus file manager and direct them to act upon selected files. To do this, you select files in Nautilus and then right-click on them to produce a list of shell scripts you've written; you then choose the scripts from this list that you want to act upon the selected files. In this section, again you might need to refer to Hour 9 if you have trouble following along with the sample scripts.

Creating and Using Shell Scripts with Nautilus

To create shell scripts that can be used with Nautilus, create and save any scripts that you want to use with Nautilus to the ~/.gnome2/nautilus-scripts directory.

When a script is called from the Nautilus file manager, the script behaves just as if it had been called from the command line. Nautilus passes the selected files to the script as arguments that can then be accessed through the usual shell variables—$1 for the first argument, $2 for the second argument, and so on, or $@ to access the entire list of arguments at once.

Sample Nautilus Shell Script

To illustrate the use of shell scripts with Nautilus, let's consider a sample script. Suppose you want to be able to create a backup copy of any file simply by right-clicking the file and selecting a script called FileBackup. This has the effect of creating a copy of the file, with the extension .bak added, in the ~/Backups directory.

Enter the script in Listing 16.3 into a text editor and save it to ~/.gnome2/nautilus-scripts.

> You may find that the ~/.gnome2/nautilus-scripts directory does not yet exist. If this is the case, use the mkdir command to create it before saving the script, or use the file manager to create it.
>
> If you need a refresher, you can learn about the mkdir command in Hour 4 and the file manager in Hour 11.

LISTING 16.3   Sample FileBackup Script for Use with Nautilus

```
1  #!/bin/sh
2
3  if [ ! -d ~/Backups ]; then
4      mkdir ~/Backups
5  fi
6
7  for BACKUPFILE in $@; do
8      cp $BACKUPFILE ~/Backups/$BACKUPFILE.bak
9  done
```

This script is reasonably short, and reasonably simple as well, but it performs as expected. Here's how it works:

- Line 1 provides the standard shell script header.
- Lines 3–5 test to see whether the ~/Backups directory exists. If it doesn't, it is created with the mkdir command.
- Lines 7–9 are a for..do loop; Line 8 is repeated once for each filename supplied to the script as an argument. Each time through, the variable BACKUPFILE contains the name of a file that has been selected in Nautilus for backing up.

After you save the script and exit your editor, don't forget to make the script file executable:

```
[you@workstation20 you]$ chmod u+x ~/.gnome2/nautilus-scripts/FileBackup
```

To test out the script, right-click a file in a Nautilus file manager window and select the Scripts menu. You will see the new FileBackup script in the menu, as shown in Figure 16.12.

FIGURE 16.12

The new FileBackup script appears in the Scripts menu after it has been marked as executable.

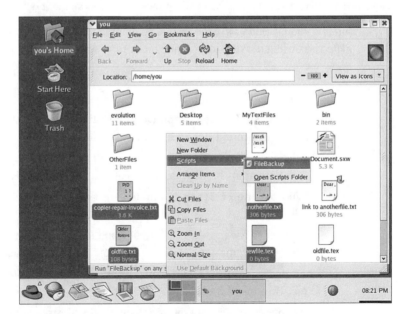

If you select FileBackup from the Scripts menu, the file you right-clicked is copied with a .bak extension to the ~/Backups folder (which is created if it doesn't already exist).

Using Nautilus scripts of this sort, it is possible to automate many types of file management functionality from the Linux desktop.

> For a collection of existing Nautlius scripts and more detailed tutorial information, visit the Web site `http://g-scripts.sourceforge.net/`.

Summary

This hour, you learned some less common but still useful and powerful techniques for using the Linux desktop.

First, you learned how to start a terminal on the desktop to have access to the command prompt on the desktop. This is especially useful if you installed a server or custom installation of Red Hat Linux with the X Window System but without GNOME or KDE. You also learned to use the terminal window to start and manage desktop applications as shell jobs.

You learned about the standard set of X Window System applications, which are also present whether or not you installed GNOME and KDE—programs such as `xterm`, `xclock`, and `xcalc`, and the desktop mode of the `emacs` text editor.

Finally, you learned to use the `xmessage` command and the Nautilus file manager to automate tasks using desktop tools while interacting with the user via the mouse.

Q&A

Q Is there a list of all the graphical applications' names, so that I can start them from the command line in a terminal window?

**A No, there is no comprehensive list. You will find desktop applications mixed in with the programs in /usr/bin, /usr/local/bin, and /usr/X11R6/bin.

Q When I use the `xmessage` command, I get an error message or an unexpected result. Why?

**A Remember to use the `-buttons` option and to enclose the following two arguments—the comma-separated list of buttons and the message text—in quotes.

Q The sample Nautlius script won't work with files that have spaces in the filename. How can I fix this?

**A In the interest of keeping the script simple for illustrative purposes, techniques for accommodating filenames with spaces or other special characters were not used. The Web site `http://g-scripts.sourceforge.net/` provides freely copyable script code that enables Nautlius scripts to work with filenames containing spaces and other special characters.

Workshop

The Workshop is designed to help you anticipate possible questions, review what you've learned, and begin learning how to put your knowledge into practice.

Quiz

1. How would you start the GNOME text editor and cause it to load the file `~/myfile.tex` from the command line?

2. What command would you use to more closely inspect very small data appearing in an area of your desktop?

3. How do you know which `xmessage` button was pressed in your shell scripts?

4. What directory contains Nautilus scripts?

Answers

1. `gedit ~/myfile.tex &`

2. `xmag`

3. After `xmessage` exits, the special variable `$?` contains an exit status of `101` if the first button was pressed, `102` if the second button was pressed, `103` if the third button was pressed, and so on.

4. `~/.gnome2/nautilus-scripts`

16

HOUR 17

Using Desktop Applications Remotely

You have learned to make effective use of the Linux desktop in many common work situations. In this hour, you learn to use one of the most powerful features of the Linux desktop's X Window System, the ability to display running applications remotely—on the monitor of a separate PC on the network. By the end of this hour, you'll know

- How the X Window System's remote display facility works conceptually
- How to use the ssh command to automate the X Window System's remote display facility
- How to use the remote display facility manually in rare cases in which the ssh command is unavailable
- How to start an entire X session on a remote computer, while displaying it on your local computer

If you can master the techniques presented in this hour, the process of using multiple Linux or Unix machines on your network, particularly for administrative tasks, will become an easy one.

> Because many of the tasks discussed in this hour occur on two computers simultaneously, illustrations are imperfect in demonstrating just what is going on at times.
>
> Some amount of imagination and familiarity with using computers in networked environments will be helpful to your understanding when illustrations fall short.

Understanding the X Window System Protocol

The Linux desktop environment, the X Window System, functions differently from the desktop environments of other operating systems, such as Microsoft Windows. X Window System applications rely on a network protocol to connect to the display on which they appear, rather than drawing to the computer display directly. Figure 17.1 shows an illustration of this concept.

FIGURE 17.1

X Window System applications communicate with the desktop using a network protocol, rather than drawing directly. Thus, applications need not run on the machine where they are displayed.

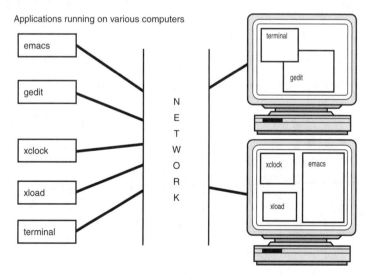

Though the network-oriented nature of the X Window System adds complexity to the desktop environment, it provides a native capability not available in any other operating system's desktop environment. You have the ability to run a program on one machine's processor while displaying the application window on another machine's desktop, automatically using the network for communication between the two. Using this technique, a system administrator working at a Linux computer can start and interact with application windows whose programs are actually running on one or more machines elsewhere on the network.

Simple examples of the uses for the networking capabilities of the X Window System include the following:

- Starting `xload` or other monitoring applications on multiple machines around the network, but displaying them all on a single computer's desktop. This allows the load or status of a number of different Linux or Unix systems to be monitored graphically from a single location.
- Running graphical administration tools for remote systems from a central location. Instead of having to walk from computer to computer, an experienced Linux administrator can manage every Linux or Unix system on the network without ever leaving his workstation.
- Creating graphical dumb terminals—computers that have little processing power or storage, but instead run only the X Window System and can thus use the storage and processing power of another, more powerful Linux or Unix computer to provide applications and a complete desktop environment.

With the networking capabilities of the X Window System, the sky and your creativity are your only limits.

Because both the GNOME and KDEs are built on X Window System technology, the network features of the X Window system work in either environment.

Networking X Using the Secure Shell

The Secure Shell (`ssh`) command makes it easy to use the remote display facilities of the X Window System, using a command format similar to the one used for general-purpose remote logins. If you've forgotten the general-purpose use of the `ssh` command, please review "Logging In Remotely Using `ssh`" in Hour 8, "Networking Without Graphics."

17

> If you find that many of the techniques in this hour don't work for your Red
> Hat Linux system, please see the section entitled "Configuring Firewall Security
> for Remote Display" later in this hour; there you learn how to alter the fire-
> walling rules on your Red Hat system to allow incoming ssh or X connections.

Displaying Single Remote Applications Using ssh

To launch a program on a remote computer, causing the application window for the program
to appear on your local Red Hat Linux system's display, call the ssh command like this:

```
ssh -l user remotehost program
```

Replace *user* with your login account on the remote system, *remotehost* with the hostname of the remote system, and *program* with the program you want to run. For example,
to launch a system load monitor to watch the activity of the processor on a system called
newton.mycompany.com where you have a login account called joeuser, you could enter
the ssh command as follows:

```
[you@workstation20 you]$ ssh -l joeuser newton /usr/X11R6/bin/xload
joeuser@newton's password:
```

After you enter your password, the xload application appears, monitoring the processor
load on the system called newton, as shown in Figure 17.2.

FIGURE 17.2

The xload *process has*
been started remotely
on the system called
newton, *but its applica-*
tion window appears
on workstation20.

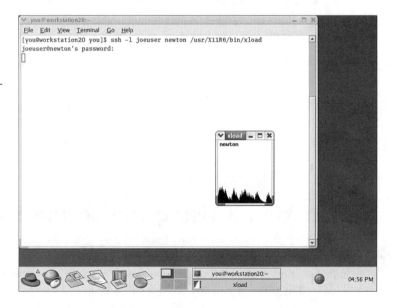

You are not limited to starting noninteractive applications like xload this way; you can
just as easily remotely interact with programs such as emacs or gedit.

Users new to Linux or Unix often wonder what will happen if they try to run applications on remote systems that are currently in use by other users.

The answer is simple: everything works as expected, for both users. Because Linux and Unix are multiuser, multitasking, network-oriented operating systems, Linux simply and securely keeps track of which processes and files belong to each user who is currently using the system, whether the user is connected over the network or sitting directly in front of the computer. No Linux user even needs to be aware of the others who might be using the same computer system.

Displaying Remote Applications Locally Using ssh

If you want to start a number of programs on a single remote system and cause each of their application windows to display on your local Red Hat desktop, you might find that calling ssh over and over again for each program you want to start is a time-consuming process.

In such cases, you will find that it is easier to start a terminal window and log in to the remote system using ssh, as you learned to do in "Logging In Remotely Using ssh" in Hour 8. After you have a command line on the remote system in your terminal window, use the command line in the terminal to start desktop applications as you normally would from the command line. Each desktop application you launch this way is displayed on your local display, as shown in Figure 17.3.

FIGURE 17.3

After logging in remotely using ssh, *the* gedit, guituner, *and* xload *have been started on a remote system to display locally.*

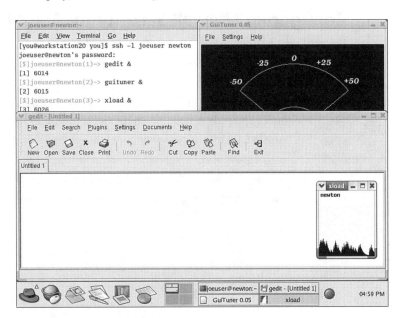

17

Notice that you can start your applications in the background using the ampersand (&) or use command-line job control techniques as you would at any shell, even though this particular command line is provided by a remote computer system. For more information on shell job control techniques, refer to "Keeping Your Shell Programs Under Control" in Hour 5, "Making the Console Work for You."

Displaying Local Applications Remotely Using ssh

You can also allow users at Linux desktops on other computers to start programs on your computer whose application windows will appear on their displays. This is done using the same technique you just learned, performed in reverse order—that is, executing the ssh command on the remote system, listing your Red Hat system as the host to connect to.

For example, if the user at a computer called workstation10.mycompany.com wanted to start the emacs program on your machine, workstation20, to be displayed on their screen using X's remote display capability, they could execute the following command from their command line:

```
ssh -l janeuser workstation20 emacs
```

As you can see, the process is symmetrical when using ssh; the system on which the ssh command is executed always displays the application, and the system to which ssh connects actually runs it. Thus, the roles of the local and remote systems are merely a matter of the location from which the ssh command was run.

Configuring Firewall Security for Remote Display

Because the technique we're using in this hour relies on ssh to manage the X Window System connections, your system must be configured to allow incoming ssh connections in order for this to take place.

Depending on the firewall options you selected when you installed Red Hat Linux, your system might not currently accept incoming ssh connections. If you find that ssh requests from other systems are refused, you need to enable incoming ssh on your system.

To do this, you should log in to the Red Hat desktop as root. In the root account, click GNOME Menu, System Settings, Security Level to display the firewall configuration tool, as shown in Figure 17.4.

FIGURE 17.4

In the firewall configuration tool, you can enable incoming ssh *connections so that remote users can use remote display.*

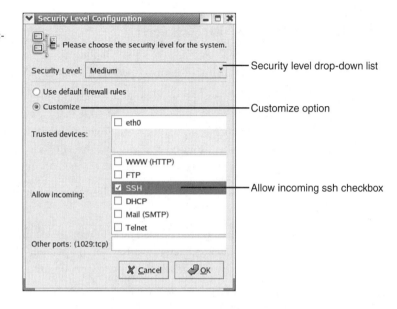

— Security level drop-down list

— Customize option

— Allow incoming ssh checkbox

17

To ensure that you can accept incoming X and ssh connections, double-check the following:

- The Medium level of security should be selected in the Security Level drop-down list.

- The Customize option should be enabled so that you can specify particular protocols for which incoming connections should be allowed.

- The SSH option should be checked in the Allow Incoming box to indicate that incoming ssh connections are to be allowed.

After all these options have been correctly configured, click OK to accept the changes, if you have made any.

It is generally a good idea to use the medium level of firewall security or to allow incoming ssh connections only on home computers that are unlikely to be subject to concerted attacks or computers that are protected from the Internet using a dedicated firewall (a computer or appliance whose only job is to relay traffic between the Internet and your local network).

Networking X Manually

Whenever possible, you should use the ssh technique already discussed for remote application display, because the ssh command performs this task both easily and securely.

If you aren't able to use ssh for some reason, and thus can't automate the security policy needs associated with the X Window System's remote display facility, you can use an alternate method—manipulation of the DISPLAY environment variable and xhost security tool—to allow and start remotely displayed applications manually. This can often be the case when interacting with older Unix systems in which ssh is not supported or economical.

To run a Linux application on one system and display it on another this way, two things must occur:

- The security features on the display system must be configured to allow remote applications to open application windows on the screen. This is done using the xhost command. By default, the Red Hat Linux desktop does not allow programs on remote systems to open application windows.

- The DISPLAY environment variable, which is used by applications to locate and use the graphical display, must be set to point to the graphical display you want applications to use.

Allowing Incoming X Connections with xhost

The xhost command is used to instruct an X Window System desktop to allow other systems to open connections (application windows) for display. Because the host-based security model that makes xhost work is somewhat insecure, you should use only xhost to allow incoming connections if your computer systems are behind a firewall and all users on your network are trusted.

 Using the xhost command to enable incoming X connections on a machine that is not behind a dedicated firewall can render your computer vulnerable to attacks leading to data theft or destruction by malicious Internet users.

To instruct a Linux desktop environment to allow incoming connections via the xhost command, start a terminal application and type

```
xhost hostname ...
```

Replace hostname with the hostname(s) of the system(s) from which application connections should be accepted. For example, to allow programs running on the computer's workstation10 and mailservera to display on the local computer's desktop, enter the following:

```
[you@workstation20 you]$ xhost workstation10 mailservera
workstation10 being added to access control list
mailservera being added to access control list
[you@workstation20 you]$
```

Fully qualified domain names and network addresses can also be used with the `xhost` command:

```
[you@workstation20 you]$ xhost sunsystem1.yourcompany.com 10.1.24.192
sunsystem1.yourcompany.com being added to access control list
10.1.24.192 being added to access control list
[you@workstation20 you]$
```

To list those systems currently allowed to connect to the local desktop and create windows on it, type the `xhost` command without arguments:

```
[you@workstation20 you]$ xhost
access control enabled, only authorized clients can connect
INET:workstation10.mycompany.com
INET:mailservera.mycompany.com
INET:sunsystem1.yourcompany.com
INET:10.1.24.192
[you@workstation20 you]$
```

The listed systems can all open application windows on the local desktop. To remove a system from the list of systems that are allowed to connect to the local desktop, call `xhost` and place a minus (-) sign in front of the system you'd like to remove:

```
[you@workstation20 you]$ xhost -workstation10.mycompany.com
workstation10.mycompany.com being removed from access control list
[you@workstation20 you]$
```

In some rare cases, it can be helpful to completely disable access control and allow all systems to open windows on your display. For example, if you're configuring a local network that is not yet connected to the Internet, you might need to open and close repeatedly remote applications from a number of different computer systems. Access control can be completely disabled by supplying the plus sign (+) alone as an argument to `xhost`:

`xhost +`

When you want to reenable access control, once again preventing systems who are not on the control list from connecting, supply the minus sign (-) alone as an `xhost` argument:

`xhost -`

You should disable access control only in completely trusted environments—
for example, if your network is not connected to the Internet at all—
because disabling access control can represent a major security risk, and can
lead to attacks leading to data theft or destruction by users outside your
network.

Displaying Local Applications Remotely

When you start a desktop application from the command line, the application decides
where it should display its application window by looking at the DISPLAY shell variable.
The DISPLAY variable should hold a value of the following format:

host:0

For example, if the desktop on the system called newton.mycompany.com has been configured with the xhost command to allow connections from
workstation20.mycompany.com (your system in this example), you can start an application on workstation20, which shows its application window on newton by executing a
command line like this one:

```
[you@workstation20 you]$ DISPLAY=newton.mycompany.com:0 emacs &
[1] 6044
[you@workstation20 you]$
```

This particular command opens an emacs window on the desktop of the computer
newton.mycompany.com on your local network, assuming that the xhost command has
been used on the newton host to allow connections from workstation20. The emacs program itself uses the processor and memory resources of your workstation (in this case,
workstation20) to run.

The :0 at the end of the DISPLAY variable's value indicates that the program
should display its application window on the first display on the remote
host. Because most PCs and workstations have only one display, you won't
find yourself using higher numbers in place of zero very often.

It can get tiresome to have to assign a value to the DISPLAY variable each time you want
to start a new program that displays remotely, particularly if you will be displaying several applications on the same remote display. In cases like this, you can set the value of
DISPLAY and then use the export command to force the value of DISPLAY to be used
even when you are starting multiple jobs from the command line:

```
[you@workstation20 you]$ DISPLAY=newton.mycompany.com:0
[you@workstation20 you]$ export DISPLAY
[you@workstation20 you]$
```

After you use export to make the value of DISPLAY apply to all jobs you start from the shell, you no longer need to set the value explicitly to cause an application to display remotely. For example, after you export the value of DISPLAY, as shown, the following command starts an emacs window, loads the file myfile.txt, and displays the application window on newton.mycompany.com so that the user sitting in front of that machine can edit myfile.txt:

```
[you@workstation20 you]$ emacs myfile.txt &
[2] 6078
[you@workstation20 you]$
```

Remember, after you set and export the value of DISPLAY to point to another workstation, any applications you start are displayed remotely, rather than locally. To restore the value of DISPLAY so that applications you start appear on your local display again, set the value of the DISPLAY variable to :0.0:

```
[you@workstation20 you]$ DISPLAY=:0.0
[you@workstation20 you]$ export DISPLAY
[you@workstation20 you]$
```

After the value of DISPLAY has been set to :0.0, any applications you start afterward from the command line appear on your local display.

Displaying Remote Applications Locally

To display remote applications locally, a similar technique can be used. Ensure first of all that you have used the xhost command to enable incoming connections on the local desktop display, as discussed earlier in "Allowing Incoming X Connections with xhost." Then, follow these steps:

1. In a terminal window on your desktop, use the telnet command to log into the remote system, from which you want to start programs that will display locally.

2. After you log into the remote system with telnet, set and export the DISPLAY variable so that it refers to your local host system.

3. Start your desktop applications as normal; they will appear on your local display.

Because the telnet command sends passwords across the network without first encrypting them, telnet is less secure than ssh. Malicious network users can steal passwords used in telnet sessions. Because of this, you should use telnet only if your network is behind a dedicated firewall, and instead should use the ssh techniques, discussed earlier this hour, whenever possible.

This process is illustrated in the following sequence of commands. Assuming that you are working at a system called workstation20.mycompany.com. This sequence starts the emacs application on a remote system called newton and displays its application window on your desktop:

```
[you@workstation20 you]$ telnet newton
Trying 10.4.26.131...
Connected to newton.
Escape character is '^]'.
SunOS Unix (newton)
login: joeuser
[joeuser@newton joeuser]$ DISPLAY=workstation20.mycompany.com:0
[joeuser@newton joeuser]$ export DISPLAY
[joeuser@newton joeuser]$ emacs &
[1] 31221
[joeuser@newton joeuser]$
```

After this sequence has been entered, the emacs application appears on your local display, running on the system called newton.

Allowing and Starting Remote X Sessions

Though it's convenient to be able to run individual applications remotely, sometimes it would be more helpful to run an entire X Window System (or GNOME or KDE) session—beginning with the graphical login screen—from a remote location. This can be especially helpful when building diskless thin clients or when using small computers with minimal Linux installations that need to function as full-fledged workstations.

By changing a setting in the Red Hat login manager configuration, you can allow remote display of entire X Window System sessions, from login through logout. After this change has been made, remote sessions can be launched by supplying a special argument to the XFree86 command.

Configuring the Login Manager for XDMCP

To allow users to remotely display entire X Window System sessions, you must configure your login manager (the program you see when you first start Red Hat Linux) to allow requests using the X Display Manager Control Protocol (XDMCP). To do this, log in to your Red Hat desktop as root and start the login screen configuration tool by clicking GNOME Menu, System Settings, Login Screen. The GDM Setup application starts. Click the XDMCP tab in this application to display the dialog shown in Figure 17.5.

Check Enable XDMCP

FIGURE 17.5

The GDM Setup application provides a way to enable XDMCP communication between your system and remote hosts.

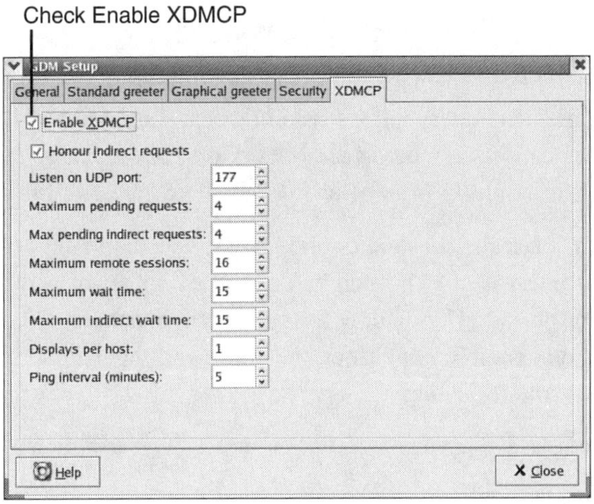

GDM Setup				
General	Standard greeter	Graphical greeter	Security	XDMCP

☑ Enable XDMCP

☑ Honour indirect requests

Listen on UDP port:	177
Maximum pending requests:	4
Max pending indirect requests:	4
Maximum remote sessions:	16
Maximum wait time:	15
Maximum indirect wait time:	15
Displays per host:	1
Ping interval (minutes):	5

Help   X Close

17

In the XDMCP tab, check the first box labeled Enable XDMCP. Then, close the dialog. This enables remote systems to query an entire X Window System session from your computer—your computer displays a login prompt on the remote machine, allowing users to log in and use applications and environments on your machine graphically.

Your firewall must also be properly configured before incoming XDMCP requests are accepted. To do this, start the security level tool as described earlier this hour and set for medium security. You must also enter the following exceptions into the Other ports entry box:

```
177:tcp,177:udp
```

This allows incoming traffic on port 177, which is the port used by the XDMCP protocol. For more information on using the security level tool to create exceptions for certain network ports, see "Managing the Red Hat Linux Firewall" in Hour 20, "Security Basics."

The warning you have become accustomed to also applies here: You should enable incoming XDMCP requests only if your local area network lies behind a dedicated firewall. Allowing incoming XDMCP requests on a machine that is connected directly to the public Internet leaves you vulnerable to attacks, which can result in data loss or theft.

Querying a Remote X Session

After XDMCP has been enabled on your machine, remote machines with the X Window System installed can query an X session (access the graphical login prompt on your machine). This allows remote users to work on your machine from login to logout, as if they were sitting right in front of it.

Normally an X session must be queried from the console, not from within an existing X Window System session. This can be done in a number of ways, depending on the version and vendor of the X Window System on the machine. On older Linux machines running XFree86 version 3.x or earlier, the command that should be entered at the console shell is one of the following:

```
X -query host
```

```
Xwrapper -query host
```

Replace *host* with the hostname or IP address of the machine on which an XDMCP session (login prompt) is to be requested. On more recent Linux machines running XFree86 version 4.x or later, the command is

```
XFree86 -query host
```

Again, replace *host* with the hostname or IP address of the machine in question. For example, assuming you have enabled XDMCP on your computer, workstation20, another Red Hat Linux 8 user on a machine called danscomputer could access your graphical login prompt by entering the following command at the console shell:

```
[dan@danscomputer dan]$ XFree86 -query workstation20.mycompany.com
```

After entering this command, the X Window System starts on danscomputer and a login prompt is displayed. When dan logs in, however, he must log in using an account on your computer, workstation20, and the desktop environment and applications dan sees are also running on your computer, workstation20. In fact, dan's entire X Window System session is running on your computer, even though it is being displayed on his.

When querying an entire session this way, none of the other techniques in this hour—such as the ssh command or the DISPLAY environment variable need to be used; applications are automatically displayed remotely as a part of the requested session.

Summary

This hour, you learned to use one of the most unique network capabilities of Unix operating systems to run applications on one machine while displaying their application windows on the graphical desktop of another machine. Specifically, you learned the following:

- How to use the `ssh` command to automate the process of launching remote applications for local display.
- How to use the `xhost` command to control connect permission to the local X Window System display on any Unix or Linux computer. Remember that the `ssh` method should be used in place of the `xhost` method wherever possible!
- How to use the `DISPLAY` environment variable in conjunction with the `xhost` command to start applications locally for remote display.
- How to use the `telnet` command when `ssh` isn't available in conjunction with `xhost` and `DISPLAY` to start applications remotely for local display.
- How to use the firewall rules editor to allow incoming connections via `ssh` and X if necessary.
- How to enable XDMCP and query entire remote X Window System sessions across the network.

When you master these techniques, your physical location in your network becomes less important, because you can access applications of all kinds, whether graphical or text-based, on any computer anywhere on your network, from the computer closest to where you are already standing.

Q&A

Q The X Window System manual page refers to another kind of security called *magic cookie authentication*, which is more secure than the `xhost` command. Why isn't it discussed here?

A The magic cookie method of authentication is indeed more secure than the `xhost` command method, but it requires the use of several additional commands, as well as the use of a secure means of network communication to transfer the security token—usually `ssh`. When you use `ssh` to display applications remotely using the techniques outlined in this hour, the magic cookie authentication method is automatically used for you anyway. In fact, `ssh` makes the process still more secure by encrypting all network transmissions. Because the magic cookie process is somewhat difficult to implement by hand and `ssh` automates it so well with added security to boot, you should simply use `ssh` whenever you can.

Q Is the remote display facility limited to a one-to-one relationship? That is to say, can I display applications from multiple remote machines on my local display, or can I display local applications on a variety of remote displays simultaneously?

A Yes. There is no limitation on the number of systems that can be involved in remote display connections; it is only required that systems have permission to connect to one another. This permission can be granted using either xhost or ssh, as described.

Q I'm still a little unclear on the basic concept. For example, if I open a file dialog on a remotely displayed application, which system's files will I see?

A Only the application window itself is displayed remotely; all other aspects of the running program occur on the system where the program was launched. So, if a program running on newton is displayed on workstation20 and a file dialog is opened, the files on newton appear in the file dialog. Remote display is simply a way to use a desktop application from a distance, taking advantage of network technology to accomplish this.

Workshop

The Workshop is designed to help you anticipate possible questions, review what you've learned, and begin learning how to put your knowledge into practice.

Quiz

1. How would you start the gedit program on a computer called server10, displaying the application on your own desktop, if your login name on server10 was admin36?

2. How would you tell your desktop environment to allow incoming application window connections from a system called robslabmachine.mycompany.com?

3. Without using ssh, what sequence of commands would you enter to start emacs in the background but display its application window on a local system called laptop6.mycompany.com?

4. Why should you use the ssh method of displaying applications remotely, rather than the xhost/DISPLAY method whenever possible?

Answers

1. `ssh -l admin36 server10 gedit`

2. `xhost robslabmachine.mycompany.com`

3. `DISPLAY=laptop6.mycompany.com:0`
   `export DISPLAY`
   `emacs &`

4. Because the ssh method is considerably more secure, using magic cookie authentication and encrypting data and passwords as they are transmitted across the network.

Activities

1. Use ssh in a terminal window to log in to a remote Linux computer system.

2. From the command line on the remote system, start an emacs window.

3. Use the emacs window to create and save a new text file on the remote system.

17

Hour 18

Command-Line System Administration

System administration is generally a skill with which even casual Linux users must become familiar, simply in the course of day-to-day work. In this hour, you learn how to perform a number of basic system administration tasks using command-line tools. By the end of this hour, you'll know

- How to list and manage running processes on your computer system by process number
- How to start and stop system and network services, both as the computer is running and as the computer starts
- How to create, mount, and unmount filesystems and how to instruct Linux to mount certain filesystems as the computer starts
- How to add and remove user and group accounts
- How to run maintenance, backup, and other tasks at regular intervals—weekly, daily, hourly, and so forth
- How to shut down or restart the system safely from the command line.

Because the tools in this hour are all carried out at the command line—whether at the console, in a terminal window, or through a remote login—there aren't any figures. However, the examples illustrate the steps involved in each type of task.

> The information in this hour is somewhat dense; it might be difficult to memorize in a single reading. Rather than try to remember it all, simply try to familiarize yourself with the topics and information presented; then, you can refer to it in the future, as the need arises.
>
> Be sure to try some of the activities at the end of this hour to help yourself become comfortable with these topics.

Using the su Command

You already know that there are many tasks in Linux that can be performed only by the root user. Most of the tasks you perform in this hour fall into this category. It can often be inconvenient to have to log out and log back in as the root user simply to perform an administration task or two.

Fortunately, Linux provides a command that can be used to temporarily perform tasks as the root user. This command is the su command, and in its basic form, it is called without arguments. When you call su, you are prompted for the root password. If you can enter the password correctly, a subshell that is owned by the root user starts and the shell prompt is displayed. Any commands you enter in the subshell work as though you were logged in as root. When you finish performing administration tasks, enter exit to close the subshell and return to the "normal user" command prompt.

The following lines show a user using the su command to become the root user, issuing a typical administration command to change the password of a user (a command you'll learn about later in this hour), and then exiting.

```
[you@workstation20 you]$ su
Password:
[root@workstation20 you]# passwd janeuser
Changing password for user janeuser
New UNIX password:
Retype new UNIX password:
passwd: all authentication tokens updated successfully
[root@workstation20 you]# exit
[you@workstation20 you]$
```

You know when you are working as the root user because the command prompt ends with a hash mark (#) instead of a dollar sign ($).

Remember to use the su command only when you need to perform an administration task that can't be performed as a normal user. Doing any real work as the root user is a dangerous proposition because Linux does exactly what root says, even if it is harmful to the system itself.

Managing System Processes

Thus far, you haven't had to worry much about which processes were running and what they were called. At most, you've used the jobs command to manage a list of jobs started from a single shell's command line.

Sometimes, however, it is necessary to list and modify running processes on a systemwide basis. Using the command line, you can list all the running processes on a system, kill processes by their process ID number, or reprioritize processes relative to other processes in the system so that you can control processor time allocation on a busy system.

Because normal users can list all processes but have access only to *modify* their own processes, management of systemwide processes is often done as the root user so that all processes can be managed and/or modified.

Listing Running Processes

The ps command is used to list processes that are currently running. Because a given Linux system might have a very long list of running processes, and because so much data can be displayed about the properties and resources of each process, the ps command supports a wide range and variety of options to modify its behavior.

The simplest way to call ps is without arguments. Whether called by root or by a normal user, this has the effect of listing all the processes owned by the current login with information in several columns:

```
[you@workstation20 you]$ ps
  PID TTY          TIME CMD
  971 pts/0    00:00:00 bash
 1028 pts/0    00:00:00 ps
[you@workstation20 you]$
```

This basic ps listing is very small because it includes only those processes owned by the user who has called ps and that were started from the command line. This listing indicates that only two processes have been started by you at the command line—the bash program (the login shell, which provides the command line) and the ps program, which lists itself because it is running, actively displaying the list of processes owned by the user. There are several columns of information in the ps output:

- The PID column displays the systemwide process ID number. When you learn to kill or reprioritize processes in the following sections, you use this number in referring to specific processes.
- The TTY column displays the system terminal from which the process was started.
- The TIME column displays the amount of real time that has been *actively* used by the process since its start. For many processes, these numbers are very small because processes like the shell are typically asleep much of the time waiting for user input, rather than actively calculating or working.
- The CMD column displays the command entered to start the process, possibly including (depending on the options you supply to ps) options or arguments supplied by the user on the command line.

The basic ps listing can be helpful when you're logged in as a normal user and simply want to manage your own processes. However, from the system administration perspective, it is often important to get information about all processes currently running on a Linux system or to get extended information about the processes being listed. This enables you to monitor the behavior of multiple users or server processes as the system functions on a day-to-day basis.

By supplying options or arguments to the ps command, you can change the types of processes that are listed and the information that is displayed about each process. The most common and useful ps options are shown in Table 18.1.

TABLE 18.1   Common Options Used to Alter the Behavior of the ps Command

Option	Description
x	Do not limit process listing to those processes launched from a terminal—include, for example, processes started from a menu or taskbar icon.
v	Include several columns of virtual memory use information in the output listing.
a	Display processes launched from a terminal owned by all users, not just by the user issuing the ps command.
-e	List all processes—those owned by any user on the system, whether launched from a terminal or not.

Table 18.1   continued

Option	Description
-f	Do a *full* listing of information, including process owner, process parent ID, and start time, among other things.
-U *user*	List only processes owned by the user whose login ID is *user*.
-G *group*	List only processes owned by the members who belong to the group known as *group*.
-H	Use indentation and sorting to show process parent and child relationships visually in the ps output.

You can mix and match the ps options listed in Table 18.1 on the command line with relative impunity.

Perhaps the two most common ways to call the ps command are with the -e and -f options or with the a and x options, in the following formats:

```
ps -ef
ps ax
```

Both of these commands have similar effects—they display a listing of processes owned by all users, including those processes not launched from a controlling terminal. These two options enable the root user (or any other user, for that matter) to get a quick listing of all running processes on the system.

> The ps command is quite powerful and flexible, and it's capable of accepting numerous options and displaying a great deal of information about running processes. The ps command is far too involved to explore fully in this hour. For more information on using ps, consult the ps manual page.
>
> A more complete printed reference for ps can be found in *Sams Teach Yourself Unix System Administration in 24 Hours*.

Adjusting Process Priority

The root user can adjust the priority of any running process upward (less CPU time) or downward (more CPU time) using the renice command and the process ID number of the related process. This enables the administrator to ensure that critical processes on an overloaded system get as much CPU time as possible, sometimes at the expense of other processes. To use the renice command, call it as follows:

```
renice priority pid
```

Replace *priority* with the desired priority, from -20 (highest priority) to +19 (lowest priority). Replace *pid* with the process ID number of the process whose priority you want to change. For example, to maximize the priority of process number 664 while minimizing the priority of process 702, you enter the following:

```
[root@workstation20 you]# renice -20 664
664: old priority 0, new priority -20
[root@workstation20 you]# renice +19 702
702: old priority 0, new priority 19
[root@workstation20 you]#
```

You can see the effects of renice operations in the output of the ps command as well because of the appearance of N (decreased priority) or < (increased priority) in the STAT column, as follows:

```
  PID TTY      STAT   TIME COMMAND
[...]
  664 ?        S<     0:00 /usr/sbin/sshd
  678 ?        S      0:00 xinetd -stayalive -reuse -pidfile /var/run/xinetd.pid
  702 ?        SN     0:00 sendmail: accepting connections
  712 ?        S      0:00 sendmail: Queue runner@01:00:00 for /var/spool/client
[...]
```

This fragment shows process 664 with a status of S<, which indicates a sleeping process with increased priority relative to other processes. Process 702, on the other hand, shows a status of SN, indicating a sleeping process with decreased priority relative to other processes.

Only the root user can adjust process priority downward (increased priority). Normal users can adjust the priorities of their own processes upward (decreased priority) if they choose.

Killing Running Processes

Sometimes it is necessary to forcefully kill a running process—for example, if a buggy piece of software has stopped responding, or if a single process has for some reason "run away" and is using vast amounts of CPU time, thus robbing the system of productivity potential.

To kill a running process, use the kill command followed by the process ID number of the process you want to kill. For example, to kill process 702, enter the following:

```
[root@workstation20 you]# kill 702
[root@workstation20 you]#
```

This sends a signal to process 702 that termination has been requested. Process 702 closes any open files and attempts to exit gracefully. From time to time, you find that even after trying to kill a process, it remains in the process list. Processes that can't be removed with a normal kill must then be terminated with the -KILL argument:

```
[root@workstation20 you]# kill -KILL 702
[root@workstation20 you]#
```

Because the -KILL argument is fairly destructive—it doesn't give a process any chance to close open files or network connections, but rather closes them forcefully as-is—it should be used only when other termination attempts fail.

From time to time, you might also see references to the commands kill -9 and kill -HUP.

The kill -9 command is equivalent to kill -KILL and works because signal number 9 is the number used by the system itself to identify the SIGKILL signal.

The kill -HUP command sends the SIGHUP or "hangup" signal to a process. In theory, this is supposed to cause a process to restart itself (often to cause recently edited configuration files to be reread). Many server and root-level processes understand this signal, but many user-level processes (for example, a gedit or an emacs process) either ignore it or treat it like a normal terminate request. The -HUP signal is thus best used only when you are very familiar with a process or when the documentation for a particular program suggests it.

Another command, the killall command, is sometimes used to kill all processes of a given name, as in the following example:

```
killall emacs
killall -KILL sendmail
```

The killall command can certainly be convenient, but use of this command is *not* recommended, especially on busy systems. Experience over decades of Unix use has demonstrated that it is too easy on a busy system to miskey or to misread the output of ps and then, using killall, to kill in one fell swoop any number of important processes that shouldn't have been killed!

As you expect, the root user is able to terminate or kill any process in the system by process ID, and normal users are able to terminate or kill only processes that they own.

18

Managing Running Services

After looking at the lengthy process lists in the previous section, you might be wondering just what most of the listed processes actually *are*. If you installed Red Hat Linux in the server configuration, you probably already know that many of them are system and network services of the sort that servers typically offer.

When Red Hat Linux is running, some of the services Red Hat Linux offers are running and others might not be. The default set of services running at any given time is determined by the system's current *runlevel*. A Linux system is always *at* a specific runlevel; available runlevels are numbered 0 through 6. Each runlevel is associated with a specific list of services, which are started when the system enters the runlevel.

Changes to the list of running services can be made by manipulating the list of services associated with the current runlevel or by changing the default runlevel at which the system operates; both of these tasks are discussed in the following sections.

Understanding Runlevels

When your Red Hat Linux system boots, the first process started by the kernel (the core of the operating system) is called init. The init process is responsible for starting all other processes in the system—from the system and network services to the graphical desktop environment. So how does the init command know what to start?

One primary file, the /etc/inittab file, controls just what init does each time the system starts. A complete description of the format of the /etc/inittab file is beyond the scope of this book, better left to an advanced text on system administration. Very near the beginning of the /etc/inittab file, however, you see a line that begins with the letters id, something like this one:

```
id:5:initdefault:
```

This line decides the default runlevel of your Red Hat Linux system. The system in this example has a default runlevel of 5. Recall that there are seven runlevels available, numbered 0 through 6. A list of these runlevels and their traditional meanings is shown in Table 18.2.

TABLE 18.2   The Linux Runlevels and Their Meanings

Runlevel	Description
0	**Halt.** When this is the current runlevel, the system is in the process of shutting down.
1	**Single-user.** This runlevel includes little more than a single virtual console running a single command line. Virtually every other service is disabled. This runlevel is

TABLE 18.2 continued

Runlevel	Description
	usually used for critical system maintenance, such as recovering from hack attacks or repairing disk corruption.
2	**Multiuser sans-file-services.** This runlevel starts most services, but does not enable network file service connections.
3	**Full multiuser.** This runlevel starts all enabled services but does not start the X Window System (or, by extension, any Linux desktop environment). Instead, users are able to use virtual consoles only.
4	**User-defined.** No conventional definition applies to runlevel 4; it is fully open to user configuration.
5	**Full multiuser with X.** This runlevel starts all enabled services *and* the X Window System and Linux desktop environments. Most Red Hat Linux users find runlevel 5 to be their default.
6	**Reboot.** When this is the current runlevel, the system is in the process of rebooting.

At any given time, a Linux system is running at a runlevel between 0 and 6. Controlling the list of automatically started services on your Linux system is a matter of setting a default runlevel and then configuring the services associated with that runlevel. You can change the default runlevel at which your system starts by editing the id line in the /etc/inittab file and inserting the runlevel number of your choice. For example, if you want to start with a default runlevel of 3, you edit the line to read as follows:

```
id:3:initdefault:
```

You learn how to control the list of services associated with each runlevel by using the chkconfig command in the next section.

18

You can change your system's current runlevel without rebooting. This has the effect of changing the list of currently active services as well. To do so, call the init command by hand, supplying the desired runlevel as an argument. For example, to switch to runlevel 3 without rebooting, you type the following:

```
/sbin/init 3
```

After entering the command, it takes a few moments for the system to settle down as processes are started and stopped before the system enters runlevel 3, where it remains until you switch again explicitly or reboot.

Selecting Automatically Started Services

In Red Hat Linux, the /sbin/chkconfig command is used at the command line to manage the list of services that are started automatically each time the system starts at a given runlevel. To see a list of available services and the current status of each with respect to each runlevel, call the chkconfig command using the --list option. The output appears in two parts, as shown in the following output fragments:

```
[root@workstation20 you]# /sbin/chkconfig --list
ntpd            0:off  1:off  2:off  3:off  4:off  5:off  6:off
syslog          0:off  1:off  2:on   3:on   4:on   5:on   6:off
httpd           0:off  1:off  2:off  3:on   4:on   5:on   6:off
netfs           0:off  1:off  2:off  3:on   4:on   5:on   6:off
network         0:off  1:off  2:on   3:on   4:on   5:on   6:off
random          0:off  1:off  2:on   3:on   4:on   5:on   6:off
rawdevices      0:off  1:off  2:off  3:on   4:on   5:on   6:off
[...]
xinetd based services:
   chargen-udp:    off
   chargen:off
   daytime-udp:    off
   daytime:off
[...]
   rlogin: off
   rsh:    off
   ntalk:  off
   talk:   off
   telnet: on
[root@workstation20 you]#
```

 Remember, you can page the lengthy output of the chkconfig --list command through a pager such as more using pipes:

/sbin/chkconfig --list | more

There are two components to the output of the chkconfig command:

- The first half of the output lists a number of system and network services in the first column; subsequent columns list the on or off status of that service in each runlevel, from 0 through 6.

- The second half of the chkconfig output lists a number of more basic services managed by the xinetd service, which is in turn managed by chkconfig and appears in the first half of the chkconfig output. Each of the more basic xinetd services is either on or off globally, for all runlevels for which xinetd is active.

A complete listing of, and set of descriptions for, all these services is beyond the scope of this book and better left to a book on Unix-style networking. However, some of the best-known services are described in Table 18.3.

TABLE 18.3 The Most Common Services Manageable by `chkconfig`

Service	Description
httpd	The Apache Web server, used to answer incoming `http` requests to your Red Hat Linux system.
sendmail	The Sendmail SMTP server, used to enable your Red Hat Linux system to act as a full-fledged SMTP mail server.
nfs	The Network File System service, used to enable your Red Hat Linux system to act as a file server to other Unix or Linux computer systems.
named	The BIND service, used to enable your Red Hat Linux system to act as a domain name server to other computers on your network.
smb	The Samba service, used to enable your Red Hat Linux system to act as a file server to Windows computer systems.
sshd	The Secure Shell service, used to enable your Red Hat Linux system to provide secure remote logins.
telnet	The Telnet service, used to enable your Red Hat Linux system to provide less secure, but more backward-compatible remote logins.
Wuftpd	The File Transfer Protocol service, used to enable your Red Hat Linux system to allow incoming File Transfer Protocol (`ftp`) logins.

Any of the services in Table 18.3 or the services in the `chkconfig --list` output can be enabled or disabled globally by calling `chkconfig` and supplying first the name of the service, and then the words on or off as arguments. For example, to completely disable both Web service and incoming Telnet service, you'd enter the following two commands:

```
[root@workstation20 you]# /sbin/chkconfig httpd off
[root@workstation20 you]# /sbin/chkconfig telnet off
[root@workstation20 you]#
```

You can easily check to see whether your changes have taken effect by using the `chkconfig --list` command again in combination with the `grep` command to filter the output. For example, to check on the new status of the `httpd` service, enter the following:

```
[root@workstation20 you]# /sbin/chkconfig --list | grep httpd
httpd           0:off   1:off   2:off   3:off   4:off   5:off   6:off
[root@workstation20 you]#
```

For services not managed by `xinetd` (those in the first half of the `chkconfig` listing), you can also enable or disable services on a runlevel-by-runlevel basis using the `--level` option, supplying the level to change as the first argument. For example, to reenable Web service for runlevel 3 only and verify the result, you enter the following commands:

```
[root@workstation20 you]# /sbin/chkconfig --level 3 httpd on
[root@workstation20 you]# /sbin/chkconfig --list | grep httpd
httpd              0:off   1:off   2:off   3:on    4:off   5:off   6:off
[root@workstation20 you]#
```

> You cannot offer services that you did not install in Hour 2, "Installing Red Hat Linux." If you find that you want to offer a service that hasn't been installed on your system, refer to Hour 21, "Installing Software."

After making changes to your chkconfig configuration, you need to reboot for the changes you've made to your current runlevel to take effect.

Stopping, Starting, and Restarting Running Services

Sometimes over the course of a network's lifetime, it is helpful to be able to temporarily stop a running service that is normally offered, to temporarily offer a service that is not normally offered, or to restart a running service on your Red Hat Linux system. Often this is the case when you have changed a configuration file or when a service seems to have become unstable or overloaded.

You do not need to use the chkconfig utility or restart your system to make temporary changes of this sort. You can use the service command to stop, start, or restart running services one by one. To do this, call the service command, supplying the service whose name matches an entry in the chkconfig service list as the first argument and either stop, start, or restart as a second argument.

For example, to start the httpd service when it hasn't already been running, enter the following command:

```
[root@workstation20 you]# /sbin/service httpd start
Starting httpd:                                            [  OK  ]
[root@workstation20 you]#
```

To stop the service once again, call service with httpd as an argument again, but with stop as the second argument instead:

```
[root@workstation20 you]# /sbin/service httpd stop
Stopping httpd:                                            [  OK  ]
[root@workstation20 you]#
```

The restart argument is used in the same way to force a running service to restart, usually after you edit its configuration file (to activate new changes) or if the service has encountered a bug and stopped responding, or encountered other problems.

The changes you make to the running status of a service this way last only until the system is rebooted; for example, if you call `service` with `httpd start` to start your Web server but don't have the `httpd` service enabled via `chkconfig`, the next time you reboot, the `httpd` service is not activated automatically.

Managing Filesystems

The ability to manage the configuration and availability of filesystems is an important system administration skill, particularly for systems heavily involved in a network's infrastructure. At various times it might be necessary to configure and add an additional hard drive to a server system, or to provide system services with access to files on a separate file server. For these types of tasks, it is necessary to know how to create, mount, and unmount filesystems.

Creating a filesystem refers to the process by which a hard drive or other storage device is made ready to store files (this process is often called *formatting* in other operating systems). *Mounting* a filesystem refers to the process of making the contents of a device or network share available to users and processes within the Linux filesystem. *Unmounting* a filesystem refers to the process of disconnecting a device or network share and its contents from the Linux filesystem.

Much of the rest of the "Managing Filesystems" section assumes that you have some familiarity with PC hardware, such as hard drives, removable storage devices, and SCSI hardware. If this is not the case, you might need to refer to additional sources of information about PC hardware to make use of the information presented here.

Creating Filesystems

Before you can mount and use a new or empty storage device with Linux, you must create a filesystem on it. For purposes of example, let's build an ext2 filesystem in this hour.

If you prefer to use metadata-journaled filesystems, such as `ext3` or `reiserfs`, or filesystems associated with other operating systems, such as `vfat` or `minix`, you need to refer to the `fdisk` and `mkfs` commands and man pages, rather than using `parted`.

18

There are two major steps involved in creating a new ext2 filesystem for use with Linux:

1. Identify the name of the device where the new filesystem is to be created.
2. Create a partition on the device and format that partition using the desired type of filesystem, such as a Linux ext3 filesystem or a Windows FAT32 filesystem.

The name of the device where the new filesystem and partition are to be created depends on the type of device and the type of connection through which the device communicates with your computer system. Most often, the device is connected either through an IDE channel or a SCSI controller.

- For IDE devices, the name of the device is /dev/hda, /deb/hdb, /dev/hdc, or /dev/hdd, depending on whether the device is connected to the primary master, primary slave, secondary master, or secondary slave channels, respectively.
- For SCSI devices, the name of the device is /dev/sda through /dev/sdg (or higher) depending on two factors—the position of the device in the SCSI ID chain and the number of earlier storage devices present. The first SCSI hard drive or random-writable (that is, not CD-R, CD-RW, or tape) device found is /dev/sda, the second is /dev/sdb, and so on, regardless of the absolute SCSI ID number.

After you identify the device on which you want to create a new filesystem for use with Linux, you call parted with the device name as an argument followed by the print option to display information about the device's size and any existing partitions that might reside on it:

```
[root@workstation20 you]# /sbin/parted /dev/sdb print
Disk geometry for /dev/sdb: 0.000-3992.717 megabytes
Disk label type: msdos
Minor    Start      End     Type       Filesystem  Flags
1        0.031    3992.717  primary    FAT
[root@workstation20 you]$
```

> If you are attempting to create a filesystem on a brand new disk, the print option of parted might give you an "unrecognized disk label" error. If this is the case, you need to run the following command first, and then proceed with the print option and the rest of this section:
>
> **/sbin/parted /dev/sdb mklabel msdos**
>
> This prepares the disk for use on a standard PC computer with Linux; you can then partition and create filesystems on the disk as usual.

In this particular example, one existing partition of the FAT (Windows) type must be removed before a new partition or filesystem can be created. The first column indicates that this is partition 1 on the device /dev/sdb. To remove it, use parted with the rm option and the number of the partition to remove as an argument. Then, call parted with the print option to verify that the partition has been removed:

```
[root@workstation20 you]# /sbin/parted /dev/sdb rm 1
[root@workstation20 you]# /sbin/parted /dev/sdb print
Disk geometry for /dev/sdb: 0.000-3992.717 megabytes
Disk label type: msdos
Minor    Start      End      Type       Filesystem  Flags
[root@workstation20 you]#
```

Be sure when you are deleting partitions that you do not delete partitions on the wrong device—you don't want to lose valuable files on a device you're already using!

With existing partitions removed, you are free to create new partitions. This is done using the parted command as follows:

```
parted device mkpartfs primary fstype begin end
```

Replace *device* with the device name where you're creating a new filesystem, *fstype* with one of fat (for a Windows filesystem) or ext2 (for a Linux filesystem), and *begin* and *end* with the begin and end positions of the new partition, in megabytes.

For example, to create a Linux filesystem the size of the entire disk shown in the examples thus far, you issue the following parted command:

```
[root@workstation20 you]# /sbin/parted /dev/sdb mkpartfs primary ext2 0 3992.717
[root@workstation20 you]# /sbin/parted /dev/sdb print
Disk geometry for /dev/sdb: 0.000-3992.717 megabytes
Disk label type: msdos
Minor    Start      End      Type       Filesystem  Flags
1        0.031    3992.717   primary    ext2
[root@workstation20 you]#
```

You can create up to four partitions on any device using this technique; Linux and Windows partitions can be freely intermixed.

You must be sure that you do not cause partitions to overlap. For example, if you create a partition from 0–300MB, your second partition must not begin earlier than 301MB. If you try to cause partitions to overlap, you will receive an error message.

18

Filesystems you create this way are referred to by appending their partition number to the device name. For example, when you learn to mount filesystems in the next section, you mount the first partition on /dev/sdb by referring to /dev/sdb1, the second partition by referring to /dev/sdb2, and so on.

> For comprehensive documentation of the parted command, visit the online parted manual, which can be found in the alphabetically sorted online list of GNU manuals at http://www.gnu.org/manual/.

Mounting and Unmounting Filesystems

Whether you want to access a newly created filesystem, the data on an existing device or filesystem, or the data on a network share, in the Linux operating system, you must first mount a data storage area before you are able to read from or write to it. There are four steps in the mounting process:

1. You must create or identify a *mountpoint*. This is an empty directory somewhere in your existing Linux filesystem that you choose and/or create where the contents of the new data storage area will eventually be accessed.

2. You must identify the device name or network source of the data area. If you have just created a filesystem on a disk device in the previous section and now want to mount it, you use a device name like /dev/hda1 or /dev/sda1. If you are mounting a network filesystem, this is supplied by your network administrator and is a hostname followed by a path, like fileserver.mycompany.com:/pub/storagearea.

3. You must identify the *type* of filesystem you are mounting. For nearly all Windows filesystems, including removable devices like floppy disks or Zip disks, this is vfat. For Linux filesystems, this is usually ext2, ext3, or reiserfs. For networked filesystems, this is usually nfs. For CD-ROM devices, this is iso9660, and for DVD devices, it's udf. If in doubt, contact your media provider or network administrator.

4. You must issue a correctly formed mount command to supply all the following information to Linux so that the data or storage area can be available to you.

The format of the mount command is as follows:

```
mount -t fstype [-o options] datasource mountpoint
```

Replace *fstype* with the type of filesystem (vfat, ext2, ext3, reiserfs, nfs, iso9660, udf, or other type you have been instructed to use). Replace *datasource* with the device name (/dev/hda1, /dev/sda1, and so forth) or network path (address:/path). Replace *mountpoint* with the place in your local filesystem where this data or this storage area is to appear. The -o *options* option is not required, but can be used to provide additional options, usually one of the following:

- -o ro to specify that the filesystem should be mounted read-only. Any attempts to write to it by anyone (even the root user) will fail. Note that CD-ROM devices are always mounted read-only, whether you supply this option or not.

- -o umask=0000 is used with Windows FAT32 filesystems to allow *all users* to read and write any data on this device. Use this option with extreme caution—it allows any user to remove any file on the filesystem in question! This option is generally used on personal Linux computers that dual-boot with Windows, to allow all the Windows files on a mounted Windows hard drive to be accessed by normal user accounts.

Additional options can be found in the man page for the mount command.

To illustrate, if you want to mount the ext2 filesystem you created on /dev/sdb1 in the previous section to a new directory called /publicspace, you first create /publicspace and then issue the mount command supplying all three as arguments:

```
[root@workstation20 you]# mkdir /publicspace
[root@workstation20 you]# mount -t ext2 /dev/sdb1 /publicspace
[root@workstation20 you]#
```

The contents of the device /dev/sdb1 can now be accessed or modified by reading or writing to files or directories in the /publicspace tree. To verify that this is the case, you can print the list of mounted filesystems by entering the mount command without arguments:

```
[root@workstation20 you]# mount
/dev/sda2 on / type ext3 (rw)
none on /proc type proc (rw)
usbdevfs on /proc/bus/usb type usbdevfs (rw)
/dev/sda1 on /boot type ext3 (rw)
none of /dev/pts type devpts (rw,gid=5,mode=620)
none on /dev/shm type tmpfs (rw)
/dev/sdb1 on /publicpsace type ext2 (rw)
[root@workstation20 you]#
```

When the mount command is called without arguments, each line of output contains the device or resource, the mountpoint, the filesystem type, and any options the device has been mounted with, in that order. Complete documentation for filesystem types and options can be found in the mount manual page.

18

Another command, df, doesn't tell you as much about the mount options of each filesystem, but when called alone, it *does* tell you how much space is free and how much space has been used on each mounted device. If you want to know how close you are to filling up one of your hard drives or another removable device, try using the df command without arguments to get a status report.

You can unmount a mounted filesystem with the umount command. The umount command simply needs one argument: either the name of the device or resource to unmount, or the name of the mountpoint where the device or resource was mounted. For example, considering the mount commands we've issued in this section, the following two umount commands are equivalent:

```
umount /dev/sdb1
umount /publicspace
```

After you unmount a device or resource, you can verify that it no longer appears in the mounted filesystems list by using the mount or df commands without arguments.

If while attempting to unmount a filesystem, you get a "device is busy" error, it means that some process or some user's current working directory still resides within that filesystem, or some process is still using a file stored on that filesystem. Until the user or process changes the current working directory or the open file is closed, you won't be able to unmount the filesystem.

Maintaining the /etc/fstab File

The /etc/fstab file is a list of devices and resources, filesystem types, and mountpoints that control which filesystems get mounted when the computer starts. This file also lists which filesystems are mountable and unmountable by regular users. Each line in the /etc/fstab file represents one mounted or mountable filesystem, and each line is formatted as follows:

device mountpoint fstype option1,option2,... dump fscklvl

Each of the fields in this file is described in Table 18.4.

TABLE 18.4   Fields in the /etc/fstab File

Field	Description
device	The name of the device or resource that contains the filesystem to which this line applies.
mountpoint	Where the filesystem should be mounted within the local filesystem tree.
fstype	The type of filesystem, usually vfat (for Windows devices), nfs (for networked filesystems), ext2, ext3, reiserfs, iso9660, or udf.
options	A comma-separated list of options, as listed in the man page for the mount command. Common options include user and owner, which let normal users mount and unmount the device; noauto, which prevents the device from being automatically mounted at start time; and defaults, which means that no special options are used.
dump	Whether this filesystem should be backed up by the dump command. This is a relic from Unix days gone by; because the dump command is obsolete as of Linux 2.4, this value should always be set to 0.
rcklvl	For all filesystems other than the root filesystem, this should be set to 2. The root filesystem should be set to 1. Filesystems that don't require checking, such as reiserfs or iso9660, can be set to 0. If in doubt, this field should contain the value 2.

18

If you would like to cause a filesystem such as the one created in the previous section to automatically be mounted when the system starts, add an entry to the bottom of the /etc/fstab file containing the device, mountpoint, filesystem type, and other information. Following the sample filesystem we created in the previous section, you add the following line:

```
/dev/sdb1  /publicspace  ext2  defaults  0  2
```

By editing the the /etc/fstab file, you can cause Linux to automatically mount added storage devices or networked filesystems each time you boot. You can also add additional removable storage devices so that users can mount and unmount them as needed.

For further documentation of the /etc/fstab file or the options that can be used in it, see the manual pages for fstab(5) and mount.

Managing Accounts

The adding and removing of users and groups is of primary importance to you as a system administrator if you are running a multiuser Red Hat Linux system or a Red Hat Linux system on a network to which many people have remote login permission.

In Hour 4, "Navigating Linux at the Console," you learned about users, groups, and permissions. Now you learn how to create the user and group accounts with which permissions work.

The process of adding or deleting users and groups at the command line is an easy one; the tasks at hand are accomplished with the adduser, groupadd, userdel, and groupdel commands.

Adding and Removing User Accounts

Whenever you want to give a new user access to your Red Hat Linux system with his or her own set of files and login information, you need to add a user account to your system. This is accomplished in two simple steps:

1. Call the adduser command, stored in /usr/sbin, supplying the name of the account you want to create as an argument and, optionally, the -c "Name" option to supply the real name of the user, which is used by email programs.

2. Call the passwd command, supplying the name of the account you just created as an argument, to assign a password to the account.

For example, to create a new account for a user named joe, you call adduser supplying joe as an argument, and then call passwd supplying joe as an argument, entering a password for joe when prompted:

```
[root@workstation20 you]# /usr/sbin/adduser -c "Joe Brady" joe
[root@workstation20 you]# passwd joe
Changing password for user joe.
New password:
Retype new password:
passwd: all authentication tokens updated successfully.
[root@workstation20 you]#
```

After you create an account for joe, he is able to log in using the password that you configured for him. His home directory has been created too: /home/joe.

To delete a user account, simply use the userdel command, which resides in /usr/sbin, supplying the name of the account you want to delete as an argument and, optionally, the -r option if you want to delete the user's home directory. To delete the account for joe that you just created, along with joe's home directory, enter the following:

```
[root@workstation20 you]# /usr/sbin/userdel -r joe
[root@workstation20 you]#
```

Without fanfare, joe's account and his home directory are deleted irrecoverably from the system.

If you want to delete an account but you're not sure which one, you can get a listing of the acounts that exist on your system by displaying the /etc/passwd file, which contains all user accounts with their account numbers, one per line.

Do not, however, delete any accounts with user numbers lower than 500 because accounts numbered below 500 belong to system services and might be critical for the proper functioning of Red Hat Linux.

Adding and Removing Groups

Groups enable users to become affiliated with one another, to work collectively on projects, or to access a specific facility or device that nongroup users can't. To create a group, use the groupadd command, stored in /usr/sbin, supplying the name of the group to create as an argument. To create a group called programmers, supply the name as an argument to groupadd as follows:

```
[root@workstation20 you]# /usr/sbin/groupadd programmers
[root@workstation20 you]#
```

The process of deleting groups is similarly easy and is accomplished using the groupdel command, also stored in /usr/sbin. To delete a group, call groupdel and supply the name of the group you want to delete as an argument:

```
[root@workstation20 you]# /usr/sbin/groupdel programmers
[root@workstation20 you]#
```

The group is deleted.

18

If you want to delete a group but you're not sure which one, you can get a listing of the groups that exist on your system by displaying the /etc/group file, which contains all groups with their group numbers, one per line.

Do not, however, delete any groups with numbers lower than 500 because groups numbered below 500 belong to system services and might be critical for the proper functioning of Red Hat Linux.

Administering Groups

Because groups are by definition a collection of individual users, they require some maintenance—you must be able to add users to a group or delete users from a group, and to assign group administration privileges to a specific user. All this is accomplished by calling the gpasswd command.

After you create a group, you can give group administration privileges to a regular user by calling the gpasswd command with the -A option, and supplying the name of the user and the name of the group as arguments. For example, to give the user joe administration privileges for the group programmers, you enter the following command:

```
[root@workstation20 you]# gpasswd -A joe programmers
[root@workstation20 you]#
```

The user joe now has administration privileges for the group programmers and can add and delete users, set the password, or clear the password for the group.

To add users, joe issues the gpasswd command with the -a option, supplying the name of the user to add and the name of the group he administers as arguments. For example, if joe adds jane to the group programmers, he enters the following command:

```
[joe@workstation20 joe]$ gpasswd -a jane programmers
[joe@workstation20 joe]$
```

The user jane is now a member of programmers until joe removes her. To remove jane from programmers, joe calls the gpasswd command with the -d option, supplying the user to remove, jane, and the group to remove her from, programmers, as arguments:

```
[joe@workstation20 joe]$ gpasswd -d jane programmers
[joe@workstation20 joe]$
```

For information on additional capabilities offered to the root user by the gpasswd command, including the ability to use group passwords, see the gpasswd manual page.

Changing Group Membership

For regular users to use their group memberships, they must use the newgrp command. The newgrp command is called with the name of a group as an argument; the user's group identity then changes to that of the specified group if the user is a member of the group. For example, if jane, a member of programmers, wants to access the files belonging to the group programmers, she calls newgrp from her command prompt, supplying programmers as an argument:

```
[jane@workstation20 jane]$ newgrp programmers
[jane@workstation20 jane]$
```

Users can return to their default (that is, login) group identity by issuing the newgrp command without arguments:

```
[jane@workstation20 jane]$ newgrp
[jane@workstation20 jane]$
```

Using cron to Manage Periodic Jobs

Every Linux and Unix system includes a service called cron that enables users to automatically run specific commands or scripts periodically, according to user-defined timing options. This service offers a range of unique tasks—periodic backups, email status reports, home directory cleanups, and so forth.

There are two levels of cron process lists: the systemwide lists and the per-user lists. The systemwide cron process lists should be used only to manage system-oriented processes; for all personal jobs that need to be periodically run, the per-user cron lists should be used instead.

Adding Systemwide cron Processes

Systemwide cron processes are most often used for tasks such as periodic backups, log rotation, and system health monitoring. To create a systemwide cron process, you create a shell script that performs the task you want to accomplish, and then, using the cp or mv commands, place it into one of several special directories in /etc:

- Shell scripts copied to /etc/cron.hourly are run once every hour at one minute past the hour.
- Shell scripts copied to /etc/cron.daily are run once every day at 4:02 a.m.
- Shell scripts copied to /etc/cron.weekly are run once every week on Sunday at 4:22 a.m.
- Shell scripts copied to /etc/cron.monthly are run once every month, on the first day of the month, at 4:42 a.m.

As is the case with all shell scripts you want to run, scripts that you copy to the /etc/cron.* folders must be marked as executable for them to work properly.

> If you are wondering what happens to your daily shell scripts when your computer isn't running at 4:02 a.m., you needn't worry. Red Hat Linux includes a system called anacron that monitors your cron tasks. When you first boot your Linux system, anacron runs those tasks that missed their last scheduled execution, ensuring that no cron job is ever missed.

Editing Per-User cron Processes

In addition to the systemwide list of cron tasks, which only the root user has permission to edit (because they reside in the /etc folder), cron provides a special way for individual

18

users to manage a personal list of periodic tasks. This is done with the crontab command. To edit your personal lists of cron tasks, enter the crontab -e command at any command line:

```
[you@workstation20 you]$ crontab -e
```

The vi editor takes over your terminal or console, pointing toward a special file that cron reads to perform the tasks you request. By editing and saving this file, you can cause cron to call any command or script for you on a periodic basis.

Each line in the file represents a separate task and must be a list of data fields of the following format:

```
min   hour   mday   month   wday   command
```

The meanings of each of these fields is described in Table 18.5. Each of them is meaningful—cron uses the values of every field on a specific line to construct the time(s) at which a task should be run.

TABLE 18.5   Fields in the crontab File

Field	Description and Format
min	The minute (from 0–60) at which this job should be run. Multiple values can be specified by separating them with commas (for example, 0,15,30,45), and a range of values can be specified to cause the job to run every minute in the range (for example, 15–40). Lists and ranges can also be mixed (for example, 0–15,30–45). An asterisk (*) indicates any minute.
hour	The hour (from 0–24) at which this job should be run. As was the case with min, lists, ranges, a combination of the two, or an asterisk may appear in this field.
mday	The day of the month (from 1–31) on which this job should be run. As was the case with min, lists, ranges, a combination of the two, or an asterisk may appear in this field.
month	The month of the year (from 1–12) in which this job should be run. As was the case with min, lists, ranges, a combination of the two, or an asterisk may appear in this field.
wday	The day of the week (from 0–7, both representing Sunday), on which this job should be run. As was the case with min, lists, ranges, a combination of the two, or an asterisk may appear in this field.

Enter each of your periodic tasks. When you have finished, save the file and exit the vi editor; the new list of jobs is read by cron and carried out at the times you specify until they are removed again—meaning when you enter crontab -e and delete them from the file.

Let's examine a few lines from a crontab file for illustration purposes:

```
* * * * * fetchmail
0 15 * * * mcopy ~/database.txt a:
1 0 1 1 * new_year_script
```

The first of these entries calls the `fetchmail` program described in Hour 8, "Networking Without Graphics," once every minute of every day. In short, this line downloads the user's new mail once per minute.

The second of these entries copies a file called `database.txt` from the user's home directory to the floppy disk in drive a: every day at 3:00 p.m., presumably for backup purposes.

The final entry runs a shell script called `new_year_script` every New Year's Day at 12:01 a.m.

Shutting Down and Restarting

The graphical Red Hat login screen provides an easy way to shut down or restart your Red Hat Linux computer system safely. However, there are times when the ability to shut down or restart from the command line is important. For example, if the system becomes overloaded or unstable, you may want to be able to restart it from a remote location through a `telnet` or `ssh` login.

The `shutdown` command is used to shut down or restart a running Linux system from the command line. `shutdown` is typically used in one of the following two ways:

```
shutdown -h time
shutdown -r time
```

Using `shutdown` with the `-h` option halts a running Linux system. Using `shutdown` with the `-r` option restarts a running Linux system. Replace `time` with one of the following:

- The word `now` to indicate that you want to shut down or restart immediately
- A time in 24-hour `hh:mm` format, where `hh` is the hour and `mm` is the minute at which the system should shut down or restart
- An offset in minutes preceded by a plus sign, such as `+30`, to indicate that the system should shut down or restart after a specific period of time measured in minutes

For example, to immediately reboot a running Red Hat Linux system, call the `shutdown` command with the `-r` option and the `now` argument:

```
/sbin/shutdown -r now
```

18

You should always use either the shutdown command or the shut down and restart tools at the graphical login prompt to stop or restart your Linux system. Using the power switch or reset button without first shutting down properly can cause data loss.

Summary

This hour, you were given a crash course in Linux and Unix system administration at the command line. Though its doubtful that you were able to absorb it all enough to fly without a net, you can refer to parts of this hour as you need them in the future.

To recount a few highlights, this hour you learned about the following:

- The su command, which enables you to access the root account to perform administration tasks without having to log out of a user account and log back in as root

- The ps, renice, and kill commands, which enable you to list running processes, adjust their priorities, or kill them forcefully

- The chkconfig utility, which enables you to edit the list of running services on a per-runlevel basis, and the /etc/inittab file, which determines your default runlevel

- The parted command, which enables you to create new partitions and filesystems on storage devices

- The mount and umount commands, which enable you to mount and unmount filesystems for access to their contents, and the /etc/fstab file, which enables you to determine which filesystems are automatically mounted at boot time

- The adduser, userdel, groupadd, and groupdel commands, which enable you to add users, delete users, add groups, and delete groups, respectively

- The gpasswd and newgrp commands, which are used by group administrators and users in the course of group management

- The cron system, /etc/cron.* directories, and crontab command, which enable both the root user and normal users to schedule tasks of all kinds for periodic execution

Linux and Unix system administration is a very involved topic, enough to have already merited volume upon volume of published documentation. You at least managed to scratch the surface in this hour.

For more involved system administration documentation for Linux systems, consult *The Linux System Administrator's Guide*, which can be found at http://www.tldp.org/LDP/sag/ and *Sams Teach Yourself Unix System Administration in 24 Hours*.

Q&A

Q **When I try to use `chkconfig` to enable some services, I get an error message about files not being found. Why?**

A In most cases, this is because you have not installed the required software to support the service in question. Refer to Hour 21 for details on how to install additional Red Hat Linux software.

Q **I have created a new `cron` task, but it doesn't seem to be running. Why?**

A First, if your task is a script, double-check to make sure that it begins with `#!/bin/sh` and is marked as executable. If your changes were made in the `vi` editor, make sure that you saved the file before exiting. Finally, depending on where your script is located, you might need to call it with a full path, such as `/home/you/bin/myscript` instead of just `myscript`.

Workshop

The Workshop is designed to help you anticipate possible questions, review what you've learned, and begin learning how to put your knowledge into practice.

Quiz

1. How would you get a listing of *all* currently running processes on a Linux system?
2. How would you forcibly kill, without questions or delay, process number `1340`?
3. How would you enable the `httpd` (Web) server for runlevel 4?
4. How do you list all filesystems on the device `/dev/hdb`, as well as its size?
5. How do you edit the personal list of periodic tasks?

Answers

1. `ps ax`

   or

   `ps -ef`
2. `kill -KILL 1340`
3. `/sbin/chkconfig --level 4 httpd on`
4. `/sbin/parted /dev/hdb print`
5. `crontab -e`

18

Activities

1. Get a list of all of the processes currently running on your system using the ps command and the ax arguments.

2. Use the chkconfig command and the -list option to get a listing of all the services that your Red Hat Linux system runs at various runlevels.

3. Use the service command and the restart argument to restart one of the services currently running on your Red Hat Linux system.

4. Add a user account called galileo and assign it a password. Log in to the account to verify that it exists. Then, log out and back in as root again and delete the account and its home directory.

5. Use the shutdown command to reboot your system.

Hour **19**

Desktop System Administration

This hour, you learn to perform a number of system administration tasks from the Red Hat Linux desktop. Though you won't always have access to the desktop environment (often the case if you've installed a server-only configuration), the desktop tools are generally easier to use than their command-line counterparts. By the end of this hour, you'll know how to use desktop tools to do the following:

- View and manage the list of running processes
- Manage the print queue as jobs are sent to it
- Manage the configuration of network interfaces
- Manage the list of services that starts automatically when your computer system starts
- Manage user and group accounts
- Read and search through the various system logs

Though most of the tools in this hour must be run as root to function properly, in most cases you don't actually need to be logged in as root to use them. If you are logged in to your desktop as another user and start one of these tools, you are prompted for the root password; if you enter the password, the tool starts. In some tools, you are prompted for the root password only if you attempt to make a change or perform an operation requiring root privileges.

Managing System Processes

As you learned in Hour 18, "Command-Line System Administration," in any running system it is important to be able to list the running processes, to change the priority at which they execute relative to other processes, and to kill those processes that need to be ended for some reason or other.

At the desktop, all these tasks are accomplished with the System Monitor tool. Open the System Monitor by clicking the GNOME Red Hat icon, and then choosing System Tools, System Monitor; the System Monitor window appears, open to the Process Listing tab, as shown in Figure 19.1.

FIGURE 19.1

The System Monitor tool (maximized here) displays a list of running processes.

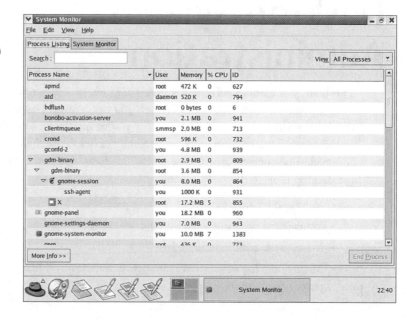

You can use the options in the Process Listing tab to list the processes that are running on your system, change the priority (amount of CPU time) given to running processes, and kill processes you decide should no longer run.

The list of displayed processes is updated on a continuous basis as system conditions evolve and the list of currently running processes changes.

You can change the View options to limit the display to certain types of running programs. That action trims the length of the displayed list and limits the display to only those files you're interested in viewing. To change the View, open the View menu (click View in the menu bar), and choose any of these options:

- The All Processes option displays all the processes running on the system, regardless of owner or whether the process is currently active (calculating or executing rather than waiting for data or input).
- The My Processes option displays all the processes owned by the user who started the System Monitor tool.
- The Active Processes option displays all processes that are currently active.

Adjusting Process Priority

The Process Listing tab in the System Monitor enables you to adjust the priority of any running process upward (less CPU time) or downward (more CPU time). This enables you to ensure that critical processes get as much CPU time as possible on an overloaded system, sometimes at the expense of other processes. For example, suppose that you are running a large spreadsheet computation involving many thousands of cells on a Linux computer that is also your small company's Web server. Because you want to ensure that customers can access your Web site as quickly as possible, you could adjust the priority of your spreadsheet application upward (less CPU time) so that it uses processing resources only when other tasks—like the Web server—don't need them.

To adjust the priority of a running process, select its entry in the Process Name list, and then choose Edit, Change Priority; the Change Priority dialog appears, as shown in Figure 19.2.

19

FIGURE 19.2

Here, the priority for sendmail is being changed. To increase the priority of the selected process, drag the slider to the left. Drag the slider to the right to decrease the process's priority.

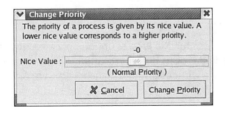

In the Change Priority dialog box, adjust the slider downward toward negative numbers to raise the priority of the process (giving it more CPU time) or toward positive numbers to lower the priority of the process (giving it less CPU time). All user processes have a default priority (also sometimes known as *nice value*) of 0. After you adjust the priority of the process relative to other running processes, click the Change Priority button to assign the priority and close the dialog box.

Killing Running Processes

If a running process becomes unresponsive or if you need to stop the process for administrative reasons, you can use the System Monitor tool to end or kill the process. When you end a process, Linux asks the process to exit. Occasionally, a process refuses to do so—sometimes because it is still busy storing information or working, sometimes because it has become unstable. When this occurs, you may decide that you want to kill the process, interrupting anything it might be doing and causing it to exit immediately. When you kill a process, any unsaved files opened by the process are lost and the process does not have a chance to close open network connections gracefully and perform other similar housekeeping tasks before exiting. Thus, it is usually a good idea to try to end a process first, killing it afterward only if absolutely necessary.

To end a process, select it in the Process Name list of the Process Listing tab and click the End Process button at the lower-right corner of the tab. The End Process confirmation dialog appears.

To confirm that you want to end the process, click the End Process button. The System Monitor tool sends a signal to the process indicating that it is time to quit.

If you find that you can't cause the process to quit using the End Process button, you can force the process to be killed. Select the offending process from the process list and then choose Edit, Kill Process; the Kill Process confirmation dialog box appears. Click the Kill Process button to kill the process.

> You should use the Kill Process option only after you try to kill a process using the End Process button; forcefully killing a process takes it out of the process table without giving it a chance to close open files or connections.

To confirm that you want to kill the process (and kill it), click the Kill Process button. The process is terminated forcefully and removed from the list of running processes.

Ending or killing a running process does not affect your ability to run the same program in the future.

Managing Running Services

If you installed your Linux system as a server system in Hour 2, "Installing Red Hat Linux," or if you included a number of server-related packages (such as Web or Windows file serving) in software customization during installation, your system is busy supplying services most of the time. As you work with your system, you might need to enable additional services to meet new work demands, or disable services you no longer need or use. These and other service management tasks are accomplished through the Services Configuration tool. You can use the Services Configuration tool to determine which services begin running when you start up your system at each runlevel (you learned about runlevels in Hour 18).

Launching and Quitting the Service Configuration Tool

The Service Configuration tool can be used to edit the list of services that are started each time your system starts. To start the Service Configuration tool, click the GNOME Red Hat icon to open the GNOME menu and choose Server Settings, Services; the Service Configuration tool is displayed, as shown in Figure 19.3.

FIGURE 19.3
The Service Configuration tool enables you to edit the list of services that are started each time your computer starts.

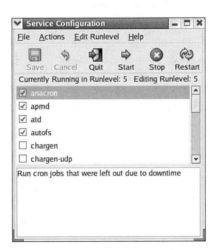

19

While using the Service Configuration tool, you are always editing the list of services for runlevels 3, 4, or 5. Because you are running in the graphical environment, you are by default editing the list of services for runlevel 5, the runlevel that boots into graphics mode. To change the runlevel you're editing, open the Edit Runlevel menu and select the runlevel you want to edit.

The following sections discuss how to use the configuration tool options to change runlevel services. After you make the configuration changes, open the File menu and choose Quit to exit the Service Configuration tool.

Enabling or Disabling Services

The Service Configuration window displays all services available for the selected runlevel. You can see descriptions for most of the services by clicking the name of the service; a description appears in the lower pane of the Service Configuration tool, as shown in Figure 19.4.

FIGURE 19.4

Clicking the name of a service in the list shows its description in the lower pane.

 For a discussion on what runlevels do and how to change the default runlevel for your Red Hat Linux system, refer to "Understanding Runlevels" in Hour 18.

Services enabled for the currently selected runlevel are marked with a check; disabled services have an empty check box. You can enable or disable individual services for the currently selected runlevel by scrolling to a service entry in the list and clicking its check box.

Stopping, Starting, and Restarting Services

Sometimes you need to temporarily stop a running service or offer a service that is not normally offered. Or you might need to restart a running service, usually to accommodate changes in the configuration file or to fix a service that is no longer responding. You can change the state of a service using the Service Configuration tool's Start, Stop, and Restart buttons, located at the right end of the Service Configuration toolbar.

To stop a currently running service, click it in the Service Configuration list of currently running services, and then click the Stop button. To start a service that isn't currently running, click it and then click the Start button. Finally, to restart a currently running service, click the service and then click the Restart button.

In each case, if the start, stop, or restart operation is successful, you see a notification of success; otherwise, you see a notification of failure, as shown in Figure 19.5.

FIGURE 19.5

When a start, stop, or restart operation fails, you see a notification of failure. Here, an attempt to stop lpd *was unsuccessful.*

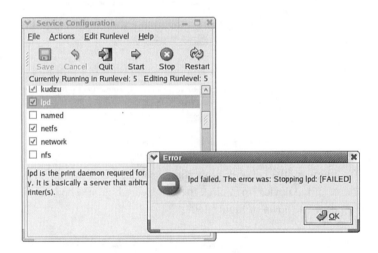

Often when a start, stop, or restart operation fails, the software for the service in question was not installed when you installed Red Hat Linux. If you know this to be the case, refer to Hour 21, "Installing Software," for details on installing the needed software. Other common causes include incomplete or incorrectly formatted configuration files, or a missing system resource of some kind. When a failure occurs, consult the system manual page for the service in question for help in diagnosing the problem. If you're still unsure about the cause, you might find hints in the system logs; refer to "Reading System Logs" later this hour for details on how to consult them.

Managing Network Interfaces

In most cases, you need to configure your network interface or interfaces only once—when you install Red Hat Linux. If you add or remove network interface hardware or the

19

configuration of your network changes, however, you might need to make additional changes to your network configuration.

Red Hat Linux provides a desktop Network Device Control tool to manage and configure your network interfaces. The Network Device Control tool enables you to configure such items as address, nameserver, and gateway configuration. Start the Network Device Control tool by opening the GNOME main menu and choosing System Tools, Network Device Control. The Network Device Control tool appears, as shown in Figure 19.6, listing all the network interfaces configured on your system.

FIGURE 19.6

Use the Network Device Control tool to configure your network interfaces.

To configure the network properties associated with a particular network device, click the name of the device, then click the Configure button. The Network Configuration dialog appears, as shown in Figure 19.7.

FIGURE 19.7

To display the Network Configuration dialog, click the device you want to configure and then click the Configure button.

Editing Static IP or DHCP Properties

To edit the address properties of the network interface you've selected, click the Edit button. The Ethernet Device dialog is displayed, as shown in Figure 19.8.

FIGURE **19.8**

Use the Ethernet Device dialog to configure the IP address of the selected ethernet hardware.

To specify that the network device in question should be automatically configured, click the Automatically Obtain IP Address Settings With option. Then, configure the rest of the automatic configuration options:

- Select a protocol type from the drop-down list. For most networks, the correct automatic configuration type is the default, dynamic host configuration protocol (DHCP).
- If your network is capable of supplying nameserver information, check the Automatically Obtain DNS Information from Provider check box.
- If you have been instructed to manually configure your system's hostname, enter your assigned hostname in the Hostname box.

If you were given an IP address, netmask, and gateway address by your network administrator, you may choose to configure the network interface manually. To do so, click the Statically Set IP Addresses option. Then, fill out the remaining fields:

- Enter your assigned IP address in the Address box.
- Enter your netmask in the Subnet Mask box.
- Enter your default gateway in the Default Gateway Address box.

After you configure your network hardware to work properly with your network, click the OK button to accept the settings you selected and dismiss the Ethernet Device dialog box.

19

Manually Configuring DNS Information

If you have not selected to have your network device's nameserver (DNS) information automatically configured, you must manually configure the DNS information. To manually configure your DNS information, click the DNS tab in the Network Configuration dialog; the DNS options are displayed, as shown in Figure 19.9.

FIGURE 19.9

At the DNS tab, you can configure the nameservice properties for your network hardware.

To configure the basic DNS properties for your network interface

- Enter your assigned hostname in the Hostname entry box.

- Enter your primary DNS address in the Primary DNS box, your secondary DNS in the Secondary DNS box, and your tertiary DNS (if applicable) in the Tertiary DNS box.

- Enter the primary domain name of your network in the Search Domain box and click Add to add the domain to the domain search list. If your network has additional domains, add them also by entering them in the Search Domain box and clicking Add after each one.

After you configure the DNS properties as desired, click the Apply button near the bottom of the window. If you configured all the network properties for your hardware correctly, click the Close button to close the Network Configuration dialog.

Enabling or Disabling Network Interfaces

Sometimes it is helpful to be able to completely disable a running network device—for example, if you are experiencing a hacking attack, or if you need to troubleshoot some aspect of network operation by disconnecting from the network. To disable a network device, click the device in the device list of the main Network Device Control tool window (refer to Figure 19.8), and then click the Deactivate button.

To activate a network device that has been deactivated, click the device in the list and then click the Activate button.

When you have made all the desired changes to your network equipment, click the Close button to dismiss the Network Device Control tool.

Managing Accounts

In "Understanding Permissions" in Hour 4, "Navigating Linux at the Console," you learned about file ownership and how file permissions relate to the user and group of each file in the Linux filesystem. Now you learn to add and delete user and group accounts using desktop tools.

In Red Hat Linux, you can add and remove users and groups using the Red Hat User Manager tool. The Red Hat User Manager tool can be started by opening the main GNOME menu and choosing System Settings, Users & Groups; the Red Hat User Manager tool opens with the Users tab on top, as shown in Figure 19.10.

FIGURE 19.10

The Red Hat User Manager (shown maximized) enables you to add and remove users and groups.

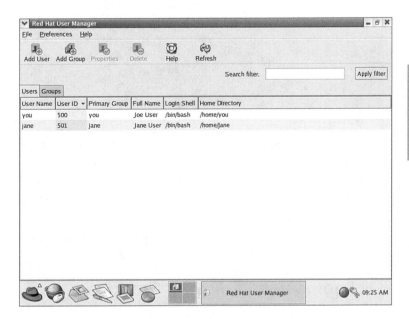

Adding and Removing Users

To add a user account in the Red Hat User Manager, click the Add User button near the top of the window. The Create New User dialog appears.

To create a new user account, fill out the fields in the top of the Create New User dialog:

- Enter the desired login name for the new account into the User Name entry box.
- Enter the user's full name into the Full Name entry box.
- Enter the desired password for the user into the Password entry box, and then enter it again into the Confirm Password entry box to verify that it has been typed correctly.

The Create New User dialog, completed to create an account for the new user (named Jack User), is shown in Figure 19.11.

FIGURE 19.11

The Create New User dialog enables you to enter the details for a new account.

After you fill out the entry boxes in the top half of the Create New User dialog, click the OK button to create a new account using the information you've supplied, automatically creating a home directory and creating a private group for the user in question. The Create New User dialog disappears and the new user appears in the Users list.

To delete a user, click the user you want to delete in the Users list and then click the Delete button near the top of the Red Hat User Manager window; the user you have selected is removed from the list of users.

Adding and Removing Groups

To add or remove groups, click the Groups tab in the Red Hat User Manager window. The list of groups is displayed in the tab.

To add a new group, click the Add Group button. The Create New Group dialog is displayed, as shown in Figure 19.12.

FIGURE 19.12

In the Create New Group dialog box, enter the name of the group you'd like to create.

Enter the name of the group you want to create in the Create New Group dialog and then click the OK button to create the group. The dialog disappears and the new group you created appears in the Red Hat User Manager Groups list.

To delete a group, click the group you want to delete in the Groups list and then click the Delete button in the Red Hat User Manager toolbar near the top of the window; the group disappears from the list of groups and is removed from the system.

Editing Group Membership

To edit the list of members in a particular group, select the group whose membership list you'd like to edit in the Groups list and then click the Properties button near the top of the Red Hat User Manager window. The Group Properties dialog appears; click the Group Users tab and the list of system users is displayed, as shown in Figure 19.13.

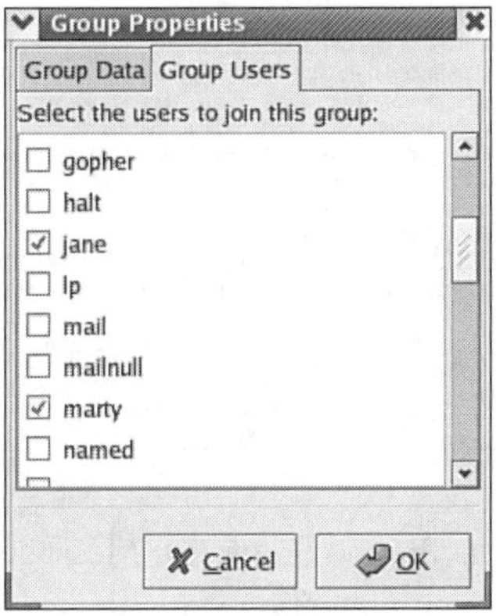

FIGURE 19.13

Use the Group Users tab in the Group Properties dialog box to edit the list of members in a group.

19

Check the boxes next to the users who should be included as members of the group; clear the check box to remove a member. When you finish editing the group membership, click the OK button to accept the updated list of users. The Group Members column in the Users list is updated to reflect the new list of group members.

After you finish adding or removing users or groups and editing group memberships, click File, Quit to exit the Red Hat User Manager.

Reading System Logs

As a matter of course, Red Hat Linux maintains a number of system logs to record activity that occurs in various parts of the system. The information in these logs can be especially helpful when you encounter trouble, such as unexpected program crashes or device errors, because most of these problems generate a log entry.

You can read system logs using the System Logs tool. Start the tool by choosing System Tools, System Logs from the main GNOME menu. To read the messages in a system log, choose a log from the list in the left pane of the window; the messages it contains appear in the right pane (see Figure 19.14).

FIGURE 19.14

The System Logs tool (shown maximized) is used to read and search through the various Red Hat Linux system logs. Here, the contents of the boot log are displayed. Use the Filter option to search for a message containing a specific keyword.

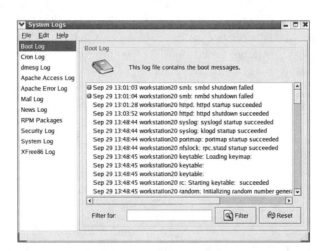

The most recent log entries appear at the top of the list. Messages that could indicate a problem of some kind are marked with attention symbols (exclamation marks in red circles). If you're experiencing trouble, these entries most likely reveal the source of the problem.

To search for a particular keyword in the currently displayed log, enter the keyword you'd like to search for in the Filter For entry box and click the Filter button. Only entries containing the keyword you enter are displayed.

When you finish viewing system logs, click File, Quit to exit the System Logs tool.

Mounting and Unmounting Filesystems

To mount and unmount filesystems according to the entries in the /etc/fstab file, you can use the User Mount tool. Start the User Mount tool by choosing System Tools, Disk Management from the main GNOME menu; the User Mount tool window is displayed, as shown in Figure 19.15.

FIGURE 19.15

The User Mount Tool screen displays a list of all filesystems that the current user is allowed to mount, unmount, and/or format.

For a discussion of the uses for mounting and unmounting filesystems and the format and use of the /etc/fstab file, see "Managing Filesystems" in Hour 18.

19

To change the mount status of one of the listed filesystems, click its entry in the User Mount Tool window. One of two things happens:

- If the filesystem is currently unmounted, the Mount button is displayed; clicking it mounts the filesystem.
- If the filesystem is currently mounted, the Unmount button is displayed; clicking it unmounts the filesystem.

Formatting a Device or Partition

If you have permission to reformat the device or partition, the Format button is activated. Clicking the Format button for a nonremovable device presents a confirmation dialog.

Because formatting deletes all information stored on a disk, Red Hat asks you to confirm that you truly want to go forward with the formatting operation. Click Yes to continue or No to cancel the format.

If you click the Format button for a removable device, the configurable confirmation dialog box shown in Figure 19.16 appears.

FIGURE 19.16

The confirmation dialog box asks you to confirm that you want to format the device or partition.

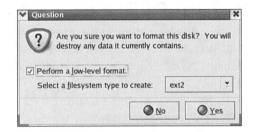

To format the device in question, follow these steps:

1. Select your desired filesystem type from the Filesystem Type drop-down list. Choose vfat for most removable devices and ext3 for nonremovable devices that will be used primarily to hold Linux files.

2. Check the Low-level Format check box if you want the tool to verify the integrity of your storage media as the format occurs.

3. Click the Yes button to begin the format.

In either case, formatting takes from a few moments to quite some time, depending on the size of the device, the filesystem it will contain, and whether a verify pass is performed. During this time, the User Mount Tool dialog buttons are grayed out. When the format is complete, the buttons are activated again.

When you have made all desired changes to the mounted or unmounted states of the available filesystems and have formatted devices and partitions as desired, click the Close button to close the User Mount tool.

Summary

This hour, you learned to perform a number of common system administration tasks using graphical tools. Specifically, you learned the following:

- How to use the System Monitor tool to list, reprioritize, and kill running processes.
- How to use the Service Configuration tool to change the list of services that are started each time your computer boots, and to start, stop, or restart running services.

- How to use the Network Device Control tool to manage your network interfaces, including selecting between static and dynamic IP configurations.

- How to use the User Manager tool to add or delete users or groups and to edit group memberships.

- How to use the System Logs tool to view the most recent entries in various Red Hat Linux logs and to identify potential problem entries.

- How to use the User Mount tool to mount, unmount, or format filesystems as they are listed in the /etc/fstab file.

Though the primary vehicle for system administration in Linux remains the command line, the graphical tools described this hour can be used to perform the more common system administration tasks you're likely to encounter.

Q&A

Q Can I create new partitions or change the filesystem type of existing partitions using the User Mount tool?

A No. For instructions on creating partitions or changing filesystem types, see "Creating Filesystems" in Hour 18.

Q How do I know the options to select or the data to enter in the Network Device Control tool?

A Information about whether you should use static or dynamic IP and the IP address, netmask, DNS, and gateway to use if you have selected static IP must be provided by your network administrator. If you need this type of information for a broadband connection at home, contact your service provider.

19

Workshop

The Workshop is designed to help you anticipate possible questions, review what you've learned, and begin learning how to put your knowledge into practice.

Quiz

1. Where do you edit group memberships using desktop tools?

2. Should the End Process button or the Kill Process option be used first in the System Monitor tool?

3. In the System Logs tool, how do you know which entries deserve your attention more than others?

Answers

1. In the Group Users tab of the Properties dialog in the User Manager tool.

2. Always try the End Process button first. Only in the rare case that it fails to end a process should you use the Kill Process option.

3. The most telling entries are marked with a small red attention icon, which indicates potential problems.

HOUR 20

Security Basics

In this hour, you learn to perform some basic security-oriented optimization on your Red Hat Linux system. Though a basic Red Hat Linux installation is reasonably secure, a few additional changes can always be made to bolster the basic level of security still further. You should at least follow the steps in this hour if you plan to use your computer on a network for any period of time. In this hour, you learn to do the following:

- Modify the firewalling configuration of Red Hat Linux to filter unwanted network activity
- Use file permissions in new ways to improve system security
- Protect the root account in several ways so that it is more difficult for malicious users to try to gain access to it
- Modify the default command-line environment to automatically log out console users or remote users after a period of inactivity

For server systems, you should also take care to read the notes in Hours 22, "Offering Network File Services," and 23, "Offering Web and FTP Service," about any network services you plan to provide.

If your system is to be an important network server or will be exposed to a large number of users, you should seriously consider studying Linux security in greater depth than can be presented in a single hour like this one.

Starting points from the Linux Documentation Project include these two online books:

- *The Linux Administrator's Security Guide*
  http://www.seifried.org/lasg/
- *Securing and Optimizing Linux*
  http://www.tldp.org/LDP/solrhe/

Managing the Red Hat Linux Firewall

If your Red Hat Linux PC will be connected to a network at any time, whether by ethernet, modem, or some other technology, the first task in securing your Linux computer should be to shore up your network security at the packet level.

Specifically, you need to be able to tell Red Hat Linux exactly what kinds of network traffic you expect and want to receive so that Red Hat Linux can discard all the rest of the network traffic it receives. This configuration is done with the Security Level Configuration tool.

Starting the Security Level Configuration Tool

The Security Level Configuration tool can be started on the Linux desktop by clicking GNOME Menu, System Settings, Security Level; the Security Level Configuration tool is displayed, as shown in Figure 20.1.

FIGURE 20.1
Using the Security Level Configuration tool, you can configure the firewalling properties of Red Hat Linux.

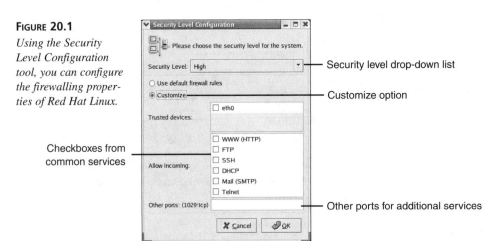

Choosing Security Level and Common Services

The first option that must be configured is the basic security level of the firewall on your system. You do this with the Security Level drop-down list in the Security Level Configuration tool. There are three options in the list—High, Medium, and No Firewall:

- If you use your Red Hat system primarily as a desktop computer and need to use streaming media software like RealPlayer or the network features of the X Window System described in Hour 17, "Using Desktop Applications Remotely," you should select the Medium security level option.

- If you use your Red Hat system as a Web server, file server, or other type of server to other computer systems on a network, you should select the High security option.

- Under very few circumstances should you select the No Firewall option, and then, only if your computer system will not be physically connected to a network.

After you select a basic security level for your firewall, you must decide whether to customize your firewall to allow specific additional types of network traffic. If you intend to provide network services of any kind, you should select the Customize option. Then, in the Allow Incoming area, check any of the common services check boxes associated with services you plan to offer. For example, if you plan to use your system as a file transfer protocol (FTP) server, check the FTP box.

Allowing Additional Traffic Exceptions

If you provide network services not listed in the Allow Incoming area of the Security Level Configuration tool, you need to enable traffic for these services by entering the details for their network port and protocol types in the Other Ports entry box.

The port and protocol details for each network service can be found in the /etc/services file, which can be viewed at the command line using a pager such as less or more. A segment of the /etc/services file is shown in Listing 20.1.

20

LISTING 20.1   A Segment of the /etc/services File

```
pop2        109/tcp      pop-2    postoffice      # POP version 2
pop2        109/udp      pop-2
pop3        110/tcp      pop-3                     # POP version 3
pop3        110/udp      pop-3
sunrpc      111/tcp      portmapper       # RPC 4.0 portmapper TCP
sunrpc      111/udp      portmapper       # RPC 4.0 portmapper UDP
auth        113/tcp      authentication tap ident
auth        113/udp      authentication tap ident
```

LISTING 20.1   continued

```
sftp             115/tcp
sftp             115/udp
uucp-path        117/tcp
uucp-path        117/udp
nntp             119/tcp        readnews untp    # USENET News Transfer Protocol
nntp             119/udp        readnews untp    # USENET News Transfer Protocol
```

The first column in the /etc/services file lists the service name. Some services are listed on more than one line; these services require more than one port or protocol. The second column in the /etc/services file lists the ports and protocols required by each service. For example, the pop3 (post office protocol version 3) network service shown in Listing 20.1 requires the availability of network port 110 using both the tcp and udp protocols.

To enable a service in the Security Level Configuration tool, you must enter each of the required port and protocol pairs mentioned in the /etc/services file for the service, separating individual pairs with commas, in the following format:

```
port1:proto1,port2:proto2,...
```

For example, to enable the nntp and pop3 services as mentioned in Listing 20.1, you'd enter the following text into the Other Ports entry box:

```
119:tcp,119:udp,110:tcp,110:udp
```

After you configure the properties of your Red Hat Linux firewall to suit your needs, click OK to save your changes, activate the new firewall settings, and close the Security Level Configuration tool.

Understanding Advanced Permissions

In "Understanding Permissions" in Hour 4, "Navigating Linux at the Console," you learned the basics of file ownership and permissions in Linux. You also learned to use the chmod command at the command line to change file permissions using symbols (letters) r, w, and x for read, write, and execute.

The basic set of read, write, and execute permissions and the basic file ownership behavior works well for most situations. However, Linux does provide a way for administrators to change the ownerships of existing files, as well as an additional set of permissions properties for more unique situations, which can provide finer-grained control over the ways in which files and directories behave.

Changing File Ownership

The chown command can be used to change the user and/or group ownership of an existing file. This can be useful if, for example, a user wants to make a file he or she has created readable to other members of a group of which he or she is a member. By changing the file's group ownership, and permissions, the file can be made readable by members of the group while remaining secure with regard to other users of the system.

To use the chown command to change ownerships for an existing file or directory, call chown as follows:

```
chown user.group file
```

Replace *user* with the user who should be given ownership of the file and *group* with the group that should be given ownership of the file. Replace *file* with the name of the file whose ownership is to be changed. For example, to change the group ownership of a file called myfile.txt to the programmers group, you issue the following command:

```
[you@workstation20 you]$ chown you.programmers myfile.txt
[you@workstation20 you]$
```

Normal users can't change user ownership. They can change only group ownership—and only to groups of which they are members.

The root user can change both user and group ownerships to any existing user account or group.

Using chmod in Numeric Mode

In "Understanding Permissions" in Hour 4, you learned that each file or directory in a Linux system is governed by three sets of read, write, and execute switches. When considered from left to right as they are usually written, these sets of switches belong to the file's owning user, the file's owning group, and everyone else, in that order. For example, the following permissions string represents a normal file that is readable, writable, and executable by everyone:

```
-rwxrwxrwx
```

In the symbolic mode of the chmod command, you use symbols such as u, g, o, r, w, and x arranged in various patterns as arguments to change these permissions. The numeric mode of chmod works somewhat differently. To call chmod in numeric mode, use the following format:

```
chmod NNN file
```

20

Each *N* must be a numeric digit. The first *N* represents the permissions for the owning user of the file, the second *N* for the owning group, and the third *N* for everyone else. Each *N* has a value of zero (0) for no permissions or a single-digit sum created from the values in Table 20.1 to indicate the absolute permissions that are to be assigned.

TABLE 20.1 Permissions Values for chmod's Numeric Mode

Value	Meaning
4	Read permission is granted for this file or directory.
2	Write permission is granted for this file or directory.
1	Execute permission is granted for this file or directory.

For example, to assign full read, write, and execute permissions for all users to a file called myfile.txt, you enter the following:

```
[you@workstation20 you]$ chmod 777 myfile.txt
[you@workstation20 you]$
```

Table 20.2 shows a number of additional examples for numeric strings, which can be provided to chmod, and their symbolic meanings.

TABLE 20.2 Examples of Numeric Values for chmod and Resulting Permissions

Number	Permissions	Description
664	-rw-rw-r--	Owning user and owning group can read and write. Other users can only read.
444	-r--r--r--	All users anywhere can read. No other permissions are granted.
700	-rwx------	Owning user can read, write, and execute. No other permissions are granted.
750	-rwxr-x---	Owning user can read, write, and execute. Owning group can read and execute. No other permissions are granted.

Though the symbolic mode of chmod is typically preferred by beginners, most longtime Linux or Unix users prefer to use the numeric mode for its simplicity and brevity.

Understanding Special Permissions

As you use Linux, you will from time to time encounter several additional types of permissions values in the output of long directory listings. It is important that you understand these special permissions because they significantly alter the way in which programs or directories behave:

- A letter s appearing in a file's user permissions' execute position indicates that when this program is run, it is granted access to files and system resources as though it had been called by its owning user, rather than by the user who actually called it. Files with this permission switch set are called *SUID (Set User ID) executables*.

- A letter s appearing in a file's group permissions' execute position indicates that when this program is run, it is granted access to files and system resources as though it had been called by a member of its owning group, rather than by the group of the user who actually called it. Files with this permission switch set are called *SGID (Set Group ID) executables*.

- A letter t appearing in the last position of a directory's permissions indicates that users who are allowed to write to this directory are allowed to remove only files or directories for which they are the owning user. This permission switch is known simply as the *sticky bit*.

The SUID and SGID bits are rarely used; the sticky bit is used more often, usually to create a public storage area in which users can create and remove their own files. The assignment of the SUID, SGID, and sticky bits to file or directory permissions can be accomplished using chmod's numeric mode by including an extra digit at the beginning of the numeric permissions code supplied to chmod as an argument. The values used in this optional first digit are shown in Table 20.3.

TABLE 20.3 Codes Used to Assign Special Permissions with chmod

Value	Meaning
4	Assigns the SUID (Set User ID) property to this executable file
2	Assigns the SGID (Set Group ID) property to this executable file
1	Assigns the sticky bit to this directory

20

Some sample numeric codes for chmod that use special permissions along with resulting descriptions can be seen in Table 20.4.

TABLE 20.4 Special Permissions Examples Using chmod's Numeric Mode

Number	Permissions	Description
4754	-rwsr-xr--	Owning user can read, write, and execute. Owning group can read and execute. Everyone else can read. When this program is executed, its user permissions behave as though it was called by its owning user.
2754	-rwxr-sr--	Owning user can read, write, and execute. Owning group can read and execute. Everyone else can read. When this program is executed, its group permissions behave as though it was called by a member of its owning group.
6554	-r-sr-sr--	Owning user can read and execute. Owning group can read and execute. Everyone else can read. When this program is executed, its user permissions behave as though it was called by its owning user and its group permissions behave as though it was called by a member of its owning group.
1777	drwxrwxrwt	All users can read, create files in, and delete files from this directory and can make this directory their current working directory. However, users can delete only files that they themselves own.

To assign the SUID or SGID properties to an executable file, you must be either the owner of the file or a member of the file's owning group, respectively—or the root user. The SUID and SGID properties are rarely used.

An understanding of the SUID and SGID properties is important for Linux security precisely because these properties are so potentially insecure—they allow users to transcend their account identities, which are fundamental to permissions. The SUID and SGID properties have been judiciously limited to a few programs like su by Red Hat Linux. You should rarely, if ever, assign them yourself.

More importantly, you should be very suspicious of SUID or SGID files that have creation dates well after the date on which you installed Red Hat Linux. You should also be very wary of SUID or SGID files that aren't in a binaries directory like /sbin, /usr/bin, or /usr/sbin.

You can get a listing of all SUID and SGID binaries by using the following two find commands:

```
find / -perm +2000
find / -perm +4000
```

You should run these commands soon after you install your system and save the output; afterward, run them again periodically to check for the emergence of new SUID or SGID files. If such a file appears, use chmod to remove its executable permissions at once and refer to Hour 24, "Backups, Troubleshooting, and Rescue."

Protecting the Root Account

The root account is one of the greatest vulnerabilities of Linux and Unix operating systems because the root account is all-powerful—root can create, read, modify, or delete any file in the system or enable or disable any resource or service. Because the root account is so powerful, the default protection for the account—a simple password—should be considered inadequate in most cases.

Fortunately, a relatively simple change to the security surrounding the root account can greatly increase the overall security of your Linux system. The change in question is the use of the wheel group to protect the su command. The wheel group is a special group whose members, by convention, are the only users given access to the su command on most Unix systems.

Enabling the wheel Group

You already learned that the su command can be called from the command line by a normal user to allow the user to take on the root identity to perform system administration tasks. This is convenient, but it is also dangerous—if a malicious user can call su repeatedly, he or she might eventually be able to guess the root password, thereby gaining unrestricted access to the entire system.

The su command provides an excellent illustration of the power and danger of SUID and SGID permissions.

The su command works because, by default, it is owned by the root user and is an SUID executable. This means that when it is called, it behaves as though it was called by the root user—thereby giving the program access to protected resources, such as those needed to change identities. To illustrate, try looking at a long directory listing of the su program:

```
[root@workstatino20 you]# ls -l /bin/su
-rwsr-xr-x    1 root       root         19092 Jul 31 07:34 /bin/su
[root@workstation20 you]#
```

20

By convention and tradition, secured Unix systems use a special group called wheel to identify an elite group of system administrators who have access to the su command. All other users are prevented from calling it. To give the wheel group teeth, you must do two things:

1. Add at least one user to the wheel group, who has administration privileges because he or she can call su.
2. Change the group ownership and permissions of the su program to restrict access to members of the wheel group.

Adding Users to wheel

To add a user to the wheel group at the command line, use the gpasswd command with the -a option, passing the name of the user to add and the group to add the user to (in this case, wheel) as arguments:

```
[root@workstation20 you]# gpasswd -a you wheel
[root@workstation20 you]#
```

> You can also use the Red Hat User Manager discussed in "Managing Accounts" in Hour 19, "Desktop System Administration," to add users to the wheel group, if you are uncomfortable with command-line tools.

If you want to give other users administration privileges, add them to the wheel group now as well. Only members of the wheel group can call su when you are done with this section.

Changing Ownership and Permissions of su

After you have added members to the wheel group as desired, change the ownership of the su command from root.root (user root, group root) to root.wheel (user root, group wheel) using the chmod command. This allows you to restrict execute permissions to members of the wheel group, removing public execute permissions entirely:

```
[root@workstation20 you]# chmod root.wheel /bin/su
[root@workstation20 you]#
```

Now that you have added administrators to the wheel group as desired and changed the ownership of su to root.wheel, assign the following permissions to su:

- Owner (root) read, write, and SUID execute
- Group (wheel) read and execute
- No permissions for nonowner, nongroup members

Using the numeric mode of the chmod command, these permissions can be assigned by supplying the numeric code 4750 as an argument to chmod, followed by the file whose permissions you want to change, /bin/su:

```
[root@workstation20 you]# chmod 4750 /bin/su
[root@workstation20 you]# ls -l /bin/su
-rwsr-x---   1 root     wheel        19092 Jul 31 07:34 /bin/su
[root@workstation20 you]#
```

The su command is now protected from all normal users. When users who are not members of the special administrative wheel group try to access the su command, permission is denied:

```
[jane@workstation20 jane]$ su
bash: /bin/su: Permission denied
[jane@workstation20 jane]$
```

Logging Out Users Automatically

It is not uncommon for a user to log into his or her account on a Linux system and to then become preoccupied with some other task or situation, forgetting that he or she is logged in at all. The user's session then sits inactive for an extended period of time.

Unfortunately, this can represent a serious security risk, especially on systems that allow remote logins. Network connections that are left open this way can eventually be hijacked by malicious users, who then have access to the user's account and, by extension, your system.

Aside from the religious use of ssh in place of telnet or other remote login commands, this type of risk can most easily be remedied by setting a login timeout—a delay after which a user automatically is logged out if he or she hasn't pressed a key.

The TMOUT variable can be used to cause the default shell to automatically log out the user after a period of inactivity, measured in seconds. For example, setting the value of TMOUT to 1800 would log the user out after 1800 seconds, or 30 minutes, of inactivity.

20

Setting a Login Timeout

To cause the value of the TMOUT variable to automatically be set whenever a user logs in, you must create a file in the /etc/profile.d directory, which contains a set of script fragments that are automatically run each time a user logs in. This file should end with .sh to indicate that it is for the standard shell and should set the value of the TMOUT variable. Use a text editor to create a file called /etc/profile.d/secure.sh, which contains only a single line:

```
TMOUT=1800
```

After you save the file and exit the text editor, don't forget to mark it as executable by everyone:

```
[root@workstation20 you]# chmod ugo+x /etc/profile.d/secure.sh
[root@workstation20 you]#
```

Red Hat Linux also includes a number of alternate shells in addition to the standard shell; advanced Linux or Unix users can use the `chsh` command to select among these for day-to-day command-line work. There are two alternate shells that provide login timeout functionality; they are called `csh` and `tcsh`. To accommodate these alternate shells, you must create another script fragment. In these, the timeout variable is `autologout`, and the timer value is measured in minutes. Use a text editor to create a file for these shells called /etc/profile.d/secure.csh, which contains only the following line:

```
set autologout=30
```

Again, don't forget to mark the file as executable:

```
[root@workstation20 you]# chmod ugo+x /etc/profile.d/secure.csh
[root@workstation20 you]#
```

Account holders who log in using any of the major shells are now logged out after 30 minutes of inactivity.

Removing Minor Shells

The list of shells from which users of the `chsh` command can select includes several shells that do not support login timeouts at all. Because of this, these shells should be removed from the list of shells available to users, which is stored in /etc/shells.

The default /etc/shells file is shown in Listing 20.2. The entries for the `ash` and `bsh` shells, which do not support login timouts, can be removed using a text editor to produce the shortened /etc/shells file shown in Listing 20.3.

LISTING 20.2   The Original /etc/shells File

```
/bin/sh
/bin/bash
/sbin/nologin
/bin/bash2
/bin/ash
/bin/bsh
/bin/tcsh
/bin/csh
```

LISTING 20.3 The Edited /etc/shells File

```
/bin/sh
/bin/bash
/sbin/nologin
/bin/bash2
/bin/tcsh
/bin/csh
```

After you edit the /etc/shells file, users can select only from shells that log them out after a period of inactivity.

Summary

This hour, you learned some simple, yet fundamental techniques to help protect your Linux computer system against break-ins, especially if your system is acting as a server or running on a network.

First, you learned to use the Security Level Configuration tool to choose a basic level of firewalling for your Linux system. You also learned to create exceptions to the firewalling rules to allow the types of network traffic you need to allow, to provide the services you want to provide.

Next, you learned about advanced use of file permissions—including some potentially dangerous types of permissions—and how to locate files that have been assigned them.

Then, you learned to restrict use of the su command, perhaps the most powerful and dangerous command in Linux security, to a special group of users who belong to the privileged wheel account.

Finally, you learned to limit the amount of time a login session can remain inactive before the system decides that it's a risky session and terminates it.

Though these security measures are only a beginning—important servers should be fully secured according to a Linux security guide or book—they do represent enough basic security to get you up and running without obvious risks.

Q&A

Q **In Hour 18, "Command-Line System Administration," I learned about cron. Can I create a cron task using the find commands in this hour that automatically searches for new SUID or SGID binaries periodically?**

A Yes, this is an ideal use of the cron system and shell scripting, and a good exercise to help you learn the ins and outs of both.

20

Q I have read other Linux security guides on the Web that recommend securing the su command by editing a file in the /etc/pam.d directory. What's the difference between implementing wheel using permissions and implementing wheel using PAM?

A The su command can be used to become any user for whom you have a valid password, not just the root user. The /etc/pam.d method of restricting su access allows only members of wheel to become the root user, but regular users can still use su to become other regular users, provided that they have the correct password. The permissions-based method discussed in this Hour puts the su command completely off limits to everyone but members of wheel—a more secure solution altogether, and without major drawbacks because legitimate uses of su by non-wheel members are rare.

Workshop

The Workshop is designed to help you anticipate possible questions, review what you've learned, and begin learning how to put your knowledge into practice.

Quiz

1. What file contains the list of network port numbers and protocol types for network services?

2. How would you add the user you to the wheel group?

3. How would you assign the following permissions to a file called myfile.txt using chmod's numeric mode: user read, user write, user execute, group read, group execute—and nothing further?

4. What timeout values would you assign to TMOUT and autologout to cause inactive users to be logged out after an hour?

Answers

1. /etc/services

2. gpasswd -a you wheel

3. chmod 750 myfile.txt

4. TMOUT=3600
   set autologout=60

Activities

1. Create a `wheel` group on your computer and implement the security techniques related to `wheel` discussed in this hour.

2. Add users who should have access to the `su` command to the `wheel` group.

3. After configuring your system for a login timeout, try logging in remotely and waiting until you are automatically logged out, to ensure that the timeout value works.

20

HOUR 21

Installing Software

In this hour, you learn how to install additional software in Red Hat Linux, either from your Red Hat Linux CDs or from Internet sites. Specifically, you learn how to do the following:

- Add or remove components of Red Hat Linux using the desktop package management system.
- Use the rpm command-line tool to add, remove, or get information about software packages, either those downloaded from the Internet or those on the Red Hat Linux CDs.
- Create new desktop program launchers for software you have installed.

As you use Linux more, you'll be able to use these skills to customize the list of software packages that are installed on your computer system, thereby enhancing your workflow considerably.

Installing and Removing Red Hat Components

Red Hat Linux comes on several CD-ROMs packed full of software. When you installed Red Hat Linux on your computer system, however, only some of this software was copied to your hard drive—those software components most commonly used in the type of installation you selected. For example, if you chose the Personal Desktop install, only software items typically useful for desktop personal computers were installed; if you chose the Server install, only software items typically useful for network servers were installed.

It is likely that at some point while using Red Hat Linux, you will want to revise the list of Red Hat software components that have been installed on your computer—either by uninstalling software you no longer use to free up space, or by installing additional software from the Red Hat Linux CD-ROMs. Fortunately, Red Hat Linux includes an easy-to-use desktop tool called the Package Management tool for installing or uninstalling Red Hat software packages.

A software package is a program or logical collection of several related programs and the data files that they require in order to operate. Packaging software in this way allows a number of files and program components to be installed or uninstalled in one operation.

Starting the Package Management Tool

The Red Hat Package Management tool can be started on the Linux desktop by clicking GNOME Menu, System Settings, Packages. If you are not logged in as root, you are asked to enter the root password, before the Package Management tool starts.

When you first start the Package Management tool, it scans the list of software packages already installed on your system so that you'll be able to remove already installed packages if you choose to do so. This check can take anywhere from a few moments to several minutes, depending on the speed of your system and the number of packages that are already installed. After the scan is complete, the main Package Management tool display appears, as shown in Figure 21.1.

FIGURE 21.1

After the scan of already installed packages is complete, the main Package Management display appears.

Package group

Package groups category

Package group checkboxes

Package group name

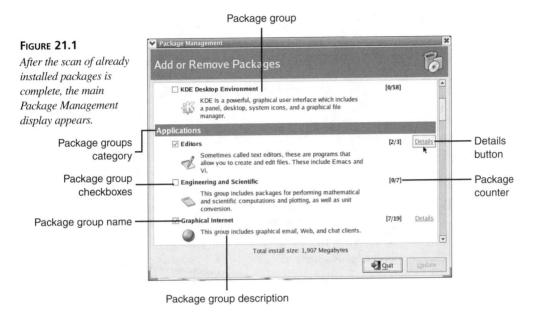

Details button

Package counter

Package group description

The main display of the Package Management tool gives you a list of available package groups. This list enables you to either add or remove software in package groups. To understand the information presented in the main display, you must be familiar with its components:

- Each *package group* is identified by a *package group name* and a *package group description*. Together, these items represent a set or category of related software components that are commonly installed or removed at the same time. Read the description to understand how the components are related and what function they perform.

- The *Package Group check box* is used to specify that a specific package group is either installed (checked) or not installed (not checked). If no check box appears next to a group, the group is installed and cannot be removed using the Package Management tool.

- Next to each package group you also see a *package counter*, which shows the number of packages (components) from the software group that are already installed on the system, as well as the total number of packages in the group. For example, in Figure 21.1 you can see from the information for the checked KDE package group that 53 of the 58 packages available in the KDE package group have been installed.

- The *Details button* next to package groups that are marked as installed is used to select components from the package group for installation or deinstallation on an individual basis.

21

Installing and Removing Software in Groups

The check box next to a package group indicates its current state. If a box is checked, at least one software package from the package group is installed on your computer. If a box is not checked, no software packages from the package group are installed on your computer.

To remove an entire package group, uncheck the box next to the group in the Package Management tool. Any software from the package group that is present on your system is marked for removal; the package counter for the group is updated to reflect this change, and the Details button next to the group disappears. To install a package group, check the box next to the group in the Package Management tool. The package group is marked for installation; the package counter for the group is updated to show that some or all of the packages for the group will be installed. When checked, some package groups install every component in the group by default, and others install only a collection of the most popular packages in the group unless you specify that additional packages should be included. A Details button also appears next to the newly checked group, as shown in Figure 21.2.

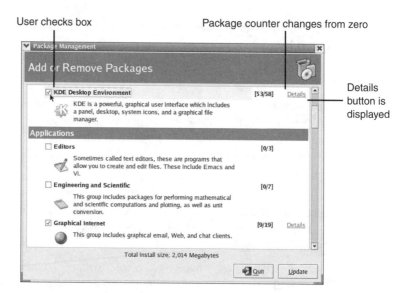

FIGURE 21.2
Checking the box next to a group marks the default selection of packages in the group for installation.

Using the Details Dialog

It can often be inconvenient to work with entire package groups. You might find that a package group's description leaves you unclear on precisely what software a package group contains. You might want to customize the list of packages to be installed when you select a group for installation, or you might want to remove only a single package from a package group while leaving the rest of its packages installed.

The Details dialog in the Package Management tool solves each of these problems. The details dialog allows you to

- List every software package in the package group so that you know exactly what will be installed or uninstalled.

- Alter the default list of packages that are installed when a group is selected for installation.

- Remove packages one by one without removing other packages in an installed package group.

To open the details dialog, click the Details button next to the installed package group you'd like to list or change. The details dialog is shown in Figure 21.3.

FIGURE 21.3

The Details dialog contains a detailed list of packages in a package group, with a check box for each package.

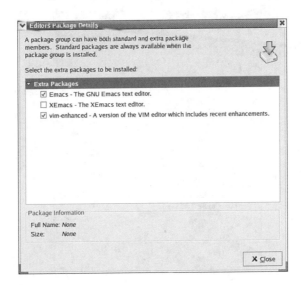

Checking an unchecked package in the details dialog marks the package for installation; unchecking a checked package in the details dialog marks the package for deinstallation.

When you have customized the list of packages for the package group to suit your needs, click the Close button to accept the list of packages you've selected for the package group.

21

Updating Your System

After you select or deselect package groups and/or individual packages to suit your needs, marking packages for installation or deinstallation in the process, click the Update button at the lower-right of the Package Management tool. The tool takes a moment to process the list of installations and deinstallations you've scheduled.

After the Package Management tool has determined how software is to be installed and uninstalled, it displays a summary of the changes you've requested, as shown in Figure 21.4. This summary lists the number of packages marked for installation, the number of packages marked for removal, and the amount of disk space required or freed by the selected installation and removal tasks. If you would like to see a detailed listing of the software packages that will be installed or removed, click the Show Details button; this alters the display to show a more detailed list of packages to be installed or removed.

FIGURE 21.4

A detailed summary of the installations and removals you've requested. In this example, one package will be removed and eight packages will be installed, using 28 additional megabytes of disk space.

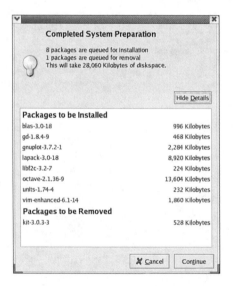

When you are ready to proceed with the changes you've requested, click the Continue button. The Package Management tool proceeds with the installations and deinstallations; a System Update indicator displays the progress of the operation.

If you've selected to install packages, you might be asked at some point to insert one or more of your Red Hat Linux CD-ROMs, as shown in Figure 21.5. When this occurs, insert the requested media and click the OK button to continue.

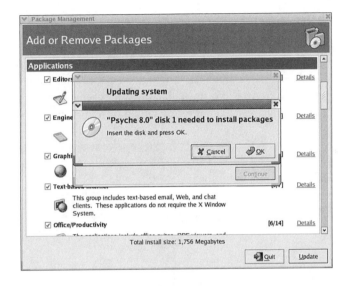

FIGURE **21.5**
You might be asked to insert your Red Hat Linux media if you are installing additional software.

After the Package Management tool has finished installing and uninstalling software, it displays a dialog box to indicate that the process is complete. Click OK to dismiss the Update Complete dialog box, and then click the Quit button in the lower-right of the Package Management tool to exit the tool and return to your desktop.

Using Third-Party Software

If you plan to use Red Hat Linux software you have downloaded from World Wide Web sites or acquired through third parties, it is likely that the software you want to install will be delivered in Red Hat Package Manager (RPM) format files.

Every RPM software package contains two major components:

- The software program and its components
- A list of package *dependencies,* system components or other software needed by the software package you're about to install for normal operation

If you attempt to install a software package that depends on other software that hasn't yet been installed, Red Hat Linux will attempt to locate and install the required software as well. Provided that all necessary dependencies can be met, installing RPM software packages is an easy task.

21

Installing Software Packages

To install an RPM software package, use the Red Hat file manager to browse to the location in your filesystem where the software package resides. For software packages you have downloaded with your Web browser, this usually is in /home/you or a subdirectory within /home/you. After you locate the software package file you want to install, double-click it to begin the installation process, as shown in Figure 21.6.

FIGURE 21.6

Double-click the RPM software package in the file manager to begin the installation process.

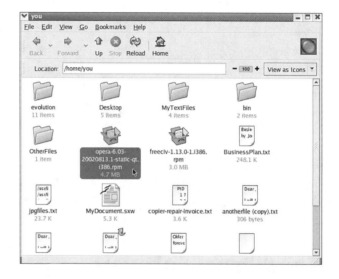

If you are not logged in as root, you are asked to provide the root password before continuing.

Before installing the software items contained in the RPM software package, Red Hat Linux checks the software package's list of requirements to ensure that all the package's needs can be met by your computer system and by Red Hat Linux. After Red Hat Linux has evaluated the requirements for the software package in question, it displays a dialog listing the number of packages that will be added to the system and the disk space the installation will consume. To see a more detailed list of the changes, click the Show Details button to switch to the detailed view. When you are ready to proceed with the installation, click the Continue button.

After you click Continue, the installation of the software package and the packages upon which it depends (if Red Hat Linux is able to locate them) begins. If Red Hat is unable to find and install some of the software upon which your package depends, you'll instead see a dialog box listing the missing dependencies. The next section contains tips for dealing with missing dependencies.

As the installation is being performed, you might be asked to insert one or more of your Red Hat Linux CD-ROMs so that additional required software can be installed. After all the needed software packages have been installed, a Completed System Preparation dialog is displayed to confirm that installation completed normally. The software package and any packages upon which it depended have now been installed on your computer system.

Click the OK button to dismiss the confirmation dialog and return to your Red Hat Linux desktop.

Dealing with Failed Dependencies

In some cases, you might find that when you try to install an RPM software package, Red Hat is unable to locate the components needed to fulfill the package's dependencies. When this happens, an error message is displayed listing the missing software components, as shown in Figure 21.7.

FIGURE 21.7

When Red Hat Linux is unable to find and install needed software packages, a dependency failure results.

In cases like this, there are several remedies you can try to rectify the problem:

- If the software you're trying to install comes in multiple separate RPM files, try changing the order in which you're installing them—first install the packages upon which other packages depend.

- Contact the vendor or revisit the Web site from which your software package came to see whether the additional needed components are available.

- Visit the `http://www.rpmfind.net` Web site and search for the names of the required packages. A wide variety of commonly needed packages can be downloaded there.

21

Using the rpm Command

If you did not install a desktop environment when you installed Linux, the desktop tools for software installation are not available to you. In this case, you need to use the command line for software installation.

The rpm command provides a way for packages to be installed or removed at the command line. It also provides several additional package management options that the desktop tools don't provide.

Installing RPM Packages with rpm

To install a package using the rpm command at the Linux command line, follow these steps:

1. Make sure you are working as the root user—use the su command if necessary to become root.

2. Make the directory containing the rpm files you want to install your current working directory.

3. Enter the **rpm** command with the **-i** (install) option, supplying the name of the package you want to install as an argument.

For example, assuming that you are working as root and want to install a package called mypackage.rpm, which is in the current directory, you'd enter the following:

```
[root@workstation20 you]# rpm -i opera-6.03-20020813.1-static-qt.i386.rpm
[root@workstation20 you]#
```

If there are no problems or errors, the package is installed and no additional messages are displayed.

Upgrading RPM Packages with rpm

If you use the rpm command to attempt to install a package that is already installed, you see an error message like this one:

```
package mypackage is already installed
```

If the package you are trying to install is a vendor-supplied upgrade or a later version of the existing package that is already installed on your system, you can automatically remove the old package and replace it with the new one using the -U (upgrade) option with the rpm command:

```
[root@workstation20 you]# rpm -U mypackage.rpm
[root@workstation20 you]#
```

Again, if the original package is successfully upgraded (replaced) by the newer package, no additional messages are displayed.

Dealing with Failed Dependencies Using rpm

When rpm is asked to install a software package that requires software not already installed on your system, an error message like this one is displayed:

```
error: Failed dependencies:
        libdvdread >= 0.9.2 is needed by ogle
        libdvdcss is needed by ogle
        libdvdread.so.2 is needed by ogle
```

Unlike the desktop package installer, the rpm command does not have the capability of automatically asking you to insert your Red Hat CD-ROMs to install needed packages that are a part of Red Hat Linux. If you are experiencing a dependency failure, you should first check the Red Hat Linux CD-ROMs to see whether the package(s) you need can be found there. To check each Red Hat CD-ROM at the command line, follow these steps:

1. Insert the CD-ROM you want to search.

2. Type **mount /mnt/cdrom** to mount the CD-ROM.

3. Type **find /mnt/cdrom | grep *dependency***, where ***dependency*** is the name of the package or software item needed—for example, **find /mnt/cdrom | grep libdvdcss** to search for a package called **libdvdcss**.

4. If the find command finds and lists any RPM packages by the needed name, use the **rpm -i** command to install the package(s).

5. Type **umount /mnt/cdrom** to unmount the CD-ROM.

6. Repeat for each Red Hat Linux CD-ROM (you might need to search all of them) and for each package required to fulfill dependencies.

> For a refresher on the mount and umount commands, refer to Hour 18, "Command-Line System Administration."
>
> For a refresher on the find and grep commands, refer to Hour 5, "Making the Console Work for You."

If you are unable to find the needed package(s) on the Red Hat Linux CD-ROMs, refer to the section earlier in this hour called "Dealing with Failed Dependencies" for more suggestions on resolving failed dependencies.

Getting Information with rpm

The rpm command can also provide you with various types of information on the software packages that are installed on your system, as well as some information about software packages that are not yet installed.

21

To get a listing of all software packages currently installed on your system, use the `rpm` command with the `-q` (query) and `-a` (all packages) options. On a typical Red Hat Linux system, this list is hundreds of lines long, so be sure to save the output to a file or to pipe it to a pager:

```
[root@workstation20 you]# rpm -q -a | more
```

You can also search the list of installed packages to see whether a specific package is installed by piping the output of `rpm` to the `grep` command, supplying the name of the package you want to search for as an argument to `grep`:

```
[root@workstation20 you]# rpm -q -a | grep bash
bash-2.05b-5
[root@workstation20 you]#
```

To learn more about any individual package that is already installed, use the `-q` (query) and `-i` (information) options, supplying the name of the package as an argument:

```
[root@workstation20 you]# rpm -q -i bash
Name        : bash                   Relocations: /usr
Version     : 2.05b                      Vendor: Red Hat, Inc.
Release     : 5                      Build Date: Fri 23 Aug 2002
Install date: Tue 01 Oct 2002 11:06:06 AM MDT      Build Host: astest
Group       : System Environment/Shells   Source RPM: bash-2.05b-5.src.rpm
Size        : 1619242                   License: GPL
Signature   : DSA/SHA1, Tue 03 Sep 2002 03:10:09 PM MDT, Key ID 219180cddb42a60e
Packager    : Red Hat, Inc. <http://bugzilla.redhat.com/bugzilla>
Summary     : The GNU Bourne Again shell (bash).
Description :
The GNU project Bourne Again shell (bash) is a shell or command
language interpreter that is compatible with the Bourne shell
(sh). Bash incorporates useful features from the Korn shell (ksh) and
the C shell (csh) and most sh scripts can be run by bash without
modification. Bash is the default shell for Red Hat Linux.
[root@workstation20 you]#
```

A number of additional information-gathering functions are available using the `rpm` command; see the manual page for `rpm` for details.

Uninstalling Software with `rpm`

If you find that you no longer use a piece of software and would like to free up the space it is using, you can also use the `rpm` command to remove installed software packages. To remove an installed software package using `rpm`, supply the `-e` option followed by the name of the package you want to remove as an argument. You do not need to supply version numbers in the package names when removing software packages. Do *not* supply the .rpm extension to the filename when you call `rpm  -e`:

```
[root@workstation20 you]# rpm -e mypackage
[root@workstation20 you]#
```

If the software package is successfully uninstalled, you see no further output.

Sometimes, you encounter dependency problems when attempting to remove a package, as can be seen in this example:

```
[root@workstation20 you]# rpm -e qt2
error: Failed dependencies
        libqt.so.2 is needed by (installed) opera-6.03-20020813.3
[root@workstation20 you]#
```

When this occurs, you have two choices:

- Begin by removing the software packages that depend on the package that you want to remove, and then remove the package.

- Leave the package in place because other installed packages depend on it.

> It's not a good idea to use rpm to "prune" your Red Hat Linux installation to save space; many packages that don't appear in desktop menus are nevertheless important system packages. Removing them might remove functionality from your Red Hat Linux installation.

Resolving Circular Dependencies

Very rarely when using rpm to install or remove packages, you encounter circular dependencies.

The term *circular dependencies* refers to a situation in which two packages depend on each other, as can be seen in this illustration:

```
[root@workstation20 you]# rpm -i mypackage-a.rpm
error: Failed dependencies:
        mypackage-b is needed by mypackage-a
[root@workstation20 you]# rpm -i mypackage-b.rpm
error: Failed dependencies:
        mypackage-a is needed by mypackage-b
[root@workstation20 you]#
```

When this occurs, you can solve the problem by supplying all the packages involved as arguments together:

```
[root@workstation20 you]# rpm -i mypackage-a.rpm mypackage-b.rpm
[root@workstation20 you]#
```

By supplying the packages to rpm simultaneously, rpm is able to resolve all the dependencies, allowing packages with circular dependencies to be installed or removed.

21

Using Application Launchers

After you successfully install a desktop application, the first thing you generally want to do is start it. To find out how, consult the documentation that came with your application or the Web site from which it was downloaded for detailed instructions. Usually, an application is launched using one of two techniques:

- If the application adds itself to the GNOME or KDE menu, you navigate to the correct submenu and click the application's icon.

- If the application doesn't add itself to the GNOME or KDE menu, you must start a terminal and start it at the command line.

If you install an application that requires the latter, you might find that launching the program from a terminal window is an inconvenience. In cases like this, you can use GNOME or KDE desktop tools to create an application launcher to streamline the process of launching the application.

Creating an Application Launcher in GNOME

To create an application launcher in the GNOME taskbar, right-click an empty part of the taskbar and choose Add to Panel, Launcher. The Create Launcher dialog is displayed and opened to the Basic tab, as shown in Figure 21.8.

FIGURE 21.8

The Create Launcher dialog box is used to create an application launcher in the taskbar.

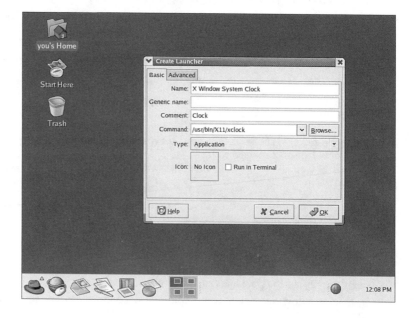

In the Basic tab of the Create Launcher dialog, fill out the entry boxes as follows:

- Enter a name for your application launcher in the Name entry box. This should be something brief but descriptive, like **Opera Web Browser** or **Civilization: Call to Power Game**.

- Leave the Generic Name entry box blank. This box isn't used for application launchers of this type.

- Enter a more general (but still brief) description in the Comment entry box—for example, **Web Browser** or **Game**.

- Enter the command you normally enter at the command line to start the application into the Command entry box.

After you fill out all the entry boxes as needed, click the Icon button to bring up the Browse Icons dialog, which enables you to choose an icon for your launcher, as shown in Figure 21.9.

FIGURE 21.9

Browse through the selection of icons provided with Red Hat Linux and choose one that seems to suit your program.

Select the icon you'd like to use for your application launcher by clicking it and then clicking the OK button. The icon dialog closes. Click the OK button in the Create Launcher dialog to create your application launcher. Your new launcher appears in the taskbar.

Now, clicking the application launcher icon launches your application.

21

Creating an Application Launcher in KDE

To create an application launcher in KDE, right-click an empty area of the taskbar and choose Panel, Add, Special Button, Non-KDE Application; the Select an Executable dialog is displayed, as shown in Figure 21.10.

FIGURE 21.10

In the Select an Executable dialog, enter or browse to the command you enter to start the application.

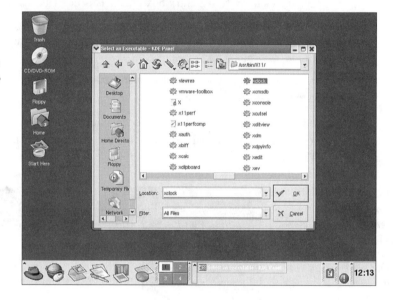

In the dialog, either enter the command you use to start the application in the Location entry box, or use the drop-down list to browse to the command in your filesystem, then select the command; click the OK button. A second dialog is displayed, as shown in Figure 21.11.

Click the select icon button (marked with a gear wheel) to bring up a dialog that enables you to choose an icon for your launcher. Click the icon you'd like to use for your application launcher to select it, and then click the OK button. The icon dialog closes. Click the OK button in the Non-KDE Application Configuration dialog to save your settings and create a new launcher in the taskbar.

You can now start your application by clicking the launcher.

FIGURE 21.11

Click the button marked with a gear wheel to select an icon for your application launcher.

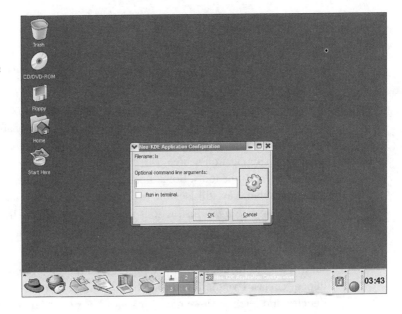

Summary

This hour, you learned how to install and remove software in a number of different contexts:

- You learned how to use the Package Management tool to install or remove components of the Red Hat Linux operating system, to allow your system to adjust as your needs change.

- You learned how to use desktop tools to install third-party software, including software that you have downloaded from the Internet.

- You learned how to use the command-line rpm tool to install or remove software packages at the command line.

- Finally, you learned how to create application launchers for applications you've installed so that you don't have to open a terminal window and enter a command to start them.

By customizing the selection of software on your system and installing third-party software of your own choosing, you can truly make your Linux system your own.

21

Q&A

Q **I have seen Linux software packages on the Internet that end in .tar.gz, .tar.bz2, .tgz, and .deb; how do I install these types of software in Red Hat Linux?**

A Software packages that end in .deb are for the Debian Linux operating system and operating systems that are based on it; they are not easily usable with Red Hat Linux. Files ending in .tar.gz, .tar.bz2, or .tgz are not software packages—they usually contain application source code that must be built using a C compiler and other command-line tools. Sometimes they also contain the finished programs themselves, but they still lack the dependency information needed to make them true software *packages*. Instructions for installing software from source code are beyond the scope of this book, but the man pages for tar and gunzip contain enough information to help you to access these types of files.

Q **I am trying to install a software package that seems to have an endless list of dependencies. I've managed to get packages to resolve some of these dependencies, but each of these new packages has dependencies of its own. What gives?**

A This often happens when a package you are trying to install was intended for a different version of Red Hat Linux or for a different Linux operating system that also uses the RPM package format. Usually, a lengthy list of dependencies, which continues to grow with each new package, indicates that the software package you began with will not be easy to install. Try instead to find a version of the software package for Red Hat Linux 8.0.

Workshop

The Workshop is designed to help you anticipate possible questions, review what you've learned, and begin learning how to put your knowledge into practice.

Quiz

1. How do you install an RPM software package using desktop tools?

2. How do you install an RPM software package at the command line?

3. Why create an application launcher?

Answers

1. Use the file manager to browse to the directory containing the RPM file; then double-click the file's icon.

2. `rpm -i mypackage.rpm`

3. So that you don't have to start a terminal and type a command each time you want to launch an application.

Activities

1. Start the Red Hat Package Management tool and browse the available software package groups and software packages. If you see some software that you'd like to install, do so.

2. Start a terminal and use the `rpm` command to list the packages installed on your system. Use the `rpm` command to find information on a few that you find interesting.

3. Create application launchers for some of the X Window System convenience applications in `/usr/bin/X11`.

21

Hour **22**

Offering Network File Services

In this hour, you learn how to enable the network file sharing services of Linux to allow your Red Hat Linux computer to act as a file server on your network. Specifically, you learn the following:

- How to enable and configure the Network File System (NFS) service to share files with other Linux or Unix computers on your network
- How to enable and configure the Samba SMB service to share files with Windows computers on your network

By the end of this hour, you will be able to share files over the network with other Linux, Unix, or Windows hosts. You will also be able to exercise some measure of control over which files get shared with whom.

Before You Begin

This hour refers often to topics covered in earlier hours. If you haven't yet read them or haven't read them recently, consider refamiliarizing yourself with the following topics and hours before continuing with this hour:

- Using the Package Management tool to install Red Hat Linux components, covered in Hour 21, "Installing Software"
- Using text editors to make changes to plain text files, covered in Hour 5, "Making the Console Work for You," and in Hour 11, "Working with Files on the Desktop"
- Using Red Hat system administration tools to enable or disable installed services, covered in Hour 18, "Command-Line System Administration," and Hour 19, "Desktop System Administration"
- Managing the Red Hat firewalling configuration, covered in Hour 20, "Security Basics"

You will find illustrations and examples in this hour as you make use of these tools, but for in-depth discussion refer to the hours listed above.

You will find that some network terminology is unavoidable when discussions of network services begin in earnest. If you are completely unfamiliar with Transmission Control Protocol/Internet Protocol (TCP/IP) networking—the type used by Linux, Unix, and most of the Internet—you should consider keeping a TCP/IP reference of some sort handy, to help you with basic concepts and unfamiliar terms.

Offering Network File System Service

The Network File System (NFS) is the de facto standard for filesystem sharing amoung Linux and Unix computers. Though there are other Unix standards for filesystem sharing that offer more security-oriented features or provide better network performance, NFS remains the most widely supported filesystem sharing service in the Unix world.

Because NFS is traditionally such a central part of any Unix operating system, NFS services are installed by Red Hat Linux 8.0 by default for every type of configuration—you do not need to have performed a server install to have the NFS service present on your Red Hat Linux computer.

Before you can enable the NFS service, you must configure it so that only the parts of your filesystem you choose to share are available on the network. There are two ways to configure your NFS service—by using the Red Hat NFS Server Configuration tool on your desktop or by editing the NFS Server Configuration files directory with a text editor.

Starting the NFS Server Configuration Tool

To configure NFS on the desktop, you must have the Red Hat NFS Server Configuration tool installed. To ensure that this is the case or to install the tool if it hasn't already been installed, follow these steps:

1. Open the Package Management tool by clicking GNOME Menu, System Settings, Packages.

2. Ensure that the Server Configuration Tools package group in the Servers category is checked, as shown in Figure 22.1. If it has not been checked, check it now.

3. Click the Details button next to the Server Configuration Tools package group to open the details view.

4. Ensure that the check box next to the NFS Server Configuration tool is checked, as shown in Figure 22.2. If it has not been checked, check it now.

5. Click the Update button if necessary to install new software. After you ensure that the NFS Server Configuration tool has been installed, click Quit to exit the Package Management tool.

FIGURE 22.1

Ensure that the Server Configuration Tools package group has been checked in the Package Management tool.

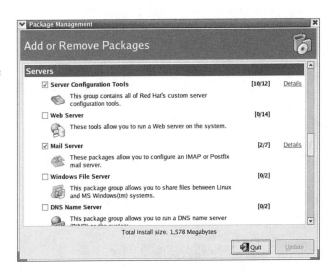

FIGURE 22.2

Ensure that the check box next to NFS Server Configuration tool has been checked in the details view.

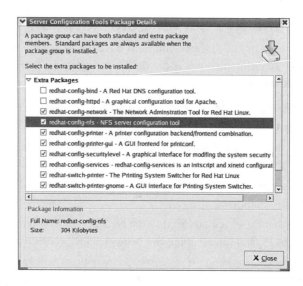

After you install the necessary software, you should log out and and log back in again to ensure that your menus have been updated to reflect the new additions to your system.

After you ensure that the NFS Server Configuration tool is present on your Red Hat Linux system, you can start the tool by clicking GNOME Menu, Server Settings, NFS Server to display the NFS Server Configuration tool.

Adding and Configuring NFS Shares

To add an NFS share (a directory tree in your filesystem that other Linux or Unix users can access), click File, Add Share in the NFS Server Configuration tool. The Add NFS Share dialog is displayed, as shown in Figure 22.3.

FIGURE 22.3

The Add NFS Share dialog enables you to add to the list of filesystem trees that are available to network users.

Enter the name of the directory tree you want to share with other users into the Directory entry box. All the directory tree's contents are available to other users via NFS after you share it.

In the Hosts entry box, you must enter a host or set of hosts on your network that are allowed to use this shared filesystem. Hosts can be specified in several ways:

- To share this directory tree with a single host, enter the host's IP address or name into the box—for example:

  `10.2.4.24`

  or

  `workstation10.mycompany.com.`

- To share this directory tree with an entire subnetwork, enter the host's IP address, then a slash, and then the network mask (you can obtain the network mask from your system administrator)—for example:

  `10.2.4.0/255.255.255.0`

  shares with every machine on the 10.2.4 subnetwork.

- To share this directory tree with an entire domain or subdomain, use an asterisk (*) as a wildcard (pattern matching) character to indicate the range of hosts you want to share with—for example:

  `*.mycompany.com`

  shares with every host on the `mycompany.com` domain.

Set the Basic Permissions option to suit your needs; if you want users to be able to read or write to files, select Read/Write; otherwise, select Read-only. Note that Linux filesystem permissions still apply, even when a directory tree is shared as read/write—users still are prevented from accessing files they don't have permission to access.

When you have filled out the Basic tab, click the OK button to dismiss the Add NFS Share dialog and add the directory tree to the list of shared filesystems. The new shared directory tree appears in the list of shared directories in the NFS Server Configuration tool, as shown in Figure 22.4.

FIGURE 22.4

After you enter share details into the Add NFS Share dialog, the directory tree appears in the NFS Server Configuration tool.

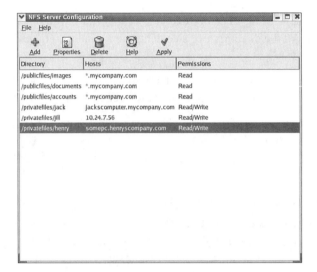

Repeat the process as many times as necessary to add other directory trees you want to share on your network, as shown in Figure 22.4. After your list of shared directory trees is complete, click the Apply button to save your changes. If your NFS service isn't currently running, you are asked whether you want to start it so that NFS is available to users on your network immediately. If you start NFS service immediately, users will be able to access the shares you've created immediately. If you do not start it immediately, users won't be able to access the shares you've created until you start the service.

After your changes have been saved, click File, Quit to close the NFS Server Configuration tool.

Starting NFS Automatically via the Desktop

Even if you chose to start the NFS service when the NFS Configuration tool prompted you, that does not guarantee that the NFS service will automatically start each time your computer system is started. To ensure that NFS service automatically starts each time your computer is started using the list of shares you created, you must enable NFS in the list of services that are associated with your default runlevel.

To do this, click GNOME Menu, Server Settings, Services to launch the Service Configuration tool. In the Service Configuration tool, ensure that the nfs service is checked, as shown in Figure 22.5.

FIGURE 22.5

The Service Configuration tool enables you to specify that the NFS service should automatically start.

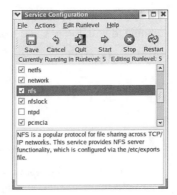

22

If the nfs service is not checked, check it now to indicate that NFS should be started when your computer starts. After you have enabled the service, click File, Quit to exit the tool.

Configuring NFS at the Command Line

The NFS service can also be configured from the command line, if you are more comfortable editing configuration files directly. The NFS service is controlled by the /etc/exports file, which is a plain text file listing the directory trees to be shared, one per line. To configure your NFS service, simply load the /etc/exports file into your favorite text editor and edit it. The format of each line in the /etc/exports file is as follows:

```
/directorytree host(access)
```

Replace /directorytree with the directory tree that should be shared, *host* with the host or set of hosts to share using the same format given in the "Adding and Configuring NFS Shares" section earlier this hour, and *access* with either ro for read-only access or rw for read-write access.

For example, to share /home/you with all the hosts directly in the mycompany.com domain, giving read-only access to the filesystem, enter the following line into the /etc/exports file:

```
/home/you *.mycompany.com(ro)
```

To also share /publicfiles/august with read-write access to all the machines on the 10.2.4 subnetwork and /tmp with read-write access to a host called barney, enter the following lines into the /etc/exports file:

```
/publicfiles/august 10.2.4.0/255.255.255.0(rw)
/tmp barney.mycompany.com(rw)
```

Enter a line for each directory tree you want to share into the /etc/exports file. When you finish editing the file, save it and exit the text editor.

If you are not already running the NFS service and want to start it immediately based on your new settings, call the `service` command with the `nfs` and `start` arguments:

```
[root@workstation20 you]# /sbin/service nfs start
Starting NFS services:                                [  OK  ]
Starting NFS quotas:                                  [  OK  ]
Starting NFS daemon:                                  [  OK  ]
Starting NFS mountd:                                  [  OK  ]
[root@workstation20 you]#
```

> If you are already running the NFS service and want the changes you've made to /etc/exports to take effect, use the `restart` argument instead of the `start` argument when calling the `nfs` script.

As the `service` command starts the NFS server, you should see four progress messages, each followed by the word `OK` in brackets. If instead at some point you see `FAILED`, check your /etc/exports file to make sure that you have formatted it correctly and your system log for diagnostic information the NFS service is returning. For further help with the format of /etc/exports, see the `exports` manual page.

Starting NFS Automatically via the Command Line

You can use the chkconfig command at the command line to cause the NFS service to start automatically each time you start your computer.

To cause NFS to automatically start for a specific runlevel, supply the `--level` option and the runlevel you want to use with NFS:

```
[root@workstation20 you]# /sbin/chkconfig --level 5 nfs on
[root@workstation20 you]#
```

After using the `chkconfig` command to enable NFS, NFS automatically starts each time you boot.

Allowing NFS Through Your Firewall

Even if you have correctly configured NFS and started the NFS service, you cannot share files with other Linux or Unix users unless you instruct the Red Hat Linux firewall to allow NFS traffic to be processed.

The mechanism NFS uses to mount shared directory trees is actually quite complex and thus requires both `tcp` and `udp` access to ports 111, 369, and 2049. These numbers correspond to the `sunrpc`, `rpc2portmap`, and `nfs` services in the /etc/services file, respectively.

RPC stands for Remote Procedure Call, UDP for User Datagram Protocol, and TCP for Transport Control Protocol. These standards are all used extensively in Internet networking and Unix operating systems. All three types of communication are essential for the proper functioning of NFS.

For more information on RPC, UDP, TCP, and other networking terms, consult a comprehensive guide to TCP/IP networking.

To allow NFS requests to reach your Red Hat Linux system, you must lower your firewalling security level to Medium, and then create special filtering exceptions for these ports. To do this, start the Security Level Configuration tool by clicking GNOME Menu, System Settings, Security Level. Then, select Medium security from the Security Level drop-down list (NFS does not work with High security), check the Customize option, and enter the following list of ports into the Other Ports entry box:

```
111:tcp,111:udp,369:tcp,369:udp,2049:tcp,2049:udp
```

A Security Level Configuration tool with these selections already made is shown in Figure 22.6.

FIGURE 22.6

Select Medium security level, opt to customize, and then open ports 111, 369, and 2049 for NFS.

If you previously allowed traffic on other ports or for other services using the Security Level Configuration tool, don't forget to enter them again—the settings you're entering now *replace* the previous security level settings, not augment them.

When you have finished with the Security Level Configuration tool, click the OK button to accept, save, and activate your changes. Remote users should now be able to mount your shared NFS directory trees without problems.

Offering Windows File Sharing Service

Red Hat Linux includes software that enables your Linux computer to share files with Windows computers on your network. This software is often referred to by its proper name, Samba, or by the type of high-level protocol it uses—Server Message Blocks, or SMB.

The Windows file server is not installed by default with Red Hat Linux unless you chose the Server installation option when you were installing Red Hat Linux on your computer. Activating your Windows file server is therefore a matter of several steps:

1. Install the Windows file server if you did not install it when you installed Linux.

2. Install the Samba Web Administration Tool (SWAT) so that you can configure Windows file service to suit your needs.

3. Use SWAT to configure the list of filesystem trees you want to share with Windows hosts.

4. Configure the Windows file server to start automatically each time you boot your computer system.

5. Configure your Red Hat Linux firewall to allow Windows file sharing requests.

Installing Windows File Sharing Service

To ensure that the Windows file server is installed or to install it if it hasn't already been installed, follow these steps:

1. Open the Package Management tool by clicking GNOME Menu, System Settings, Packages.

2. Ensure that the Windows File Server package group in the Servers category is checked, as shown in Figure 22.7. If it has not been checked, check it now.

3. Click the Update button if necessary to install the new software. After you ensure that the Windows file server has been installed, click Quit to exit the Package Management tool.

FIGURE 22.7

Ensure that the
Windows File Server
package group has
been checked in the
Package Management
tool.

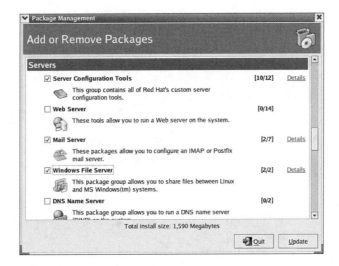

Using Desktop Tools to Install SWAT

After installing the Windows file server, you must install the Samba Web Administration Tool (SWAT), which is used to configure the Windows file server. SWAT is contained in a software package on disc 3 of the Red Hat Linux install media. To install it using desktop tools, follow these steps:

1. Insert Red Hat Linux disc 3 and open a file manager window.

2. Enter **/mnt/cdrom/RedHat/RPMS** in the Location entry box in the file manager window.

3. Scroll your file manager window until you locate the samba-swat package.

4. Double-click the package, as shown in Figure 22.8, to launch the package installer and proceed with package installation.

FIGURE 22.8

Double-click the samba-swat *package to launch the package installer and install the package.*

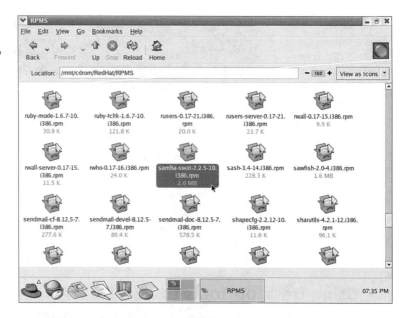

After the SWAT package has been installed, you must activate the SWAT service before you can use it to configure the Windows file server. To activate SWAT, start the Service Configuration tool by clicking GNOME Menu, Server Settings, Services and ensure that the swat service is checked. If it is not checked, check it now.

After you make sure that the swat service is checked, click Save to save your changes and then File, Quit to exit the Service Configuration tool. Both your Windows file server and the SWAT Configuration tool are now ready for use.

Using the Command Line to Install SWAT

If you feel more comfortable installing the package using command-line tools, follow these steps at the command line:

1. Insert Red Hat Linux disc 3 and mount the CD-ROM.

2. Make /mnt/cdrom/RedHat/RPMS your current working directory.

3. Use the rpm command with the -i option to install the samba-swat package.

Perform these steps at the command line as follows:

```
[root@workstation20 you]# mount /mnt/cdrom
[root@workstation20 you]# cd /mnt/cdrom/RedHat/RPMS
[root@workstation20 you]# rpm -i samba-swat*.rpm
[root@workstation20 you]#
```

After the SWAT package has been installed, you must activate the SWAT service before you can use it to configure the Windows file server. You can do this at the command line with the chkconfig command; use the --level argument to indicate the runlevel for which you want to enable SWAT and supply swat and on as arguments:

```
[root@workstation20 you]# /sbin/chkconfig --level 5 swat on
[root@workstation20 you]#
```

Both your Windows file server and the SWAT Configuration tool are now ready for use.

Starting SWAT and Configuring Samba Basics

The SWAT tool is used to configure every aspect of the Windows file server; it can be accessed only from within a Web browser. To start SWAT, start your Web browser and instruct it to load the URL http://localhost:901. You are asked to log in with the root account and root password. After you do so, the main SWAT page is displayed, as shown in Figure 22.9.

FIGURE 22.9

The main SWAT page contains buttons to enter configuration areas and links to Samba documentation.

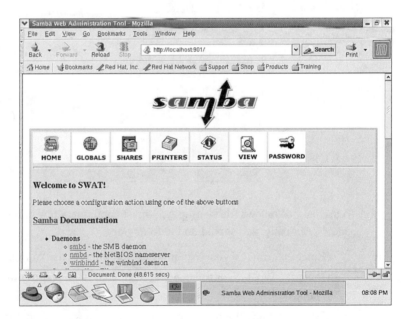

Because the Mozilla Web browser remembers values you've recently entered into dialog boxes, if you enter your root password incorrectly, you have to exit the Web browser and restart it before attempting to start SWAT again.

On the main SWAT page, you find links to a number of Samba-related documents as well as several buttons that take you to various configuration or monitoring areas within SWAT.

Before configuring the list of directory trees you want to share, you must configure a few global options to allow Red Hat Linux to look more like a Windows host to the Windows computers on your network. Click the Globals configuration button to display the page shown in Figure 22.10.

FIGURE 22.10

Clicking the Globals buttons displays a page that enables you to configure the way Linux appears to Windows hosts.

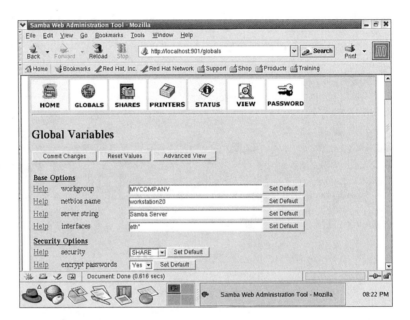

To use basic Windows file sharing, you must configure a few options near the top of this page. Specifically, you should do the following:

- Enter the name of your Windows workgroup into the Workgroup entry box.
- Enter the Windows hostname you want your computer to use into the Netbios Name box.
- Enter **eth0** into the Interfaces box. If you have more than one ethernet interface and want to offer Windows file sharing on both interfaces, enter **eth***, or if you only want to share on the second interface, enter **eth1**.

- Choose SHARE from the Security drop-down list. There are other security modes available in Windows networking, but the SHARE mode is the easiest to administer and is therefore the one discussed here.

When you finish configuring these options, click the Commit Changes button to save your changes. Now you are ready to begin choosing the filesystem trees you'd like to share with Windows machines on your network.

Configuring Samba Shares

Click the Shares configuration button near the top of the page to load the page that enables you to configure the directory trees Samba will share, shown in Figure 22.11.

FIGURE 22.11

Clicking the Shares configuration button displays this page, which enables you to add or configure Windows shares.

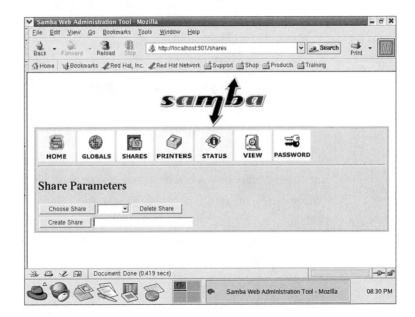

To add a directory tree to the list of Windows shares that your Red Hat Linux computer offers to the Windows computers on your network, enter the name you want to use for the share into the Create Share entry box and click the Create Share button. The page is refreshed and a number of new configuration options appear, as shown in Figure 22.12.

FIGURE 22.12

After you create a new share, a number of new options are displayed to enable you to configure it.

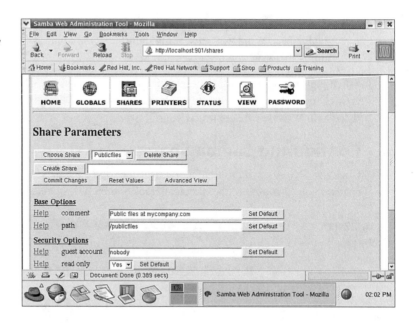

To configure the new share, do the following:

- Enter a plain English description for the share into the Comment entry box.
- Enter the directory tree you want to attach to this share into the Path entry box.
- If this share is read-only, select Yes from the Read Only drop-down list; otherwise, select No.
- If this share should be accessible to guests—meaning that Windows users won't have to enter account or password information to access it—select Yes from the Guest OK drop-down list; otherwise, select No.

For a guest share to be accessible from Windows hosts, its directory tree must have permissions set to allow public (any user) reading. If you want Windows hosts to be able to write to a guest share, you must also ensure that the directory tree in question has its permissions set to allow public writing.

When you finish configuring your share, click the Commit Changes button to save the configuration of this share. To create additional shares, enter the name of the share you want to create into the Create Share entry box, click the Create Share button, and repeat the entire process. Do this until you have created all the Windows shares you intend to create.

If you find that you want to edit a share after you've moved on, use the Choose Share drop-down list to display the share you want to edit, and then click the Choose Share button to bring up the page containing share options.

If you simply want to delete a share, use the Choose Share drop-down list to display the share you want to delete, and then click the Delete Share button to remove it.

22

Starting and Autostarting Windows File Service

To start the Windows file server after you configure it, click the Status button near the top of any SWAT page. A page containing status information about the Windows file server is displayed, as shown in Figure 22.13.

FIGURE 22.13

Clicking the Status button displays a page containing status information about the Windows file server.

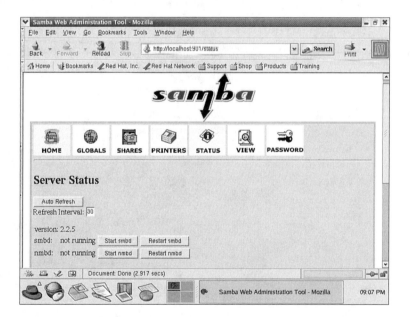

If SWAT shows the status of both smbd and nmbd (two components of the Windows file server) as not running, click the Start smbd button, and then the Start nmbd button, to start the Windows file server. If both are already running, click the Restart smbd button, and then the Restart nmbd button, to activate the configuration changes you've made.

Your Windows file server is now up and running, but if you want it to automatically start each time you start Red Hat Linux, an additional change must be made.

To use desktop tools to configure the Windows file server to automatically start each time Red Hat Linux starts using desktop tools, click GNOME Menu, Server Settings, Services to display the Service Configuration tool. Then, ensure that the smb service is checked.

After you check the smb service, click Save and then File, Quit to exit the Services Configuration tool.

You can also configure the Windows file server to start automatically for your default runlevel by using the chkconfig command at the command line along with the --level option, supplying smb and the word on as arguments:

```
[root@workstation20 you]# /sbin/chkconfig --level 5 smb on
[root@workstation20 you]#
```

If you created only guest shares for your Windows file server, you are finished configuring for Windows file service after you configure it to start automatically. If you created some nonguest shares, however, you must also add accounts for those users.

Creating Windows File Service Accounts

The Windows file server uses a different accounts file than does Red Hat Linux. Because of this, if you have created any nonguest shares, you have to create accounts in the Windows file service for the the Linux users who should be able to access these shares.

To create Windows file service accounts, click the Password button near the top of a SWAT page. A new page is displayed containing tools for working with user accounts, as shown in Figure 22.14.

FIGURE 22.14

Clicking the Password button displays a page that enables you to add new users to your Windows file service.

To add a user to the Windows file service, enter the user's existing account name in Linux into the Server Password Management User Name entry box. Then, enter a Windows file service password for the user in the New Password entry box and reenter it in the Re-type New Password entry box. Then, click the Add New User button to add the user. The user can then use his or her Linux username plus his new password to access nonguest shares from Windows hosts on your network.

> To remove a user account from the Windows file service, enter the user's name into the User Name entry box and click the Delete User button.

Allowing Windows File Service Through Your Firewall

Though your Windows file server is now fully configured and running, users on your network won't be able to access your Windows shares until you tell the Red Hat Linux firewall to allow Windows file service traffic.

To enable Windows file service traffic, start the Security Level Configuration tool by clicking GNOME Menu, System Settings, Security Level. As shown in Figure 22.15, configure your firewall as usual but enter the following additional ports into the Other Ports entry box at the bottom of the tool:

137:tcp,137:udp,138:tcp,138:udp,139:tcp,139:udp

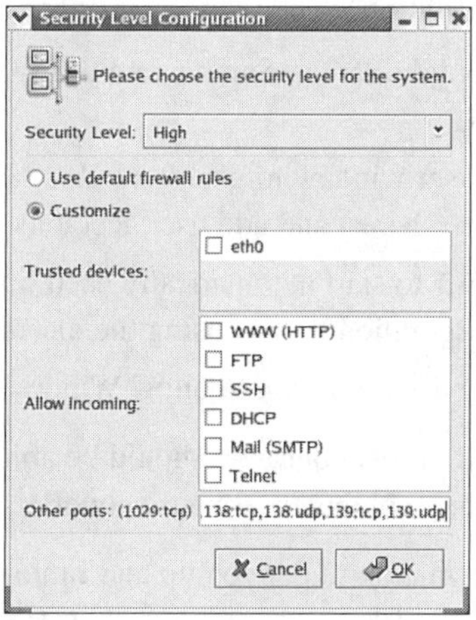

FIGURE 22.15

Enter ports for the netbios *services from* /etc/services—ports *137, 138, and 139, respectively—into the Other Ports box.*

If you want to make SWAT accessible remotely so that you can access it on any computer on your network by connecting to `http://hostname:901` where *hostname* is the name of your computer, you can also add port `901:tcp` to the list of Other Ports.

Be sure to enter these ports in addition to any other special ports you configured for your firewall because each time you run the Security Level Configuration tool, it replaces the previous settings rather than augmenting them. After you configure your firewall, click the OK button to save and activate your firewall settings and close the Security Level Configuration tool.

Summary

This hour, you learned how to configure a Red Hat Linux computer to act as a file server for other Linux or Unix computers, as well as for Windows computers on your network.

To enable your Network File System (NFS) service, you did the following:

- Installed the NFS Server Configuration tool
- Added NFS shares, either via the NFS Server Configuration tool or by editing the /etc/exports file directly
- Configured the NFS server to start automatically each time you boot Linux, either via the Service Configuration tool or using the `chkconfig` command
- Edited your packet filtering configuration to allow NFS network traffic

To enable your Windows file sharing service, you did the following:

- Installed both the Windows File Server, Samba, and the Samba Web Administration Tool (SWAT)
- Used SWAT in a Web browser window to give your Red Hat Linux computer a Windows identity, configure shares, and add user accounts
- Configured the Samba server to start automatically each time you boot Linux, either via the Service Configuration tool or using the `chkconfig` command
- Edited your packet filtering configuration to allow Windows networking traffic

Using the techniques you learned in this hour, you should be able to efficiently and naturally exchange files with nearly any computer on your network.

This hour presented enough information to get you up and running. However, if you plan to run a high-volume or high-profile file server, you should seriously consider consulting more advanced documentation for these services and for Linux network security. One of the favorite sources of documentation in the Linux world is *The Linux Documentation Project* at `http://www.tldp.org`.

Q&A

Q How do I access NFS shares from another Linux or Unix system?

A As explained in Hour 18, you can mount a remote filesystem on a Linux or Unix computer using `mount -t nfs` *host:/tree /mnt/point*, where *host* is the hostname of the server, */tree* is the shared directory tree, and */mnt/point* is the mountpoint on the local system where you want the shared files to appear. For example, to mount the `/publicfiles` directory on a host called `mack` on the local directory `/network/publicfiles`, you enter the following:

```
Mount -t nfs mack:/publicfiles /network/publicfiles
```

Q Do I need to have a Web server running to use SWAT?

A No. SWAT operates inside any Web browser, but it does not require a Web server to run; it is fully independent.

Q Can I also use Samba to share my printers with other Windows machines?

A Yes, but because of driver issues related to printing in Windows, the process is somewhat more complex. Please consult the online Samba documentation in SWAT and the extensive list of Samba documentation resources at `http://www.samba.org` for details on printing with Samba.

Q Can I use Red Hat Linux to serve files to Mac OS computers?

A Yes. Mac OS X includes the capability of sharing files using either Windows file sharing or NFS—you can choose whichever you prefer. Consult your Mac OS X documentation for details on mounting NFS or Windows shares in Mac OS.

Workshop

The Workshop is designed to help you anticipate possible questions, review what you've learned, and begin learning how to put your knowledge into practice.

Quiz

1. What does the /etc/exports file do?

2. What general security level must be used for NFS to function properly?

3. How do you start the Samba Web Administration Tool (SWAT)?

4. How can I make SWAT remotely accessible?

Answers

1. /etc/exports contains a list of the NFS shares offered by your computer system.

2. To offer NFS services, you must use the Medium security level and accept ports 111, 369, and 2049.

3. Enter `http://localhost:901` into your Web browser.

4. Accept port 901 in the Red Hat firewall.

HOUR 23

Offering Web and FTP Service

In this hour, you learn how to configure your Red Hat Linux computer system to act as a World Wide Web server or an FTP server. By the time this hour is over, you'll be able to do the following:

- Install and enable the Apache World Wide Web server.
- Configure the basics of the Apache World Wide Web server so that you can provide content of your choice to people of your choice.
- Configure the FTP service to allow users to log in and access their home directories.
- Configure the FTP service to allow anonymous logins for distribution files.

These services represent the most visible uses of the Internet, beyond simple email. Together, they can turn your Red Hat Linux computer into an ideal Internet server platform.

Before You Begin

This hour refers often to topics covered in earlier hours. If you haven't yet read them or haven't read them recently, consider refamiliarizing yourself with the following topics and hours before continuing with this hour:

- Using the Package Management tool to install Red Hat Linux components, covered in Hour 21, "Installing Software"
- Using text editors to make changes to plain text files, covered in Hour 5, "Making the Console Work for You," and in Hour 11, "Working with Files on the Desktop"
- Using Red Hat system administration tools to enable or disable installed services, covered in Hour 18, "Command-Line System Administration," and Hour 19, "Desktop System Administration"
- Managing the Red Hat firewalling configuration, covered in Hour 20, "Security Basics"

You will find illustrations and examples in this hour as you make use of these tools, but for in-depth discussion please refer to the hours listed above.

You will find that some network terminology is unavoidable when discussions of network services begin in earnest. If you are completely unfamiliar with Transport Control Protocol/Internet Protocol (TCP/IP) networking—the type used by Linux, Unix, and most of the Internet—you should consider keeping a TCP/IP reference of some sort handy, to help you with unfamiliar terms or basic concepts.

Running a Web Server

Using Red Hat Linux, you can configure your computer to act as a World Wide Web server—a computer that delivers Web content to Web browsers running on computers around your network or around the Internet at large.

The Web server software included with Red Hat Linux is the single most popular Web server platform in use today and is known as the Apache Web server. To use your Red Hat Linux system as a Web server with existing Web content, you must complete the following tasks:

- Ensure that the Apache Web server and the tools used to configure it have been installed.
- Configure Linux to automatically start the Apache Web server each time Linux starts.
- Configure your Red Hat Linux firewall to allow traffic related to World Wide Web requests.

Installing Apache

You can ensure that the Apache Web server is installed or install it if it isn't by using the Package Management tool. Start the Package Management tool by clicking GNOME Menu, System Settings, Packages. In the Package Management tool, scroll down to the Servers category and ensure that the Web Server package group is checked, as shown in Figure 23.1. If it isn't checked, check it now to mark it for installation.

FIGURE 23.1

Use the Package Management tool to install the Apache Web server that comes with Red Hat Linux.

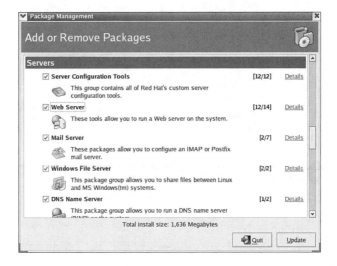

You might notice in Figure 23.1 that only 12 of 14 components from the Web Server packages group have been marked for installation by default. The other two packages, which can be enabled in the package group's Details view, allow the Web server to be used with the PostgreSQL database service. If you plan to use the PostgreSQL database in conjunction with your Web server, you should use the Details view to mark these components for installation as well. This book does not cover the PostgreSQL database.

In addition to the Web Server package group, you must also ensure that the Red Hat Linux configuration tool for the Apache Web server has been installed. Ensure that the Server Configuration Tools package group check box is checked.

Click the Details button for the Server Configuration Tools package group to bring up the details view, where you can mark individual packages within the group for installation. In the details view, ensure that the box next to redhat-config-httpd is checked, as shown in Figure 23.2. If it isn't checked, check it now to mark the configuration tool for installation.

FIGURE 23.2

If the redhat-config-httpd box isn't checked in the Server Configuration Tools Package Details window, check it.

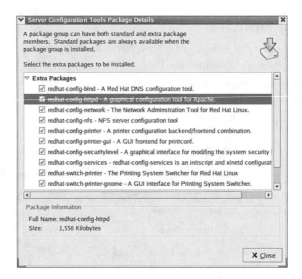

After you mark the Web Server package group and the Apache Configuration tool for installation, click the Update button in the Package Management tool to install the software.

After you install the necessary software, you should log out and and log back in again to ensure that your menus have been updated to reflect the new additions to your system.

Configuring Apache to Start Automatically

To use your Red Hat Linux computer as a Web server after you have installed the Apache Web server software, you must configure Apache to start automatically each time you start Red Hat Linux. To configure Apache to start automatically using desktop tools, click GNOME Menu, Server Settings, Services to start the Service Configuration tool. Ensure that the httpd service is checked, as shown in Figure 23.3. If it isn't checked, check it now.

FIGURE 23.3

*Use the Service
Configuration tool to
configure the Apache
Web server to start
each time Linux starts.*

After you check the box next to the httpd service, click File, Quit to exit the Service
Configuration tool.

If you prefer to use command-line tools, you can use the chkconfig command to configure the Apache Web server to start automatically each time Red Hat Linux starts at your
default runlevel. Call the chkconfig command, supplying httpd and the word on as
arguments:

```
[root@workstation20 you]# /sbin/chkconfig --level 5 httpd on
[root@workstation20 you]#
```

You have now configured your Web server to start automatically when Red Hat Linux
starts, but if you've just installed it, it isn't running yet. To start it, either reboot Linux or
call the service command, supplying httpd and the word start as arguments to cause
the server to start now:

```
[root@workstation20 you]# /sbin/service httpd start
Starting httpd:                                          [  OK  ]
[root@workstation20 you]#
```

Allowing Web Requests Through Your Firewall

Now you have the Apache Web server running, but before it can answer World Wide Web
requests from machines on your network or from the Internet at large, you must configure your firewall to allow World Wide Web requests. To do this, start the Security Level
Configuration tool by clicking GNOME Menu, System Settings, Security Level.

In the Security Level Configuration tool, select your desired level of security, and then
select the Customize option and ensure that you also check the WWW (HTTP) option in
the Allow Incoming area.

23

When deciding on a security level, remember that if you are using the network capabilities of the X Window System, the Network File Service (NFS), or streaming media tools like RealPlayer at your desktop, you must choose the Medium security level rather than the High security level.

Remember also to enter exceptions for the ports of any services you're using that require them because any ports you entered are lost each time you use the Security Level Configuration tool.

Be sure to reenter your list of ports for other services (if you have them) into the Other Ports entry box because each time you run the Security Level Configuration tool, it replaces your old settings. Click the OK button to exit the Security Level Configuration tool when you are done.

Using the Apache Web Server

Your Web server is now up and running and allowing requests from the outside world. The default Apache configuration is adequate and correct for most users—no need for additional up-front configuration when starting out. The properties of the Web server in its default configuration are as follows:

- Your Web content goes in the /var/www/html directory tree. Note that any files your Web server should deliver must be set to have publicly (all users) readable permissions.

- The contact email address, which is displayed to visitors when errors occur, is root@hostname, where hostname is your computer's hostname.

- The default index files, which will be loaded for any visited directory, are index.php, index.html, index.htm, and index.shtml, in that order.

- Your Common Gateway Interface (CGI) /cgi-bin/ scripts should be placed in the /var/www/cgi-bin directory.

- Secure Sockets Layer (SSL) https:// connections are supported.

Because your Web server is already online if you've followed the steps outlined thus far in this hour, you can begin copying your content to or creating your content in /var/www/html; any files you place there from now on will be instantly available to the world.

Enabling Home Directory Web Sites

If your Red Hat Linux computer system serves a number of users, you might want to give each user the opportunity to host his or her own home page. Although it is possible to do this while still keeping all content in the /var/www/html directory tree, it is certainly not convenient.

The Apache Web server has the capability of giving each user on a Linux system his or her own HTML content directory, by default in /home/*user*/public_html. Visitors can then load the index page at /home/*user*/public_html/index.html by constructing a URL using the host name of your Web server followed by a slash (/), a tilde (~), another slash, and the name of the user whose home page should be loaded, as follows:

```
http://host.mycompany.com/~jane/
```

For example, this URL loads the file index.html stored in the /home/jane/public_html directory.

To enable this functionality in Apache, you must edit the Web server configuration file, /etc/httpd/conf/httpd.conf. Load the file into your favorite text editor and search for the text shown in Listing 23.1.

LISTING 23.1   Text to Change to Enable Home Pages

```
<IfModule mod_userdir.c>
    #
    # UserDir is disabled by default since it can confirm the presence
    # of a username on the system (depending on home directory
    # permissions).
    #
    UserDir disable
```

Notice the text UserDir disable; if user home directories are to be enabled, you must change this to read UserDir public_html, as shown in Listing 23.2.

LISTING 23.2   Text Changed to Enable Home Pages

```
<IfModule mod_userdir.c>
    #
    # UserDir is disabled by default since it can confirm the presence
    # of a username on the system (depending on home directory
    # permissions).
    #
    UserDir public_html
```

Then, save the httpd.conf file and exit. To cause the changes to take effect, restart your Web server using the service command, supplying httpd and restart as arguments:

```
[root@workstation20 you]# /sbin/service httpd restart
Stopping httpd:                                         [  OK  ]
Starting httpd:                                         [  OK  ]
[root@workstation20 you]#
```

> On a busy World Wide Web server, you should use the graceful argument
> instead of the restart argument to restart the Web server:
>
> /sbin/service httpd graceful
>
> When a Web server is restarted using the graceful argument, it might not
> restart and update its configuration immediately; instead, it processes all
> pending requests before restarting, to make sure that everyone who has
> requested to view your Web site is able to do so.

Before a user's public_html directory can be used, the permissions for the user's home
directory, the ~/public_html directory, and the contents of the ~/public_html directory
must be correctly configured:

- Using chmod in numeric mode, the user's home directory must be set to 711—user
  read, write, and execute; group execute; and other (public) execute.

- Using chmod in numeric mode, the user's ~/public_html directory and all subdirectories must be set to 755—user read, write, and execute; group read and execute; and public read and execute.

- Using chmod in numeric mode, all the content files in the user's ~/public_html
  directory tree, such as HTML files and images, must be set to 644—user read and
  write, group read, and public read.

> If you're administering a system with many users, always warn a user before
> changing the permissions of any files or directories in his or her home direc-
> tory. Using administration privileges to change a user's file or directory per-
> missions without first warning them of which files and directories will be
> changed might make public files that were intended to remain private or
> endanger the files in other ways! By warning users first of the changes that
> will be made to their home directory, you give them a chance to move criti-
> cal files or directories to other areas, or to ask you, the administrator, not to
> make the change in the first place.

If permissions are incorrectly set or if a user does not have a public_html directory, visitors who try to load a user's home page get an error message saying that the page in
question is Forbidden.

Introducing the Apache Configuration Tool

The default configuration of the Apache Web server is sufficient to provide a small amount of public Web content. The default configuration should not be used, however, when business interests or large amounts of content are at stake. You can use the Apache Configuration tool to configure many of the options related to the Apache Web server and its level of security and performance while operating.

23

To start the Apache Configuration tool, click GNOME Menu, Server Settings, HTTP Server; the Apache Configuration tool is displayed, as shown in Figure 23.4.

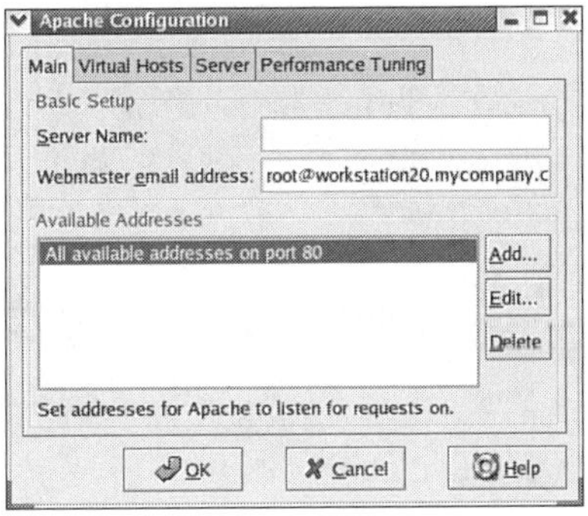

FIGURE 23.4

The Apache Configuration tool provides a graphical interface for configuring the Apache Web server.

The Apache configuration tool contains four basic tabs—Main, Virtual Hosts, Server, and Performance Tuning—which function as follows:

- The Main tab contains general systemwide configuration options, including the fully qualified domain name of your Web server, the email address of the administrator, and the set of ethernet addresses on which your Web server will *listen* for incoming requests.

- The Virtual Hosts tab enables you to configure the default host (most commonly used for small Web servers) or a number of user-definable virtual hosts, such as are commonly used by ISPs or larger companies.

- The Server tab enables you to configure some basic housekeeping properties, such as the directory in which Apache will write machine-readable error information if it crashes, and the user and group identities under which Apache should run; as a general rule, it is not a good idea to change these options.

- The Performance Tuning tab enables you to fine tune your Apache installation for the amount of traffic you expect to receive; it includes options such as the maximum number of connections Apache will manage at one time before it begins turning down requests for Web content.

The two most important tabs are the Virtual Hosts tab, where most security control occurs and where multiple hosts are managed if you are running a larger server, and the Performance Tuning tab, which enables you to adjust Apache's workload to suit your computer system hardware and the set of scripts (if any) you'll be using on your Web site.

Basic Apache Security

As you run your Web server on a day-to-day basis, you will likely want to be able to control which Internet users can view which parts of your Web site. Some areas of a site are meant for public consumption and other parts are intended for certain viewers only. You can control viewership of your site by filtering Web requests based on the Internet addresses from which viewers originate.

This can be accomplished through the Virtual Hosts tab. Because we're covering only the basics this hour, let's assume that you are running only a single Web host that provides you with basic Web server functionality.

To control which visitors will be able to see files delivered by your default virtual host, follow these steps:

1. Click the Virtual Hosts tab, and then click the Edit Default Settings button to display the Virtual Host Properties dialog box.

2. Click the Directories item in the left pane of the Virtual Host Properties dialog to display the Directory configuration pane shown in Figure 23.5.

FIGURE 23.5

In the Directories item of the Virtual Host Properties dialog box, you can configure directories on your Web site to have specific security features.

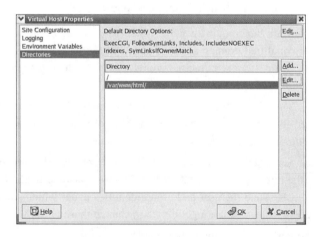

The primary directory for your Web site is its root directory (`/var/www/html`). With that directory highlighted, click the Add button to display the Directory Options dialog box shown in Figure 23.6.

FIGURE 23.6

The Directory Options dialog enables you to give specific security properties to directories within your Web content directory tree.

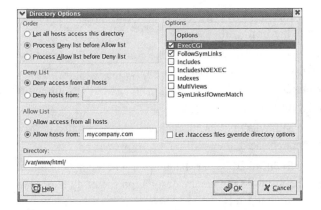

23

There are a number of settings on the left side of the Directory Options dialog related to access control based on the IP address or domain name of connecting hosts. These settings are configured as follows:

- The Deny List and Allow List panes enable you to specify that all requests for content from this directory should be accepted, that all should be denied, or that only certain hosts should be accepted or denied. You can enter hosts as IP numbers, partial IP numbers, or partial domains. The Allow entry shown in Figure 23.6 would allow connections from all hosts in the domain mycompany.com.

- The Order pane enables you to specify whether the list of denials or the list of allowed hosts should be processed by Apache first. You should think of the first processed list as the general rule and the second processed list as exceptions to that rule. The Order, Deny, and Allow configuration shown in Figure 23.6 would result in all requests being denied except those requests from machines inside mycompany.com.

In the Options list box, you can choose from a number of options to enable or disable certain capabilities for the specified directory. Select or deselect check boxes to control the following capabilities:

- If the ExecCGI box is checked, scripts requested from files in this directory will be called. If it is not checked, they won't.

- If the FollowSymLinks box is checked, symbolic links in this directory that point to other files or directories will be followed and used. If it is not checked, they will be ignored.

- If the Includes box is checked, server-side includes in content files will be honored. If it is not checked, they will be ignored.

- If the IncludesNOEXEC box is checked, server-side includes will be honored everwhere but from within scripts.

- If the Indexes box is checked, the contents of the directory (a directory index) will be displayed to the Web visitor requesting the index if no index file is present in the directory. If it is not checked, attempts to visit directories without an index file will return an error.

- If the Multiview box is checked, content-negotiated multiviews will be allowed. If it is not checked, they will not be allowed.

- If the SymLinksIfOwnerMatch box is checked, symbolic links in the directory will be followed only if the destination file or directory has the same owner as the symbolic link itself.

> Do not check any option box unless you know for sure that you need the capability it provides. Each of these options represents additional vulnerability that could conceivably be exploited by a malicious World Wide Web user.

When you finish configuring the host security options for the directory in question, click the OK button to save your changes and return to the Virtual Host Properties dialog's Directory pane. If you want to configure additional security properties for directories within your Web content tree, click the Add button to bring the Directory Options dialog back up; in the Directory box of the Directory Options dialog, enter the name of the directory to which these options should apply, and then set the options for that directory just as you did for your root content directory.

When you finish making changes to your Apache configuration, click OK in the Virtual Host Properties Dialog and OK in the Apache Configuration tool to exit and save your changes.

Additional Apache Configuration Information

The Apache Web server can also be configured using your favorite text editor by editing the files stored in /etc/httpd/conf and /etc/httpd/conf.d. These files are large and fairly involved, however, so you shouldn't venture into editor-based configuration unless you have an Apache reference volume handy.

Because the Apache Web server is a relatively complex application, further Apache configuration is beyond the scope of a beginning-level book like this one. A great deal of in-depth documentation for Apache can be found on the main Apache Web site, at http://httpd.apache.org/docs-2.0/.

Running a File Transfer Protocol (FTP) Server

The File Transfer Protocol (FTP) service enables users to download files from—and in some cases upload files to—your Red Hat Linux system using special programs called FTP clients, or in some cases using a standard Web browser.

Red Hat Linux includes several FTP servers; because the Washington University FTP server, known as wu-ftpd, is very common in the Linux and Unix world and because it is installed by default, it is the one you look at in this section.

23

> Use wu-ftpd only inside a local area network that is protected from the Internet by a firewall. A large number of successful theft and/or destructive attacks against hastily configured or buggy FTP servers have taken place, and the wu-ftpd server does not encrypt usernames and passwords as it sends them across the network. If you plan to use wu-ftpd to offer anonymous FTP, you should use a dedicated machine with no other user accounts on it.
>
> Alternatively, if you have installed and configured the sshd service (also included with Red Hat Linux), you can use the sftp service to offer FTP service beyond your firewall; sftp includes additional security features and encryption. Because sftp isn't compatible with all FTP clients, however, we haven't documented it here.

To offer FTP service on your Red Hat Linux computer, you must do the following:

- Ensure that the FTP Server packages on the Red Hat Linux media have been installed on your system.
- Configure Linux to automatically start wu-ftpd when incoming FTP requests are received.
- Configure your Red Hat Linux firewall to allow traffic related to FTP requests.

Enabling or Disabling FTP

To offer FTP service, you must ensure that the FTP Server package group has been installed from the Red Hat Linux media. To ensure that the package group is installed or to install it if it isn't, start the Package Management tool by clicking GNOME Menu, System Settings, Packages. In the Package Management tool, scroll down to the Servers category and ensure that the box next to FTP Server is checked, as shown in Figure 23.7. If it isn't, check it now if you want to offer FTP service.

FIGURE 23.7

Make sure that the FTP Server package group is checked if you want to offer anonymous FTP service.

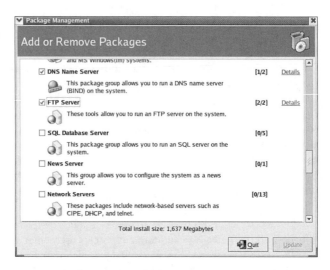

Configuring `wu-ftpd` to Answer Requests

For users to log in to your computer system using FTP, the `wu-ftpd` server must be configured to automatically start when an incoming FTP request occurs. To do this using desktop tools, click GNOME Menu, Server Settings, Services to start the Service Configuration tool. In the tool, ensure that the box next to `wu-ftpd` is checked, as seen in Figure 23.8.

FIGURE 23.8

The `wu-ftpd` server must be configured to start automatically when incoming FTP requests are received.

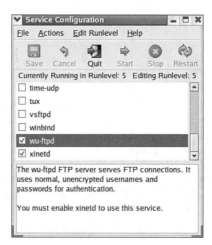

If you are more comfortable using command-line tools to enable wu-ftpd, call the chkconfig command, supplying wu-ftpd and the word on as arguments:

```
[root@workstation20 you]# /sbin/chkconfig wu-ftpd on
[root@workstation20 you]#
```

The wu-ftpd server automatically answers incoming FTP requests.

Allowing FTP Through Your Firewall

Before incoming FTP requests can be received, you must configure your Red Hat Linux firewall to allow FTP-related traffic. To do this, click GNOME Menu, System Settings, Security Level to start the Security Level Configuration tool.

In the Security Level Configuration tool, select your desired basic level of security, and then select the Customize option and check the box next to FTP in the Allow Incoming area.

Don't forget to enter your list of ports, if you have any from other services you're offering, in the Other Ports entry box. You should do this because running the Security Level Configuration tool replaces your previous firewall configuration rather than augmenting it.

Controlling FTP Access

The FTP server normally allows users to log in with their account and password information, thereby gaining full read and write access to your system—limited only by filesystem permissions—just as if they were accessing files directly. If certain users have no valid need to access their files remotely via FTP, you should disable FTP logins for their accounts as a precautionary measure.

The /etc/ftpusers file contains a list of login accounts, one per line, that are not allowed to log in to FTP using their account. To shut off FTP access for a specific user on your system, use your favorite text editor to add a line to /etc/ftpusers containing only the name of the account. For example, to prevent you from logging in via ftp, add the following line to /etc/ftpusers:

you

The user you is no longer allowed to log in to FTP via his or her account.

Using or Disabling Anonymous FTP

File Transfer Protocol is a special kind of File Transfer Protocol service that allows connecting users to log in as the user ftp or the user anonymous without supplying a password, in order to access a set of files you have provided for public download. Anonymous FTP is commonly used to distribute large software or media files to the general public via the Internet.

By default, the Red Hat Linux FTP server is configured to allow anonymous logins. The files that users will be able to download when they log in anonymously are those stored in /var/ftp.

There is no reason to allow anonymous logins, however, if you don't plan to distribute files publicly via FTP. If this is the case for you, you should disable anonymous FTP. This can be done simply by editing the /etc/ftpusers file and adding the user ftp to the end of the file.

> Anonymous FTP is a service with a relatively poor security history. In order to avoid data loss or theft, it is recommended that Linux and Unix beginners or users without a dedicated and properly configured FTP host not run Anonymous FTP servers.
>
> If you do plan to offer anonymous FTP, you *must* take care to remove write permission from all directories in /var/ftp and write and execute permission from all files in /var/ftp.

Summary

This hour, you learned to install and use the Apache Web server and Washington University FTP server, which come with Red Hat Linux. Specifically, you learned the following:

- How to install and start the Apache Web server
- How to allow World Wide Web requests through your firewall
- Where to place your HTML content so that Apache can deliver it to users who request it
- How to install and enable the wu-ftpd server for FTP service
- How to control the list of users who can log in to FTP

Q&A

Q When I try to load my Web pages (or the Web pages of one of my users), I get a 403 Forbidden error. How can I fix this?

A Any content that Apache delivers to the outside world must be set to be readable by everyone so that the account under which Apache runs will be able to read it. Please also refer back to the special list of permissions required for users' home directories in the "Enabling Home Directory Web Sites" section.

Q I've added a user to the /etc/ftpusers file, but he or she can't log in via FTP. Why?

A Counterintuitively, the /etc/ftpusers file is a list of users who are *forbidden* from using FTP, not a list of users who are *allowed* to use FTP. Remove the user from /etc/ftpusers and he or she should be able to log in.

Workshop

The Workshop is designed to help you anticipate possible questions, review what you've learned, and begin learning how to put your knowledge into practice.

Quiz

1. Where should your system's Web content be stored?

2. Where should your individual users' Web content be stored if you are offering home pages to your users?

3. How do you disable anonymous FTP logins?

Answers

1. `/var/www/html`

2. `~/public_html`

3. Add the user `ftp` to the end of the `/etc/ftpusers` file.

HOUR 24

Backups, Troubleshooting, and Rescue

In your last hour, you learn how to deal with some of the tedious chores of computing life—making backups of your valuable data, restoring from these backups, and knowing just when to do either. By the time you've finished this hour, you'll know how to do the following:

- Make backups of your data, either on magnetic tape or on disk-style storage media.
- Automate backups using shell scripts and the cron service.
- Restore data that you have previously backed up.
- Recognize some telltale signs of hacking or data corruption, indicating that it might be time to reinstall Linux and make use of your backups.
- Use the Red Hat Linux rescue system to salvage data even if your computer isn't starting normally any longer.

Though discussions of backing up or restoring data and performing rescue operations often get lost in the shuffle of more immediately useful topics, you should pay as much—or perhaps more—attention to this hour as you have to all the rest. This book is only 24 hours long—but it can take much longer than 24 hours to re-create months or years of data that was lost because you didn't maintain regular backups.

Backing Up and Restoring Your Data

By the time you have used Linux for a few months, you will have built a collection of important files of various kinds—important spreadsheets, documents in progress, Web content, or any number of other types of files. What an annoyance—or worse—it would be to lose them!

Modern hard drives are remarkably reliable, especially when compared to the storage devices used by early computers. However, for every handful of users who have never lost an important file due to circumstance or hardware failure, there is at least one user who has seen hours and hours of work lost in the void. That user inevitably regrets not having made backups of his data.

There are a number of common types of backup media in widespread use today, but they all fit into one of three major categories:

- Tape drives, such as 8mm or 4mm DAT drives or DLT cartridge streamers. These devices typically have very large storage capacities, which must be accessed in a single, extended read or write operation, rather than a file at a time.

- Removable disk drives, such as Zip, Jaz, Orb, DVD-RAM, Magneto-Optical, or LS-120. These devices act like a cross between a floppy drive and a hard drive— they are removable and easily accessible like floppy drives but hold much more data than can fit on a single floppy disk.

- CD-R and DVD-R drives, which can be written to only once (or in some cases, several times) and which must also be written in a single, extended write operation using special software tools. Because of the special tools required, this book does not discuss this type of backup medium. If you need to use a CD-R or DVD-R drive in Linux, see the manual pages for `mkisofs` and `cdrecord`.

If your Linux computer is acting as a personal workstation or small server, most of the files you want to save will be documents—OpenOffice files, World Wide Web content, LaTeX source files, or similar things that you have invested your time and effort in creating. These types of files don't take up much space and are relatively easy to back up simply by copying them to your backup medium.

If you need to back up a larger amount of data or a large number of files, a tool specially designed for backing up large amounts of data, like the `tar` command, can be extremely helpful.

Both of these techniques are discussed in the sections that follow.

Backing Up to Disk

In Hour 7, "Working Without the Mouse," you learned how to use mcopy to copy files from your home directory to a floppy disk. It is sometimes helpful, however, to be able to back up larger amounts of data. Many users have access to Zip, Jaz, or other removable storage devices that can be accessed like a hard drive. These devices are an ideal backup medium for small-to-medium amounts of data.

Backing up files or entire directory trees to removable disk devices is simply a matter of using the mount and cp commands in three steps:

1. Use the mount command to mount the removable disk device so that you can copy files to it.

2. Use the cp command to copy individual files or the cp command with the -R option to copy entire directory trees to the removable disk, or use the file manager to copy files and directories you want to back up.

3. Unmount the removable disk and file it away for safekeeping.

> The information in this section refers to material covered in earlier hours.
>
> The mount command and common SCSI and IDE device types are discussed in Hour 18, "Command-Line System Administration."
>
> The cp and mkdir commands are discussed in several places in Hour 4, "Navigating Linux at the Console."
>
> The process of copying files and directories using the file manager is discussed in several places in Hour 11, "Working with Files on the Desktop."
>
> Additional information can also be found in the mount, cp, and mkdir manual pages.

To illustrate, let's step through a sample backup session at the command line. For this example, assume that you are using a removable disk drive connected as the master device on your secondary IDE channel. The disk you're using is formatted for Windows using the common "superfloppy" format, meaning that it has no partitions—most removable device disks come from the factory formatted this way.

Your first order of business is to mount the disk. First, make a mountpoint where your files will appear using the mkdir command. By convention, mountpoints for removable devices usually reside in the /mnt directory:

```
[you@workstation20 you]# mkdir /mnt/removable
[you@workstation20 you]#
```

24

Now, insert and mount the disk so that you can copy files to it. Because it was formatted for Windows, the correct filesystem type to supply to the mount command is vfat:

```
[you@workstation20 you]# mount -t vfat /dev/hdc /mnt/removable
[you@workstation20 you]#
```

Now that your disk has been mounted, you can begin to copy files to it using the cp command. Let's assume that you want to copy the file /var/www/mypage.html and the entire contents of your home directory to the disk. You can use the cp command with the -R argument to copy entire directory trees—simply supply a list of files and directory trees you want to copy as arguments, listing the destination directory as your final argument. If you want to see the files listed as they are copied, use the -v (verbose) argument:

```
[root@workstation20 you]# cp -R -v /var/www/mypage.html /home/you /mnt/removable
'/var/www/mypage.html' -> '/mnt/removable/mypage.html'
'/home/you/myfile.txt' -> '/mnt/removable/you/myfile.txt'
'/home/you/document-1.tex' -> '/mnt/removable/you/document-1.tex'
'/home/you/document-2.tex' -> '/mnt/removable/you/document-2.tex'
'/home/you/old/budget-jan.sxw' -> '/mnt/removable/you/old/budget-jan.sxw'
'/home/you/old/budget-feb.sxw' -> '/mnt/removable/you/old/budget-feb.sxw'
[root@workstation20 you]#
```

You can see by the output of the cp command that your files have been copied to the /mnt/removable directory, which is where your removable disk is mounted. Now that your files have been backed up, unmount your removable disk:

```
[root@workstation20 you]# umount /mnt/removable
[root@workstation20 you]#
```

Eject your disk and file it away for safekeeping. Your files bave been backed up.

Creating Backups with tar

Backups to disk devices are relatively easy to perform. However, depending on the format of your disks—they are generally formatted for Windows—there is a good chance that any file permissions connected with your files will not be preserved when you back them up with the cp command.

Furthermore, the cp command can't be used to copy files to magnetic tape devices, which are necessary tools for backing up larger amounts of data because magnetic tape is available in sizes that far exceed anything removable disks can offer.

These problems can be solved by using the tar (Tape ARchive) command, which can communicate with magnetic tape drives and can also be used to save the permissions of files you back up on Windows-formatted media. The tar command must be used entirely from the command line; it has no graphical equivalent. To create a backup with the tar command, call tar in the following format:

```
tar -c -v -f dest /path1 [/path2 ...]
```

The required -c option tells tar that you want to *create* a backup. The optional -v option causes tar to display the name of each file as it is backed up.

Replace *dest* with the device or file that should hold the backed-up data. Table 24.1 lists some common magnetic tape devices; *dest* can also simply be the name of a file, however, as is the case if you are backing up to a mounted removable disk device.

Replace */path1* with the directory tree that tar should back up, the optional */path2* with the second directory tree tar should back up, and so on.

TABLE 24.1 Common Magnetic Tape Device Names

Device	Description
/dev/st0	First SCSI magnetic tape device
/dev/st1	Second SCSI magnetic tape device
/dev/ht0	First IDE magnetic tape device
/dev/ht1	Second IDE magnetic tape device

24

Backing Up with tar Examples

Given what you've just learned about using the tar command, let's step through some examples for purposes of illustration.

To back up the /home directory tree (which backs up all user home directories) to the first SCSI tape device, listing each file as it is being processed, you use the following command:

```
tar -c -v -f /dev/st0 /home
```

To back up the files in /var/www/html and /var/www/cgi-bin to the first IDE tape device, listing each file as it is being processed, you use the following command:

```
tar -c -v -f /dev/ht0 /var/www/html /var/www/cgi-bin
```

To back up the /home, /var/www, and /var/ftp directory trees to a backup file called backup-oct52002.tar, which is to be stored on a removable disk mounted on /mnt/opticaldisk—without bothering to list the files as they are stored—you use the following command:

```
tar -c -f /mnt/opticaldisk/backup-oct52002.tar /home /var/www /var/ftp
```

Because tar is a relatively quick command that does little processing of your files, you will find that the speed of your backups is limited only by the speed of your storage device or streaming tape device.

> If you want to create a list or index of the files you're backing up, use the -v
> option and then save tar's output to a file, like this:
>
> ```
> tar -c -v -f /dev/st0 /home > filelist.txt
> ```

> If you have read the tar manual page and found the compress (-z) option,
> you might be tempted to use it for your tape backups.
>
> Don't.
>
> When you use the tar compress option, tar doesn't compress files individu-
> ally; it compresses the entire *stream* of files as they are written out. This is
> great, unless your backup media develops an error.
>
> If tar finds a read error when restoring from an uncompressed backup, tar
> can often recover, losing only the file in which the error occurred. When tar
> finds a read error when restoring from a compressed backup, *all of the files*
> *in the backup are lost.*
>
> You should thus *never* use the compress (-z) option for creating critical
> backups.
>
> Most modern tape drives (4mm, 8mm, and DLT) compress your data as it is
> written anyway—so using -z generally produces little in the way of space
> savings.

Restoring tar Backups

To restore files from a backup with the tar command, call tar in the following format:

```
tar -x -v -f source [pattern ...]
```

The required -x option tells tar that you want to *extract* (restore from) a backup. The
optional -v option causes tar to display the name of each file as it is restored.

Replace *source* with the device or file that should hold the backed-up data. Refer to
Table 24.1 for some common magnetic tape devices; and once again, *source* can also be
the name of a backup file rather than a device.

If you don't supply a *pattern*, tar restores every file stored on the streaming tape device
or in the backup file. Sometimes, however, you want to restore only a single file or small
list of files. When this is the case, replace *pattern* with a list of quote-enclosed filenames you want to restore, or patterns you want to use to select which files are to be
restored.

> When you restore a tar backup, any existing files to which you have write
> permission will be overwritten by the files being restored.

Note that when you restore using tar, the files in the backup are restored *relative to your current working directory*. This means that if you backed up the /var/www directory tree using tar and now want to restore the files to /var/www, you must first make the root directory (/) your current working directory using the cd command. If, for example, you try to restore the backup while /home/you is your current working directory, the restored files will end up in /home/you/var/www.

Restoring tar Backups Examples

Using what you've just learned about the tar command, let's step through a few restoration examples to illustrate.

To restore all the files on the magnetic tape in the first SCSI tape drive, listing each file as it is restored, use the following command:

```
tar -x -v -f /dev/st0
```

To restore only the files from the /var/www tree stored on the magnetic tape in the second IDE tape drive, listing each file as it is restored, use the following command:

```
tar -x -v -f /dev/ht1 "var/www/*"
```

To silently (without listing) restore only the plain text (.txt) files from the /home/you directory stored on the magnetic tape in the second SCSI tape drive, use the following command:

```
tar -x -f /dev/st1 "home/you/*.txt"
```

Silent backups or restores of this kind are often useful when writing scripts because you often want to keep output from shell scripts to a minimum.

To silently restore all the files from the tar backup file called backup-oct52002.tar stored on the removable disk mounted on the /mnt/opticaldisk directory, use the following command:

```
tar -x -f /mnt/opticaldisk/backup-oct52002.tar
```

Using tar's backup and restore capabilities, you can preserve any file on your system that you want to save and restore it later if something should happen to it.

24

If you are restoring only one or two particular files from a large backup, you might find that the tar command takes some time to complete. This is because tar must read through every file in a backup, regardless of whether you chose to restore every file.

Testing and Listing Backups

Sometimes you want to verify the integrity of a magnetic tape, to make sure that the files on it can still be restored. This can be accomplished by calling tar using the -t (test) option:

```
tar -t -f source
```

Replace *source* with the name of the device containing the magnetic tape or the name of the tar file that you want to test. If there are any errors in the backup (meaning that some of the files stored in it can't be restored), an error message is displayed. If tar reads the entire tape or the entire backup file and then exits silently, the backup is problem free.

By also supplying the -v option to a test operation, you can list the contents of a backup because the -v option causes the name of each file in the backup to be displayed as it is tested. To create an index of an existing backup tape or file, save the output of the tar command to a file.

For example, to save a list of the contents of the tape in the first SCSI tape drive to the file tape1contents.txt, use the following command:

```
tar -t -v -f /dev/st0 > tape1contents.txt
```

If while testing a backup, tar reports errors, you should throw the media away immediately and begin backing up to a new tape or disk because tar errors usually indicate aging or failing magnetic media.

Though media verification does have its place, you shouldn't use it as a way to store information on magnetic media for *archival* (long-term preservation) purposes.

Magnetic media of all kinds should be considered useful only for short-term *backup* purposes.

Automating tar Backups

One of the biggest advantages of tar's command-line nature is the fact that it can easily be used in scripts or called using the cron service. This makes automating a single backup or a series of backups very easy to do—use your favorite text editor to create shell scripts that use the tar command as outlined in previous sections, and then call those shell scripts using cron.

> The cron service, which is used to schedule tasks to be carried out repeatedly at specific intervals, is discussed in "Using cron to Manage Periodic Jobs" in Hour 18.
>
> Shell scripting is discussed in Hour 9, "Harnessing the Power of the Shell."

24

Let's step through a detailed example for illustration purposes. Suppose that your computer system has two tape drives in it, one SCSI tape drive and one IDE tape drive. You are the system administrator and are responsible for backups, so you create the following backup policy:

- Every morning at 2:30 a.m., you back up the entire /home directory tree, which contains all your users' files, to the tape in the SCSI tape drive, verifying the contents of the tape afterward and saving any error messages displayed during verification in a file called /var/log/NightlyErrors.txt.

- Once a week at 5:00 p.m. on Sunday afternoon, you back up the contents of the /var/www tree to the tape in the IDE tape drive, verifying the contents of the tape afterward and saving any error messages displayed during verification in a file called /var/log/WeeklyErrors.txt.

While logged in as root, using vi (or emacs, if you prefer) you create a script called system-backup, shown in Listing 24.1; then you copy it to ~/bin and mark it as executable.

LISTING 24.1 The system-backup Script Created by You As Administrator

```
#!/bin/sh

if [ "$1" = nightly ]; then
    tar -c -f /dev/st0 /home
    tar -t -f /dev/st0 2> /var/log/NightlyErrors.txt
fi
```

LISTING 24.1   continued

```
if [ "$1" = weekly ]; then
    tar -c -f /dev/ht0 /var/www
    tar -t -f /dev/ht0 2> /var/log/WeeklyErrors.txt
fi
```

When called with the `nightly` argument, the `system-backup` script shown in Listing 24.1 performs the described nightly backup task; when called with the `weekly` argument, it performs the described weekly backup task.

After you have created the script, you issue the `crontab -e` command to edit the root user's list of periodic jobs. In the special `cron` control file, you enter the following lines:

```
30 2 * * * ~/bin/system-backup nightly
0 17 * * * ~/bin/system-backup weekly
```

After entering these lines, you save and exit. Your backup regimen is now in place; you need to remember only to load or switch tapes as necessary. Linux, `cron`, and `tar` take care of the rest, and any errors encountered are saved as `/var/log/backup.daily` and `/var/log/backup.weekly`. Remember to check these logs often to make sure that your backups are being completed without media errors!

Your own backup automation techniques using `cron`, shell scripts, and `tar` can of course be much more complex and nuanced than these; you are limited only by your imagination and your ability to master shell scripting.

Dealing with Catastrophic Failures

Most anyone who has worked with computers for any length of time knows that sometimes our worst fears come true—a computer system suffers a failure of some kind, which prevents it from even starting properly any longer.

Though Linux is a very stable operating system, if you use Linux long enough, you are still likely to encounter a situation at some point in which Linux is unable to start properly, even though your computer can at least be powered on and your hard drive appears to be functioning.

Red Hat has provided a special tool called `rescue` that can be used to try to salvage some of your data in situations like this.

Starting Rescue

To start the `rescue` tool, you insert your Red Hat Linux Install CD-ROM and allow it to boot your system. At the `boot:` prompt at the Red Hat title screen, type the phrase **linux rescue**.

If your computer doesn't have bootable CD-ROM capability, you need to use the installation floppy disks that you created near the end of Hour 1, "Preparing to Install Red Hat Linux."

You're asked whether you want to test your CD-ROM media; unless you have some reason to suspect that your media is bad, choose the Skip option by pressing your Tab key until Skip is highlighted, as shown in Figure 24.1, and then press Enter.

FIGURE 24.1

Skip the media test unless you have some reason to suspect that your Red Hat Linux media is bad.

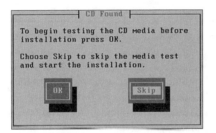

Next, you'll be asked to select a language and keyboard; press Enter to accept the default selections (English, us)—because we aren't installing but are instead intending to use the rescue mode, the language and keyboard selections don't matter. A few moment's later, you see the Red Hat Linux Rescue dialog shown in Figure 24.2.

FIGURE 24.2

The Rescue dialog offers to try to find your Red Hat Linux installation. Select the Read-Only option and press Enter.

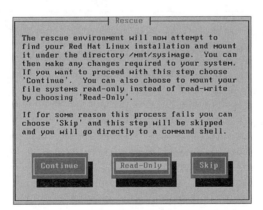

The dialog offers to have rescue try to find and mount the filesystems that make up your Red Hat Linux installation. Use the Tab key here to select the Read-Only option and then press Enter, thereby allowing rescue to try to access your data while ensuring that it won't be damaged any further. When rescue has found your Linux filesystem, it displays a message telling you that the filesystem has been mounted on /mnt/sysimage.

Press Enter to go to a Linux command prompt, where you are able to try to salvage your data, a process you explore in the next section.

> If instead you receive a message saying that rescue was unable to find or unable to mount your Linux filesystem, there is little more that you can do to salvage any current data stored in your Linux filesystem.
>
> Simply reset your system (starting with the install CD), and re-install Linux. Then, restore data from whatever backups you do have using the instructions earlier in this hour.

Attempting Filesystem Repairs

If rescue is able to find and mount your Linux filesystem, you can try to use a technique that often restores nonbooting Linux systems to full functionality—the filesystem check. The e2fsck command can be used to thoroughly check your Linux filesystem for structural problems and attempt to repair them.

To use e2fsck in rescue, you call it with the -f option (to force a full filesystem check) and supply the name of the device you want to check as an argument. There is, however, one catch—e2fsck must never be run on mounted filesystems. Therefore, to test your filesystems using e2fsck in rescue, follow the following steps.

> You learned about data pipes and the grep command in Hour 5, "Making the Console Work for You."

First, enter the mount command without arguments to list the mounted filesystems; pipe the output of mount to the grep command and search for the text sysimage. This gives you a list of the devices that make your Linux filesystem because, as rescue told you, all of your Linux filesystem is mounted under /mnt/sysimage.

```
-/bin/sh-2.05b# mount | grep sysimage
/dev/sda2 on /mnt/sysimage type ext3 (ro)
/dev/sda1 on /mnt/sysimage/boot type ext3 (ro)
none on /mnt/sysimage/dev/pts type devpts (ro)
none on /mnt/sysimage/proc type proc (ro)
-/bin/sh-2.05b#
```

Ignore lines that begin with none; these are virtual filesystems and no real devices are connected to them. In this case, the Linux filesystem is stored on two devices, /dev/sda1 and /dev/sda2. Before using the e2fsck utility, all these filesystems must be unmounted. To do this, issue the umount for each filesystem in the list, beginning at the bottom and moving upward:

```
-/bin/sh-2.05b# umount /mnt/sysimage/proc
-/bin/sh-2.05b# umount /mnt/sysimage/dev/pts
-/bin/sh-2.05b# umount /mnt/sysimage/boot
-/bin/sh-2.05b# umount /mnt/sysimage
-/bin/sh-2.05b#
```

Your Linux filesystem has now been unmounted and you can proceed to check each device by using the e2fsck command, supplying the -f option followed by the device name for the device you want to check each time through. For example, to start with /dev/sda1, this user enters

```
-/bin/sh-2.05b# e2fsck -f /dev/sda1
e2fsck 1.27 (8-Mar-2002)
Pass 1: Checking inodes, blocks and sizes
[...]
/: 76751/434592 files (0.2% non-contiguous), 346776/867510 blocks
-/bin/sh-2.05b#
```

The output e2fsck produces varies depending on the type and number of problems (if any) that e2fsck finds on the device. If you are asked any questions by e2fsck, press Enter to accept the default choice. The guts of the Linux filesystem are beyond the scope of a book like this one and perhaps more importantly, choices *other than* the default choice are almost *never* the correct choice for the best chance at full repair. When e2fsck finishes checking a device, it prints a brief, somewhat cryptic summary of the number of files, noncontiguous files, and used blocks on the system.

After you check all your devices, enter exit and the command prompt to exit rescue and reboot your system. If you are now able to boot normally into Red Hat Linux, your problem has been solved.

Salvaging Files

If you are able to start rescue mode, it is able to find your Linux filesystem, you are able to run filesystem checks using e2fsck, and yet your system *still* doesn't start normally, there is likely nothing left to do but try to save any current files in your Linux filesystem before reinstalling Red Hat Linux. Though a Linux expert might still have been able to repair the system, more advanced types of repairs are beyond the scope of a book like this one and beyond the reach of Linux beginners.

24

Restart Red Hat's rescue in the same way you did before. After your filesystems have been mounted on /mnt/sysimage again, you can proceed to use the backup techniques described in "Backing Up and Restoring Your Data" earlier in this hour to save any current files you might want to save from your filesystem tree—commands such as mount, cp, and tar are all available to you in rescue. Remember, however, to adjust for the fact that your filesystem is now mounted on /mnt/sysimage. For example, to back up what is normally your /home tree to a SCSI tape drive using the tar command, you would now have to enter the following:

```
tar -c -f /dev/st0 /mnt/sysimage/home
```

After you save the files you want to save from your Linux filesystem, exit rescue mode, reinstall Linux following the directions in Part I, and then restore your important data from the backups you've just made.

Recognizing Other Critical Problems

Sometimes it's obvious that you need to go into "emergency mode" and try to preserve your data and rescue your system—for example, if you suffer a complete hard drive failure, or if you are unable to boot Linux at all. There are, however, two times when it is desirable to preemptively take drastic action to save your system even though your system still appears to be mostly functional:

- Situations in which your hard drive is displaying symptoms of filesystem corruption or approaching failure
- Situations in which you can determine that your Red Hat Linux system might have fallen victim to network "hacking" or so-called trojan-horse or worm programs

Left unchecked, either of these situations can lead to eventual unexpected downtime, data loss, or even data theft. The following sections detail how to spot these types of situations and what to do should they occur.

Recognizing Filesystem Trouble

Filesystem corruption occurs when the organization of the data on your hard drive is unexpectedly damaged, thereby causing Linux to begin to lose track of where some files begin or end, or of which files contain what data. After your filesystem becomes corrupt, continued access to the disk usually *increases* the spread of filesystem corruption, thereby endangering and potentially damaging still more files with every passing minute.

There are a few telltale signs that indicate that you are likely beginning to experience filesystem corruption:

- You begin to encounter files that contain *garbage,* a mishmash of nonsensical data that doesn't represent the content that you were expecting a file to have—the content that you remember actually *storing* in the file in the first place.

- You begin to encounter directory problems—filenames containing garbage, spontaneously appearing or disappearing files, files or directories that can't be removed or edited even when permissions would seem to indicate that such things should be possible.

- You find files that, when accessed, seem to crash your computer system or the program you're using every time, without fail, in the same way.

- You begin to lose files or directories entirely, even though you have not deleted them—they're just suddenly gone.

If you believe that you are experiencing filesystem corruption, follow the steps earlier in this hour in the "Dealing with Catastrophic Failures" section to start the rescue tool and perform checks on your filesystems using e2fsck; this should repair the corruption that has occurred on your filesystem and make it safe for use again—though any data that was corrupted has been lost forever.

If e2fsck is unable to find any problems in your Linux filesystems, whatever symptoms you are experiencing are not due to filesystem corruption. In some cases, they might be due to malicious activity (we'll deal with this topic in the next section); in other cases, they might simply represent an aspect of the normal functioning of the Linux operating system that is unfamiliar to you.

If you are experiencing repeated bouts of filesystem corruption, you find that your system often hangs with the hard drive activity light on, or you begin to find log entries that refer to I/O errors or missing sectors on one of the devices used by your Linux filesystem, you are likely going to experience a catastrophic hard drive failure in the near future.

You should back up your data immediately and replace your hard drive to avoid unexpected downtime and/or data loss!

Recognizing Malicious Network Activity

There is one other type of critical problem that some unfortunate Linux users no doubt experience—particularly those who are connected to busy networks or directly to the Internet. Linux systems are often targeted by hackers or other types of malicious network users. This is because most Linux systems on networks are not just PCs, but are typically servers—configured to accept incoming requests while providing important services to many users.

In general, Red Hat Linux should be very good at repelling attacks, especially if you have properly configured your firewall as described in Hour 20, "Security Basics." However, from time to time it is inevitable that some attacks are successful. Recognizing the symptoms of having been successfully attacked can help you avoid extensive amounts of data loss or unwilling participation in Internet crimes. So long as your Red Hat Linux system is connected to a network, you should stay vigilant in watching for all of the following:

- Newly appearing SUID/SGID files, which indicate that someone is trying to access or has already accessed root-level functionality on your system. For more information on SUID/SGID special permissions, see "Understanding Special Permissions" in Hour 20.

- The appearance of new accounts in the /etc/passwd file or new groups in the /etc/group file that you did not create.

- System log records of users remotely logging in using accounts that don't seem to exist or that you did not create.

- Unexplained heavy network traffic that doesn't appear to be connected to any service you're running, or unfamiliar processes in the output of the ps command that always eventually return even after you kill them repeatedly.

- Any of the above combined with symptoms of filesystem corruption—disappearing files, undeletable files, or unreadable files or directories in spite of correct permissions, and so on.

If you find yourself experiencing any of these symptoms, it is likely that your system has been compromised. Unfortunately, this counts as a catastrophic failure. When a computer system is compromised by a malicious network user, he or she usually replaces many of the operating system components with modified components, which allow them to steal your data, use your computer in attacks on other computers, or other unwanted behavior.

If you think your system has been compromised, you should *immediately* shut down your computer system to prevent further unknown malicious activity. Boot into rescue as described in "Dealing with Catastrophic Failures" earlier in this hour. Save your important data files *only* (no programs or applications—they might have been replaced by dupes) using the techniques described in "Backing Up and Restoring Your Data" earlier in this hour. Then, reinstall Red Hat Linux from scratch as described in Part I and restore your data from the backups you made.

After your Linux system is running again, review Hour 20 and implement the techniques described there. Afterward, contact Red Hat about the availability of updates to the version of Red Hat Linux you're using.

Summary

This hour, you gained the final set of administrative tools and skills needed for you to become a safe and happy longtime Linux user. Specifically, you learned the following:

- How to back up and restore your important data files using removable disk media and simple copying
- How to back up and restore your important data files to magnetic tape or to special backup files using the `tar` command
- How to try to rescue a system that has experienced a catastrophic failure of some sort and no longer boots correctly
- How to salvage files from a broken system if you are unable to rescue it
- How to recognize other situations in which data salvage and subsequent reinstallation and restoration might be apropos, including situations caused by filesystem corruption and malicious network activity

Congratulations! You've survived all 24 hours. You've learned how to install and configure Linux to work on your computer system, you've mastered a basic set of applications and techniques at the Linux command line, you've learned how to make efficient use of Linux desktop applications, and you've learned how to perform most basic administration tasks in Linux.

Though you might not feel like a guru yet, keep working at it and you will eventually become one. Experiment, read manual pages, and consult the documentation at `http://www.tldp.org` often. In time, you will find that you can make Linux work for you on your terms, efficiently and reliably.

When you are ready to become a guru, consider reading *Red Hat Linux 8 Unleashed*, also a Sams title.

Q&A

Q I have a magnetic tape device, but it isn't connected to a SCSI controller or an IDE controller. How can I access it?

A Though Linux does include drivers for many older tape devices, there are so many of them—and they behave in so many different ways—that use of such devices in Linux is best left to the pros. Consider upgrading to an industry-standard SCSI or

IDE streamer instead; the newer drives are much more reliable, and using them with Linux and the `tar` command is relatively easy.

Q Can I back up my entire system, rather than just my data files, using `tar`?

A Yes; you can back up every directory tree but /proc using the `tar` command. Restoring from a systemwide backup of this sort is a matter of booting `restore`, using `parted` and `mount` (both of which you've learned about) to create and mount a new filesystem, and then streaming the data back on to the hard drive with `tar`. Beware, however—if you have experienced hacking activity, any compromised files might also be restored in such an operation. It is usually therefore a better idea to back up data files only.

Q I have experienced filesystem corruption several times, but each time, rescue and `e2fsck` are able to repair the problem. Why should I buy a new hard drive?

A Because repeated bouts of filesystem corruption indicate that your hard drive is *losing data* that has been stored there. Aside from the fact that some of your data is disappearing forever, it is very likely that a hard drive that is losing data will fail completely in short order.

Workshop

The Workshop is designed to help you anticipate possible questions, review what you've learned, and begin learning how to put your knowledge into practice.

Quiz

1. What command would you use to back up the /var/www, /var/logs, and /home directory trees to the only IDE tape drive on a Linux computer system?

2. How do you start the Red Hat rescue tool?

3. What command is used to perform filesystem checks of the Linux ext2 and ext3 filesystems?

4. Finding "garbage" in your files is a symptom of what type of critical problem?

Answers

1. `tar -c -f /dev/ht0 /var/www /var/logs /home`

2. Boot from your install media (floppy or CD-ROM) and enter the text **linux rescue** at the `boot:` prompt.

3. `e2fsck`

4. Filesystem corruption.

Activities

1. Design and implement a backup regimen for your data—either an automatic one using shell scripts and `cron` or simply a manual one that you decide to abide by faithfully.

2. Try booting into the rescue tool just to test it out and become familiar with the process.

3. Use the `tar` command to store a few files of your choosing in a backup file, and then restore them to another directory.

24

APPENDIX **A**

Installer Troubleshooting

In general, Anaconda, the Red Hat Linux installer, is a reasonably foolproof tool, which does a good job of installing Linux. However, to enjoy the benefits it provides, you must first be able to start it. This appendix deals with two subjects related to the Red Hat Linux installer:

- The installer's failure to find hard drive or CD-ROM drive devices to install to or from, respectively
- The use of the text-based installer, which can be seen as a last resort when you are unable to start the default installer

Loading Modules at Install Time

In some cases—most notably when either your hard drive or CD-ROM drive is connected to your computer via a SCSI controller—Red Hat Linux cannot start the installer right away because either it isn't able to find your CD-ROM drive or it isn't able to find your hard drive. This occurs because none of the drivers in the installer's default driver list is able to communicate with your hardware. When this occurs, the installer asks about the nature of your hardware and then asks you to select a driver, as shown in Figures A.1 through A.3.

FIGURE A.1

The installer can't find a CD-ROM drive; it asks where the install media are located.

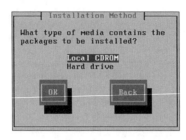

FIGURE A.2

The installer guesses that the CD-ROM drive is a SCSI drive.

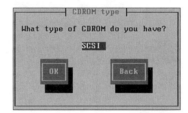

FIGURE A.3

The installer asks you to choose the driver for the controller to which your CD-ROM is connected.

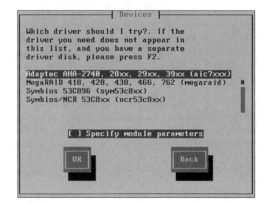

When you are given a list of driver modules, scroll up and down through the list until the one that matches your hardware is highlighted; then press Tab until the word OK is highlighted and the driver will be loaded.

Generally, if you can't find the module in a list, you can press your F2 key to search from an additional list of modules. After you press F2, a message box appears, asking you to insert your driver disk; insert the disk and press Enter. A list of drivers is displayed, as shown in Figure A.4.

After you select the correct driver, the Red Hat Linux installer finds your hardware and the installation process proceeds as outlined in Hour 2, "Installing Red Hat Linux."

FIGURE A.4

After you insert a driver disk, a different list of drivers is displayed for your selection; select one using your arrow keys and press Enter.

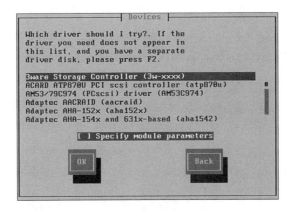

Last Resort: Module Parameters

If a module fails to load, you do not get an error message, but the installer asks again how to locate the missing piece of hardware and continues to offer you the same list of drivers. If you are sure about the type of hardware you possess and yet your driver is failing to load, you might need to supply extra information to the driver to get it to load correctly. Unfortunately, the list of values needed by each driver can be found only in the source code of the Linux kernel itself or from the driver's author (or manufacturer). The source code of the Linux kernel can be downloaded from the anonymous FTP site ftp.kernel.org. Because navigating the Linux kernel source requires some experience in dealing with programming in the C language, module parameters are best used by experienced users or those with previous Linux experience.

To supply parameters to a module, use the Tab key to highlight the Specify Module Parameters option and then press Space to select it; an asterisk appears in the selection box, as shown in Figure A.5.

FIGURE A.5

If the driver doesn't load the first time, try again, but choose to specify module parameters.

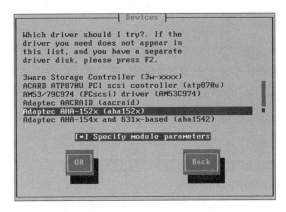

A

When you attempt to load a driver after selecting that you want to specify module parameters, the Module Parameters screen is displayed before the driver is loaded; in this screen, you can enter various types of configuration data, as shown in Figure A.6.

FIGURE A.6

You can configure the device driver in the Module Parameters screen if you are familiar with your hardware.

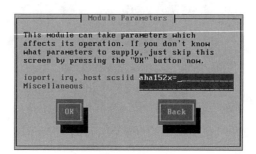

The set of options that can be configured varies from device to device, but generally some indication is provided for how to proceed, though it might at first seem obtuse. The format of the Module Parameters screen is a list of input lines, each of which supports a specific type of option. For example, in Figure A.6, there are two main datapoints that can be configured for the controller in question. In this case, the correct action is to tab to the field beginning with aha152x= and finish the line with the input/output base address (ioport), interrupt request line (irq), and host adapter's SCSI ID (host scsiid) in the supplied format—separated by commas:

```
aha152x=0x340,11,7
```

In some cases, the module's request for information is more explicit—a module might ask only for an IRQ, a base address, or a revision level for your hardware. If in doubt, feel free to experiment with values in order to try to get your hardware working. Obviously, you must be reasonably familiar with PC hardware in general, with your own hardware in particular, and with the conventions in use in Linux and the C programming language to be able to configure module parameters effectively during the install process. Regrettably, every driver is different, so the information you must provide and the format in which it should be provided varies from driver to driver (and from manufacturer to manufacturer, if you have manufacturer-supplied driver disks for Red Hat Linux). Try to follow the visual cues and supplied values for each driver as guidelines. In the end, it is nearly always easier for inexperienced users to replace an undetected hardware item than to try to load a driver manually in this fashion.

Using the Text Mode Installer

Some computers are not capable of running the standard Red Hat installer that runs in graphical mode. When this is true, one of two things happens:

- The Red Hat installer detects that your computer is not compatible with its graphics mode and the text mode installer starts instead.

- Your computer crashes, displays the installer screens incorrectly, or otherwise prevents you through abnormal circumstances from completing the install process as it is shown in Hour 2.

If the latter is true in your case, you need to force the text mode installer to start preemptively so that the graphical installer is never started. To do this, boot from your Red Hat Linux install media and enter the phrase **linux text** at the boot: prompt. This causes the Red Hat installer to bypass the graphics mode entirely and begin the text mode installer after the media check, shown in Figure A.7.

FIGURE A.7

The text mode installer doesn't use graphics and doesn't use your mouse; it relies on your keyboard exclusively.

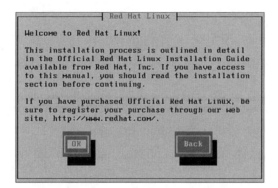

Fortunately, the text mode installer functions almost identically to the default installer discussed in Hour 2. The program flow and offered choices and options are the same; only the appearance is different. You should therefore be able to navigate the text mode installer using Hour 2 as a guide, provided that you keep the following in mind:

- Highlighted text (red letters on gray background) serves the same purpose as the mouse in the default installer; any highlighted text is currently being "pointed at."

- The Enter key serves the same purpose as your mouse button would in the default installer; pressing the Enter key chooses the currently highlighted (pointed at) option.

- Pressing the Tab key repeatedly is like moving the mouse—each time you press the Tab key, it moves the highlight to the next choice on the screen. When offered a choice, press Tab until the highlight points to the option you want to select; then press your Enter key to select it.

- When using the text mode installer, you are not asked for a default display resolution and color depth until you boot Linux for the first time, just before the

A

graphical login described in Hour 3, "Booting, Logging In, and Configuring," is displayed. This contrasts with the normal install process, in which resolution and color depth are configured as a part of the regular install process.

The fact that you are forced to use the text mode indicates a greater chance that Red Hat Linux is not compatible with your display hardware. You might find that after you finish the text mode installer, Red Hat's graphical mode doesn't work when you boot your system. If this is the case, you might want to consider upgrading your graphics hardware to be compatible with Red Hat Linux. After you have done so, I hope you'll attempt to install Red Hat Linux again!

INDEX

Symbols

100-megabyte boot partition, 36
(&) ampersand, 369
(*) asterisk, 68, 114
(\) backslash character, 149
(^) carat character, 201
($) dollar sign, 405
($) dollar sign character, 78, 201
(..) double period, 88-89
/etc/fstab file, 421-422
.fetchmailrc file, creating, 177-178
(/) forward slash, 80-82
(#) hash mark, 405
(|) pipe, 122-123
(.) single period, 88
(/) slashes, 513
() tilde, 513
() tilde character, 83, 105, 117

A

About option, 323-324
About to Install screen, 53

access, FTP, 522
Accessibility icon, 349
accessing
    e-mail attachments, 314
    Windows files, GNOME, 316-317
    Windows networks, 316
accounts
    configuring, installer, 47-49
    group
        adding, 423-424
        administering, 424-425
        memberships, 425
        removing, 423-424
    root, 457
        su command, 457-459
    user
        adding, 422-423
        group memberships, 95
        identity, 95
        removing, 422-423
    Windows file server, creating, 503-504
activating SWAT, 496
Add a User Account dialog box, 48
Add Group button, 444
Add Partition dialog box, 36
Add User button, 442-444

adding
  group accounts, 423-444
  printers, 67
  user accounts, 422-444
addresses
  e-mail, Pine program, 182
  IP, editing, 439-440
adduser command, 422
administering group accounts, 424-425
Advanced Micro Devices (AMD), 8
Advanced tab, 352-353
advantages
  GNOME environment, 237
  KDE environment, 237
AMD (Advanced Micro Devices), 8
AMD processors, 8
ampersand (&), 369
anonymous FTP, 522-523
Apache Configuration tool, 515-516
Apache Web servers
  Apache Configuration tool, 515-516
  configuring, 517-519
  firewalls, 511-512
  home directory Web sites, 513-515
  installing, 509-510
  running, 512-513
  security, 516-519
  starting automatically, 510-511
Apache Web site, 519
appending standard output of commands, 120
Application tab, 344
applications
  color, configuring, 356-357
  displaying
    ssh command, 389-390, 394-395
    xhost command, 396
  gFTP, 317
    copying files from remote systems, 319
    copying files to remote connections, 318
    exiting, 319
    remote connections, 318
  GNOME, multiple windows, 230-231
  help, 322
  launching, 226-227, 237
  menus, 229

  OpenOffice Calc, 279-280
    copying formulas, 290-291
    entering formulas, 286-288
    entering numeric data in cells, 284-286
    entering text labels, 282-284
    functions in formulas, 288-290
    modifying spreadsheets, 291
    starting, 280-282
  OpenOffice Writer, 267
    components, 268-269
    editing text, 270-271
    entering text, 269
    launching, 268-269
    modifying text, 271-273
    opening files, 278
    page layout, 275
    paragraph formatting, 273-275
    printing files, 278-279
    saving files, 275-278
  remote
    displaying, 390-392
    ssh command, 388-389
  routine, relative paths, 89-90
  terminal. *See* terminal applications
  X Window System. *See* X Window System
    applications
  xbiff, 374
  xclock, 374
  xeyes, 374
  xload, 376
  xmag, 376
arguments
  command-line, 207-208
  graceful, 514
  restart, 514
asterisk (*), 68, 114
Attach button, 311
attachments, e-mail files, 311-314
authentication, configuring, 49

B

Background dialog box, 358-361
Background Preference dialog box, 346

Background Properties dialog box, 348
backslash (\) character, 149
backups, data, 526-527
    tar command, 533-534
    testing, 532-533
    to disks, 528-532
basic input/output system (BIOS), 7-8
bc command, 163-164
    automating calculations, 164-165
    controlling script flow, 165
\begin command, 150
bg command, 126-127
binary calculations. *See* bc command
BIOS (basic input/output system), 7
BIOS display, 7-8
bookmarks, 298
    Lynx Web browser, 176
Boot Diskette Creation screen, 55-56
boot disks, installer, 55-56
boot floppy disks, crcating, 22-23
Boot Loader Configuration screen, 40-42
boot loaders, 40-42
boot partition, creating, 36-37
booting, 60, 535-536
    CD-ROM, 535
    dual, 12
    GRUB boot display, 60-61
    GRUB boot loader, 60
    Red Hat Linux installer, 61
BootIt Next Generation Web site, 21
braces ({}) character, 204
brackets ([]) character, 204
browsers
    Help, 328-330
        info pages, 335
        manual pages, 332-334
        printing from, 338
    Mozilla
        browsing Web, 294-300
        launching, 294
browsing
    Mozilla Web browser, 294-298
        tabbed browsing, 299-300
        URLs, 295-298

Web
    console, 172-176
        Lynx, 173-176
buttons
    Add Group, 444
    Add User, 442-444
    Attach, 311
    Details, 51
    Edit, 439-440
    End Process, 434
    Format, 447
    Kill Process, 434
    Language, 65
    Properties, 445
    Scaled, 347
    Session, 65
    System, 65

C

Calc icon, 267
Calc window, 280-282
calculations, 163-164
    automating with bc command, 164-165
    controlling script flow with bc command,
        165
    variables, assigning values to, 164
carat (^) character, 201
case-sensitivity, 82
cd command, 85
CD-ROM, booting, 535
CD-ROM media, testing, 535
Change Priority dialog box, 434
characters
    asterisk (*), 114
    backslash (\), 149
    braces ({}), 204
    brackets ([]), 204
    carat (^), 201
    dollar sign ($), 201
    LaTeX documents, 159-160
    parentheses (()), 204
    tilde (), 105, 117

chkconfig command, 412-414

chmod command, 98, 178, 380, 453-457

    numeric method, 98

    numeric strings, 454

    symbolic method, 98

chown command, 453

chsh command, 460-461

client systems, 186

Colors dialog box, 356-357

command lines

    console, 366

    NFS, 492

    NFS configuration, 491

    SWAT, installing, 496-497

    terminal applications, launching, 368-370

    terminals, 366

command mode, 105

command prompts, 78

    terminal applications, 367

command substitution, 123-124

commands

    adduser, 422

    bc, 163-164

        automating calculations, 164-165

        controlling script flow, 165

    \begin, 150

    bg, 126-127

    cd, 85

    chkconfig, 412-414

    chmod, 98, 178, 380, 453-457

        numeric method, 98

        numeric strings, 454

        symbolic method, 98

    chown, 453

    chsh, 460-461

    Copy File, 250

    cp, 86, 528-532

        destination arguments, 101

    creating

        command-line arguments, 207-208

        conditional statements, 209-211

        myscript command, 208-209

        predefined sets, 214-216

        shell scripts, 206-207, 216

        tests, 212-214

crontab, 426

df, 420

\documentclass, 150-152

Duplicate context menu, 250

e2fsck, 536

echo, 198

emacs, 374

emacs editor keystrokes, 111-113

\end, 150

expr, 198-199

fetchmail, 177

fg, 126

find, 117-118

formatting LaTeX, 160-162

ftp, 189

    commands, 191

    logging in, 189-191

    sample sessions, 191-193

gedit, 369

gpasswd, 424-425

grep, 121, 166

groupdel, 424

head, 199

help messages, 141-143

info system keystrokes, 137-138

init, 410-412

job, 405

kill, 127, 408-410

killall, 409

latex, 153

LaTeX sections, 156-158

LaTeX text formatting, 158-159

less, 133

less pager keystrokes, 143

locate, 118-119

lpq, 147

lpr, 146-147

lprm, 147-148

ls, 81, 94, 124

    displaying information, 101

    existing directories/files, 101

Lynx Web browser keystrokes, 173-174

\maketitle, 154

man, 132-135, 332

mkdir, 86

mount, 419-420, 528, 537
mv, 86
  destination arguments, 101
myscript, 208-209
\newline, 155
nohup, 370
output
  appending, 120
  command substitution, 123-124
  dequeing print jobs, 147-148
  listing print jobs, 147
  pipes, 122-123
  printing, 146-147
  redirecting, 119-120
\pagestyle, 154
parted, 416-418
passwd, 422
print, 416-418
ps, 405-407
pwd, 84
read, 165
Rename, 252
renice, 407-408
rm, 90
sed, 200-201
service, 414-415, 492
shell, 78-79
shutdown, 428
smbclient, 193
  connecting to Windows shares, 194
  copying files, 195
  listing shares on Windows hosts, 194
sort, 167
ssh, 188-189, 387
  displaying applications locally, 389-390
  displaying local applications remotely, 390-395
  remote applications, 388-389
su, 404-405, 457
  permissions, 459
  wheel group, 458
tail, 199
tar, 528-530, 542
  automating data backups, 533-534

restoring data backups, 530-532
  testing data backups, 532-533
telnet, 186-188
textedit, 380
touch, 84, 371
twm, 373
umount, 420-421
vi editor keystrokes, 106-107
xhost, 392-394, 400
  displaying applications locally, 396
xmessage, 376-380, 383
communications hardware, 9-10
components
  chkconfig command, 413-414
  default installer, 27
  GNOME desktop, 223-224
  GNOME file dialog box, 240
  OpenOffice Writer, 268-269
composing e-mail
  Evolution, 308-310
  Pine program, 182-183
computers, starting, 534, 538
  filesystem check, 536-538
  filesystem corruption, 539-540
  filesystem files, 538
  hackers, 540-541
  rescue tool, 535-536
conditional statements, 209-211
configuring
  accounts, installer, 47-49
  Apache Web servers, 517-519
  application color, 356-357
  authentication, installer, 49
  date and time, 61-62
  desktop taskbar, 362-364
  desktop wallpaper, 346-348
  DNS information, 440-441
  Evolution, 302-304, 308
  firewalls, 450
    installer, 44-46
    security levels, 451
    traffic, 451-452
  graphics, installer, 57-58

Internet services, 66
  Internet Configuration Wizard, 70-72
  logging out, 72
  Network Configuration tool, 72
  root accounts, 66
monitors, installer, 57
mouse, 340-343, 351-353
network interfaces, 438-439
network settings, 70
networks, installer, 42-44
NFS, 487-488
  at the command line, 491-492
printers, 66-69
Samba shares, 500-502
screensavers, 348-349
title bar, 358
window borders, 358
windows, 343-346, 353-356
Windows file sharing, 499
wu-ftd, 521
Congratulations screen, 58
connections
Ethernet, 70
filesystems, creating, 416
printers, 68
remote systems, gFTP applications, 318
X Window System, 392-394
consoles, 366
e-mail, 176
  .fetchmailrc file, 177-178
  Pine program, 179-185
  retrieving from servers, 177
defined, 76
switching between, 77
virtual, 77, 232
  logging in, 77-78
  switching between, 124
Web browsing, 172
  Lynx, 173-176
context drag operation, 259-260
context menu, 247-248
controls
Print dialog box, 279
windows, 228
convenience applications, 374-376

cookie jar (Lynx), 175
cookies, Lynx Web browser, 175-176
Copy File command, 250
copying
files, 249
  from remote systems, 319
  to remote systems, 318-319
OpenOffice Calc formulas, 290-291
Core Desktop section, 329
corruption, filesystem, 539-542
hackers, 540-541
cp command, 86, 528-532
displaying information, 101
CPU, speed, 8
Create New User dialog box, 443
creating
boot disks, 55-56
boot floppy disks, 22-23
boot partition, 36-37
command output print jobs, 146-147
commands
  command-line arguments, 207-208
  conditional statements, 209-211
  myscript command, 208-209
  predefined sets, 214-216
  shell scripts, 206-207, 216
  tests, 212-214
cron processes, 426
directories, 255
.fetchmailrc file, 177-178
file copies, 250
filesystems, 416
  connections, 416
  devices, 416-418
LaTeX-2e documents, 149-150
root partition, 37
substitution variables, 202-204
  quotation marks, 204-206
swap partition, 37
symbolic links, 92-93, 252
text files, 104-105, 240, 243
  emacs editor, 108-113
Windows file server accounts, 503-504
cron processes, 425-426
crontab command, 426

crontab file, fields, 426-428

current directory drop-down, 242

current working directories, 97. *See also* present working directories

current working directory, 84-85

Cursors tab, 341

Custom installation, 30

Customize Graphics Configuration screen, 57-58

customizing desktops, 340, 349-350
  mouse configuration, 340-343
  screensavers, 348-349
  wallpaper, 346-348
  window configuration, 343-346

D

data
  backing up, 527
    tar command, 533-534
    testing, 532-533
    to disks, 528-532
  backups, 526
  sorting lists, 167-168

Date and Time Configuration screen, 61

Date and Time Update Agent screen, 62

default desktops, KDE, 224-225

default installer, components, 27

default printer, 67

defragmenting hard drives, 13-14

deleting
  directories, 90-91, 253
  files, 90-91, 253
  partitions, 417

dequeing command output print jobs, 147-148

desktop applications, 322

desktop files, accessing from command lines, 370

desktop selector, 233

desktop taskbars, configuring, 362-364

desktop terminal applications. *See* terminal applications

desktop wallpaper
  configuring, 346-348
  modifying, 358-361

desktops, 223
  customizing, 340, 349-350
    mouse configuration, 340-343
    screensavers, 348-349
    wallpaper, 346-348
    window configuration, 343-346
  files, 239-240
  files, moving to, 257-258
  FTP, 317
    closing connections, 319
    connecting to remote systems, 318
    copying files from remote systems, 319
    copying files to remote systems, 318-319
  GNOME, 223-224
  help, 322
  KDE, 224-225
  logging out, 236
  login prompts, 223-224
  navigating, 225
  networking on, 293-294
  screensavers, configuring, 348
  taskbars, 225-226
  virtual, 232-233
    application windows, 234
    desktop selector, 233
    GNOME environment, 234
    KDE window management menu, 235
    switching between, 234

destructive repartitioning, 19-21

Details button, 51

device-independent files, 153

devices
  filesystems, creating, 416-418
  formatting, 447

df command, 420

dial-up Internet services, configuring, 66
  Internet Configuration Wizard, 70-72
  logging out, 72
  Network Configuration tool, 72
  root accounts, 66

How can we make this index more useful? Email us at indexes@samspublishing.com

dialog boxes
Add a User Account, 48
Add Partition, 36
Background, 358-361
Background Preferences, 346
Background Properties, 348
Change Priority, 434
Colors, 356-357
Create New User, 443
Directory Options, 517-518
Edit Partition, 38
Ethernet Device, 439-440
Format Floppy, 15
Functions, 289
GNOME file, 240-243
Group Properties, 445
Mouse, 351
    Advanced tab, 352-353
    General tab, 352
Mouse Configuration, 27
Mouse Preferences, 341
Mouse Properties, 341
Network Configuration, 72, 439-441
NFS Share, 488-490
Open, 278
Page Style, 275
Print, 279
Properties, 13, 253
Rescue, 536
Save As, 276-277
Screensaver, 362
Screensaver Preferences, 348
Style
    Effects tab, 354
    Miscellaneous tab, 355-356
System Properties, 8
Theme Preferences, 344
Virtual Host Properties, 517
Window Decoration, 358
directories, 80-83
creating, 255
current working directory, 84-85
deleting, 90-91, 253
file manager, 245-247
files, moving between windows, 258-259
files, moving to, 257-258
home, 83
    existing directories/files, 101
    files, copying, 85-86
    permissions, modifying, 98-100
    user accounts, 83
navigating, 84-86
ownership, 95-97
parent, 89
permissions, 253-255
relative paths, 87-89
renaming, 252
root, 80-83
searching, 117
directory navigation pane, 240
Directory Options dialog box, 517-518
Disk Druid tool, 32
freeing partition space, 34-36
partition list, 33-34
    checking, 39
disk partitioning, installer, 30-32
disk setup, installer, 32-33
partition list, 33-34, 39-40
disks
backing up data to, 528
    tar command, 528-532
boot, creating, 55-56
DISPLAY variable, 394-395
displaying manual pages, 132-133
sections, 133-135
DNS (network device's nameserver), 440
documentation, /usr/share/doc tree, 139-140
\documentclass command, 150-152
dollar sign ($), 405
dollar sign ($) character, 78, 201
double period (..), 88-89
double-clicking, 231-232
downloading e-mail messages, 312-314
drag-and-drop files, 257-258
context drag, 259-260
moving between directories, 258-259
drive letter, filesystems, 79
dual booting, 12
Duplicate context menu command, 250

E

e-mail, 301
    addresses, Pine program, 182
    composing, Pine program, 182-183
    console, 176
        .fetchmailrc file, 177-178
        Pine program, 179-185
        retrieving from servers, 177
    downloading messages, 312-314
    Evolution
        composing e-mail, 308-310
        configuring, 302-304, 308
        launching, 301
    file attachments, 311-314
    forwarding messages, 314
    HTML message formatting, 310-311
    ISPs, 301
    reading, Pine program, 184-185
    replying to messages, 314
    sending messages, 312
e2fsck command, 536
echo command, 198
Edit button, 439-440
Edit Partition dialog box, 38
editing
    cron processes, 426
    files, 248
    group accounts, 445
    text, 148-149
        OpenOffice Writer, 270-271
    text files, 104-107
editors
    emacs, 104
        creating text files, 108-113
        LaTeX-2e, 149
        switching between applications, 125-126
    text, 104
    vi, 104
        creating text files, 104-105
        editing text in text files, 106-107
        inserting text in text files, 105-106
        LaTeX-2e, 149
        resuming jobs, 126
        running background jobs, 126-127
        saving text in text files, 107-108
        switching between applications, 125-126
    viLaTeX-2e, 149
    vim, 107
Effects tab, 354
electronic spreadsheets, OpenOffice Calc, 280-282
    copying formulas, 290-291
    entering formulas, 286-288
    entering functions in formulas, 288-290
    entering numeric data in cells, 284-286
    entering text labels, 282-284
    modifying spreadsheets, 291
emacs command, 374
emacs editor, 104, 374
    creating text files, 108-110
        keystroke commands, 111-113
        menu system, 110-111
    LaTeX-2e, 149
    switching between applications, 125-126
empty text files, 104
emptying trash, 261
\end command, 150
End Process button, 434
entering
    OpenOffice Calc formulas, 286-288
    OpenOffice Calc functions in formulas, 288-290
    OpenOffice Calc numeric data in cells, 284-286
    OpenOffice Calc text labels, 282-284
environment variables, 205-206
Ethernet connections, 70
Ethernet Device dialog box, 439-440
ethernet hardware, 9-10
Evolution, 301
    composing e-mail, 308-310
    configuring, 302-304, 308
    exiting, 315
    launching, 301
    sending e-mail, 312
Evolution Setup Assistant, 304
executable files, 91-92

exiting
Evolution, 315
gFTP applications, 319
Mozilla, 301
expr command, 198-199

F

fetchmail command, 177
fg command, 126
fields
crontab file, 426-428
/etc/fstab file, 421-422
file attachments, e-mail, 311-312
accessing, 314
file dialog, 240-243
file manager (Nautilus), 380-383
file managers, 243
directories, 245-247
Linux tasks, 243
windows, 244-245
file navigation pane, 242
File Transfer Protocol. *See* **FTP**
File Types icon, 349
filename entry box, 242
filename expansion, 114-116
preventing, 116-117
filenames, grouping files, 114
filename expansion, 115-117
pattern matching characters, 115-116
files
context menus, 247-248
copying, 249
crontab, fields, 426-428
deleting, 90-91, 253
desktops, 239-240
accessing from command lines, 370
device-independent, 153
drag-and-drop operation, 257-258
context drag, 259-260
moving files between directory windows, 258-259
duplicates, creating, 250

editing, 248
empty text, 104
/etc/fstab, 421-422
exchanging between Linux and Unix, 189
ftp command, 189-193
executable, 91-92
.fetchmailrc, 177-178
filesystem repairs, 538
filesystem trees, 80-83
grouping, 114
filenames, 114-117
home directories, copying files, 85-86
listings, 94-95
multiple, selecting, 251
opening, 249
OpenOffice Writer
opening, 278
printing, 278-279
saving, 275-278
output
appending, 120
redirecting, 119-120
ownerships
chmod command, 453-455
chown command, 453
permissions, 93, 253-255
permissions, modifying, 98-100
properties, 93-94
renaming, 252
restoring, 260
searching, 117
find command, 117-118
single words, 121-122
word patterns, 120
sharing, with Windows computers, 494
symbolic links, 92-93
text
creating, 240-243
emacs editor, 104, 108-113
vi editor, 104-108
Windows
accessing, 316-317
copying, 195
exchanging with Windows hosts, 193-194
filesystem check, 536-538

filesystem corruption, 539-542

filesystem files, 538

filesystem trees

  files, 80-83

  mounting, 80

filesystems, 415

  creating, 416

    connections, 416

    devices, 416-418

  defined, 79

  directories, 80-83

  drive letter, 79

  /etc/fstab file, 421-422

  Linux, 80

  metadata-journaled, 416

  mounting, 416-420, 446

  ownership, 95-97

  roots, 79

  searching, locate command, 118-119

  trees. *See* filesystem trees

  unmounting, 416, 420-421

find command, 117-118

FIPS, 12-13

  running, 14-16

    floppy disks, 14-16

    partition backups, 16-19

fips tool, 34-36

Firewall Configuration screen, 44-46

firewall security, remote application display, 390-392

firewalls, 44, 450

  Apache Web servers, 511-512

  configuring, 450

    installer, 44-46

    security levels, 451

    traffic, 451-452

  FTP, 521

  NFS, 492-494

  Windows file server, 504

floppy disks

  boot floppies, 22-23

  FIPS, 14-16

Font icon, 349

Format button, 447

Format Floppy dialog box, 15

formatting

  devices, 447

  LaTeX commands, 160-162

  LaTeX documents, 153

    characters, 159-160

    paragraphs, 154-156

    sectioning commands, 156-158

    text, 158-159

  partitions, 447

  text, 148-149

formulas, OpenOffice Calc

  copying, 290-291

  entering, 286-288

  functions, 288-290

forward slash (/), 82

forward slash character (/), 80

forwarding e-mail messages, 314

FTP (File Transfer Protocol), 519

  access, 522

  anonymous, 522-523

  desktops, 317

    closing connections, 319

    connecting to remote systems, 318

    copying files from remote systems, 319

    copying files to remote systems, 318-319

  firewalls, 521

ftp command, 189

  commands, 191

  logging in, 189-191

  sample sessions, 191-193

FTP Server package group, 521

FTP servers, 519-521

  enabling/disabling, 521

  wu-ftd, configuring, 521

FTP services, 507

functions

  OpenOffice Calc formulas, 288-290

  sum(), 288-289

Functions dialog box, 289

G

garbage, 539
gedit command, 369
General tab, 352
gFTP application, 317
  exiting, 319
  remote connections, 318
    copying files from, 319
    copying files to, 318-319
Ghz (gigahertz), 8
GNOME
  desktop taskbars
    icons, adding to, 363
    icons, moving, 363
    icons, removing, 363
  Windows files, accessing, 316-317
GNOME applications
  Help Browser, 328-330
    info pages, 335
    manual pages, 332-334
    printing from, 338
  Help menu, 322
    About option, 323-324
    viewing contents, 325-326
GNOME Control Center, 340
GNOME desktop, 223
  applications, running, 230-231
  components, 223-224
  logging out, 236
GNOME environment
  advantages, 237
  Konqueror file manager, 243-245
GNOME environments, 65, 222
  virtual desktops, 234
GNOME file dialog box, 240-243
GNOME Menu icon, 226-227
gpasswd command, 424-425
graceful argument, 514
Graphical Interface Configuration screen, 56-57
graphical interfaces, installer, 56
Graphical User Interface (GUI), 10
graphics, configuring, 57-58
grep command, 121, 166

group accounts
  adding, 423-424
  administering, 424-425
  memberships, 425
  removing, 423-424
group memberships, identity, 95
Group Properties dialog box, 445
groupdel command, 424
grouping files, 114
  filenames, 114-117
groups
  adding accounts, 444
  editing accounts, 445
  removing accounts, 444
  wheel group, 458
GRUB boot display, 60-61
GRUB boot loader, 41, 60
GUI (Graphical User Interface), 10

H

hackers, 540-541
handbooks, viewing, 326-327
hard drives
  capacity requirements, 9
  Linux installation, 11-22
  partitions, 11-12
    defragmenting, 13-14
    FIPS, 12-13
    Windows installation, 11
  repartition alternatives, 21-22
  repartitioning, 19-21
  troubleshooting, 538
hardware
  BIOS display, 8
  communications, 9-10
  ethernet, 9-10
  installing Linux, 6-10
  Linux, requirements, 10-11
  modem, 9-10
hash mark (#), 405
head command, 199

help
applications, 322
commands, 141-143
desktops, 322
Pine program, 185
Help Browser, 328-330
info pages, 335
manual pages, 332-334
printing from, 338
Help menu, 322
About option, 323-324
viewing contents, 325-326
viewing handbooks, 326-327
What's This? item, 324
HelpCenter (KDE), 330-332
home directories, 83, 513-514
existing directories/files, 101
files, copying, 85-86
permissions, 514
permissions, modifying, 98-100
user accounts, 83
Home icon, 225
hosts, newton (Windows), 316
HTML, e-mail message formatting, 310-311

I

icons
Accessibility, 349
Calc, 267
desktop taskbar, 225-226
desktop taskbars, 363
GNOME, 363
KDE, 363
File Types, 349
Font, 349
GNOME Menu, 226-227
Home, 225
Impress, 267
Keyboard Shortcuts, 349
Keyword, 349
Menus & Toolbars, 349
Password, 349

Screensaver, 362
sorting, 256
Sound, 349
Start Here, 226
Style, 353
Trash, 226, 260
emptying trash, 261
restoring files, 260
Window Focus, 350
Writer, 267
identity, 95
group memberships, 95
user accounts, 95
IMAP server, 302-304
Impress icon, 267
info documents, 335-337
info pages, 335-337
info system, 136
navigating, 136-138
/usr/share/doc tree, 138
init command, 410-412
insert mode, 105
inserting text files, 105-106
Install Additional Software screen, 62
installation type, installer, 29-30, 35
installer, 26-27
account configuration, 47-49
authentication configuration, 49
boot disks, 55-56
Boot Loader Configuration screen, 40-42
default, components, 27
disk partitioning, 30-32
disk setup, 32-33
partition list, 33-34, 39-40
fips tool, freeing partition space, 34-36
graphical interfaces, 56
graphics configuration, 57-58
installation type, 29-30, 35
keyboard configuration, 27
language selection, 27
language support, 46-47
monitor configuration, 57
mouse configuration, 27-29
network configuration, 42-46
package group selection, 50-53

packages, 53-55
time zones, 47
installing
Apache Web servers, 509-510
KDE environment, 237
Linux
hard drive space, 11-22
hardware, 6-10
software, 62
Windows file systems, 24
SWAT, 495-496
command lines, 496-497
Windows file server, 494
Intel processors, 8
interfaces
graphical, installer, 56
network
configuring, 438-439
configuring DNS information, 440-441
editing address properties, 439-440
enabling/disabling, 441
Internet. *See also* **Web**
configuring dial-up services, 66
Internet Configuration Wizard, 70-72
logging out, 72
Network Configuration tool, 72
root accounts, 66
e-mail, 301
composing, 308-310
downloading messages, 312-314
Evolution, 301-304, 308
file attachments, 311-314
forwarding messages, 314
HTML message formatting, 310-311
ISPs, 301
replying to messages, 314
sending messages, 312
Internet Configuration Wizard, 71
Internet Service Providers (ISP), 301
IP addresses, editing, 439-440
ISPs (Internet Service Providers), 301

J-K

job command, 405

KB (kilobytes), 6
KDE, desktop taskbars, 363
KDE applications
Help browser, 330-332
Help menu, 322
About option, 323-324
viewing handbooks, 326-327
What's This? item, 324
Konqueror
info pages, 336-337
man pages, 336-337
KDE Control Center, 351
application color configuration, 356-357
desktop wallpaper modification, 358-361
launching, 351
mouse configuration, 351-353
screensaver modification, 362
title bar configuration, 358
window border configuration, 358
window configuration, 353-356
KDE desktop, 224-225
KDE environment
advantages, 237
installing, 237
KDE Control Center, 351
application color configuration, 356-357
desktop wallpaper modification, 358-361
launching, 351
mouse configuration, 351-353
screensaver modification, 362
title bar configuration, 358
window border configuration, 358
window configuration, 353-356
Konqueror file manager, 243-245
KDE environments, 65, 222
KDE window management menu, 235
keyboard configuration, installer, 27
Keyboard Shortcuts icon, 349
keystroke commands, vi editor, 106-107
keystrokes, emacs editor command, 111-113
Keyword icon, 349

kill command, 127, 408-410
Kill Process button, 434
killall command, 409
kilobytes (KB), 6
Konqueror
    info pages, 336-337
    man pages, 336-337
Konqueror file manager, 243-245

L

Language button, 65
languages
    installer, 27
    support, installer, 46-47
LaTeX. *See also* LaTeX-2e
    characters, 159-160
    commands, 150-151
    formatting commands, 160-162
    formatting documents, 153
    online sources, 162
    page styles, 154
    paragraph formatting, 154-156
    printing documents, 153
    sectioning commands, 156-158
    text formatting, 158-159
    title pages, 154
latex command, 153
LaTeX-2e, 149. *See also* LaTeX
    creating documents, 149-150
    document classes, 151-152
launching. *See also* starting
    application help, 322
    applications, 226-227, 237
    Evolution, 301
    Help Browser, 328-330
        info pages, 335
        manual pages, 332-334
    HelpCenter (KDE), 330-332
    KDE Control Center, 351
    Konqueror
        info pages, 336-337
        man pages, 336-337

Mozilla Web browser, 294
OpenOffice, 267
OpenOffice Writer, 268-269
Red Hat Linux installer, 22-23
terminal applications, 366-367
    command prompts, 367
    from command lines, 368-370
less command, 133
less pager, 133
    keystroke commands, 143
levels, firewall security, 451
linking commands, pipes, 122-123
links, symbolic, 92
    creating, 92-93, 252
    renaming, 252
Linux. *See also* Red Hat Linux 8.0
    case-sensitive, 82
    files, exchanging with Unix, 189-193
    filesystems, 80
    hardware, requirements, 10-11
    history, 76
    installation
        hard drive space, 11-22
        hardware, 6-10
        Windows file systems, 24
    paths, 83
Linux Administrator's Security Guide Web
    site, 450
Linux Documentation Web site, 10
Linux modems Web site, 10
listings
    command output print jobs, 147
    conditional statements, lxprint command,
        210-216
    files, 94-95
    LaTeX document commands, 160
    rm —help Command output, 142
    running processes, ps command, 405-407
    shell scripts, myscript command, 207
    Windows hosts, smbclient output, 194
lists
    searching, 166
        specific entries, 166-167

sorting, 166
    data, 167-168
    specific entries, 166-167
ln command, 92
local applications, displaying, 389-390, 396
    remotely, 390, 394-395
locate command, 118-119
logging in, 64-65
    desktop prompts, 223-224
    ftp command, 189-191
    languages, 65
    Red Hat Linux graphical login prompt, 64
    remotely, 185-186
        client systems, 186
        server systems, 186
        ssh command, 188-189
        telnet command, 186-188
    virtual consoles, 77-78
logging out, 72
    automatically, 459-460
    GNOME desktops, 236
    login timeouts, 460-461
Login screen, 66
logs, system
    restarting, 428
    shutting down, 428
lp (line printer), 67
lpq command, 147
lpr command, 146-147
lprm command, 147-148
ls command, 81, 94, 124
    displaying information, 101
    existing directories/files, 101
Lynx Web browser, loading Web pages, 173
    bookmarks, 176
    cookies, 175-176
    keystroke commands, 173-174

M

magnetic tape devices, 542
Main tab, 515
\maketitle command, 154

man command, 132-135, 332
man pages, 336-337
man system, /usr/share/doc tree, 138
manual pagers, 133
manual pages, 132, 332-335
    displaying, 132-133
        sections, 133-135
    pagers, 133
    reading, 133
    topic searches, 135-136
MB (megabytes), 6
media, CD-ROM, 535
megabytes (MB), 6
megahertz (Mhz), 8
memberships, group accounts, 425
memory, 6
    capacity
        BIOS display, 7
        requirements, 6-8
    Windows, 7
menus
    applications, 229
    context, 247
        files, 247-248
        options, 248
    desktop taskbars, KDE, 363
    emacs editor, 110-111
    Help, 322-324
Menus & Toolbars icon, 349
messages, e-mail
    downloading, 312-314
    forwarding, 314
    replying, 314
    sending, 312
meta-documentation, /usr/share/doc tree, 139
metadata-journaled, filesystems, 416
Mhz (megahertz), 8
Microsoft Intellimouse, 29
Miscellaneous tab, 355-356
mkdir command, 86
models, printer, 69
modem hardware, 9-10
modes
    command, 105
    insert, 105

modifying
   desktop wallpaper, 358-361
   screensavers, 362
   taskbars, 231
   windows, 228-229
monitors, configuring, 57
Motion tab, 343
mount command, 419-420, 528, 537
mounting
   defined, 80
   filesystems, 418-420, 446
   partitions, 38-39
mouse, configuring, 27-29, 340-343, 351-353
Mouse Configuration dialog box, 27
Mouse dialog box, 351
   Advanced tab, 352-353
   General tab, 352
Mouse Preferences dialog box, 341
Mouse Properties dialog box, 341
Mozilla, 294
   exiting, 301
   pop-up windows, 300
Mozilla Web browser
   browsing Web, 294-300
   launching, 294
mv command, 86
   displaying information, 101
myscript command, 208-209

N

naming
   directories, 252
   files, 252
   symbolic links, 252
Nautilus file manager, 380-383
Nautilus scripts Web site, 382
navigating desktops, 225
network configuration, installer, 42-44
Network Configuration dialog box, 72, 439-441
Network Configuration screen, 42

Network Configuration tool, 72
network device's nameserver (DNS), 440
Network File System. *See* **NFS**
network interfaces
   configuring, 438-439
   configuring DNS information, 440-441
   editing address properties, 439-440
   enabling/disabling, 441
network settings, configuring, 70
networks
   desktops, 293-294
   hackers, 540-541
   Windows, accessing, 316
\newline command, 155
newton, Windows host, 316
NFS (Network File System), 486
   configuring, 487-488
     at the command line, 491-492
   firewalls, 492-494
   services, 486
   starting automatically, 490-492
NFS Server Configuration tool, 487-490
NFS Share dialog box, 488-490
NFS shares, 488-490
nohup command, 370
numeric data, OpenOffice Calc, 284-286
numeric method (chmod command), 98

O

online sources, LaTeX, 162
Open dialog box, 278
opening
   files, 249
   OpenOffice Writer files, 278
OpenOffice, launching, 267
OpenOffice 6.0, 265-266
   OpenOffice suite, 267
OpenOffice Calc, 279-280
   copying formulas, 290-291
   entering formulas, 286-288
     functions, 288-290

entering numeric data in cells, 284-286
entering text labels, 282-284
modifying spreadsheets, 291
starting, 280-282
OpenOffice suite, 266
OpenOffice Writer, 267
  components, 268-269
  editing text, 270-271
  entering text, 269
  launching, 268-269
  modifying text, 271-273
    paragraph formatting, 273-275
  opening files, 278
  page layout, 275
  printing files, 278-279
  saving files, 275-278
output
  commands
    dequeing print jobs, 147-148
    listing print jobs, 147
    pipes, 122-123
    printing, 146-147
    substitution, 123-124
  files
    appending, 120
    redirecting, 119-120
ownership
  directories, 95-97
  filesystems, 95-97

P

package group selection, installer, 50-51
Package Group Selection screen, 50
package groups, installer, 51-53
Package Management tool, 494
packages, installer, 53-55
page layout, OpenOffice Writer, 275
Page Style dialog box, 275
page styles, LaTeX documents, 154
pagers, 133
  keystroke commands, 143
\pagestyle command, 154

pages
  info, 335-337
  man, 336-337
  manual. *See* manual pages
paragraphs
  LaTeX documents, 154-156
  OpenOffice Writer, 273-275
parallel port printer, 68
parent directories, 89
parentheses (()) character, 204
parted command, 416-418
Partition Magic Web site, 21
partitioning
  boot loaders, 40-42
  Windows, 19-21
partitions, 11-12
  100-megabyte boot, 36
  boot, creating, 36-37
  deleting, 417
  destructive repartitioning, 19-21
  FIPS, backups, 16-19
  formatting, 447
  freeing space, 34-36
  mounting, 38-39
  root, creating, 37
  root filesystem, 36
  swap, 35-37
  Windows
    defragmenting, 13-14
    FIPS, 12-13
  Windows installation, 11
passwd command, 422
Password icon, 349
passwords, root accounts, 66
paths
  defined, 83
  relative, 86
    directories, creating, 87-88
    present working directories, 88-89
    routine applications, 89-90
patterns, text files, 120
  single words, 121-122
Performance Tuning tab, 516
period (double) (..), 88-89
period (single) (.), 88-89

permissions, 93, 96-97, 452
  defined, 95-97
  directories, 253-255
  file ownership
    chmod command, 453-455
    chown command, 453
  files, 253-255
  modifying, 98-100
  types, 455-457
Permissions pane, 253
Personal Desktop installation, 29
Pine program, 179
  composing e-mail, 182-183
  e-mail addresses, 182
  help, 185
  preferences, 180-181
  quitting, 185
  reading e-mail, 184-185
  running, 179-180
Pine Web site, 185
pipes (|), 122-123
piping, 119
POP servers, 302-304
pop-up windows, Mozilla, 300
POP3 (Post Office Protocol 3), 177
ports, printers, 68
Post Office Protocol 3 (POP3), 177
preferences, Pine program, 180-181
present working directories, relative paths,
  88-89. *See also* **current working directory**
preventing filename expansion, 116-117
print command, 416-418
Print dialog box, 279
printers
  adding, 67
  configuring, 66-69
  connections, 68
  default, 67
  line (lp), 67
  models, 69
  parallel port, 68
  ports, 68

printing
  command output, 146-147
  Help Browser, 338
  LaTeX documents, 153
  OpenOffice Writer files, 278-279
processes
  cron, 425
    creating, 426
    editing, 426
  running, 405, 432-433
    editing lists, 435-438
    kill command, 408-410
    listing, 405-407
    prioritizing, 407-408, 433-434
    ps command, 405-407
    renice command, 407-408
    stopping, 408-410, 434-435
processors
  Intel, 8
  speed, 24
programs
  Pine, 179
    composing e-mail, 182-183
    e-mail addresses, 182
    help, 185
    preferences, 180-181
    quitting, 185
    reading e-mail, 184-185
    running, 179-180
  shell, 125
    resuming jobs, 126
    running background jobs, 126-127
    switching between open applications,
      125-126
properties, 93-94
Properties button, 445
Properties dialog box, 13, 253
protocols, X Window System applications,
  386-387
ps command, 405-407
pwd command, 84

Q-R

quitting Pine program, 185
quoting shell, 201-202
   variables, 204-206

read command, 165
reading
   e-mail, Pine program, 184-185
   manual pages, 133
   system logs, 445-446
Red Hat Config tool, 68
Red Hat GNOME desktop. *See* **GNOME desktop**
Red Hat KDE desktop, 224-225
Red Hat Linux 8.0, 10. *See also* **Linux**
Red Hat Linux 8.0 installer, 6
Red Hat Linux desktop. *See* **desktops**
Red Hat Linux graphical login prompt, 64
Red Hat Linux installer, 61. *See also* **installer**
   launching, 22-23
Red Hat User Manager tool. *See* **User Manager tool**
relative paths, 86
   directories, creating, 87-88
   present working directories, 88-89
   routine applications, 89-90
remote applications, displaying, 388-389
   firewall security, 390-392
remote logins, 185-186
   client systems, 186
   server systems, 186
   ssh command, 188-189
   telnet command, 186-188
removing
   group accounts, 423-444
   user accounts, 422-423, 442-444
Rename command, 252
renice command, 407-408
repartitioning
   alternatives, 21-22
   destructive, 19-21
replying to e-mail messages, 314

requirements
   hard drive capacity, 9
   Linux hardware, 10-11
   memory capacity, 6-8
Rescue dialog box, 536
rescue tool, 535-536
restart arguments, 514
restarting
   running services, 414-415
   system logs, 428
restoring files, 260
rm command, 90
root accounts, 66, 457
   passwords, 66
   su command, 457
      permissions, 459
      wheel group, 458
root directories, 80-83
root filesystem partition, 36
root partition, creating, 37
root user, 404-405
roots, defined, 79
routine applications, relative paths, 89-90
runlevel services, enabling/disabling, 436-438
runlevels, 410
   chkconfig command, 412-414
   init command, 410-412
running
   FIPS, 14-16
      floppy disks, 14-16
      partition backups, 16-19
   GNOME applications, 230-231
running processes, 405, 432-433
   editing lists, 435-438
   listing, ps command, 405-407
   prioritizing, 433-434
      renice command, 407-408
   stopping, 434-435
      kill command, 408-410
running services, 410
   restarting, 414-415
   runlevels, 410
      init command, 410-412
      starting automatically, 412-414
   starting, 414-415
   stopping, 414-415

S

Samba, 494
  configuring shares, 500-502
Samba Web Administration Tool. *See* **SWAT**
Save As dialog box, 276-277
saving
  files, 538
  OpenOffice Writer files, 275-278
  text files, 107-108
Scaled button, 347
Screensaver dialog box, 362
Screensaver icon, 362
Screensaver Preferences dialog box, 348
screensavers
  configuring, 348-349
  modifying, 362
scripting, shell, 198
  command-line arguments, 207-208
  commands, 206-207, 216
  conditional statements, 209-211
  echo command, 198
  expr command, 198-199
  head command, 199
  myscript command, 208-209
  predefined sets, 214-216
  sed command, 200-201
  tail command, 199
  tests, 212-214
searching
  directories, 117
  files, 117
    find command, 117-118
    single words, 121-122
    word patterns, 120
  filesystems, locate command, 118-119
  lists, 166-167
  manual page topics, 135-136
  /usr/share/doc tree, 141
sections
  LaTeX documents, 156-158
  manual pages, 133-135
Secure Shell, 387
secure shell client. *See* **ssh command**

Securing and Optimizing Linux Web site, 450
security, 449-450
  Apache Web servers, 516-519
  firewall, remote application display, 390-392
Security Level Configuration tool, 450, 493, 504
sed command, 200-201
selecting multiple files, 251
sending e-mail messages, 312
Server installation, 30
Server Message Blocks (SMB), 494
server systems, 186
Server tab, 516
servers
  FTP, 519-521
    enabling/disabling, 521
    wu-ftd, configuring, 521
  IMAP, 302-304
  POP, 302-304
  retrieving e-mail from, 177
  Web, 508
    Apache, 509-512
    Apache Configuration tool, 515-516
    configuring, 517-519
    home directory Web sites, 513-515
    running, 512-513
    security, 516-519
    software, 508
service command, 414-415, 492
Service Configuration tool, 490-491
  editing running processes lists, 435-436
  enabling/disabling running processes services, 436-438
services
  FTP, 507
  NFS, 486
  running, 410
    restarting, 414-415
    runlevels, 410-414
    starting, 414-415
    stopping, 414-415
  Web, 507
Session button, 65
sessions, defined, 77

settings, Directory Options dialog box, 517-518
shading (windows), 231-232
shares
    NFS, 488-490
    Samba, configuration, 500-502
    Windows, 194
        connecting to, 194
        copying files to, 195
sharing files with Windows computers, 494
shell
    command interpreter, 78
    commands, 78-79
    defined, 78
shell programs, 125
    resuming jobs, 126
    running background jobs, 126-127
    switching between open applications, 125-126
shell quoting, 201-202
    variables, 204-206
shell scripting, 198
    commands, 206-207, 216
        command-line arguments, 207-208
        conditional statements, 209-211
        myscript command, 208-209
        predefined sets, 214-216
        tests, 212-214
    echo command, 198
    expr command, 198-199
    head command, 199
    sed command, 200-201
    tail command, 199
shell scripts
    Nautilus file manager, 380-383
    xmessage command, 377-380
shell variables, 201-202
    creating, 202-204
        quotation marks, 204-206
shutdown command, 428
shutting down system logs, 428
single period (.), 88
slashes (/), 513
SMB (Server Message Blocks), 494

smbclient command, 193
    connecting to Windows shares, 194
    copying files, 195
    listing shares on Windows hosts, 194
software, Web servers, 508
sort command, 167
sorting
    icons, 256
    lists, 166
        data, 167-168
        specific entries, 166-167
Sound icon, 349
speed
    CPU, 8
    processors, 24
spreadsheets, OpenOffice Calc, 280-282
    copying formulas, 290-291
    entering formulas, 286-288
    entering functions in formulas, 288-290
    entering numeric data in cells, 284-286
    entering text labels, 282-284
    modifying, 291
ssh command, 188-189, 387
    displaying applications locally, 389-390
    displaying local applications remotely, 390-395
    remote applications, 388-389
standard output, commands
    appending, 120
    redirecting, 119-120
Start Here icon, 226
starting. *See also* launching
    Apache Web servers, 510-511
    computers, 534-538
        filesystem check, 536-538
        filesystem corruption, 539-540
        filesystem files, 538
        hackers, 540-541
        rescue tool, 535-536
    NFS, 490-492
    OpenOffice Calc, 280-282
    running services, 414
        automatically, 412-414
        service command, 414-415
    SWAT, 498-499
    Windows file server, 502-503

statements, conditional, 209-211
stopping
    running processes, kill command, 408-410
    running services, 414
        service command, 414-415
storage devices, filesystem trees, 79
Style dialog box
    Effects tab, 354
    Miscellaneous tab, 355-356
Style icon, 353
su command, 404-405, 457
    permissions, 459
    wheel group, 458
substituting variables, 201-204
    quotation marks, 204-206
suites, OpenOffice, 266
sum() function, 288-289
swap partition, 35-37
SWAT (Samba Web Administration Tool), 495
    activating, 496
    installing, 495-496
        command lines, 496-497
    starting, 498-499
symbolic links, 92
    creating, 92-93, 252
    renaming, 252
symbolic method (chmod command), 98
System button, 65
system logs
    reading, 445-446
    restarting, 428
    shutting down, 428
System Logs tool, 445
System Monitor tool, 432-433
    prioritizing running processes, 433-434
    stopping running processes, 434-435
System Properties dialog box, 8
systems
    info, 136
        navigating, 136-138
        /usr/share/doc tree, 138
    keystroke commands, 137-138
    man, /usr/share/doc tree, 138

T

tabbed browsing, 299-300
tabs
    Advanced, 352-353
    Apache Configuration tool, 515-516
    Application, 344
    Cursors, 341
    Effects, 354
    General, 352
    Main, 515
    Miscellaneous, 355-356
    Motion, 343
    Performance Tuning, 516
    Server, 516
    Virtual Hosts, 516
    Wallpaper, 359
    Window Border, 345
tail command, 199
tape devices (magnetic), 542
tar command, 528-530, 542
    automating data backups, 533-534
    restoring data backups, 530-532
    testing data backups, 532-533
taskbars
    desktop, 225
        configuring, 362-364
        icons, 225-226, 363
        menus, 363
    sizing, 231
telnet command, 186-188
terminal applications, launching, 366-367
    command prompts, 367
    from command lines, 368-370
terminals, 366
test expressions, 209
testing
    CD-ROM media, 535
    data backups, 532-533
text, LaTeX documents, 158-159
text cursors, OpenOffice Writer, 269
    editing text, 270-271
    entering text, 269
    modifying text, 271-273

page layout, 275
paragraph formatting, 273-275
text editing, 148-149
text editor, 104, 226
Text Editor
files
editing, 248
opening, 249
text files, creating, 240-243
text files
creating, 240-243
emacs editor, 104, 108-110
keystroke commands, 111-113
menu system, 110-111
empty, 104
searching
single words, 121-122
word patterns, 120
vi editor, 104
creating files, 104-105
editing text, 106-107
inserting text, 105-106
saving text, 107-108
text formatting, 148-149
text labels, OpenOffice Calc, 282-284
textedit command, 380
Theme Preferences dialog box, 344
tilde () characters, 83, 105, 117, 513
time zones, installer, 47
title bar, configuring, 358
title pages, LaTeX documents, 154
TMOUT variable, 460
tools
Apache Configuration, 515-516
Disk Druid, 32
freeing partition space, 34-36
partition list, 33-34, 39
Network Configuration, 72
NFS Server Configuration, 487-490
Package Management, 494
Red Hat Config, 68
rescue, 535-536
Security Level Configuration, 450, 493, 504
Service Configuration, 490-491
editing running processes lists, 435-436
enabling/disabling running processes services, 436-438

System Logs, 445
System Monitor, 432-433
prioritizing running processes, 433-434
stopping running processes, 434-435
User Manager, 442
adding/removing groups, 444
adding/removing users, 442-444
editing groups, 445
User Mount, 446
topics, 135-136
touch command, 84, 371
traffic, firewall security, 451-452
Trash icon, 226, 260
emptying trash, 261
restoring files, 260
trees, defined, 79
troubleshooting, starting computers, 534, 538
filesystem check, 536-538
filesystem corruption, 539-540
filesystem files, 538
hackers, 540-541
rescue tool, 535-536
twm command, 373
TWM environment, 372-373
convenience applications, 374-376
types
installation, installer, 29-30, 35
permissions, 455-457

U

umount command, 420-421
Uniform Resource Locators (URLs), 295-298
Unix
files, exchanging with Linux, 189-193
history, 76
unmounting filesystems, 416, 420-421
Upgrade Existing System installation, 30
URLs (Uniform Resource Locators), 295-296
bookmarks, 298
USB printer ports, 68
user accounts
adding, 422-423
home directories, 83

identity, 95

removing, 422-423

User Manager tool, 442

adding/removing groups, 444

adding/removing users, 442-444

editing groups, 445

User Mount tool, 446

users

adding accounts, 442-444

logging out

automatically, 459-460

login timeouts, 460-461

removing accounts, 442-444

root, 404-405

/usr/share/doc tree, 138

documentation, 139-140

searching, 141

V

values, assigning to variables, 164

variable substitution, 201-202

creating, 202-204

quotation marks, 204-206

variables

assigning values, 164

DISPLAY, 394-395

environment, 205-206

shell, 201-202

creating, 202-204

quoting, 204-206

TMOUT, 460

vi editor, 104

creating text files, 104-105

editing text in text files, 106-107

inserting text in text files, 105-106

LaTeX-2e, 149

resuming jobs, 126

running background jobs, 126-127

saving text in text files, 107-108

switching between open applications, 125-126

vim editor, 107

virtual consoles, 77, 232

logging in, 77-78

switching between, 124

virtual desktops, 232-233

application windows, 234

desktop selector, 233

GNOME environment, 234

KDE window management menu, 235

switching between, 234

Virtual Host Properties dialog box, 517

Virtual Hosts tab, 516

VMWare Web site, 12

W

wallpaper

configuring, 346-348

modifying, 358-361

Wallpaper tab, 359

Web, 176, 301. *See also* **Internet**

browsing

console, 172-176

Lynx, 173-176

e-mail. *See* e-mail

Web servers, 508

Apache

Apache Configuration tool, 515-516

configuring, 517-519

firewalls, 511-512

home directory Web sites, 513-515

installing, 509-510

running, 512-513

security, 516-519

starting automatically, 510-511

software, 508

Web services, 507

Web sites

Apache, 519

BootIt Next Generation, 21

Linux Administrator's Security Guide, 450

Linux Documentation, 10

Linux modems, 10

Nautilus scripts, 382
Partition Magic, 21
Pine, 185
Securing and Optimizing Linux, 450
VMWare, 12
Win4Lin, 12
Yahoo!, 173, 295
Welcome to Red Hat Linux! screen, 61
What You See Is What You Get (WYSIWYG), 148
What's This? item, 324
wheel group, 458
Win4Lin Web site, 12
Window Border tab, 345
window borders, configuring, 358
Window decoration dialog box, 358
Window Focus icon, 350
window shading, 231-232
windows
    Calc, 280-282
    configuring, 343-346, 353-356
    controls, 228
    file manager, 244-245
    GNOME applications, running, 230-231
    sizing, 228-229
    virtual desktops, 234
        KDE window management menu, 235
Windows
    destructive repartitioning, 19
    file systems, 24
    files
        accessing, 316-317
        copying, 195
        exchanging with Windows hosts, 193-194
    hard drive capacity, 9
    installation
        defragmenting, 13-14
        FIPS, 12-13
        hard drive partitions, 11
    memory capacity requirements, 7
    networks, accessing, 316
    partitioning, 19-21
    sharing files with, 494

Windows file server
    accounts, creating, 503-504
    firewalls, 504
    installing, 494
    starting automatically, 502-503
Windows file sharing, configuring, 499
Windows hosts, newton, 316
wizards, Internet Configuration, 71
word processor, 104
Workstation installation, 29
World Wide Web servers. *See* **Web servers**
Writer icon, 267
wu-ftd, configuring, 521
wu-ftpd, 519
WYSIWYG (What You See Is What You Get), 148

X-Z

X Display Manager Control Protocol (XDMCP), 397-399
X Window System, 76
    connections, 392-394
    networking manually, 392
X Window System applications, 372-373
    convenience applications, 374-376
    protocols, 386-387
    XDMCP, 397-399
X Window System environments, 65
xbiff application, 374
xclock application, 374
XDMCP (X Display Manager Control Protocol), 397-399
xeyes application, 374
xhost command, 392-394, 400
    displaying applications locally, 396
xload application, 376
xmag application, 376
xmessage command, 376-380, 383

Yahoo! Web site, 173, 295

Installing Red Hat Linux

You may need to change your BIOS settings to boot directly from a CD-ROM drive. If you are not sure if you can boot from a CD-ROM, you should start or reboot your computer and go into the computer's BIOS setup utility. Pressing the DEL (Delete) or the F2 key usually accesses this utility while the computer is starting up. Once in the BIOS setup utility, look for a boot priority option. If your computer is capable of booting from a CD-ROM, your CD-ROM drive will be listed. Make sure the CD-ROM drive has a higher boot priority than your hard drive(s) to enable booting from a CD-ROM.

Once you have determined that you can boot from the CD-ROM, start or reboot your machine with the Installation Disc (Disc 1) in your CD drive. After a few moments, you should see the Red Hat Linux installation routine. Follow the onscreen prompts to finish the installation.

If your computer cannot start the Red Hat Linux installation program from the CD-ROM, you will need to create boot disks to launch the installation program. You will find instructions for how to do this on Disc 1.

NOTE: The Red Hat setup program requires your system to have 48 or more megabytes of memory to launch into a full screen graphics mode. If you have less than 48 megabytes of memory, the setup program will go to a text-only mode, which is functionally identical to the graphical install.

License Agreement